AUTHORS,
PUBLISHERS
AND POLITICIANS

AUTHORS, PUBLISHERS AND POLITICIANS

THE QUEST FOR AN ANGLO-AMERICAN COPYRIGHT AGREEMENT
1815–1854

James J. Barnes

OHIO STATE UNIVERSITY PRESS
Columbus

Library of Congress Cataloging in Publication Data

Barnes, James J
Authors, publishers, and politicians.

1. Copyright, International. 2. Copyright—United
States—History. 3. Copyright—Great Britain—History.
I. Title
Law   346.048'2   74-12489
ISBN 0-8142-0210-1

Printed in Great Britain by
The Camelot Press Ltd, Southampton

To J. C. B. and G. P. B.

CONTENTS

PREFACE

In 1838 Parliament passed legislation enabling Great Britain to become a party to international copyright agreements, and in the following decades a number of such treaties were signed with European states. However, Americans were suspicious about international copyright and feared that it meant exploitation and domination of their book trade. As a young nation the United States wanted the freedom to borrow literature as well as technology from any quarter of the globe, and it was not until 1891 that Congress finally recognized America's literary independence by authorizing reciprocal copyright agreements with foreign powers.

Well before Anglo-American relations were disrupted by the Civil War of 1861-5, a number of authors, publishers, and politicians in both countries emphasized the advantages of copyright between these two English-speaking nations. At times their efforts seemed close to success, reinforced as they were by political intrigue and diplomatic manœuvres. In 1854 the issue even became the subject of a legal decision before the House of Lords. That same year an Anglo-American copyright treaty already signed by the American Secretary of State and the British Minister in Washington awaited final confirmation by the Senate. This volume deals with why failure attended these many efforts during the years 1815-54. A good deal of attention is also given to describing the ways in which authors and publishers functioned in the absence of an Anglo-American agreement.

In the chapters which follow I have taken minor liberties with the spelling and punctuation of quoted passages in the interest of clarity and intelligibility. This in turn serves to remind me how enormously indebted

I am to those who facilitated my research into previously unpublished materials on both sides of the Atlantic. In the section of Acknowledgments I mention these sources by name, but here I should like to express my deep sense of gratitude to those who helped to finance my undertaking. During the past ten years Wabash College has been most generous in supporting my project in its various phases. I am also greatly indebted to grants from the American Council of Learned Societies, the American Philosophical Society, and the Social Science Research Council.

May I also take this opportunity to mention a few of the many individuals who have sustained me throughout the past decade with advice and encouragement: Mr Simon Nowell-Smith of Oxford; Mr Ronald E. Barker of the Publishers' Association in London; Dr Marjorie Plant, former Deputy Librarian of the London School of Economics and Political Science; Professor Robert K. Webb of Columbia University; Professor Richard D. Altick of Ohio State University. Finally, only those who know something of my working and writing habits can begin to appreciate Patience Barnes's contribution to this project. As wife, editor, and critic, she has also served as intrepid travelling companion and documentary sleuth. Together we dedicate this volume to our children, Jennifer and Geoffrey, who have crossed the Atlantic many times, sharing our preoccupation with writing and research.

J. J. B.
Wabash College
Crawfordsville, Indiana

ACKNOWLEDGMENTS

The notes throughout this volume are an eloquent testimony to the many individuals and institutions who assisted me in my research. I am extremely grateful to have been allowed to examine materials in their possession and when appropriate to quote extracts from them.

American Antiquarian Society, Worcester, Massachusetts, for the fine collection of nineteenth-century periodicals.

American Philosophical Society Library, Philadelphia, Pennsylvania.

Amherst College Library, Amherst, Massachusetts.

Assistants. To the many who have worked with me over the years as research assistants, readers, and typists, I would like to express my very great appreciation: Richard Adlof, Roberta Berry, Ronald Brown, Ann Dillon, Lynn Fairfield, James Gibson, Susan Glennon, Ariel Gordus, Elaine Greenlee, William Harader, Ruth Hepler, Mrs William B. Jackson, Marina Justice, Valdina Koller, Larry LeSeure, Terry Meyer, Stuart Miller, Linden Nicoll, Patricia Ponte, Patricia Radinger, Marsha Remsen, Edward Shorter, and Virginia Zachary.

Professor James F. Beard, for his assistance with the J. F. Cooper Papers.

Wm Blackwood and Sons Ltd, in particular Wing-Commander G. D. Blackwood.

Bodleian Library, Oxford. Over the years Mr D. S. Porter and others have been most helpful in making available to me such materials as the Clarendon Papers, the Crampton Papers, the Bentley Papers, and the G. P. R. James Papers.

British Museum, London. This volume would scarcely be possible were it not for the fine collection and co-operation of the Department of Printed Books. I am also much indebted to the Department of Manuscripts for such collections as those relating to Richard Bentley, W. E. Gladstone, and Sir Robert Peel.

Buffalo and Erie County Historical Society of New York for assistance with the Millard Fillmore Papers.

Cambridge University Library.

The Rt Hon. the Earl of Clarendon.

The Papers of Henry Clay: those currently engaged in editing the Papers of Henry Clay, especially Professor James F. Hopkins of the University of Kentucky, were most cordial to me in the course of my researches.

Lady Hermione Cobbold, with respect to the Papers of the Lytton family.

Columbia Law School Library, New York, especially for their outstanding collection on literary copyright law.

Columbia University Library, New York, and Kenneth A. Lohf of Special Collections, for access to the John Jay Papers and Park Benjamin Papers.

Connecticut Historical Society, Hartford.

Connecticut State Library, Hartford.

Cornell University Library, Ithaca, New York.

Professor Thomas J. Curran, St John's University, New York, for sharing information about L. C. Levin.

Customs and Excise. I am most grateful to the library staff of HM Customs and Excise for allowing me to examine some of their nineteenth-century records and publications.

Harrison P. Dilworth III, for assistance with my inquiry concerning L. C. Levin.

Seth Dubin, for helping to locate the John Jay Papers.

Duke University Library, Durham, North Carolina.

Sir William Gladstone.

Greater London Record Office, Middlesex Section, for Papers of G. P. R. James.

Harper & Row, and Mr Eugene Exman, for their co-operation and suggestions.

Harvard University, Cambridge, Massachusetts: Widener Library for its outstanding collection of printed books; Houghton Library for the papers of Longfellow, Emerson, Sparks, and Sumner. Also Miss Carolyn E. Jakeman for her able assistance.

Hertfordshire County Record Office: Peter Walne and Eileen Lynch for their great help in locating and examining the Lytton Family Papers.

Professor and Mrs Walter Houghton, for kindly making accessible the files of the Wellesley Index to Periodicals.

Hudson's Bay Co., London: Mrs J. Craig, archivist, for the correspondence of Sir George Simpson.

Huntington Library, San Marino, California, for letters of Washington Irving, L. C. Levin, and G. P. R. James.

University of Illinois Library: Professors Royal Gettmann and Scott Bennett for their assistance in examining the Bentley Papers. The Library's collection of printed materials for the nineteenth century is outstanding.

Indiana State Library, Indianapolis.

Indiana University Library, Bloomington.

Institute of Historical Research, London: Mr Kellaway and his colleagues.

John Jay Homestead, Katonah, New York. I am greatly indebted to the Trustees and to the curators, Messrs Lewis Rubenstein and L. S. Lipinsky, for permission to examine and make use of the fine collection of Jay Papers.

Johns Hopkins University Library, Baltimore, Maryland.

Lea & Febiger, Philadelphia, Pennsylvania: Messrs John and Christian Spahr who allowed me to examine the surviving records of Carey & Lea.

Library of Congress, Washington D.C. Both the manuscript and the printed collections of the Library are indispensable for anyone studying American political and diplomatic history.

The Rt Hon. the Earl of Malmesbury.

Maryland Historical Society, Baltimore, especially the J. A. Pearce and Brantz Mayer Papers.

Massachusetts Historical Society, Boston. Of the many major holdings, I found most valuable for this volume the papers of Edward Everett, Robert C. Winthrop, William H. Prescott, George Bancroft.

University of Michigan Library, Ann Arbor.

Pierpont Morgan Library, New York.

John Murray Ltd: Messrs John G. and John R. Murray for their cordial co-operation over the years.

National Archives and Records Office of the General Services Administration, Washington D.C. This great repository of government documents has enhanced its value to scholars over the years by making many of its collections available for purchase on microfilm.

National Book League, London. Its library contains a large number of standard works on the history of the book trade.

National Library of Scotland, Edinburgh, for the extensive papers of the Blackwood publishing firm.

National Reference Library of Science and Inventions, London, in particular, the Patent Office Library.

National Register of Archives (Scotland), Edinburgh.

New Hampshire Historical Society, Concord, for materials relating to Daniel Webster.

New York Bar Association, New York, for indexes to legal periodicals.

New York Historical Society, New York, for a wide and varied collection of manuscript and printed materials.

New York Public Library, New York, for the Berg Collection and the Department of Manuscripts.

New York State Library, Albany, for the Marcy Papers.

Newberry Library, Chicago, Illinois.

North Carolina State Department of Archives and History, Raleigh.

University of North Carolina Library, Chapel Hill. The Southern Historical Collection has a wealth of materials on nineteenth-century America.

Historical Society of Pennsylvania, Philadelphia. Among their impressive holdings are the papers of James Buchanan and the publishing firm of Carey & Lea.

University of Pennsylvania Library, Philadelphia.

Pilgrim Edition of the Dickens Letters: Madeline House, Graham Storey, and Kathleen Tillotson, the Editors, to whom I am most grateful for their cordial exchange of information.

Pratt Free Library, George Peabody Branch, Baltimore, Maryland, for the John P. Kennedy Papers.

Princeton University Library, Princeton, New Jersey.

Public Record Office, London. Transcripts of Crown copyright records in the Public Record Office appear by permission of the Controller of Her Majesty's Stationery Office. In the course of reading this volume it will become apparent how indebted I am for access to the archives of the different departments of government, especially the Foreign Office, the Colonial Office, the Board of Trade, the Treasury, the Court of Chancery, and the Post Office.

Purdue University Library, Lafayette, Indiana.

University of Rochester Library, Rochester, New York, for the Seward Papers.

Routledge & Kegan Paul Ltd, London. Margaret Selley was most helpful in my search through older records of the firm.

Royal Commission on Historical Manuscripts; and the National Register of Archives, London. Any scholar doing research in Britain comes to value the indexing services of the National Register as well as the work which the Commission has done in organizing the Palmerston Papers.

Mr and Mrs Rollo G. Silver, for their lively interest in my researches.

Mrs Theodore Silverstein. I am extremely grateful for the trouble taken to facilitate my perusal of new material relating to J. F. Crampton and the copyright issue.

The Rt Hon. Baron and Lady Stratheden and Campbell, for their kind and generous access to the diaries of John, Lord Campbell.

Miss V. M. Synge, for friendly interest in my research concerning her grandfather, W. W. F. Synge.

Syracuse University Library, Syracuse, New York.

United States Post Office Archives, Washington D.C.

University College Library, the University of London, for the Brougham Papers.

Victoria and Albert Museum, London, for the correspondence of John Forster and Charles Dickens.

Virginia Historical Society, Richmond.

University of Virginia Library, Charlottesville.

Wabash College Library, Crawfordsville, Indiana. I can scarcely express my deep appreciation for all the help and co-operation given to me over the years by Donald Thompson and the staff of the Lilly Library. They have made my task infinitely easier.

The Papers of Daniel Webster: G. E. Carter, Editor, and Mr K. C. Kramer of the Dartmouth College Library.

William and Mary College Library, Williamsburg, Virginia.

Yale University Library, New Haven, Connecticut.

Chapter I

THE DEPRESSION OF 1837–43 AND ITS IMPLICATIONS FOR THE AMERICAN BOOK TRADE

Perhaps nothing in the nineteenth century so influenced the American book trade as the depression of 1837–43. Established firms faltered but somehow carried on. New publishers sprang up only to disappear a few years later amidst the ranks of debtors and insolvents. Editors moved from one journal to another, seeking to stave off the inevitable. Prices for books and periodicals fell lower and lower, till proprietors began to wonder if it would not be cheaper to suspend business altogether. A mania for cheapness had descended upon the trade, and things would never be the same again.

England was undergoing a rather similar time of trouble, but this was small comfort to the average American bookman. If he paid any attention to the economics of the situation, he knew that British sterling was at a high premium, and American bank notes almost worthless. This was especially true in the spring and summer of 1837. It was brought home to even the largest and most prosperous of the American publishers when they could neither secure credit nor transact business in London. Harper & Bros of New York had agreed to pay the English novelist, Edward Lytton Bulwer, for advance sheets of his latest work: a history of ancient Athens. To their great chagrin they had to write and explain:[1]

By the packet which sails tomorrow, we were desirous of sending you a bill of £150 for 'Athens' – but upon consultation with some of our friends, we are told that a bill cannot be safely purchased at present. Nearly all of our bankers have failed – and it is feared that the remainder must fail before long. We were treating with one of our large Houses for a bill – but before the sailing of the packet the House failed! We cannot remit the specie, as the banks have suspended specie payments. Under these circumstances, we shall defer purchasing a draft until we hear further from England, and ascertain something more respecting the solvency of our bill drawers. We shall procure a bill as soon as we can possibly do so with safety, and of course will include interest for the delay.

Two months passed, but the Harpers' financial predicament persisted. Resorting to more bizarre channels of procuring funds, they advised Bulwer:

It mortifies us greatly that, owing to the present deranged state of affairs, we cannot remit to you as usual. As yet there is no ascertaining the fate of our bill drawers – Those generally considered good, will not draw upon any reasonable terms. –

We have just received a letter from our agent in Calcutta, (Mr. Henry T. Hall), advising us, that he should place in the hands of Messrs. Baring, Brothers, & Co. some funds (941 sicca rupees) on our account, – the exact value and amount of which we cannot ascertain – for which, however, we beg leave to enclose a draft. In case the funds have not arrived, or for any other cause, Messrs. Baring, Brothers, & Co. should decline paying the draft, we do not wish it protested – but beg that you will inform us of its reception, or otherwise, the amount received, &c. &c.

The crisis in credit and banking which overshadowed the year 1837 was only the prelude to something worse. The American economy recovered for a time and 1838 looked promising. Then in 1839 panic set in again: a depression whose severity, according to one recent economic historian, 'can most accurately be compared to that of 1929'. The signs were apparent enough. Major banks failed, companies went bankrupt, and even States of the Union defaulted on their debts. By 1842 there was still no interest forthcoming on bonds issued by Pennsylvania, Maryland, Michigan, Indiana, Illinois, Arkansas, and Mississippi. Much of the capital for these bonds had been raised in Britain to permit various states to finance the building of roads, canals, railways, and other public works. Once constructed, these works would have yielded a sufficient profit to cover both principal and interest. This plan might have worked had the depression not come along, making the bonds seem worthless since the public works were incomplete and the major political parties could not agree on how to repay the debts.

Some looked for help from the Federal Treasury. Others, especially the Democrats, advocated an increase in local taxation combined with a reduction in expenditure and a general lessening in the power of the

Federal Government. The Whigs thought money could be raised from the sale of public lands, the Government making up for lost revenue by substantially raising tariffs. However, nothing was done. The crisis continued: the states were in default and British creditors cursed the day that they had been tempted by the speculative prospects in America.

The depression was deeper than met the eye. The nation's economy had become heavily dependent upon the growth, financing, and exportation of cotton. Between 1831 and 1836 the value of cotton exports almost trebled. More and more marginal land was pressed into its cultivation, the market in slaves boomed, plantation banks over-extended credit; all combining to encourage Eastern merchants to finance shipments to Liverpool and there set up their own commercial exchange. The panic of 1837 changed all this. With the contraction of credit and the consequent mistrust of American currency, cotton prices inevitably fell. Production was over-committed, so that each year as prices declined and demand slackened more and more raw cotton came on to the market, depressing the price still farther.[2]

The book trade in America may not have been hit harder than any other business, but the depression certainly took its toll among authors, editors, and publishers. Horace Greeley, later proprietor of the *New York Tribune*, told how his magazine, the *New Yorker*, was progressing fairly well 'till the Commercial Revulsion of 1837 swept over the land, whelming it and me in the general ruin'.[3] When he married in 1836 he fancied himself modestly but comfortably secure. His assets were worth about $5,000, and his magazine provided an annual income of $1,000. Then came the depression:

instead of that, or of any income at all, I found myself obliged, throughout 1837, to confront a net loss of about $100. per week. . . . It was in vain that I appealed to delinquents to pay up; many of them migrated; some died; others were so considerate as to order the paper [magazine] stopped, but very few of these paid; and I struggled on against a steadily rising tide of adversity that might have appalled a stouter heart. Often did I call on this or that friend with an intent to solicit a small loan to some demand that could no longer be postponed nor evaded, and after wasting a precious hour, leave him, utterly unable to broach the loathsome topic. . . . Most gladly would I have terminated the struggle by a surrender; but, if I had failed to pay my notes continually falling due, I must have paid money for my weekly supply paper – so that would have availed nothing. To have stopped my journal (for I could not have given it away) would have left me in debt, besides my notes for paper, from fifty cents *to two dollars each, to at least three thousand subscribers who had paid in advance; and that is the worst kind of bankruptcy.*

The experience of Park Benjamin was not much happier. As editor of the *American Monthly Magazine*, he became increasingly involved in its survival and found himself pouring what money he had, plus what he could borrow from relatives, into the venture. The *Magazine* survived the first wave of 1837 only to succumb in the backwash of 1838. Benjamin long remembered this personal disaster to his own fortunes, and it is not surprising that he turned his efforts to editing a cheap newspaper which would be more likely to meet the cut-throat competition.[4]

Even the major publishing houses struggled to stay afloat. In 1837 the Harpers seriously considered bankruptcy as the best means of extricating themselves from the effects of the panic. The better alternative seemed to be one of retrenchment, in an effort to cut costs and overheads. Other firms contracted their operations and tried to ride out the storm.

Though a crude measurement of business stagnation, the numbers of titles published by these firms is some indication of their plight. In the early 1830s Harpers were averaging over fifty titles a year. The annual number fell below this figure for the years 1837, 1839, and 1842. In the last of these, some thirty-six works were published, many of which reflected earlier commitments to schoolbook publications. Their general trade sank to an unprecedented low. By contrast, the next few years testified to the restoration of confidence: 75 titles for 1844; 87 for 1845; 94 for 1846; 113 for 1847.[5]

The *Cost Book* or Paper and Print Book of Ticknor & Fields reveals a parallel struggle This Boston firm, a much smaller one than Harpers, was expanding its publishing in the early 1830s only to find its progress severely checked by economic conditions. Table 1 shows approximations of their yearly output.[6]

It was also an epoch of ever-diminishing retail prices. Whereas books averaged about $2.00 in the 1820s, they dropped to around 50¢ by the depression of 1837-43. Readers were also victims, and the amount of spare income allocated to reading matter was drastically reduced. Naturally tempted by the fall in book prices, they were even more attracted by cheaper periodicals and newspapers.

Perhaps most marked was the effect which the depression had on the leading Philadelphia firm of Carey & Lea (see Table 2).[7] Unfortunately the later cost books are not published, but the production curve is plain

TABLE I *Yearly output*

YEAR	NO. OF TITLES
1833	55
1834	13 (year of sharp recession)
1835	22
1836	5
1837	9
1838	11
1839	22
1840	13 (reflecting the growing panic of the previous year)
1841	24
1842	14
1843	36
1844	23
1845	33
1846	42
1847	48
1848	55
1849	57
1850	77
1851	105

TABLE 2 *Carey & Lea*

YEAR	NO. OF TITLES
1828	50
1829	46
1830	45
1831	69
1832	69
1833	106
1834	38
1835	112
1836	91
1837	52

enough. Even when one takes into account that some titles obviously sold more readily than others and that several best sellers offset a score of nonentities, the overall trend of the times emerges clearly. Popular novelists such as James Fenimore Cooper also felt the effects. In an effort to compete with price-cutting, Carey & Lea, Cooper's publishers, ripped the hard covers off thousands of his unsold volumes and replaced them with cheap paper ones. Until 1837 Carey & Lea successfully held their own against the rising competition from the Harpers of New York. However, in trying to adjust to reduced circumstances, they decided to lessen their dependence on both fiction and foreign reprints; the Harpers were geographically closer to the source of supply of imported books, and fiction was more volatile than other forms of literature. They reasoned that doctors, lawyers, engineers, and teachers would continue to order books even when the fickle reading public ceased buying new romances. Their strategy paid off. Within a decade Carey & Lea were leaders in the publication of medical and technical books. Gone were their editions of Dickens, Irving, and Cooper. Gone too, as of 1838, was Henry C. Carey himself from the ranks of prominent publishers. In spite of family tradition – he was the son of the illustrious publisher Mathew Carey – Henry increasingly turned his attention to the field of political economy. The substantial profits and opportunities for expansion which so characterized the latter 1820s and early 1830s had evaporated. The depression brought with it the passing of an era.

During these years of trade distress, cheap newspapers and periodicals came into their own. They dominated the book trade and came to symbolize both the best and the worst in American journalism. Two weeklies set the pace. These were *Brother Jonathan* and the *New World*, followed by a host of rivals and imitators, and contemporaries began to speak of a revolution in the production and marketing of literature. Their rise to prominence was meteoric; their decline almost as swift.

The first to make its appearance was *Brother Jonathan*. The capital for the venture seems to have come from a New York printer-publisher, James Gregg Wilson, while the editorial inspiration belonged to Park Benjamin and Rufus W. Griswold. As so often happened in these years, weekly journals were the offshoot of daily newspapers. Thus, Wilson's primary undertaking was the *Evening Tattler*, which he began to publish on 8 July 1839. On 13 July he announced his intention to publish a weekly as well. *Brother Jonathan* would be 'the largest folio sheet in the world', and would combine important news from the daily issues of the *Tattler* with 'as much more original and selected, prepared exclusively for the JONATHAN'.[8] A keynote was sounded on 24 July when the *Tattler* prepared its readers for the first of sixteen instalments of Dickens's *Nicholas Nickleby*. The *Great Western* steamship had brought this first instalment from Liverpool, while the slower sailing packets from London would supply the *Tattler*'s competitors. Taking pride in their accomplishment, the Editors informed their readers that their agent in London would be sure to send 'by the big ships, all the original sayings and original productions that are indigenous to that capital'.

These ingredients spelled radical change in the American book trade. The excess capacity of printing presses so frequently idle during the years of depression had great potential for rapidity and volume. People could ill afford to pay much for their reading, but the *Tattler* for a penny or the *Jonathan* for 6¢ were attractive bargains. For such modest outlays of cash, readers were to enjoy the advantages of both news and periodical literature. Few papers could boast of an agent in London, especially one who could make good use of the regular steamship service begun the previous year. Now British literature could make its way to the American shores in a matter of two weeks instead of the usual but uncertain thirty to sixty days. To be sure, most of these characteristics were not new, and other newspapers and periodicals exploited some of them. However, it took the peculiar combination of circumstances associated with the trade, technology and reading tastes of the late 1830s, to produce *Brother Jonathan* and the *New World*.[9]

A step-child of *Brother Jonathan*, the *New World* made its first appearance on 26 October 1839. Their similarity was hardly coincidental. Feeling unappreciated, Benjamin and Griswold deserted *Jonathan*, and with the backing of another printer, Jonas Winchester, launched this new venture. As before, there was to be a daily newspaper in conjunction with the weekly, and Winchester's *Evening Signal* duly made its appearance a fortnight before the *New World*. As the demand for stories and poems grew, these literary periodicals began to overshadow their daily counterparts. The weeklies in turn spawned monthlies. As early as January 1840 *Evergreen* appeared as a compilation of the *New World*'s best articles. *Brother Jonathan* was somewhat slower, but by January 1841 it could point with pride to its *Dollar Magazine*. In the early 1840s the same pattern was repeated elsewhere. George Roberts, the Boston publisher, combined the daily *Boston Times* with the weekly *Boston Notion* and *Roberts' Semi-Monthly Magazine*.

The distinctive feature of the new weeklies was their inordinate size. They all vied with each other to be the largest folio sheet in the world. On 30 November 1839 the *New World* brought out the first of its Leviathans, and claimed thereafter to lead the pack. Leviathans were issued sporadically and eventually became extra issues for which an additional charge was made. By the beginning of 1841 they had reached the absurd dimensions of five feet eight inches long by four feet four inches wide. This in turn gave way to the record-breaking Christmas Leviathan of 1841, measuring a modest six feet seven inches by four feet four inches! The surface area was 3,500 square inches, and subscribers were confronted by forty-eight columns; each a solid four feet of small type. The term 'mammoth' was applied to them, and even in their ordinary folio size they were more than a handful for the average reader. One had to spread out an issue on a table, or better yet, on the floor.

There was more than mere gimmickry in these large folios, however. The newspaper format held distinct advantages for the publisher of a weekly journal. A single sheet of printing paper could go through the post at newspaper rates instead of those for magazines, and such large sheets could be cheaply printed, required no binding or stitching, and yet had more reading matter than most literary periodicals. As the *New World* was not slow to point out, one of its issues contained more material than six daily newspapers. The editors of *Brother Jonathan* liked to make invidious comparisons with ordinary books: why not purchase as much reading for 6¢ as would otherwise cost $2.00 in a duodecimo volume? One volume of Irving's *Columbus* or Bancroft's *History* at $3.00 contained no more than a weekly issue of the *Jonathan*.[10]

The unwieldiness of the folios eventually induced publishers to issue quarto editions as well. Within the trade there was a relentless pressure for bigness, and subscribers had to be continually reassured that they were receiving as much reading matter as before. Having begun a quarto edition in June 1840, the *New World* ushered in a 'large quarto' one year later, with four columns to the page instead of three. The next year *Brother Jonathan* pointed out that the size of its printing sheet was larger than that used by its competitors. The quarto editions generally had sixteen pages, but the *New World*'s three or four columns per page held more print than the *Jonathan*'s two columns. By 1842 quarto editions had pretty well replaced folios in most people's libraries.[11] They lent themselves to binding in one or two volumes a year, which reinforced their publishers' claim that they contained literature worth preserving. The seemingly innocuous decision to emphasize the quartos had one unforeseen effect. It was but the first of many steps to deprive the 'mammoths' of their uniqueness and eventually to relegate them to the mass of undifferentiated cheap periodicals.

In the meantime the weeklies took everyone by storm. Increasingly they filled their columns with stories from abroad and capitalized on readers' anticipation of coming instalments. Emulating the newspapers of the day, they sent newsboys on to the streets to hawk the latest issues. In large cities arrangements could be made to deliver copies to subscribers' doors, or people could pick them up at designated outlets. Unlike newspapers, they developed not only a local but also a national market. They did this by appointing local agents in major cities throughout the country. In this respect the *New World* seems to have been more successful than *Brother Jonathan*. In 1840 it had about thirty-five agents, one to a town, scattered throughout a dozen states. By the beginning of 1841 there were fifty-two in seventeen states and the District of Columbia plus an additional five in Canada. Most of these were concentrated in the North-Eastern quadrant of the country where readers could avail themselves of the same price of 6¢ charged in New York, while Southern and Western agents supplied their customers for as little as 12½¢ per copy. *New World* agents in the North-East were supplied copies at the rate of one hundred for $4.00, giving them a profit of 2¢ on each copy sold. They were also encouraged to solicit annual subscriptions for $3.00 each, from which they could retain 75¢. Towns without an agent were urged to provide themselves with one, and if this were not possible, to use the authorized travelling representatives. However, since there were only three of these throughout the United States and Canada, subscribers were cautioned against imposters.[12]

The other important means of developing a national market was through the post. This proved particularly convenient for communities lacking an authorized agent, in as much as *Brother Jonathan* or the *New World* could be mailed to subscribers for $3.00 a year. To be sure, payment had to be made in advance and sent to the publishing offices in New York, but this was facilitated by one of the regulations of the Post Office: local postmasters were allowed to use their franking privilege when forwarding subscriptions and payments to newspapers and periodicals. Similarly, renewals required no postage as long as the local postmaster transmitted them.

Clearly, it was an easy step to convert postmasters into unofficial subscription agents, and as with authorized city agents, they could also retain 75¢ from every $3.00. Payments to publishers were to be made in 'funds current in New York', a reminder of the currency and banking instability of the time.[13] A few months later even these qualifications were relaxed in the interest of encouraging new subscriptions. 'We are quite willing to receive "Red Back" bills, in spite of the machination of the New York Brokers.' They went on to explain that the panic over currency was not as bad as it was pictured by those who stood to profit from it.[14]

By the summer of 1841 a very different tone was assumed towards subscribers and their payments. 'We have paid during the past year more than *fifteen thousand dollars* in discounts on uncurrent or Southern and Western money, a sum quite too large, and which ought to be diminished.' Even the North-East subscribers were henceforth charged an extra 8 to 20 per cent if their banks were unchartered. By the same token, outlying agents would have to content themselves with 50¢ instead of 75¢ commission on each $3.00 subscription.[15]

Once having established a nation-wide clientele, the weeklies launched further campaigns of expansion. As precursors of twentieth-century Madison Avenue, the columns of the *New World* trumpeted valuable premiums for those who renewed their subscriptions promptly or secured new ones. The multi-volume edition of *Sears' Illustrated Bible* was offered as tempting bait. Each volume was said to be worth $2.00 and was awarded in exchange for two new subscriptions. Alternatively, one could begin to collect the eight-volume set of the *American Family Magazine* with its one thousand woodcut illustrations; the really ambitious might acquire the whole set by collecting merely fifteen new subscribers. Somewhat later, seven new subscriptions qualified for a $5.00 premium in the form of Stephens's *Incidents of Travel in Central America*.[16]

Absolutely essential to the successful functioning of *Brother Jonathan* and the *New World* was the notion of narrow profit margins based on volume sales. The *New World*, for example, made an impressive beginning in October 1839, when its first printing of 15,000 quickly sold. A month later, the first Leviathan realized a sale of 20,000. Gradually, in the next six months, the regular weekly issues and occasional Leviathans climbed to the imposing figure of 25,000. During the course of 1841 the average weekly circulation was somewhat under 20,000, although the special Leviathan issues might reach as high as 30,000.[17] *Brother Jonathan* was more discreet about its weekly circulation figures, and while they were no doubt imposing, they were probably somewhat less than those of the

New World. Both journals far exceeded the circulation of other American periodicals, with the exception of *Graham's Magazine* and a few of the leading daily newspapers. Neither were there many publications in Great Britain which approximated these figures.

Large sales depended in turn on rapid and efficient printing presses. Never modest in its accomplishments, the *New World* crowned its wave of success by moving to larger premises. This was in the spring of 1840 and a year later it could boast of two Napier presses capable of printing 20,000 sheets in three or four days. From rather humble beginnings, Jonas Winchester had become one of the leading printers in New York City.[18] It was only a matter of time until this increased printing capacity was put to additional use. What began as a premium for new subscribers eventually turned into a whole new publishing industry. The beginnings were rather unspectacular: in the *New World* of 19 June 1841 appeared an announcement for Charles Lever's Irish novel, *Charles O'Malley*, to be issued complete in a special quarto edition, distinct from the regular weekly issue. This would be sent free to new subscribers or to anyone renewing a subscription. Of course there was nothing unusual about reprinting British novels, but till now they had been presented in weekly or monthly instalments. A few long poems or plays by Bulwer, Knowles, or Moore, were sometimes printed complete in one weekly issue, but now for the first time readers had a whole novel squeezed into the many columns of a single printed sheet.

The implications of this experiment were not immediately grasped, and it was not until the following spring that novels began appearing in supplements of one, two, or three sheets, comprising 16, 32, or 48 quarto pages. *Brother Jonathan* followed suit as did other newspapers and periodicals to a lesser extent. During the course of 1842 the *New World* put out twenty-one works of fiction and non-fiction in the form of 'extras', followed by thirty-six separate reprints the next year. Regular subscribers were charged $1.00 or $2.00 in addition to the normal subscription fee for these supplements and were reminded that a typical novel occupied the the space of two or three sheets. In major cities including New York, a single number would usually cost 12½¢; a double number 18¾¢ or 25¢. Prices in the country would be proportionally higher. To interest agents, special rates were offered for quantity orders.

What was most remarkable about these special supplements was the size of their sales. The *New World*'s edition of Bulwer's *Zanoni* had sold 26,000 copies within a few weeks of its appearance, while some months later *Brother Jonathan* reported 33,000 for its edition. The usual number of copies for a first printing was 10,000, as in the case of G. P. R. James's *Jacquerie* and *Morley Ernstein*, but during 1842–3 there was always the firm expectation that further printings would be called for. Even a volume of Bulwer's poems, *Eva*, provided *Brother Jonathan* with a sale of 16,500, at a time when most poetry was thought to be a drug on the market. Another *Jonathan* extra, *Gasper the Pirate*, totalled 28,500; *Father Connell* reached 21,000; and *The Butchers of Ghent*, 25,000. Dickens's *American Notes* brought the *New World* over 50,000 customers, while a similar number was confidently anticipated for Bulwer's *Last of the Barons*.[19] With James's *Morley Ernstein*, the *New World* outdid itself. Winchester's presses took only sixty hours to turn out the entire American edition of 10,000, notwithstanding its use of 600,000 'ems' and 320 tokens.[20]

Popular French novels in translation were also a favourite target for reprinting. Sometimes, when no convenient translation was available, a special American one might be commissioned. In the case of Borgaerts's *The Butchers of Ghent*, the translator turned out to be the Editor of *Brother Jonathan* himself.[21]

Occasionally, in a burst of literary nationalism or by way of countering criticism against piratical publishers, the weeklies sponsored an original American work. Such was *Jonathan*'s edition of *Puffer Hopkins* by Cornelius Mathews, and no opportunity was lost to point out that the copyright had been purchased by the journal. Another was Walt Whitman's *Franklin Evans, Or the Inebriate*, which the *New World* published in the autumn of 1842.[22]

For a time these supplements became so spectacularly successful that their publishers began to curtail the weeklies in order to concentrate on book-length extras. At the beginning of 1843 the *New World* decided to discontinue serialized stories in its weekly issues. It had already stopped publishing the daily *Signal* and the monthly *Evergreen*. Now the weekly was to be cut back in the interest of selling complete works at low prices, and the publisher claimed that this would not injure the quality of the weekly but would only enhance the supplements.[23]

For the next few years supplements were all the rage. As a contemporary observer noted, there were distinct advantages to any publisher who could carry on this kind of cheap mass-circulation competition.

The change in the mode of publishing has brought about this result. Formerly, when the production of a book required capital and credit, there was a natural limit in the resources of the trade. Many books went through some of the regular forms of announcement, printing, binding, circulating from city to city, a tithe of the best English publications supplied the market. Correspondents and agencies had to be created, and credit had to be given.

The coming of paper-covered unbound reprints changed all this. Printer-publishers like Winchester and Wilson did not extend credit but accepted cash over the counter or from advance subscriptions. New outlets were created which placed no obligation upon the publisher. 'One of the most flourishing . . . in Broadway is a candy shop!',[24] wrote a correspondent in New York to the *Athenaeum* in London. He went on:

Where there is no copyright charge, no binders' charge, where one sheet of paper does the work of four, where there are no losses by credit, where there is no store-hire chargeable, where there are no old shopkeepers on hand, the edition being at once disposed of for ready money – books may well be cheap, and cheap they are.

With the resources of a large newspaper establishment and the need to keep labour and machinery constantly employed, the cheap weeklies paid no attention to publishing seasons or other considerations of traditional book production and distribution. Any competitor would be forced to slash prices and narrow profit margins. Few orthodox book-publishers were inclined to risk this, especially in view of the protracted trade depression.

As long as large impressions were sold, profits could be made. The correspondent for the *Athenaeum* estimated that the break-even point came at about 2,000 copies sold. After that, from $40.00 to $50.00 clear profit could be made on every thousand copies. Thus a sale of 20,000 copies would return a handsome profit of $1,000.

What was particularly significant to the *Athenaeum*'s observer was the wide range of cheap republication in America.[25]

The class of works is very far from being limited to the fashionable novels. The republications of this week in New York alone are O'Connell's 'Memoir of Ireland,' (25 cents); Dr Arnold's 'Lectures on History,' (25 cents); Mrs Ellis's 'Wives of England,' (25 cents); the last number of the Edinburgh Review, (25 cents); and 'The Roué,' (12½ cents), an old novel now published as Bulwer's on the faith and recommendation of some former advertisements in the Times. There have been four cheap editions of Borrow's 'Bible in Spain' by two publishers, and three of the 'Zincali;' at least 35,000 copies in all. The translation of

D'Aubigné's 'History of the Reformation' has been widely circulated. Alison's 'History of Europe' will be soon entirely published for four dollars, with some additions by the author. Taylor's 'Edwin the Fair' was published for 6¼ cents. The whole twenty parts of 'Martin Chuzzlewit' will be published by the Messrs Harpers, with fourteen well executed plates, for forty-four cents, less than the cost of two numbers in England, and the edition is as good as that of Ballantyne's 'British Novelists,' in double columns. Of Bulwer's 'Last of the Barons,' at least 50,000 were circulated. Bulwer's 'Eva, and other Poems' attained a large edition at sixpence – in the old form it would have remained on the shelves. Brande's 'Encyclopaedia' may be had complete for three dollars. 'The Pictorial History of England' will soon be republished. What think you of Liebig's works and old Froissart in this popular form? Several editions of the former have been published, and the latter is in hand. So you will see that the Commissioners of Customs will have full employment for at least one sub-official in keeping the list of contraband books.

Many contemporary Americans criticized the cheap weeklies and their supplements not only because of the shoddy appearance and eye-straining type but also because of the impact they had on traditional modes of authorship and publishing. The weeklies were not slow to justify themselves. In fact one might say they even anticipated such charges. In the second issue of the *New World* for 2 November 1839 they set down their credo.

The 'New World' will be found to be worthy of its name from its full summary of all the important events that may transpire between Behring's Strait and Cape Horn! ... The whole World of letters, Old and New, will be ransacked for the best and richest stores. Every book and every periodical of merit, whether published in Great Britain or the United States, will be received at this office, and faithful selections made from them all. Our chief aim will be to be entertaining.

From the beginning the weeklies emphasized their unique contributions to American literary life in order to set themselves apart from the other eclectic journals. As often as possible they avoided printing extracts and instead reprinted the whole of foreign articles, plays, and poems. In this way the *New World* could claim that it had introduced to the American reading public some thirty-five complete works in the space of one year. Any two of these would have cost subscribers more in London than they paid for their year's subscription.[26]

It was argued that the cheap weeklies were a particular boon to the country subscriber. No longer need he wait endlessly for journals and books to arrive at the nearest bookseller's shop. Now he could receive the latest in American and foreign literature carried as quickly as possible by the post. Furthermore, whether subscribers and readers lived in country or town they were all victims of hard times. In these circumstances, cheapness was a virtue.[27]

The community . . . owes us a debt of gratitude for reducing the prices of works of light literature to the means of the poorest classes. We have begun a great literary revolution, which will result in enlightening the understanding of the masses. It is truly democratic – utterly subversive of that intellectual aristocracy which has hitherto controlled the energies of the nation.

To those cynics who accused the weeklies of debasing taste and corrupting morals, the *New World* had its own self-righteous answer.[28]

This influence of the press is a powerful auxiliary to the great temperance movement. Joined with them, it is fast robbing the rum-palace of its victims; it renders the neglected home pleasant; restores to the dejected inebriate a true sense of his own real worth; and is, in fact, the very essence of civilization. The seed thus unwittingly scattered by the way-side, will bring forth a thousand fold, and the harvest will be – the human mind redeemed, regenerated, disenthralled.

And to the chorus of voices raised within the book trade in protest against the ruinous competition which cheap reprints had brought, the *New World* charged: was it not these same critics who consistently opposed an international copyright agreement in the name of cheap literature for America? All that the mammoths were doing was to extend low prices to their logical conclusion. Well might the American reading public wonder why the book trade had not long since followed *Brother Jonathan* and the *New World*.[29] In fact, the *New World* had nothing but scorn for one of the older eclectic journals, the *Albion*, and baited it by asking whether it was not content with its share of literary piracy: 'Born stealing, has lived by stealing, and will die stealing!'[30] Besides, the *Albion* contained a third less reading at twice the price.

The *New World*'s challenge to the book trade did not long go unheeded. In 1842 the largest American book publishers, Harper & Bros of New York, decided to do battle. Perhaps this eminent firm on Cliff Street might never have entered the conflict had they not felt provoked. A fire

broke out in their bindery on the first of June and it seemed to be the work
of an arsonist. The Harpers became convinced that Winchester's *New
World* was connected with the fire in an effort to steal a copy of James's
Morley Ernstein, which Harpers were soon to publish.[31] Despite the fire
Harpers issued a cheap edition of *Morley Ernstein* and began to cut prices
on its other English reprints. The *New World* was not impressed. The
Editor informed his readers that he would 'keep cool' and would gladly
give Harper notice 'the moment we are in a fair way of "being done for" '.[32]

By the end of the year Harpers had issued twelve cheap reprints, most
of them by Bulwer, and made it clear that this was only the beginning.
It reduced the price of its popular Family Library from 45¢ to 25¢. This
series, begun in the early 1830s, had reached about 150 titles by the end of
1842. Though most of the works had long been in print, they were now
available at very tempting prices. A note of concern combined with
combativeness crept into the *New World*'s rhetoric by late autumn.[33]

*Surely, they [Harpers] make money enough in their District School Library
and other works of a similar character to leave production of a transitory
interest to others. . . . About twenty-five hours after our edition of Dickens'
American Notes was out . . . they came lagging along with a shilling [12½¢]
edition, without doubt, with the intention of injuring our sales . . . If we see
more of this, we will . . . republish all the most valuable books in their list,
at a cost barely sufficient to cover the smallest expenses – viz: compositors'
wages, paper, ink, and presswork. We rather think we could give most of their
dollar books for sixpence a piece.*

Now it was the Harpers' turn to scoff. They knew that they vastly
exceeded Winchester and the others in assets and publishing capacity.
They also did their own printing and were not dependent, as the cheap
reprinters were, on only one kind of market. They could well afford to
take a loss on their Library of Select Novels and a number of other
publications and still make up for it on school books. Due to general trade
conditions 1842 had not been a good year for them and they had little to
lose by cut-throat competition. They might even be able to beat the
pirates at their own game. Their resolution was no doubt quickened when
an early copy of Bulwer's *The Last of the Barons* was stolen from their
premises on Christmas Day.

Competition became more reckless during 1843. The pages of the *New
World* were sprinkled with caustic comments about Harpers' publications.
Readers were especially warned to avoid the inferior Harper editions of

Alison's *History of Europe* and Sue's *Mysteries of Paris* in favour of the superior Winchester versions. In the case of Dickens's *Martin Chuzzlewit*, they met the *New World* on its home ground by sending newsboys into the streets selling part-issues for 6¢ each and stretching the work over seventeen instalments.[34]

Increasingly during 1843 and 1844 it became apparent that Harpers would withstand the competition and that the *New World* might not. *Brother Jonathan* succumbed at the end of 1843 and was acquired formally by Winchester in January 1844. By the summer of 1844 the strain on the *New World* was clearly apparent. Competitors arose on all sides. As Prescott put it: the 'bigger sharks' were beginning to complain now that 'the smaller ones are running away with the game'.[35] The predicament for the *New World* revolved around their having paid Sue 15,000 francs in order to receive advance sheets of his *Wandering Jew*. It was their intention to issue the work in instalments as it appeared in Paris. Before long it became apparent that few others in America were prepared to respect Winchester's priority of claim on the work. Two other versions in French appeared in America plus English translations based on a London edition. How ironic it was for the *New World* to condemn the latter as a 'pirated edition'.[36]

There were others who were less successful than the Harpers in weathering the competition with the *New World*. One such was Horace Greeley. During 1839 and 1840 his energies were absorbed in journalistic support of Henry Clay and in the literary fortunes of a periodical, the *New Yorker*. Writing to Griswold in early 1841, Greeley lamented the impact which the mammoths had. 'The great beasts murder me in the way of circulation.'[37] Soon thereafter the *New Yorker* folded and Greeley in effect adopted the motto: if you can't beat them, join them. He saw all too clearly what had to be done to survive in that time of trade depression and rampant price-cutting. Somewhat reminiscent of Winchester in 1839, he began a daily newspaper in April 1841. His *Tribune* was to have a weekly version as well; one that could be posted to subscribers in the country. The pattern was repeating itself and Greeley showed that Wilson's and Winchester's formula was a good one if strictly adhered to. By 1860 the *Weekly Tribune* had reached the unprecedented circulation of 200,000.[38]

Another apparent casualty of these years was the literary magazine, the *New York Mirror*. As a weekly it had been in existence since 1823 and survived the hardships of 1837–9 only to founder in 1842. Its proprietor,

BAP

Gen. George Pope Morris, managed to revive it for a while in 1843-4 but finally gave up and launched a daily newspaper, the *Evening Mirror*, and the natural corollary, a *Weekly Mirror*. As such, the two publications continued for some years.[39]

Keen competition was not the only threat facing the cheap weeklies in the years 1842-3. Ominous rumblings began to come from the United States Post Office. This was unexpected since special low rates of postage for newspapers had been a long-standing concession from the American Congress. According to the Act of 1825, which was still in force in the early 1840s, newspapers were charged only 1¢ for distances under one hundred miles and 1½¢ for greater distances. Although the mammoths came out weekly, they were only one printing sheet and easily qualified for this low postage. Another problem arose in defining just where a newspaper left off and a magazine began. This was especially true for the quarto editions of the *New World* and *Brother Jonathan*, folded like magazines and containing sixteen or thirty-two pages. However, since they were unstitched, they avoided paying the higher magazine rates of 1½¢ or 2½¢.[40]

The extras which the *New World* and *Brother Jonathan* began to issue defied definition. Their publishers saw no reason why these supplements in one, two, or three sheets should not go through the post at newspaper rates. Since they were not published on a regular basis they could hardly be regarded as magazines and were thus not subject to the somewhat higher postage for periodicals. But Section 30 of the Act of 1825 also made provision for magazines or pamphlets which appeared sporadically. Four cents was to be charged for shorter distances and 6¢ for longer ones. At that rate a two-sheet supplement would cost *New World* subscribers 8¢ instead of 2, or 12¢ instead of 3, depending upon distance. In fact this is what eventually happened with *Brother Jonathan*'s edition of Bulwer's *Zanoni*. The Post Office ruled that it was a three-sheet pamphlet and subject to 12 or 18¢ postage.[41]

The question was strictly one of interpretation, and it was up to the Postmaster General, Charles A. Wickliffe, to construe the Act of 1825. On the surface it looks as though he had decided to undermine the cheap weeklies. One might reasonably suspect that influence was brought to bear upon him from the more traditionally-minded members of the book trade. However, there is nothing in the surviving Post Office records to suggest this. What is evident is that the Post Office was plagued by a whole class of irregularly published materials which needed definition.

Wickliffe decided to seek the opinion of H. S. Legaré, the United States Attorney-General, and in a letter of 12 March 1842 he set forth the problem. There was no mention of *Brother Jonathan* nor the *New World* in it. Instead, he was preoccupied with *Shipping and Commercial List and New York Prices Current*, *New Orleans Prices Current*, *Savannah Prices Current*, *Charleston Prices Current*, and other similar commercial publications.[42] On 18 March Legaré duly rendered an official opinion which sought to clarify the ambiguities.[43]

On the whole, the only requisites of a newspaper which I think must be judicially held indispensable are –

1st That it be bona fide published, that is, for everybody's use. For example, the Price Currents, &c., printed at stated intervals, and sent by great Banking and Commercial houses to their customers, are not newspapers: they are not pro bono publico, but for private use.

2nd That they be published in numbers, not perhaps with exact regularity, but something approaching to it. Occasional sheets, placards, &c., are not newspapers.

3rd That they convey news, not mere dissertations and discussions, or literary and poetical miscellanies.

4th That they be in sheets, and in rather a cheap form.

But cases will be perpetually arising in which the Chief of the Post Office Department or the Stamp Bureau would be at a loss what to do without express legislative instructions. If you think them required by the service, I have no doubt they are called for by the state of the law.

With this opinion in hand, Wickliffe informed the New York Postmaster that *Brother Jonathan*'s supplement of *Zanoni* was liable to pamphlet postage because it was not in sheets but stitched and in a paper cover. The *New World*, however, successfully made out a case to exempt its edition of *Zanoni* on the grounds that it had no cover and was not stitched. Needless to say, *Brother Jonathan* did not make the same mistake twice, and for another year both reprint publishers enjoyed the usual newspaper rates of postage.[44]

Then came a sudden reversal of policy. As the *New World* described it, the New York Post Office received instructions to charge pamphlet rates 'on all the cheap publications of the day, issued as extras'.[45] This time it really seemed as if the Postmaster General was out to get the cheap weeklies. And little wonder. The weeklies had grown progressively abusive in their criticism of Post Office procedures and inefficiencies.

Why was it, they had rhetorically asked the previous year, that a barrel of flour could be shipped from New York to Boston, Massachusetts, or Portland, Maine, for only 10¢ or 12½¢, while the letter postage to these cities cost 18¾¢? In 1841 the editor of the *New World* wondered when Postmaster General Granger would resign from the Tyler cabinet, and pointed out that mail service had grown worse in the past four months than during the previous ten years. 'Mr. Granger may be a very good intriguing politician, a first-rate abolitionist, and a great Minister of State, but he is a miserable manager of the Post. The deputies, whom he has appointed, are constantly making the most vexatious blunders; and it is high time that the newspaper press should expose them.'[46]

Obviously there was no love lost between the weeklies and the Post Office. This in itself might have been sufficient provocation to bring about some form of Post Office retaliation. However, the *New World* detected another source of grievance: the Postmaster General wished to penalize publishers for employing private express companies rather than the United States mail.

Prior to 1825 the problem of private versus public conveyors of the mail had not loomed large. Both modes were allowed by law. Then by the nineteenth section of the Act of 1825 the Post Office was given a near monopoly. Any stagecoach, vehicle, or boat travelling on legally designated Post Roads or waterways was forbidden to carry letters, newspapers, and magazines. Only agents and contractors employed by the Post Office were permitted to do so. Two years later Congress tried to tighten the restriction by excluding private mail carriers on foot or on horseback. Yet private express companies multiplied and continued to compete with the United States Post Office. They did so by one of several ways. Though the more direct Post Roads were closed to them, they could use any other route from city to city. Furthermore, the law made no provision for railway conveyance, and this became increasingly important despite its relatively high cost. Finally, in some areas the Post Office subcontracted its business to private agents, which meant that under certain circumstances they could be given permission by the Postmaster General to carry private consignments of newspapers, magazines, and pamphlets over and above those items officially allocated to the Federal mail. The Post Office's consignment came first, but if there was still room, other things could be conveyed as well.[47]

The problem of private expresses became Wickliffe's prime concern during the Tyler Administration. Especially after Britain reduced her rates of postage in 1840, the American Post Office came under considerable fire from many quarters demanding it do likewise. Wickliffe was willing to contemplate a rate reduction if he could secure a monopoly to the Post Office. Thus it was that he began to marshal evidence against the express companies. In his annual report to Congress for 1843, he assigned two main reasons for a fall in postal revenues. He admitted that the poor trade conditions of the time might have had some influence, but by far the greater loss was ascribed to the competition from the expresses. He called for stricter enforcement of existing laws and a strengthening of the Post Office's rights by new legislation.[48] He also referred to a letter which he sent out to subcontractors on 1 September 1843. In this he reminded them that their right to carry newspapers and magazines in bulk apart from the regular mail was contingent on formal approval by the Postmaster General. Many contractors had not obtained such permission or were operating under the misapprehension that cheap newspapers might go in bulk on Post Roads whereas more expensive papers and periodicals had to pay postal rates. He also asked the Attorney-General if an express company such as Adams & Co. of New York and Boston could be prosecuted. It was known to have illegally carried some mail amounting to $3.00. Needless to say, the amount was trivial but Wickliffe felt that a matter of principle was at issue. He seemed to be on firm ground, gaining support for his position from the Attorney-General.[49]

Congress was slow in tightening the laws against express companies, and in the meantime relations worsened between the cheap reprint trade and the Post Office. Upon learning in May 1843 that their supplements could no longer travel at newspaper rates, the New World assumed a stance of defiance. Henceforth they would send everything they could by private express: 'we will not send even a letter by mail, if we can get it carried in any other way'. It was high time the Post Office was disbanded and private enterprise allowed to prevail.[50]

The columns of the New World provide a commentary on the running battle with the Post Office. They urged the Postmaster General to emulate Britain's low postal rates, and condemned his forbidding local postmasters from serving as publishers' agents or using their franking privilege to forward subscriptions. In 1844 they protested against proposed legislation that would substantially increase the postage on pamphlets and magazines, and they viewed any legislative effort to limit the overall dimensions of newspapers as an overt attack upon the mammoths.[51] There was also personal abuse. In their eyes the Postmaster General was: 'a stupid, fat

man, with no more "go-aheadness" in him, than a somniferous mud-turtle'.[52]
The cheap periodicals had one very powerful weapon in their arsenal. Private express rates were generally cheaper than Post Office rates. The *New World* recommended one of the private carriers to the attention of the public. It disclosed that the American Mail Letter Co. was prepared to offer attractive rates to specified cities, implying that publishers might supply their customers with bulk mailings via private express. A few weeks later it noted: 'Soon a line of [private] mails will be established, extending from Bangor to New Orleans, and letters will be sent to those places for 5 or 10 cents'. At about the same time another reprint publisher, E. Littell, recalled how he 'had offers to carry [his journal] at one quarter the government price', admitting that 'this would not have been available for the scattered residences of very distant subscribers – but it would have taken away most of what is profitable to the Post Office'.[53]

In the struggle between the Post Office and the mammoth press, Postmaster General Wickliffe had the satisfaction of witnessing the downfall of both Wilson and Winchester. Wilson sold *Brother Jonathan* to Winchester in early 1844, but later that year Winchester himself went bankrupt. When Congress finally passed the new Post Office bill a few months later, Wickliffe achieved some of his aims. Newspapers were to be limited in size to 1,900 square inches, a significant reduction from the Leviathans of recent memory. Trains as well as coaches and boats were now designated as official conveyors of the post, but they could only carry magazines and pamphlets in bulk when intended for retail outlets rather than individual subscribers.[54]

The competition between private and public carriers was by no means over. Before the Act of 1845 the *New World* observed: 'The prosecutions of the Post Master General seem to have little or no effect, for the ablest judges in the land have decided against the Department.' Following the passage of the 1845 Act, the new Postmaster General, Cave Johnson, was not much more successful in curbing extra-governmental mail carriers. Private expresses were still depriving the Post Office of revenue, and it was very difficult to enforce the law against them. It was a pyrrhic victory for the reprinters, however, many of whom ceased to ply their trade during those frantic early years of the decade.[55]

Why this decline or demise of the mammoths and their book-length supplements? The question has preoccupied many observers then and since. F. L. Mott, who has done more than anyone else to further our knowledge of nineteenth-century periodicals, has two key explanations to offer. First, the mammoths were badly hurt when the Post Office imposed higher rates on the supplements in the spring of 1843, and second, the Act of 1845 lowered book rates thus allowing other publishers to compete more effectively with the cheap reprinters through the post.[56] In the first instance there is no doubt that the change in postage hurt the reprinters, but as we have already seen they were not slow to react. By shifting as much of their mail-order business as possible to private expresses they may even have saved sufficient money to offset the higher official charges on country subscriptions. As for Mott's second point, it is difficult to know what to make of it. The Act of 1845, as with previous acts, forbade the sending of bound books through the United States mail,[57] and since serious weight limitations were placed on parcels of printed matter, it is difficult to imagine publishers dispatching large quantities of unbound books. It is true that the Act of 1845 significantly reduced the rate on pamphlets, which in turn would apply to single copies of cheap reprints. Had *Brother Jonathan* or the *New World* continued their book-length extras, they could have availed themselves of these reductions. Other firms exploited these cheap rates with pamphlet-like reprints. Thus it would seem that reduced pamphlet rates fostered what remained of the cheap reprint trade rather than gave any new advantage to the more traditional book publishers. If book publishers were to win out in their struggle against the cheap weeklies, they would have to do so on their own ground of retail outlets, not through the post.

Competition was certainly an important ingredient in Wilson's and Winchester's decline. More threatening than the Harpers, however, may have been the appearance of numerous smaller firms or 'little sharks'. Individually none of them was a match for *Brother Jonathan* or the *New World*, but collectively they made deep inroads into the reprint market. Editions of twenty or twenty-five thousand were becoming rare; the correspondent for the *Athenaeum* estimated that the average had dropped to five thousand. Even if this figure is conservative, the mammoths could not long sustain a narrowing of their profit margins resulting from a host of imitators.

Under ideal trade conditions the mammoths might have been able to withstand such competition, but they were victims as well as exploiters of the economic depression. They were continually over-extended and under-capitalized. The shoe-string nature of their business is seen in Benjamin's apology to Longfellow for not being able to publish his poems.[58]

since I saw you in Cambridge, we [New World] *have entered into so costly an arrangement for a foreign correspondent in England, on the Continent of Europe and in South America that the publisher* [Winchester] *fairly* [?] *declared his inability to pay the proper price* [*for the poems*].

By the spring of 1844 Benjamin saw the writing on the wall and resigned as Editor of the *New World*.⁵⁹

I think Winchester an unsafe man – I do not mean dishonest but rash and imprudent. Before I left the New World establishment, he had managed to get himself considerably into debt by his careless and venturesome way of transacting business.

So I managed to get out of the concern by absolutely giving away my interest, so as to obtain a full release from the creditors and ample security for money lent by my brother to the finance-ring; a mortgage on the whole establishment, which cost $40,000 and would sell at auction at $15,000 to secure $8,000. This mortgage expires in a couple of months and will be foreclosed, unless $4,000 is paid – which I am confident cannot be. Winchester has been greatly assisted by Letsfield [?] *but that bubble has burst – and, unless something as lucky turns up, he must be wound up.*

Ironically, when times began to improve in late 1843, the weeklies sustained a further setback. What economists call a shift in the income elasticity of demand took place: people began to find more employment, to feel they had more disposable income, and to prefer better looking books and magazines to the cheapest editions possible. In this respect, prosperity proved to be their final undoing. Like prehistoric mammals, the mammoths had become over-specialized and unable to adapt to new circumstances. Beginning as daily and weekly newspapers and then monthly periodicals, they gradually sloughed off the dailies and monthlies and reduced the value of the weeklies by depriving them of serialized stories. This inevitably put the emphasis on cheap book production. But book production, even in the form of cheap supplements through the post, was too complex an enterprise to develop and stabilize in a few hectic years. By falling into this trap, the mammoths unwittingly courted the competition of the major book publishers as well as the newspaper and magazine proprietors. Given more time and tranquillity, they might well have made a success of it, as Greeley's *New York Tribune* was to do. But these were volatile times. Traders and merchants of all sorts were in and out of business, bankruptcies abounded, and it is small wonder that the reprinters went under.

The commercial disruption of 1837–43 ultimately took its toll among those who most profited from it. The biographer of Park Benjamin states: 'the greatness of his editorial career with the *New World* never returned; he was to have a hand in many editorial ventures, but only as an associate more or less recognized at the time, and most frequently as a hack writer and special contributor'. This fate was much less apparent in 1844, however, especially when Benjamin withdrew as editor of the *New World*. Towards the end of 1845 he arranged to edit a new weekly folio financed by some printers in Baltimore. This necessitated moving from his familiar New York, and in January 1846 the first issue of the *Western Continent* was published. It was patterned on the *New World* as it had been in its earlier and more successful days. The experiment was short-lived. Within six months Benjamin sold his interest in the venture and left Baltimore.

Another year passed with nothing very promising in the offing. Then in October 1847, in conjunction with a printer, Ross Wilkinson, Benjamin resuscitated the *New World*. It was presented in its early folio garb, trying desperately to recapture its former glory at a time when the nation's economy was sluggish but not heavily depressed. Unfortunately it collapsed in the spring of 1848, this time for good. Benjamin never found anything to take its place.

Jonas Winchester fared no better. Six months after Benjamin quit as editor of the *New World* Winchester declared bankruptcy. His son and another partner took over, but by May 1845 Ebenezer Winchester was forced to sell the New World to Ward & Co. who merged it with their *Saturday Emporium*.[60] Once the Winchesters sold their interest in the *New World* they had no further use for the extensive printing facilities at 30 Ann Street. They moved into smaller premises at 44 Ann Street and in time published a masonic periodical known as the *Golden Rule and Family Companion*. A few years later a contemporary observed that Jonas Winchester was still poor, and by the early 1850s both father and son had disappeared from New York City. From a modest beginning as a junior partner in Horace Greeley's printing firm, Jonas Winchester rose to considerable heights in the early 1840s, only to subside into oblivion with equal dispatch.[61]

The man who took over as editor of the *New World* from Benjamin in 1844 was Henry Champion Deming (1815–72). A graduate of Yale College and Harvard Law School, Deming came to New York to practise law. For a while he shared a residence with Park Benjamin, and it was probably the latter who suggested that he occupy his leisure moments

translating Eugène Sue's *Mysteries of Paris* from French into English. This
sort of sensational novel endeared itself to the readers of the cheap weeklies,
and as noted earlier, the *New World* had made special arrangements in the
summer of 1844 to secure advance sheets of Sue's *Wandering Jew*. Deming
presumably translated these sheets upon arrival in order to publish them
simultaneously with the Paris edition. But Deming's editorial career was
cut short by Winchester's bankruptcy, and he returned to the law. By
1847 he was an attorney in Hartford, Connecticut, and shortly thereafter
entered the lower house of the Connecticut legislature. His brief encounter
with cheap journalism only diverted his career, and unlike Benjamin and
Winchester, he had a good alternative to fall back on.[62]

James Gregg Wilson, the proprietor of *Brother Jonathan*, seems to have
continued in other printing and publishing ventures after disposing of the
weekly to the *New World* in late 1843. He sold cheap publications through
the post facilitated by the Act of 1845, and by 1848 claimed to be one of
the leading mail-order firms in the United States. In the mid-1840s he
also published special annual or semi-annual issues of *Brother Jonathan*.
From premises at 15 Spruce Street, New York, he advertised teach yourself foreign language books for 25¢; a reprint of an English work on sheep
by William Youatt for 50¢; plus old-time favourites like G. C. Knowlson's
Horse Doctor and *Cow Doctor*. Even more reminiscent of the past was Henry
William Herbert's *The Maiden's Rescue* for 12½¢ and *Lucy Neal, a Romance
of Negro Life* for 12½¢ or ten copies for a dollar. All these cheap editions
could be sent to any part of the United States for as little as 2 to 5¢ postage.
In 1848 Wilson resumed regular publication of *Brother Jonathan* at about
the same time that Park Benjamin revived the *New World*. Unlike its
erstwhile competitor, *Brother Jonathan* did not appear weekly but only
monthly. Wilson also published another cheap monthly, the *Dispatch*,
whose circulation of 70,000 exceeded *Brother Jonathan*'s by 40,000. Size
was still at a premium, and the *Dispatch* was reputed to be the largest
paper appearing regularly in America. *Brother Jonathan* continued to put
out special issues at Christmas and 4 July. In its number celebrating
Independence Day 1848, it featured the largest wood engraving ever
published: 22 by 44 inches; seven square feet depicting the storming of
the castle of Chapultepec! There was even some of the old fervour for
the blessings of cheapness: 'The business of forwarding books, prints, etc.
by mail, commenced by us many years ago, has been exerting a great and
salutary influence, in the spread of popular intelligence — the only safe-
guard of the Republic.'[63] Wilson relinquished his business to his partner,

Benjamin H. Day, in 1851 and what became of him thereafter is uncertain but it seems that he developed an interest in the invention of a knitting machine about 1857-8 and purchased a partnership in the enterprise, spending the Civil War years trying to defend his patent. He apparently did not return to the book trade.[64]

Although it was not realized at the time, Benjamin H. Day was probably the financial mainstay of *Brother Jonathan* and Wilson & Co. as early as 1841. In that year Park Benjamin gloated in the columns of the *New World* how poor struggling *Jonathan* was secretly up for sale, and how he had been obliquely approached to buy it. At this time Benjamin would not deign to consider such a marriage of convenience when the *New World's* fortunes were riding so high. Sometime during 1841 Day stepped in with enough financial aid to rescue *Brother Jonathan* and later to sustain Wilson & Co.'s other activities.

Day had made his reputation as a printer and editor in the 1830s by inaugurating the *Sun*, the first successful penny daily newspaper in America. When the depression of 1837 struck, he sold out and took his losses rather than hold on tenaciously like Greeley. He was later to regret parting with such a potentially profitable newspaper, but in so doing he kept his assets liquid for a few years and eventually invested them in Wilson's printing and publishing enterprise. When Wilson finally sold out in the early 1850s Day assumed the firm entirely in his own name. He continued publishing the *Jonathan* and, if anything, enlarged the mail-order business and the distribution of cheap publications. Ironically, *Brother Jonathan* had the satisfaction of seeing the revived *New World* of 1848 fall by the wayside while it kept going for another decade.[65]

The editing of *Brother Jonathan* was primarily in the hands of Horatio Hastings Weld (1811-88). Before joining *Brother Jonathan* he had acquired editorial experience with several Massachusetts newspapers as well as having been employed as a printer. It may be recalled that Benjamin and Griswold were the first editors of the *Jonathan* and the *Tattler*, remaining only briefly in this capacity. After their departure Weld took over the editorial duties and remained with the enterprise until sometime in 1843. Upon his departure he seems to have remained in newspaper editing for several more years, and then entered the ministry of the Protestant Episcopal Church, where he combined the life of a parish priest with that of author and editor of religious works. Like Deming of the *New World* Weld's experience with the cheap weeklies had been only an interlude in his life.

Attached to *Brother Jonathan* as a regular contributor from May 1840 to September 1841 was Nathaniel Parker Willis. Nominally one of its editors, Willis was still at the height of his popularity and one of the best paid journalists of the day. As he became more closely associated with *Brother Jonathan* he diverted more and more of his energies to editing rather than to writing. He helped revive the *New York Mirror* in 1842 and a few years later took on the editorship of the *Family Journal* which he retained till his death. Having originally cast his fortunes with the cheap press, Willis was one of the few who survived the many upheavals and carried on more or less in the tradition.[66]

By the late 1840s and early 1850s there was scarcely a trace of the cheap weeklies and their supplements. With the exception of B. H. Day and *Brother Jonathan*, all else from that era of rampant price-cutting had receded into obscurity. Even the men who exploited the times most successfully seemed to have disappeared. Yet a closer examination reveals the profound impact which the depression of 1837-43 had upon the American book trade. There is a tendency among some literary historians to ignore these years of trade upheaval and to concentrate almost exclusively on the broad themes of American intellectual development such as romanticism, transcendentalism and the frontier. Yet the lives of virtually every American author and publisher were deeply touched by the economic dislocations of this depression and the drastic decline in book prices.

On the other hand, there is the opposite tendency to equate American literary development with the cheap literature which characterized these years of economic panic. Contemporary British observers were most prone to assume that American book production before, during and after 1837-43 was epitomized by *Brother Jonathan* and the *New World*. Charles Dickens was particularly susceptible to this fallacy. His trip to America in 1842 coincided with the deepest years of distress and he tended to generalize thereafter on the basis of his limited exposure. Typical of his attitude for some years to come was a circular letter which he sent to various British periodicals shortly after his return. He urged his fellow writers not to sell advance sheets of their forthcoming works to American editors and publishers who:

can gain a very comfortable living out of the brains of other men, while they would find it very difficult to earn bread by the exercise of their own. . . . They are, for the most part, men of very low attainment and of more than indifferent reputation; and I have frequently seen them, in the same sheet in which they

*boast of the rapid sale of many thousand copies of an English reprint, coarsely
and insolently attacking the author of that very book, and heaping scurrility
and slander upon his head.*

He admitted that some American publishers were respectable but the
general tone was set by the opportunists. *Brother Jonathan's* reply was
caustic.

*If Mr. Dickens prefers dollars and cents to literary fame – selfish, sordid grati-
fication to a position of commanding respect – and a flash waistcoat to a laurel
wreath, it is his own misfortune – the result of traits inseparable from his
character. . . . Mr. D. has not strength of character and mind enough to prove
the European axiom that a parvenu must betray himself by his vulgarity*

And the *New World* concluded that Dickens was 'either a fool or a knave';
'insolent and malignant'; a 'low-bred vulgar man'.[67]

By the early 1850s the American book trade was a very different scene
from what Dickens and others in Britain thought. It had become far
more stable; prices of most new books had risen; cut-throat competition
had given way to more gentlemanly agreements within the trade; and
various amicable arrangements had been made with British authors and
publishers. This new equilibrium would eventually be shattered by another
major depression, but in the meantime the book trade enjoyed its image of
prosperity and respectability.

Chapter II

BRITISH PERIODICALS IN AMERICA

The cheap weeklies certainly satisfied the reading tastes of many Americans during the first half of the nineteenth century. Yet there were always those who wished to peruse British periodicals in their entirety rather than content themselves with the scissors and paste eclectics. For such Americans there were two alternatives: either they imported copies directly from Great Britain, or they availed themselves of American reprints of the more popular British journals. Securing periodicals from abroad was expensive. An annual subscription to the Edinburgh edition of *Blackwood's Magazine* cost about $11.00 to $12.00, or somewhat over £2 sterling. A few Americans indulged themselves and insisted upon the *bona fide* British publication rather than the cheaper American reprint, but they numbered well under a hundred throughout the country for any given periodical.

In these circumstances, it is not surprising that a New York printer, Edward B. Clayton, of 64 Pine Street, hazarded a reprint of *Blackwood's*. Since no one in America had previously tried to put out a facsimile edition of a British periodical, Clayton's venture was risky indeed. The first number appeared in September 1819, and to his great relief it did very well. Circulation during the first year rose to about one thousand, and with annual subscriptions costing $8.00, he began to realize a handsome profit.[1] Some time in 1820 William Blackwood became aware of Clayton's undertaking and sought to persuade him to import the monthly direct from Edinburgh. No doubt he offered him a special rate, but Clayton declined. He was enjoying the pleasant notoriety of success. There was something almost patriotic in putting out an American reprint which employed native workmanship and materials at a time when little or no stigma was attached to 'literary piracy'. However, once the novelty wore off subscriptions began to flag. Now it was Clayton's turn to approach Blackwood about the possibility of importing copies. Six months passed; no answer from Edinburgh; and Clayton struggled on as best he could. Only then did he learn that his letter to Edinburgh had been sent by mistake to one of his debtors in Washington D.C. By this time he had resolved to carry on by himself, which he did for another year. But with subscriptions down to about five hundred, the venture of three years failed, and it was a decade before anyone else reprinted another British periodical.[?]

Meanwhile, in 1824, two new booksellers in New York decided to import copies directly from Blackwood. Messrs Wilder & Campbell of 142 Broadway were unique, because unlike other American booksellers who imported a few copies of various periodicals from wholesale houses in London, they were prepared to make a formal agreement with the Edinburgh publishers. This was tendered in an exchange of letters. William Blackwood agreed to supply Wilder & Campbell with 100 copies at 1s. 6d. each, or 500 copies at 1s. 3d. each. At this rate Wilder & Campbell would be paying a wholesale price of $4.50 a year for twelve issues, excluding freight and tariff charges. On top of this they had to add their profit of a third or more, so that it is hard to imagine that they could have sold the imported magazine for less than $8.00 a year. A month's notice was necessary whenever larger or smaller quantities were required, and the New York firm was obliged to pay its bills on a London bank every two months. Blackwood was also prepared to supply back numbers at 1s. 6d. each and divide whatever profit was made on their sales.

There was one thing Blackwood wished to make perfectly clear. Under no circumstances should copies which had been sent to America be permitted to return for sale in Great Britain. He further stipulated:

Being satisfied that you will do everything in your power to promote the sale of my magazine, I hereby bind myself not to send either directly or indirectly any copies to America; and you on the other hand bind yourself not to be concerned directly or indirectly with any American edition of the work.

Finally, there was a penalty clause whereby either party would forfeit £100 if it failed to abide by the terms.[3] The beginnings of this arrangement were auspicious enough, but nothing more is heard of it. Wilder & Campbell seem to have been in business in 1825 but were no longer so by the end of the following year – the victims, no doubt, of the 1825–6 financial panic.

Until 1833 there was a distinct lull in the reprint trade, but a remarkable revival occurred in that year. One of the British journals which attracted bargain-conscious Americans was the *Penny Magazine*, the extremely successful brain-child of the London publisher Charles Knight and the Society for the Diffusion of Useful Knowledge. Begun in 1831, it did not take long for imported copies to find their way to the United States under an agreement with a gentleman in Philadelphia named Condé Raquet.[4] However, by 1833 Raquet's imported original yielded to an American reprint by a New York bookseller. Although it is not entirely clear, the reprint was most likely the result of an arrangement between the New York publisher, William Jackson of 71 Maiden Lane, and the SDUK in London.[5] Jackson's *Penny Magazine* sold for 3¢ and appeared as soon as it arrived by sailing ship and could be reprinted. It was moderately successful and Jackson managed to carry it on till 1841. By that time he was located at 102 Broadway and apparently negotiated to sell his business to Edmund Baldwin who relocated at 155 Broadway the following year. As far as one can tell Baldwin continued to reprint the *Penny Magazine* until it ceased publication in London in 1846.

The year 1833 ushered in two other reprints of British periodicals: *Blackwood's Magazine* and the *New Monthly Magazine*. They were both put out by Allen and Ticknor of Boston, and as with Clayton a decade before, there were no arrangements with British publishers. Three volumes of each journal were printed spanning the period January 1833 to June 1834 before they were discontinued, presumably victims of another year of notable trade depression.[6]

A somewhat longer-lived effort begun in 1833 was the *Metropolitan and Foreign Quarterly*. The bookselling firm of Peck & Newton in New Haven, Conn., had the novel idea of taking three British periodicals, the *Metropolitan Magazine*, *Blackwood's Magazine* and the *Quarterly Review*, and combining parts of each into this weekly reprint. It appeared in the form of a royal octavo pamphlet on cheap paper, each issue roughly divided into thirds. At the end of a year subscribers could collate the various sections which were separately paged and have replicas of three complete British periodicals.

Peck & Newton's interest in the reprint side of their business was bought in 1835 by a newcomer to the New York publishing scene, Theodore Foster.[7] Like so many young men at this time he counted on the cheap reprint trade to reward him for his initiative and hard work, despite slender cash reserves. He began by expanding his new business and presenting the public with six different British periodicals: *Edinburgh Review*; *Foreign Quarterly Review*; *London Quarterly Review*; *London and Westminster Review*; *Blackwood's Magazine*; and *Metropolitan Magazine*. Annual subscriptions ranged from $3.00 to $5.00 and, for a time, it seemed as if Foster had discovered the secret of successful republication. He even ventured upon a few reprints of complete books, charging 50¢ for what otherwise cost well over a dollar. However, that grim reaper, the financial crisis of 1837, brought him down along with so many others.[8] His business at 2 Pine Street was then taken over by his clerk, William Lewer, who 'undertook to manage the business for the benefit of Foster's creditors, on commission, being bound when they were paid off to return the business to Foster'.[9] To the six British periodicals already published by Foster, Lewer added a seventh, *Bentley's Miscellany*, but he managed to accomplish little else before he died in 1838 with none of Foster's debt repaid. In fact, he left his widow, Jemima M. Lewer, with additional debts incurred in the procurement of paper, printing, and binding. Much to everyone's surprise, Jemima managed nevertheless to carry on the business with the assistance of two men: Leonard Scott and Joseph Mason. Scott collected the bills, solicited new subscriptions, and generally dealt with matters outside the office; Mason specifically managed the business for her. Manager and widow got on so well together that some time in 1839 they were married. For a few years they retained the same business premises at 2 Pine Street, and then in 1842 moved to 102 Broadway which had been recently vacated by Edmund Baldwin, the reprinter of the *Penny Magazine*. The business went as well as could be expected during the depression although they were forced to discontinue the *Metropolitan Magazine* and *Bentley's Miscellany* in 1841 because of declining sales. However, the following year they were able to add the *Dublin University Magazine* to their list of reprints.

Having weathered the economic storm, the Masons' position seemed secure, but appearances were deceptive. The ostensible success of the periodical reprint trade stimulated competition from an unexpected quarter: the New York publishers, Wiley & Putnam, decided to negotiate with various British publishers to import their periodicals on special terms. This was facilitated by a decision in 1840 to send their junior partner, George Palmer Putnam, to London to set up a branch office in Paternoster Row. Putnam took this opportunity to contact periodical

publishers as well, and in early October he was in communication with
John Murray, publisher of the *Quarterly Review*. He succeeded in persuading Murray to supply each issue at 2s., or a yearly wholesale price of
$2.00. He made similar arrangements with other publishers, and during
the course of 1841 quarterlies were made available at $4.00 a year and
monthlies such as *Blackwood's*, $5.00. One advantage which Wiley &
Putnam exploited was variety. They offered a wider selection than Mason
did. To his list they added: *British Critic* at $4.00; *British and Foreign
Review*, $4.00; *British and Foreign Medical Review*, $5.00; *Fraser's Magazine*,
$6.00; *Monthly Magazine*, $6.00; *New Monthly Magazine*, $10.00; *United
Service Journal*, $10.00; *Ainsworth's Magazine*, $6.00; *Civil Engineer and
Architect's Journal*, $5.00; *Practical Mechanic and Engineer's Magazine*,
$2.50.

The Masons soon felt the effects of such competition and in an effort
to counter it reduced the rates of their subscriptions from $5.00 to $4.00
on the monthlies and $4.00 to $3.00 on the quarterlies. Unfortunately
this had little effect, and in 1842 they found themselves on the brink of
insolvency. In a desperate effort to salvage their affairs they called upon
their employee, Leonard Scott, for assistance.

Scott had long been in the printing business. A Canadian by birth, he
found employment with Theodore Foster in 1835. Over the years he had
acted as clerk, bill collector, and canvasser of subscriptions. While in these
positions he managed to save several thousand dollars which Mason now
asked to borrow in return for a long-term mortgage on the business.
Scott was led to believe that Mason would eventually withdraw, and
that he would take over as proprietor. Imagine Scott's dismay when he
was told a year later (1843) that Mason intended to retain control and had
mortgaged the business to other creditors.

Scott realized that if he did not act promptly he would lose his whole
investment. He foreclosed his own mortgage but to no avail because
Mason had possession of the account books and was determined to carry
on. Scott considered taking the matter to court, but soon became aware
that the value of the mortgage would easily be consumed in legal costs.
He then hit upon a bold course of action.

*I proposed to Mason's other creditors to give them a share of whatever I might
recover if they would share with me in the expense of litigating the suit. Two
of them, Messrs. Walker and Craighead, accepted the proposition and, after
a few weeks of hard fighting, a compromise was effected with Mason and his*

assignee, by which, in consideration of the relinquishment of our several demands in full, the payment of all the costs that had accrued, and the giving our notes for some $1,500, besides, we obtained the possession of a broken down business out of which we hoped to build up something which should ultimately prove successful and restore to us the large amounts we had lost.

Robert Craighead and Edward Walker were valuable partners for Scott. The former was a printer at 112 Fulton Street and the latter a bookseller and binder next door at 114. By the beginning of 1844 Mason's reprint business was firmly in the control of these three partners who occupied Craighead's premises on Fulton Street.

Alas, a further impediment arose. While Scott consolidated his affairs, Jonas Winchester, the publisher of the *New World*, ever restless for expansion, had begun his own reprint of *Blackwood's Magazine* and the *Edinburgh Review*. He offered these for the unprecedentedly low price of $2.00 a year each, and if subscribers took the *New World* with its monthly supplements and *Blackwood's*, they could have the lot for $5.00. His reprint of *Blackwood's* was a quarto newspaper form . . . very badly printed and utterly unfit to preserve. . . . Still its cheapness among a certain portion of Mason's [former] subscribers was sufficient to induce them to drop Mason's edition and take Winchester's.

Thus when Scott and his partners took over Mason's reprint business their best-selling product, *Blackwood's Magazine*, was reduced to a circulation of about 1,200, thanks to the inroads of Wiley & Putnam and Jonas Winchester. One of the first things Scott did was to reduce the price of *Blackwood's* to $3.00. Wiley & Putnam had already brought their price down to $4.50. But even more threatening, Winchester considerably improved the appearance of his facsimile while still retaining the $2.00 price.

At this point Joseph Mason evidently secured the financial help of a new partner, Edmund B. Tuttle, and proceeded to break his agreement with Scott by importing periodicals from abroad. Instead of the original British format these were the cheaper 'colonial edition' which had recently been made available to the North American possessions. John Murray, for example, was willing to supply Mason with 100 copies of the *Quarterly Review* at 2s each, the same terms on which he supplied the Montreal firm of Armour & Ramsay. No doubt Wiley & Putnam resented British publishers supplying Mason & Tuttle with a somewhat cheaper edition on inferior paper but they were left with no alternative but to lower the price on *Blackwood's* to $4.00. Mason & Tuttle reduced their price in turn to $3.00, and the familiar descending spiral of price-cutting set in. In the early months of 1844 New York City could offer four alternatives of *Blackwood's*: Winchester's reprint at $2.00; Scott's reprint at $3.00; Mason & Tuttle's import at $3.00; and Wiley & Putnam's import at $4.00.

It is scarcely surprising that this state of affairs could not continue long. Within six months Mason & Tuttle stopped importing British periodicals altogether and started an advertising agency.[13] At about the same time Wiley & Putnam raised the price of their imported periodicals and gradually reduced their number, finding that this side of their business had ceased to prove very remunerative. Scott tenaciously held on, and in order to compete with the rapidity of Winchester's presses farmed out his reprints to four different printers. This lasted until the summer of 1844 when Winchester unexpectedly offered to sell his interest in the reprint of *Blackwood's* to Scott for $1,500. Six weeks after the transaction Scott discovered that Winchester was bankrupt. Had he suspected, Scott could have witnessed Winchester's downfall *gratis*.

During the years 1845–7 Scott found that he had the British periodicals trade virtually to himself, but there was much ground to make up in order to compensate for expenditures and losses of the previous few years. His momentary sense of triumph was then again upset by rumblings from a quarter completely unknown to him, and involved his most profitable reprint, *Blackwood's Magazine*. Two strangers, one a lawyer and the other an Episcopal priest, took him to task in the first decisive case involving copyright.

John Jay was a practising attorney in New York City. The grandson of the renowned diplomat and Supreme Court Justice, and the son of Judge William Jay, he was born in 1817 and after graduating from Columbia College was admitted to the Bar. While an undergraduate at Columbia he had acquired the reputation of a reformer, especially with regard to the issues of slavery and the Protestant Episcopal Church.[14] His close friend and Rector of a church in Hartford, Connecticut, was a writer named Arthur Cleveland Coxe.

Coxe was born in 1818 and graduated twenty years later from the University of the City of New York. For a year or two he wrote poetry, succeeding especially with a volume entitled *Christian Ballads* which went through five printings between 1840 and 1845. Authorship as a career didn't satisfy him, however, and in the early 1840s he entered General

Theological Seminary to become an Episcopal priest. Shortly thereafter he became Rector of St John's Church where he intended to combine parochial duties with occasional literary labour. One of his first projects stemmed from his respect for *Blackwood's Magazine*. He greatly admired this monthly journal and wished to establish some connection with it. Feeling that the publisher of *Blackwood's* should receive his rightful due, he determined to harass Leonard Scott for freely reprinting 'Maga'. Accordingly, he hit upon a plan whereby he could write a few articles for the magazine and at the same time render the Edinburgh publisher a signal service. In April 1846 he wrote to the firm suggesting a way to trap Scott.[15]

Coxe offered to pose as an Englishman temporarily resident in America who would send Blackwood several articles describing what he saw in the new world for inclusion in the magazine. In due course these would be reprinted by Scott along with the rest of *Blackwood's*. Only then would Scott be informed that the articles by Coxe had been copyrighted in America and that he would be served with an injunction and liable for damages. Depending upon Scott's response, Blackwood could apply pressure in one of three ways, according to Coxe. The first would be to force an arrangement on Scott whereby he would have to pay for the privilege of reprinting the *Magazine* with Blackwood supplying him with advance sheets. If Scott did not agree to this, Blackwood could by-pass him entirely and appoint another agent to handle the authorized reprint. If this occurred, Coxe recommended that his own publisher in New York, Daniel Appleton, should be given the job. Appleton already had a good reputation for handling British publications of high quality and could either set up in type in New York as Scott did, or import stereotype plates from Edinburgh. Coxe showed a preference for Appleton over the other New York importer of British publications, Wiley & Putnam, because he felt the latter firm was too much associated with various Protestant groups and thus not sufficiently sympathetic with the conservative tone of 'Maga'. A third alternative was for either Scott or Appleton to import entire copies of the Edinburgh edition at a low enough rate to compete with other unauthorized reprints in the United States.[16]

During the summer of 1846 Coxe discussed this project with his good friend, John Jay, but no provocative action was undertaken. In the meantime Blackwood seems to have acquiesced to the plan, acknowledging his confidence in Coxe's literary talent by publishing one of his articles in March 1847.[17] By June preparations were under way to carry out the copyright scheme. The article which was to become the test case left New York on 10 June, with Coxe not knowing in which issue of the magazine it would appear. He warned Jay to be ready at any time, however, to register the title, 'Maga' in America', and to follow this by depositing the article itself with the Clerk of the Court. Both Coxe and Jay had studied the laws relating to copyright in the United States. They knew that the first step was to register the title page with the nearest United States District Court, in their case the Southern District Court of New York. Then, within three months they had to deposit the published version with the Clerk of the Court.

To be sure, there were uncertainties. What if Scott did not believe that the article was written by an Englishman resident in the United States? Must Coxe then divulge his anonymity which he was particularly anxious to maintain? He had warned Jay to tell no one, not even his wife, and although the secret was shared with a few intimate friends, he wanted no one else to know. Perhaps he felt it unbecoming for a parish priest to engineer such literary skulduggery. After all, when he had asked the Bishop of Connecticut to write a letter of introduction for him to Blackwood the previous year he had certainly not intimated his intentions. But his wish for secrecy also had its mischievous side. He rather relished his anonymity and privately delighted in the fact that no one would know that a Yankee had put one over not only on the readers of the *Magazine*, but also on Leonard Scott. More seriously, if Coxe pretended to be a resident alien, could he then convince Scott that he had a valid copyright? The law said either citizens or residents, and there was no indication as to what constituted residence. He did know of Capt. Marryat's attempt a decade before to secure copyright through temporary residence and the failure of that stratagem. Yet the law seemed plain: a resident was entitled to copyright. Thus Coxe felt secure as long as he did not have to be brought into personal negotiations with Scott.

There was another problem, though. Would Coxe be subject to a libel action for what he wrote about Scott in the forthcoming article? He had taken precaution not to identify Scott by name but rather as 'Reprint and Co.', but there could be little doubt as to who this was since Scott was the only one who published a facsimile of the *Magazine*. Jay assured Coxe that his statements were not libellous, and that he need not worry because Scott could not sue for libel on the basis of an article that he had willingly published.[8]

Coxe's article was slated to appear in the October issue and as soon as proof sheets arrived, Jay registered the title. That was on the twelfth. A few days of suspense ensued until a regular copy of the *Magazine* reached Scott. Then on 21 October Jay deposited a copy of the article itself with the Clerk of the District Court and before Scott had had time to reprint, Jay confronted him.

To muddy the waters a bit and keep Coxe out of the picture Jay saw to it that Coxe transferred the copyright of the article to Jay. Going one step further, so as not to seem the author himself, Jay re-assigned the copyright to a New York printer, William Van Norden. Van Norden paid the princely sum of $1 for the right to print as many copies as he wished above and beyond the fifty that Jay purchased from him. Van Norden also agreed to sue any infringement of the copyright, although Jay was to reimburse him for such legal expenses. Finally, he promised to yield the copyright to Jay or someone else upon demand.

Scott proved to be surprisingly accommodating, and turned out not to be the reprint knave that Coxe had made him out to be in his article for *Blackwood's*. Within a few days he capitulated to the extent of telling Jay that he was willing to pay Blackwood $200 for the privilege of receiving advance sheets and reprinting an authorized version. Jay apparently was not prepared for such a prompt acquiescence, and responded by saying that he was not authorized by Blackwood to conclude an agreement but he would forward Scott's offer to Edinburgh. In the meantime, however, Scott wanted to get on with the reprinting of the October number of the magazine which had been suspended by Jay's sudden intrusion. For the consideration of $20 Jay permitted Scott to go ahead, but made it clear that there would be another copyrighted article appearing in November and that he reserved the right to take Scott to court should negotiations break down. Since letters going by steamship across the Atlantic took about ten days, and it required several exchanges of correspondence before details could be worked out, Jay settled on a temporary accommodation: Jay agreed not to harass Scott for the issues of October, November and December, if Scott would pay $20 for each of the three issues, even if the December issue had no American copyrighted article.

So far Scott figured that his position remained intact. He had nothing to lose by being accommodating, and he had bought time by agreeing to negotiate with Blackwood. There was nothing to be gained by risking a court injunction which would force him not only to cease publication for a time but also to pay damages of $1 per printed sheet. Besides, he conceived that Jay's position was not all that impregnable. What was to prevent him simply omitting any copyrighted article from a future issue, since all he need do to find out which one to leave out was to inspect the District Court's Registers which were open to the public.

Jay's counter to this was to label Scott's issue a facsimile of the Edinburgh periodical 'a lame and halting imitation' of what it claimed to be, subject to 'occasional mutilations'. He further stated that, if need be, *Blackwood's* would carry more American articles or even devote a whole issue to American writers. In other words, the Blackwoods were determined to put an end to unauthorized reprints whatever it would take.

Scott guessed that Jay was bluffing somewhat but he never knew quite how much. When he had time to consult his lawyer he presented a more sophisticated argument as to why Jay's tactics would not work. Had not Jay overlooked the fact that he had waited too long to deposit a copy of the article, since the Edinburgh edition had appeared in Britain prior to 21 October? Jay was prepared for this and cited a little-known court decision which held that an American could have his work printed and published abroad as long as a copy of the work was deposited with the District Court before the work appeared in America. Since Jay had deposited the copy before Scott reprinted the October issue, Jay seemed to be on firm ground. However, he took no chances with Coxe's next article for the November issue and had Van Norden's printed copy ready for deposit prior to its appearance in Edinburgh.[21]

Besides using veiled threats, Jay kept hammering away at the advantages which Blackwood could offer Scott. The Edinburgh firm would provide him with advance sheets rather than his waiting for the published version to reach New York. He could hope to have the American edition in print more or less simultaneously with the British. He would have the satisfaction which comes from the enhanced respectability of being an authorized agent instead of a pirate. The only thing Scott would have to do was pay Blackwood more than $200 a year.

Scott saw no great advantage in being the exclusive agent for *Blackwood's* because no one else in the United States was publishing a facsimile, and these issues imported from Great Britain were more expensive than his reprint. Scott's real problem came more from the so-called 'eclectics' such as the *Albion* and *Littell's Living Age*. The latter was a particular threat since it came out weekly, selling for 12½¢ as compared with his own reprint which sold for 25¢, and it reprinted the choice articles not only from *Blackwood's* but also from other British reviews and magazines.

This galled Scott, especially as there was nothing which Blackwood or Jay could do to trap Littell in the way they had cornered him. It was not worth carrying a number of American copyrighted articles in 'Maga' on the off-chance that Littell would reprint one of them, and once it was known how Scott had been foiled, Littell and the others would keep close track of the District Court registrations.

Scott had one predicament that neither Jay nor Coxe nor Blackwood could gainsay: he was not making much money from his reprint and therefore could not make grandiose payments to Blackwood. Coxe and Jay had predicated much of their reasoning on the large sales and handsome returns that they supposed Scott would make. In his first article for Blackwood, Coxe placed the likely circulation of the American reprint at 10,000 copies. Eventually they had to face up to the sobering fact that only about 4,250 copies were printed and that no profit accrued until the first 3,000 were disposed of.

As negotiations progressed, Jay, Coxe and Blackwood became persuaded that Scott wanted to come to an honest compromise. His candour concerning his firm's ledgers and accounts was remarkable. In a letter to Blackwood he set forth all his printing and binding expenses:[22] on the basis of 3,000 copies it cost him about \$335–40 per issue, or about $11\frac{1}{2}$¢ per copy. Thus, with an average monthly printing and binding outlay of \$336, his yearly publication costs amounted to \$4,032. Adding to this his fixed costs of rent, salaries, advertising, carriage, etc., at \$700, his expenses totalled \$4,732.

As to income, 300 copies of the first 3,000 printed were gifts and exchange copies given to editors of other journals and newspapers. A further 100 copies had to be written off as dead stock. Therefore, of the original 3,000, only 2,600 would bring in revenue from subscriptions. Complicating the picture further, there were two subscription rates: \$3.00 for those who took only Blackwood's Magazine, and \$10.00 for those who received Blackwood's plus the reprints of four other British journals. From the first group, Scott derived \$5,700 from about 1,900 subscriptions; from the second, \$1,400, with 700 subscriptions. Thus, total gross sales of 2,600 copies amounted to \$7,100. When the usual trade discount of one-third off the subscription price was figured in, it left a net return on sales of \$4,733.34, or about 15¢ per copy. This then was Scott's break-even point, with costs amounting to \$4,732, with an income of \$4,733. Consequently, only beyond the first 3,000 copies would he begin to make a profit. Then, for every copy over 3,000 he had to pay for press work, paper, covers and stitching, which he estimated cost 8½¢ per copy, leaving a clear profit of only 6½¢ each. As Scott usually printed 4,250 copies each month, he figured his profit on only the last 1,250. Thus he made slightly over $80 a month or about $1,000 a year. Of this he was prepared to pay Blackwood a quarter, either in the form of a royalty on copies sold above 3,000, or outright payment of $250 annually.

Jay suggested that Scott raise subscription rates to $4.00 per annum in order to increase profits, but Scott doubted that this would work, since such a rate had been charged prior to 1843 and had only attracted about 2,000 subscribers.[23] Jay also recommended that Scott might effect some saving by importing stereotype plates from Edinburgh rather than setting type in New York. Scott was perfectly willing to consider this alternative but pointed out that it would necessitate not only an extra set of plates but also paying duty and freight from Edinburgh to New York. Importing the finished copies from Britain might cut costs but Scott questioned whether Blackwood could supply them cheaply enough to compete in the American market. Furthermore, as Scott took special pride in the quality of his reprint as well as the paper he used, he wondered if Blackwood wouldn't be forced into using inferior paper in order to bring down the price.

In addition to everything else there was a tariff on imported books and journals to be reckoned with. Works which had already been reprinted in the United States were subject to a duty of 20 per cent. As far as *Blackwood's Magazine* was concerned, if no one else reprinted before Scott imported it, the duty was 10 per cent of the trade or wholesale price on each copy. To Blackwood's trade price in Britain of 2s. per copy had to be added the import duty of 5¢ plus the cost of printing extra copies in Edinburgh and shipping them to New York. Scott's trade price was only 16½¢ or 8d. and consequently it seemed obvious to him that resetting type in New York was the better course.[24]

Admittedly disappointed by the realization that Scott's profits were modest and that there would be no great windfall, the Edinburgh publishers nevertheless instructed Jay to secure the best agreement he could, and for this purpose issued him with a Power of Attorney.

For a brief moment Blackwood wondered whether Scott might be playing him false because of a difference in the way each calculated composing costs. Jay was asked to clarify Scott's estimates which had been based on a rate of 40¢ per thousand 'ems' (i.e. the space taken up by the letter 'm'), because a journeyman printer in Britain who was familiar with the New York scale of composing charges claimed that the usual charge was from 10 to 14¢ per thousand, depending on whether the text was handwritten or printed. The explanation was that American compositors based their charges on 'ems' whereas the British did so on 'ens', the latter obviously using less space. Furthermore journeyman printers in New York received only 25¢ per thousand 'ems' whereas master printers got 40¢.[25]

Jay verified these charges by comparing them with those of Wiley & Putnam, and being satisfied negotiated a formal agreement with Scott which was duly signed on 30 December 1847. The two main points concerned the payment which Scott would make to Blackwood and the duration of the agreement. Blackwood, counselled by Coxe, wanted a one-year contract only, so that some other arrangement could be made if circumstances proved disadvantageous. Scott, on the other hand, wanted from three to six years so that he had some long-term assurance to continue his reprint. They compromised at two years, 1848 and 1849, with provision for either termination or renewal. Scott agreed to make an annual payment of $300, and Jay, on behalf of the Blackwoods, promised not to prosecute Scott for any violation of American copyrighted articles during the course of the agreement.[26]

Gradually it became known throughout the trade that Scott had ceased his pirating and become legitimate. Coxe outlined the way it came about in his facetious article on 'American Copyright' for the November number of *Blackwood's*. However, it became official in an announcement by Blackwood in the January 1848 issue, which Scott confirmed by inserting a special announcement into his reprint for that month. Scott related that he would be turning over a portion of his profits to the Edinburgh firm in return for early sheets, and asked other 'republishers' to refrain henceforth from printing articles from *Blackwood's*. 'This is a courtesy which has generally been observed by the trade when the foreign author of a book is known to have an interest in its republication, and we trust that it will not be overlooked in the case of a periodical republished under similar circumstances.'[27]

For a time it looked as though Scott might not be pirated by others in America, and so in March 1848 he suggested to Jay that he would not copyright American articles for the time being, as this tended to provoke opposition from the other reprinters. 'We *now* appeal to their sense of justice and to the usages of the trade, and we have reason to believe that the appeal is having its effect in the proper quarters.' However, by the beginning of May it became clear that Littell was prepared to help himself to whatever he wanted of *Blackwood's* – the age-old story of honour among thieves until it suits them otherwise – and Scott could do nothing about it.[28]

In the months and years to come Scott continued reprinting an authorized edition of 'Maga', paying Blackwood $300 a year. When the initial two-year agreement came to an end, another was negotiated but with no cut-off point and each reserved the right to cancel.[29] Once an opening wedge had been made by Coxe, Jay and Blackwood, other publishers of British periodicals sought similar arrangements with Scott. The first to act was John Chapman of London.

Besides being publisher of the *Westminster Review*, Chapman was a major importer and publisher of American books. He was thus naturally in close touch with the American literary scene. In 1851 he decided to authorize a reprint of the *Review* in America, although Jay cautioned him 'not to anticipate from this source any but the most trifling income'.[30] Jay based this warning in part on the relatively small number of subscribers to reprints of British periodicals, and pointed out that Scott's sales had declined in recent years: 'in consequence of the fatal rivalry of eclectic magazines, such as *Harper's* and the *International*, professing to give choice selections from all the British miscellanies and quarterlies and in addition a current history of the times, political, literary and scientific in both hemispheres.' Apparently such eclectics were 'preferred by numerous readers to any single reprint of a foreign review'. *Harper's Monthly Magazine*, although only about a year old, was said to be printing over 10,000 copies, and Jay knew that the *Westminster* could not hope for more than several thousand subscribers. If, under these circumstances, Chapman still wanted Jay to instigate formal negotiations with Scott to produce an American reprint, Jay agreed to proceed.[31]

Meanwhile, Chapman seems to have tried the same tactic on Scott as Blackwood had done: find an American contributor who was willing to write for the *Westminster* and thus secure a copyright in America. He thus proceeded to instruct Jay to register such articles and he agreed to send copies of the *Review* printed in London for sale in the United States. The first article appeared in January 1852 and dealt with American literature.

Before Jay could conclude an arrangement between Chapman and Scott the situation was further complicated by the *Eclectic Magazine* reprinting one of the supposed copyright articles from the *Westminster*. A warning notice had not been inserted, and so Jay was inclined not to confront the *Eclectic* but instead hasten negotiations with Scott; his reasoning being that once Scott was known to be the authorized reprinter, at least some of the other journals would respect his claim.

By mid-March Jay was able to announce that all was well. Scott agreed to pay Chapman $100 for each quarterly issue of the *Westminster*, which amounted to more than Scott paid Blackwood. There was no indication why this was the case, but it may have been because the quarterly issues of the *Westminster* contained fewer aggregate pages than the monthly issues of *Blackwood's*, making Scott's printing costs lower.[32]

By 1853 John Jay was less active as an intermediary between Scott and the British publishers, and his place was gradually filled by Henry Stevens of Vermont. Since the late 1840s, Stevens had established himself in London as an importer and exporter of books. Most of the leading American book collectors and librarians were his customers. Thus it was not surprising that he included among his shipments to the United States copies of the latest British periodicals.

For a time Leonard Scott and Henry Stevens seemed to be working at cross purposes. By the autumn of 1853, however, Stevens had managed to negotiate an arrangement which seemed satisfactory to all parties.[33] To Scott he explained the details concerning not only *Blackwood's* and the *Westminster* but also the *Quarterly Review*, the *Edinburgh Review*, and the *North British Review*.

The publishers of the five periodicals, which you reprint, have all at last, I believe, concluded to accept your proposition for continuing the reprints, and I doubt not that all of them except Mr. Murray and Messrs. Longman have written you in accordance.

Your proposition was to give each of the publishers $500 a year for early sheets and the permission to reprint, etc. and also to give me $500 a year. This matter involves an entirely new arrangement between the publishers and myself, yet after weighing everything I have concluded to accept your offer. . . .

I am authorized by Murray and Longman to inform you that they will supply you through me with early sheets to be sent by post.

Stevens concluded by lamenting the fact that Murray and Longman still insisted that he take one hundred copies of their London editions and export them to America. Nevertheless, he was sure that these copies of the *Quarterly Review* and the *Edinburgh Review* would not interfere with Scott's cheaper reprints.

Thus, by the beginning of 1854 Leonard Scott was the 'authorized' reprinter of the five major British periodicals. The transition from piracy to respectability had taken only six years, and no one in America was in a position to dispute his pre-eminence.

Ever since Scott's co-operation with Blackwood was publicly avowed in January 1848, the name of John Jay was linked with the proceedings as Blackwood's attorney. Anyone wishing to know more about this arrangement or to be put in touch with the Blackwoods went through Jay. Always in the background, however, was the shadowy figure of the man who started the whole thing by writing articles for 'Maga' – Arthur Cleveland Coxe. Not even Scott was allowed to know his identity. Coxe insisted on this, and yet his attitude to the whole affair and his involvement in it changed substantially as time went on. As Jay became more emotionally committed to the enterprise as well as being its public spokesman, Coxe withdrew increasingly into his rectory and parish for reasons which perhaps were very much bound up in his motives for launching the experiment.

Coxe had literary talents and wanted to demonstrate them, if not to the public at large then at least to his intimate friends. He had an inordinate fondness and respect for 'Maga' dating back to his adolescence, and shared the religious and political conservatism of the Blackwoods. It undoubtedly appealed to him to link his pen, if not his name, to the journal. At first all went well, as his articles were accepted and paid for by Blackwood, and he had the satisfaction of knowing he had outwitted one of the leading literary pirates. He thought it enormously amusing that an American reprinter could be trapped in the pages of the *Magazine* by means of the very articles that the offending New York publisher himself printed. But Scott turned out to be too co-operative and too forthright: the potential loser by the arrangement with Blackwoods. It didn't take long for Coxe to feel pangs of conscience for the outlandish caricature that he had drawn of Scott in the pages of *Blackwood's*. To put things right became a dilemma: he could not apologize directly to Scott because that would give away his identity. Perhaps he could write something for the *Magazine* which would inform the readers of the honourable way in which Scott negotiated for the authorized reprint. Months dragged on and he grew ever weary of the task of an official if veiled apology. In April 1848 it was still a 'duty'; by August, 'I hate that Godfrey business so heartily that I don't

date finish my letter though I could do it in a few hours.[34] Apparently he
never did.

Other things troubled Coxe besides a guilty conscience. He found he
just didn't have the time to be an unofficial American contributor to
Blackwood's though the Edinburgh firm seemed quite prepared to publish
his articles. His parochial duties were many; he was busy raising a family;
and the glamour began to pale. After the two articles on copyright in
October and November 1847, he published five others between March
1848 and May 1849, but thereafter did not appear in 'Maga'.

Long before he wrote his last article other sources of irritation arose.
He began to realize that he might have to share the honours with other
American authors who wished to appear in the distinguished pages of the
Edinburgh monthly. As early as November 1847, well before a final
agreement was worked out between Blackwood and Scott, this happened.
Coxe wrote to Jay:

*On thinking over Bristed's offer of a contribution, I think you had better decline
the responsibility of introducing him, or anybody else as a contributor. . . . I
don't want to appear as if connected with a clique, or with any other writer at
all; and it is much for our dignity and our pleasure too, to let no one into our
affairs at all. . . . There will be a great rush for Maga's favour; and let them
that desire it succeed.*

Jay, however, felt obliged to transmit Bristed's article to Blackwood
since he was the publisher's agent. Rather than providing a standard
letter of introduction he merely forwarded Bristed's article to Blackwood
without explanation. Unwittingly he also enclosed a letter from Coxe in
the same parcel and, since the Bristed article was anonymous, it was
assumed to have been written by Coxe. The article dealt with American
periodical literature and appeared in January 1848. Coxe received proof
sheets and later payment, Blackwood thinking it was his. To Jay he
wrote: 'Do pray undeceive them and get them to keep him [Bristed] out,
in future', and characterized the article as 'a poor, shabby thing'.

Coxe and Jay gradually came to consider their partnership a closed cor-
poration, and warned Blackwood against indiscriminately accepting articles
by Americans. In all likelihood Blackwood probably would not have taken
the Bristed article had he known, as he was anxious to be highly selective.

*Your advice to be on our guard against a deluge of Yankee contributions is
excellent. We are fully alive of the possibility of a storm of MSS. from the
States. . . . We always pay particular attention to keeping the general tone of*

the Magazine uniform, and it was the complete Buchanan spirit in which you
wrote, that first satisfied us that you would make an excellent contributor.

In March 1848 Coxe advised Jay,

I hope, if you agree with me, that you will tell him [Blackwood], you are
adverse to having any new contributor at present: and that every additional
American contributor will detract so much from the charm of Maga, in American
eyes. That is my conviction . . . the fewer the better; and none should come in
but men with whom we would like to associate as friends.

Coxe harped on this theme of exclusiveness relentlessly. He hesitated to
see Blackwood take on too many American contributors; personally he
intended to write only occasionally, but he feared 'Maga' might lose its
distinctive 'charm' and 'its preeminently *British* character'. 'It is on this
account, that I always write with an assumed John Bullism.' He could
think of only two or three American writers, 'the Danas, for instance',
and Charles Fenno Hoffman who could 'naturally fall into the "Buchanan"
tone and style of light writing and *thinking*'.

A little later a slightly political note crept into his argument. America
needed a magazine like *Blackwood's*. 'I want the *other* [the conservative] *side*
to get fairly before our Yankee public, through this means. . . . All the
nonsense about "Egalité – liberté" will come to nothing; and thinking
men will settle down upon the views and principles of Burke, as they will
now be expressed and expounded in Maga.'

During the course of 1848 and the immediate years thereafter, Jay
found himself in the position of having to function as Blackwood's agent
and therefore obliged to transmit those articles placed in his keeping.
These only amounted to a few, and of course it was always up to Blackwood to decide whether or not to publish them.

In view of Coxe's concern that American writers did not 'deluge' Blackwood with contributions, it is particularly ironic to come across a letter
from Blackwood to Jay in May 1852 asking whether Coxe might be
prevailed upon to write for 'Maga' again as so few manuscripts had been
forthcoming from America. Two years later, during the summer of 1854,
Blackwood asked Jay to secure an article by an American on the Crimean
War. Jay asked several authors, but without success; few men in New
York, he observed ruefully, had the leisure to write. His implication was
clear: America had not bothered to cultivate her men of letters and had
not made any effort to provide them with international copyright
protection, without which few could make a living from writing.[35]

Chapter III

COPYRIGHT IN AND OUT OF
CONGRESS, 1815–42

In the years immediately following the Napoleonic Wars, the issue of international copyright was of little concern to America. She imported most of her general literature from England at a time when comparatively few books were published at home. By the mid-1820s the situation had changed considerably. The writings of Porter, Edgeworth, Scott and Byron had become extremely popular and were the subject of many an American reprint. An increase in the tariff on imported books had also encouraged the American manufacture of books. Carey & Lea of Philadelphia dominated the reprint market; a pre-eminence they were not to relinquish to Harper & Bros of New York until the mid-1830s.

Occasionally during the 1820s some slight interest in international copyright was manifested. James Fenimore Cooper, one of the few American authors to make an impression on the British reading public, quite naturally showed some sympathy for the cause. In 1826 he raised the question with his London publisher, John Miller:[1]

We are about to alter our [copyright] law and I hope to make it more liberal to Foreigners – Verplanck (the author) is in Congress, and chairman of the Committee – he is a friend, and indeed, connexion of mine, and has written me on the subject – As I shall go to Washington in a few days I hope to be in time to throw in a hint to that effect – There are some strong Literary Men in both Houses at present, and as the President [John Quincy Adams] is a good deal of a Scholar, I am in hopes of a more liberal policy; than heretofore will prevail.

Cooper's interest in international copyright was certainly not typical.
CAP

If Americans thought of the topic at all they were concerned with protecting domestic copyright and not the rights of foreigners. As a country, nineteenth-century America was akin to a present-day underdeveloped nation which recognizes its dependence on those more commercially and technologically advanced, and desires the fruits of civilization in the cheapest and most convenient ways. Reprinting English literature seemed easy and inexpensive, and so America borrowed voraciously.

Some Americans took an interest in improving the terms of domestic copyright as an incentive to native authors. Both the Federal Government and the States had shown an early willingness in this direction. As far back as the 1780s, prior to the adoption of the Constitution, several States had their own copyright laws or conferred copyright on the works of specific authors. The Constitution itself embodied a general provision for the encouragement of literature and science, and in 1790 specific federal legislation was passed establishing literary copyright throughout the nation. Citizens and residents of the United States only were guaranteed protection for fourteen years, with the option of a further fourteen years if the author was still living. In the latter 1820s, there was some wish to extend the term of copyright and to allow the heirs of a deceased author to renew the protection.[2] On 3 February 1831 'An Act to Amend the Several Acts Respecting Copyright' was signed. The normal term was extended from fourteen to twenty-eight years, again with the option of renewal for an additional fourteen. If an author died, his widow or children could apply for the extension. For the first time musical compositions were covered by copyright legislation. But not a word on international copyright. In fact, foreign authors were explicitly barred from protection, which in essence safeguarded reprints.

The details concerning the passage of the Act of 1831 indicate what sort of battle was ahead for the advocates of international copyright. Among the American *literati*, Guilian C. Verplanck was best placed to promote copyright legislation. Elected to the House of Representatives in 1824, he was, as Cooper noted, Chairman of a committee considering the subject. He later summarized his role in the affair at a banquet honouring him for his stewardship of the successful bill.[3]

My only merit is that of having almost four years ago during the first session of the 20th Congress [1827–8], called public attention to this subject of having with some industry collected the requisite information from those who had practically experienced the difficulties and imperfections of the laws then in force, and of

*having framed and introduced a bill for the purpose of correcting those evils.
. . . Although, therefore, the bill I prepared received the approbation of some of
the most distinguished Senators and Representatives, of both political parties,
I found it utterly impossible during the whole of that Congress to act upon the
bill, or even to draw the attention of any large portion of either house to the
measure. . . . [During the next session of Congress] the Judiciary Committee
of the House of Representatives, at an early period, consented to adopt my bill
of the last year, and, with some useful modifications, introduced it as their own.
In doing this, they not only gave to it the great weight of their unanimous
sanction, but also added to its support the very ardent and able assistance
of the member of their body [Judiciary Committee] who reported the bill, Mr
Ellsworth, of Connecticut.*

Verplanck did well to give some of the credit to William W. Ellsworth
(1791–1868). He had been a practising lawyer in Hartford, Connecticut,
and then a teacher of law at Trinity College. Elected to the House of
Representatives in 1828, he was to supersede Verplanck as the member of
the Judiciary Committee most dedicated to promoting the cause of domestic copyright. Ellsworth came by his interest, one might even say vested
interest, quite naturally since he was married to the eldest daughter of
Noah Webster, the patriarch of American school books and dictionaries.
As long ago as 1783–5 her father had trudged from one state legislature
to another seeking copyright protection for his spelling books. When the
1831 law was passed Noah gave his son-in-law most of the credit, and in
this case parental pride was not misplaced, for Ellsworth seems to have
been one of the most conscientious supporters of the bill.

Webster himself contributed much to the effort. He prodded Congress
from time to time and devoted about ten weeks of 1830–1 to supervising
the measure personally in Washington. Once the bill passed both Houses
of Congress and was waiting the President's signature, he wrote,

*This law will add much to the value of my [literary] property. . . . My presence
here has, I believe, been very useful and perhaps necessary to the accomplishment of the object. Few members of Congress feel much interest in such a law,
and it was necessary that something extra should occur to awaken their attention
to the subject. When I came here I found the members of both houses coming to
me and saying they had learned in my books, they were glad to see me,
and ready to do me any kindness in their power. They all seemed to think,
also, that my great labors deserved some uncommon reward. Indeed, I know of
nothing that has given me more pleasure in my journeys, the last summer and*

this winter, than the respect and kindness manifested towards me in consequence of the use of my books. It convinces me that my fellow citizens consider me as their benefactor and the benefactor of my country.

And elsewhere he noted,[4]

In my journeys to effect this object, and in my long attendance in Washington, I expended nearly a year of time. Of my expenses in money I have no account.

From his description several things emerge. Members of Congress were generally indifferent to copyright, and it took something 'extra', in Webster's word, to goad them into legislative action. It was convenient to have men like Verplanck and Ellsworth placed on key committees, but even more important was their willingness to devote much time and trouble to the measure. A distinguished author like Webster being present in Washington fostered good public relations. On the other hand, the Act succeeded partly because it avoided high controversial issues such as protection for foreign authors.

In the 1820s there was still confusion over the rights of foreign authors, but by the mid-1830s the policy was clear. In 1826 Cooper wrote to Carey & Lea, his American publishers, describing his recent conversation with Sir Walter Scott.[5]

I was of opinion that by proper assignments and with sufficient care in publishing, copyrights might be obtained by an English subject for the same work both in England and the United States. – I fell into the error by my recollections of an examination which I had once made with a view to ascertaining what privileges an American might enjoy, in a similar situation – I still think that he [a foreign author] is permitted to control the sale of his works in the two countries, but I regret to see that a narrow, and as I conceive an impolitic jealousy, has confined the rights to works which are written by Citizens in our statute on the subject.

American authors may have been confused, but any American publisher could have told Cooper that foreign authors had no rights in America. The best they could hope for was an occasional honorarium for advance sheets. Carey & Lea were apparently the first to make a systematic effort in this direction. In the 1820s they paid their London agent, John Miller, to forward the novels of Sir Walter Scott to them as soon as they were published. However, due to the vagaries of trans-Atlantic sailing, it was feared that some other American publisher would receive copies before Miller's found their way to Carey & Lea, so the Philadelphia firm decided to go straight to the source of supply, the Edinburgh publisher, and contracted to receive the sheets in instalments as they were printed, not waiting for the complete volume before setting type.[6]

During the last decade of his life Scott or his publishers generally received some sort of payment from Carey & Lea for advance sheets. The amounts paid varied from as little as $250 for *Canongate* to $1,475 for the *Life of Napoleon*, the usual reimbursement for a three-volume novel being $375 or £75. In due course this arrangement proved valuable to the Philadelphia firm because other American reprinters abandoned the competition for Scott's writings and purchased complete copies from Carey & Lea at wholesale prices. For example, Carey & Lea reprinted 5,750 copies of *Ann of Geierstein* in 1829, of which they kept only 3,250 for their own customers. Another 1,250, on cheaper paper and without title pages, went to Harper & Bros, and a further thousand to J. Crissy of New York. These firms subsequently inserted their own title pages and imprints before distributing them to their own customers. So although Scott's income from the sale of advance sheets was modest, it is certainly inaccurate to say, as the *Knickerbocker* did in 1835, that 'Walter Scott never received a cent on the sale of his works in America'.[7]

At about the time Scott died, Edward Lytton Bulwer began receiving similar payments from Harper & Bros of New York. This culminated in a formal written agreement dated 7 April 1835.[8]

Memorandum of Agreement between Edward Lytton Bulwer Esq of London, and Harper & Brothers, publishers, of New York. Mr Bulwer agrees to forward to Harper & Brothers early copies in sheets, as they come from the press in London of all works hereafter to be written and published by him, so as to ensure to them possession of the said copies, a sufficient time before the works can be received by any other person in America, to enable them to reprint for publication in that country. And Harper & Brothers in consideration thereof, agree to pay for the said copies at the rate of Fifty pounds sterling per volume, to be remitted by Bill of Exchange or otherwise, on the receipt of the first sheets forwarded by Mr Bulwer.

Since Bulwer's novels usually consisted of three volumes he received £150 for each new work of fiction with lesser amounts for short stories, poetry, or plays.

The first work to come under the provisions of this Agreement was the historical novel, *Rienzi*. Published at the end of 1835, it sold well in America and Bulwer received his £150. The Harpers pointed out, however, that something had gone wrong with the transmission of the early sheets resulting in the Philadelphia firm of Carey & Hart procuring a copy of the book before all the sheets from Bulwer had reached the Harpers.[9] This was not the first time that Bulwer had been urged to take more adequate precautions. Since English copyright could be secured only if a work was first published in Britain, Harpers often had to hold back their reprint in order not to anticipate the date of publication in England. But as soon as the English edition was out, Harpers rushed into print before any other American publisher. The same communiqué which reprimanded Bulwer for allowing a competitor to reprint *Rienzi* also presented another awkward problem. In an attempt to impress Bulwer with their strong position among American publishers, Harpers warned him not to accept offers from competitors.[10]

We have invested a large amount of capital in your productions, having stereotyped them all – an unusual measure by the way – and given assurances, both publicly and privately, to our customers in all parts of the United States, that they should be supplied by us with uniform editions of all you might write hereafter. For our own interest, as well as to redeem this pledge, we should be under the necessity of reprinting them upon the publisher to whom you might give the preference; and as delay would necessarily subject us to the risk of loss, by suffering the market to be stocked before we could appear in it with our editions, we should, of course, put in requisition all our means of competition; from the magnitude of our disposable force, we could throw before the public one of your novels in twenty four hours after obtaining a copy – which no other house in the U.S. could do – and even then sell it cheaper than any other, getting it up in the same form. Add to this the fact that the booksellers who have hitherto been supplied by us, would give our Editions the preference, and we think that no responsible publisher would feel willing a second time to pay a higher sum than we could afford, for a priority which would be little more than nominal. We have always made it a rule not to pursue any course that must prove injurious to another publisher, unless driven to it by aggression, but in this case we should have no alternative. We have too much already invested, and you will perceive at once how important it is for us that booksellers who have been for years dependent on our press for suppliers of a popular series, should still be able to obtain them from us.

Not unnaturally, Bulwer took offence at what he considered an implied threat. In the heated exchange that followed Harpers reiterated their position.[11]

Nothing could be farther from our intentions than presenting to you anything that even savoured of a threat; neither our respect for you nor our judgment would permit us to think of adopting such a course. We presented that postscript to you, merely as a plain and candid statement of facts, serving to show, first how much we feel and acknowledge it to be for our interest to continue the publication of your works; for although we have said, and truly, that we could prevent the priority from being any great advantage to any other publisher, we have not said, and do not say, that we should not be the losers by the operation. Our only motive for doing it would be the imperious necessity of keeping our editions complete, for the sake of continuing to sell those which we have already incurred the expense of stereotyping, and of maintaining our connection with the booksellers who now look to us for supplies. Secondly that it was likely to be quite as advantageous, to say the least, to you, to have your works republished by us as by any other, inasmuch as our interests are identified with yours to a certain extent, and therefore yours would be studied by us with a vigilance proportioned to that we should bestow upon our own. And lastly we designed, with the best intention in the world, to furnish you a criterion by which you might judge whether it would be any respectable and responsible publisher in this country who would interfere between you and us, knowing as they all do, how much capital we have invested in your works, how much it would be in our power and how strongly interest would urge us to diminish or prevent the injury we should sustain from a transfer of them from us. We know perfectly well that there are publishers, who, having nothing to lose would be willing to incur any risk – agree to any terms – make any promises. But we also know that there would be but small advantage to you in having the promise of higher terms from men whose performance would depend upon the issue; who would remit if they made money by the publication, but fail to remit if, from any cause, it should not prove equal to their expectations.

This warning was not without substance, for in the spring of 1836 Nahum Capen, one of the partners in the Boston firm of Marsh, Capen & Lyon, was in London and sought out Bulwer with just this purpose in mind. By way of vouching for his firm's reliability, Capen asked the representative of another American publisher, William H. Appleton, to write to Bulwer. Appleton gave assurances that Capen's firm was one of the oldest and most respected in America and that they would honour any agreement. Bulwer was somewhat receptive to Capen's overtures. Although he had an agreement with Harpers, he was always seeking higher remuneration because he felt that the Harpers undervalued his writings.

A new proposal to reprint his forthcoming works in America pleased and flattered him. Furthermore, a confusion among the Harper Brothers led to their rejecting one of Bulwer's new plays.[12] Although the details are vague, it seems that James Harper personally turned it down when passing through London on his way back to New York from Italy. This presumably occurred in late February or early March 1836, about the same time that Capen approached Bulwer. Six months later the Harpers apologized but the damage was done. Had Bulwer directed the volume to the New York office rather than submitting it to James Harper personally, it would have been published in accordance with the terms of the agreement.[13]

By August 1836 a draft of a contract between Bulwer and Marsh & Co. was drawn up. Although no specific remuneration was mentioned, Bulwer probably would have received as much if not more than he did from the Harpers. Capen, who by this time had returned to the United States, insisted that distinct safeguards be taken in the transmission of advance sheets: the London printers were to enforce strict security regulations so that no unauthorized person would obtain them; duplicates should be sent from London and Liverpool; publication in London had to be postponed for at least twenty to thirty days in order to give enough time for the advance sheets to reach America. In a letter accompanying the draft contract, Capen alluded to some correspondence between Bulwer and the Harpers which might be injurious to Harpers if the contents were known. Capen seemed to suggest that Bulwer publish them if Harpers tried to intimidate him for having had dealings with Capen. The letters referred to may well have been those in which the Harpers told Bulwer that they would brook no resistance in the American reprint market.

Three months later Capen temporarily suspended negotiations with Bulwer as there was no legal way to prevent the Harpers from interfering with Marsh & Co.'s reprints, and he had decided that the best tactic would be to lend support to the proposed Anglo-American copyright agreement. 'Perhaps it would be quite as well for your interest not to take your books from the Messrs. Harpers until Congress shall have decided on the new bill.'[14]

By this time things were even further complicated by Bulwer's London publishers, Saunders & Otley, opening a branch office in New York. If they had succeeded in this endeavour they would have been able to pay Bulwer more than either Harper & Bros or Marsh & Co.

To appreciate Bulwer's predicament fully one must realize the events which led Saunders & Otley to attempt the New York venture. The idea seems to have originated with the American author and publicist, Nathaniel Parker Willis. [15] During the mid-1830s he spent a good deal of time in Britain sending home newspaper dispatches describing whom he met and what he saw. He also arranged to publish several of his own volumes with Saunders & Otley. [16] This liaison provided Willis with a natural and convenient opportunity to discuss Anglo-American literary relations with his London publishers. He urged them to establish a branch office in New York, in part in order to shame the Americans into acknowledging the legitimate rights of British authors and publishers. Accordingly Simon Saunders, the senior partner, persuaded his son Frederick to manage such an office. Frederick later recalled,

I had but little time for preparation and, after a hurried farewell to wife, child and home circle at 16 Argyle Street, I, accompanied by my father, soon reached Portsmouth and saw the packet ship, the 'Montreal'; Capt. Champlain, was to carry me across the broad Atlantic. After parting with my father, I found myself for the first time in my life on the deck of an ocean-going ship; I know a feeling of utter loneliness came over me.

After thirty-nine days at sea he reached New York on 14 May 1836 and relates how he would have preferred to take things slowly and size up the New York book trade, [17]

but I was compelled to follow instructions of the London house and commenced my business agency by opening an office in Ann Street near William Street, where I had my operations arranged for the publishing of my father's London publications simultaneously with him in London. This was a work of no easy accomplishment however, for it took too long to correspond on the subject.

Saunders was frustrated by the problems arising from distance, but he always felt that the chief obstacle to success came from the 'opposition of some unscrupulous publishers'.

A good start was made with the agency; but soon trouble began; for the N.Y. publishing firm of Harper & Bros got hold of proof sheets of our books; our own pressmen having been tampered with; and published books that were the property of Saunders & Otley, several days sooner than we could get them out ourselves. This action of the N.Y. firm was widely announced with placards proclaiming 'great American enterprise'.

His only recourse, he felt, was to appeal to the American conscience through the public press.

Mr William Cullen Bryant kindly gave me free access to the columns of the 'Evening Post' and that afforded me an excellent opportunity for urging upon the public the Equity of our claims in seeking simply the protection of our personal property.

But even this aroused a spate of letters to the editor criticizing the interloping London firm and its attempted invasion of the American book trade. Saunders sometimes stood next to the compositor of the *Evening Post* and dictated his replies to such letters so that his rejoinders would appear alongside the incoming letters.

Among the works which Saunders & Otley brought out during the summer of 1836 were the *Memoirs* of Prince Lucien Bonaparte, two plays by Bulwer – *Cromwell* and the *Duchess de la Valliere* – Hazlitt's *Literary Remains, Memorials of Mrs Hemans* by Chorley, and *Madrid in 1835*: a guidebook. Unfortunately the Harpers were in direct competition over Bulwer's plays and Bonaparte's memoirs. In an attempt to buttress his moral claim to the Bonaparte work, Saunders published a letter in the *Evening Post* from the author stating that Saunders & Otley were his only authorized agents. An anonymous parody of this appeared soon thereafter.[18]

PROCLAMATION TO THE WORLD – The Americans are a ridiculous people, and their Government is a ridiculous government; both which facts are abundantly proved by the absurd laws made by that government, excluding foreigners from the advantage of copyright in books, charts, etc., and the pertinacity of the people in availing themselves of the benefits thus reserved and secured to them, especially in the matter of getting books at fifty cents a copy, for which, but for those laws, they would have to pay two dollars and fifty cents, and as much more as the London publisher could squeeze out of them. The American publishers are ridiculous too, in preferring the system of large sales and small prices, to that of small sales and high prices, so wisely and properly followed in Europe, and especially in London. – It must be evident that nothing can be more preposterous than the notion entertained by the American people, government and publishers, namely that the interests of the American people should be consulted in preference to that of the foreign author and publisher. Clearly it is better that these last should get a few thousand dollars more by the sale of a book than that the ridiculous Americans should be able to buy it for a fifth of the price that they would have to pay, if it were not for the absurd Laws aforesaid. These barbarians of the western world are getting knowledge at little cost, and the system must be amended.

Therefore, Pope Joan, Prince Cunningo, of the Pope's bedchamber, and the Hon. Lady Dorothy Dawdling, authoress of 'Flirtation and Philosophy', being of a high distinction in rank and literature, and having very important secrets to communicate, but determined that the Western barbarians shall not have them without paying handsomely, hereby declare that they have appointed Messrs Pica and Blackletter, of London, to be the publishers of their 'Memoirs' and other invaluable productions in England, France, Kamschatka, the land of the Hottentots, all the rest of the universe, and that anywhere and everywhere, they, the said Messrs P. and B. are the only authorized publishers of the same. And the deuce is in it if the Americans get cheap books much longer.

J. POPE OF ROME,
D. DAWDLING, A.O.F.A.F. ETC.,
I. PRINCE DE CUNNINGO.

Theodore Foster, the periodical reprinter, also harassed Frederick Saunders. A new work about London entitled *The Great Metropolis* was published by Saunders & Otley in New York for the very low price of $1.25. Foster reprinted the work in a 50¢ edition, adding some notes especially directed towards the American reader. In a letter of 31 January 1837 to the *Evening Post*, Foster reminded readers that the passage of an Anglo-American copyright agreement would preclude such an inexpensive reprint and that they would be forced to pay much more for their reading.

Bulwer became the pivot around which all of these recriminations revolved. As Harpers began to receive advance sheets of his next work, *Athens: Its Rise and Fall*, they reacted predictably.[19]

Your favour of the 27th of July has been received. In reply, we beg leave to inform you, that only ninety-four pages of the copy of 'Athens' have as yet arrived – And we are at a loss to know (not having been informed) of how many volumes the work will consist. This, of itself, would be a sufficient reason for not making the payment in advance. But, in the present instance, there are other reasons why we prefer delaying to remit. You are probably aware that your publishers in London have established a branch House in this city. Its agent has claimed it as his right, and has announced it as his intention, to republish exclusively in this country the works published by the House in London. We can recognise no such right. But we are threatened, by Mr Saunders, in case we do not respect his claims – (which we shall certainly feel ourselves under no obligations to do) – that, among other works, he will reprint upon us your 'Athens' – We expect him to do so. But if we pay for the work, we wish to be put in possession of the first copy that arrives in the country. This, you will recollect, was the main condition of our agreement. We were to receive the copy 'a sufficient time before the work could be received by any other person in America to enable them to reprint for republication'. With Mr Saunders' facilities for obtaining an early copy, and thus executing his threat we trust that you will not consider us unreasonable in wishing to receive the work in the manner and time specified, before we render the consideration therefor.

Thus Bulwer had three options which, on the face of it, were mutually exclusive. He could continue with the Harper arrangement; accept a new one from Marsh, Capen & Lyon; or work through his London publishers, Saunders & Otley. Quite understandably, he was reluctant to sever his connection with the Harpers before knowing whether either of the other two alternatives would succeed. His only hope was to temporize and await a clarification of events.

By the autumn of 1836 it was becoming increasingly apparent that Saunders & Otley would have to abandon their agency in New York if an international copyright law was not soon forthcoming. With the accumulation of gloomy reports from Frederick Saunders, the London firm did what it could to enlist the help of its prominent authors like Harriet Martineau. She agreed to ask a number of distinguished British writers to sign two formal petitions which would be submitted to the American Congress – one to the Senate and the second to the House of Representatives.

In a letter to Henry Brougham she related,

I never met with an American (not a bookseller) who did not agree with me on this subject. Mr Webster and Col Preston moved for a copyright law in the Senate the winter I was at Washington [1835–6]. They only want to be backed by the English authors. Messrs Saunders & Otley set up a house in New York a few months ago. They have been stoutly fighting our battle but such aggressions are made upon their property that they must give up unless the desired law can be obtained.

She then went on to explain that Saunders & Otley hoped to have his name at the head of the list along with that of Maria Edgeworth and William Wordsworth. She argued that the signatories to the petition would form a glittering array and added 'I rather think both Houses [of Congress] will fall on their knees on the receipt of our petition'. This was on 5 November, and when Brougham failed to respond Miss Martineau urged him on.

We are disposed to persevere, – but have changed our petition to an address. This removes the objection about us who are not legislators. I am afraid it will not remove yours but we can but try. I believe this mode will succeed. If it does not, the other remains – by the one you propose, we could not have the law for a year and a half: whereas, the excitement in America is now great, and favourable to our object; and the publishing house there [Saunders & Otley] must be sustained, if it is in human power to do it. The Americans in London give us their sanction completely so far.

Brougham was never fully convinced, and therefore apparently did not sign, but fifty-six other British authors led by Thomas Moore eventually put their signatures to the statement.[20]

Before all the British signatures were collected, Harriet Martineau sent a number of printed copies of the memorial to influential acquaintances in America. Among those who received them were the scholar, Edward Everett; the editor of the *Evening Post*, W. C. Bryant; former President of the United States, John Quincy Adams; Supreme Court Justice, James M. Wayne; the physician, Dr James Rush; and the historian, Jared Sparks. Each printed text was accompanied by a personal letter from Miss Martineau along the lines of her letter to Brougham. She asked their support in petitioning Congress and promoting an international copyright agreement.[21]

On 16 January 1837 Everett acknowledged Harriet Martineau's letter. He wrote that he was under the impression that John Quincy Adams intended to make a formal presentation of the British authors' memorial to the House of Representatives but that he doubted that anything could come of it during this session. Congress was due to adjourn in early March and there were major issues demanding attention. 'You propose a petition of American writers in aid of that of their British brethren. A movement to that end was talked of, last autumn, but I have not lately heard anything of it.' He promised to speak with a few authors in Boston to see what could be done.[22]

The signed copies of the British Address made their way to Washington through the assistance of Frederick Saunders. Senator Henry Clay of Kentucky presented one of them to the Senate on 2 February 1837, while a Representative from New York State, Churchill Cambreleng, submitted the other to the House on 13 February.[23]

In response to the presentation of the British authors' Address, the Senate approved the appointment of a Select Committee on 2 February to look into the question of international copyright. Clay became its Chairman, with William C. Preston of South Carolina, James Buchanan of Pennsylvania, Daniel Webster of Massachusetts, and Thomas Ewing of Ohio, as co-members. Two days later Clay presented another petition favouring international copyright signed by American citizens, and we now know that it was Frederick Saunders who supplied the Senator with these signatures. Clay also requested that another Senator be added to the Select Committee, and John Ruggles of Maine was duly designated. Finally Clay submitted additional signatures of British authors which had just reached him and which reinforced the already imposing list of two days before.[24]

When the members of the Select Committee scrutinized the British authors' memorial they could not help noticing the allusion to Saunders & Otley.

That certain authors of Great Britain have recently made an effort, in defence of their literary reputation and property, by declaring a respectable firm of English publishers in New York to be the sole authorized possessors and issuers of the said works, and by publishing, in certain American newspapers, their authority to this effect. That the object of the said authors has been defeated by the act of certain persons, citizens of the United States, who have unjustly published for their own advantage the works sought to be thus protected under which grievance the said authors have at present no redress.

The British authors went on to urge the adoption of an international copyright bill which would end the indiscriminate pirating and mutilation of their writings.

On 16 February Clay's Committee reported that justice required protection for foreign authors and it was time that America entered into an agreement to this effect with Britain and France, both of whom were in a position to give reciprocal safeguards to American authors. It also suggested that copyright legislation need not raise the price of books, but even if it did Americans would not begrudge fair compensation to foreign authors. American publishers in turn could look forward to protection through increased tariffs. The Committee buttressed its case with a popular analogy.[25]

A British merchant brings or transmits to the United States a bale of merchandise, and the moment it comes within the jurisdiction of our laws, they throw around it effectual security. But if the work of a British author is brought to the United States, it may be appropriated by any resident here and republished without any compensation whatever being made to the author. We should all be shocked if the law tolerated the least invasion of the rights of property, in the case of the merchandise, whilst those which justly belong to the works of authors are exposed to daily violation, without the possibility of their invoking the aid of the laws.

Their report concluded with the recommendation that copyright legislation be adopted. Clay presented Senate Bill 223 which extended copyright privileges to British and French authors on condition that their works were reprinted and published in the United States within a month of their appearance abroad. As one historian has noted:[26]

Thus, by making the protection of foreign authors' works dependent upon the manufacture of their books in the United States, the first American measure for international copyright attempted the task of reconciling the rights of authors with the interests of the American book trade. Its failure to do so to the satisfaction of the latter was, and continued to be, the chief obstacle in the path of the movement for international copyright.

Before the close of the second session of the Twenty-Fourth Congress a few more petitions arrived favouring international copyright. There were none for the opposition. On 16 February Clay's Bill had its first and second readings in the Senate and was passed by unanimous consent, but there was scarcely any time to submit it for a third reading and full discussion since the session was due to end on 3 March. Even though the Senate could be persuaded to stay longer in executive session, the House of Representatives would adjourn, and as the Bill required the sanction of both Houses of Congress, it was virtually doomed during the shortened 1836–7 session. Clay knew this when he proposed the Bill, but he apparently thought the gesture would enhance the cause of international copyright.

During the following few decades Clay's achievement stood out as a landmark of hope. Between 1837 and 1868 Congress issued but two reports on international copyright, Clay's being the only favourable one. Coming on the eve of the panic of 1837, his was not tainted by that melancholy event. Advocates of international copyright later looked back with envy to the masterful way in which he had presented the various petitions from British and American authors, secured a Select Committee, issued a favourable report and Bill.

The realities of the situation were far different. Clay actually had planned no clear strategy. He was probably taken by surprise when Harriet Martineau entrusted the task to him, and when he submitted the British petition to the Senate he casually referred it to the Library Committee. In the debate that ensued Senator Preston disagreed on this designation, and proposed that the Judiciary Committee consider it. But Senator Grundy, the Chairman of this Committee, said that it had quite enough business on hand and could not be bothered; why not a Select Committee? Had Clay given more thought to it, he could have arranged with the President of the Senate to appoint a committee friendly to the matter at hand, since this was the usual courtesy extended to members of both Houses. Instead the President of the Senate asked both friends and foes to serve on the Select Committee. One of the latter was James Buchanan who clearly indicated his negative position during the course of the debate.[27]

he saw an interest involved far beyond that of publishers, . . . and that was the interest of the reading people of the United States. Cheap editions of foreign works were now published and sent all over the country so as to be within the reach of every individual; and the effect of granting copyrights asked for by this [British] memorial would be, that the [British] authors who were anxious to have their works appear in a more expensive form would prevent the issuing of these cheap editions; so that the amount of republications of British works in this country . . . would be at once reduced to one half. But to live in fame was as great a stimulus to authors as pecuniary gain; and the question ought to be considered, whether they [British authors] would not lose as much of fame by the measure asked for, as they would gain in money.

Although one cannot be certain, it is quite probable that Clay and Preston were the only two supporters of international copyright on the Select Committee, while the other four demurred. If this was so, how did it happen that the Committee issued both a report and a Bill supporting the rights of foreign authors? The answer was revealed by Clay in a conversation with the young New York attorney, John Jay, ten years afterwards. Knowing that the Select Committee was divided, Clay persuaded them to endorse the report and the Bill with their 'permission' but not their 'concurrence'. Since the Senate as a whole must have discovered this discrepancy, it is no wonder that it never took action on Bill S. 223.[28]

Once it was apparent that the efforts to petition Congress had failed, Saunders & Otley began to limit their operations in New York. The exact termination date is unclear since Frederick Saunders remained in the city to take up permanent residence.[29] In 1838–9 he was in partnership with George Adlard, a New York bookseller, and for a time thereafter had his own bookshop. By 1846 he was employed as a publisher's reader by, of all firms, Harper & Bros of New York. He stayed with them for three years and then went into journalism, eventually securing the post of Assistant Librarian for the newly created Astor Library.

In the meantime, Bulwer had seen the handwriting on the wall. He decided to retain his connection with the Harpers and made sure that they were supplied with advance sheets of *Athens*. Although their relationship was sometimes uncertain and occasionally stormy, it continued virtually intact until Bulwer's death. Capen was undaunted by his failure to wean Bulwer from Harpers and tried to work out a publishing agreement with Frederick Marryat. As for the Harpers, they managed to emerge from the various episodes stronger than ever, and continued to dominate the reprint trade for decades to come.

By 1837 it was also apparent that the quest for an Anglo-American copyright agreement was not a purely national affair. Authors, publishers, and politicians on both sides of the Atlantic were taking an active role in its support or opposition. This interrelationship was part of a growing sense of an Atlantic community in which both Britain and America shared the same language, the same literature, and even the same economic cycles. There were times when these similarities fostered as much antagonism as co-operation, but in either case the significant areas of contact and influence increased.

During the spring and summer of 1837, there were still some, like Harriet Martineau, who remained optimistic about a forthcoming copyright agreement. As she told Clay on 15 May:

It gives me great pleasure to acknowledge, on behalf of many authors, besides myself, your exertions on the copyright business. I thought I was sure, both of what your convictions and your efforts would be; and I rejoice that my confidence has been justified. We are exceedingly pleased with your Report, and have strong hope that our object may be obtained next session. The American newspapers seem to show a more and more favourable disposition toward our claim, and some solid proofs have reached the hands of one, at least, of our authors (Professor Lyell), of the feeling which honorable American publishers entertain of the injury we suffer. Several hundred copies of Lyell's fifth edition of his Geology, in four volumes, have been ordered from England by booksellers in Boston, New York, and Philadelphia, and the money, in full, transmitted with the order. A highly creditable proceeding. It was transacted through Professor Silliman.

Edward Everett and Jared Sparks were not so hopeful. For one thing they complained that it was far from clear whether an American could secure a valid copyright under existing British law, and urged Miss Martineau to seek clarification on this point.[30]

A special session of Congress was summoned in the autumn of 1837, primarily to cope with the banking crisis and collapse of the currency. There was no time to deal with such peripheral matters as copyright. But once the regularly scheduled session in December opened, Clay lost little time. He reintroduced his Copyright Bill on 13 December and this time it was assigned to the Standing Committee on Patents. As a normal session of Congress would continue until the following summer, there was ample time to consider the Bill. Clay himself was far from confident, however, as revealed in a letter to Epes Sargent.

I concur with you in opinion entirely about the expediency of passing the bill. But the Booksellers, or rather some of them, are making effort to defeat it by procuring signatures against it, and if they are not counteracted they may possibly succeed.

His words were prophetic, for two days later the first of a flood of negative memorials reached Washington. Both Houses of Congress were deluged by petitions objecting to the Bill. Not until the latter half of April did the supporters of international copyright begin to make themselves known. However, the petitions continued to be clearly against Clay's Bill in a ratio of about three to one.

Clay's tactic throughout was to speed things along and secure an early report. The more delay, the greater the opportunity there would be for organized opposition. On 24 April he said:

The Committee to which this subject had been referred, had had it under consideration for some time, and he believed that they had been working with very proper motives under a desire that all the parties interested should be fully heard, before making their report. But as every thing that could be said or written on the subject had been exhausted, he hoped they would report the result of their deliberations to the Senate at an early day.

By contrast, the opponents of international copyright played for time. On 19 March petitioners urged the Senate not to act hastily but to await the report of the Patent Committee. Philip H. Nicklin, in his *Remarks on Literary Property* published at about the same time, wrote:[31]

It is therefore to be hoped, that Congress will do no more at this session than appoint committees of inquiry, to report at a future time, when enough information has been obtained to form a solid basis for sound legislation.

The *New World*, temporarily advocating international copyright, described the rise of the opposition:

In the meantime, some of the great publishing houses in Philadelphia saw fit to raise an alarm on this subject. . . . A counter-petition was got up, and a host of artisans connected with the business of printing and publishing were called upon, and not without success, to attach their names. Every person, who came into the book-stores to buy a book, was also requested to subscribe to the memorial.

Few were surprised by the report of the Patent Committee issued on 25 June 1838. While reporting Clay's Bill out of committee without amendment, it issued a supplementary report emphatically rejecting the intention of the measure. This was scarcely to be wondered at, at a time when trade was stagnant throughout the country and many members of the book trade unemployed. Few Senators were brave enough to invite competition from abroad when American commerce languished.[32]

Nevertheless, it is valuable to explore the composition of the Patent Committee in order to assess their predilection in the matter of copyright and to trace some of the ideas expressed in their report. Prior to the Civil War no other Congressional committee was to bring itself to the point of issuing a report, thus giving added significance to the remarks of 1838.

The Patent Committee contained five Senators, most of whom were far more obscure than those who served with Clay the year before. The Chairman was John Ruggles, a Democrat from the state of Maine who had been in the Senate since 1835. He had helped to frame the law for the the reorganization of the Patent Office in 1836, but had secured little reputation beyond that. Like so many of his Congressional colleagues he was a lawyer by training. It will be recalled that he was co-opted on to Clay's Select Committee of 1837 and was probably one of those who basically disliked the prospect of an Anglo-American copyright agreement. If this was the case, Clay would have been well advised to direct his Bill to another committee.

John M. Robinson of Illinois and Samuel Prentiss of Vermont were not necessarily predisposed one way or the other. But John Davis of Massachusetts had already established himself as an ardent protectionist, and so one might infer that he extended these principles to safeguarding the American book trade. On the other hand, he was the brother-in-law of George Bancroft, the promising young historian, and perhaps Bancroft influenced him to support international copyright. However, in these years the historian took little interest in the topic, therefore the likelihood was that Davis opposed the measure.

The fifth member of the Committee was the only potential supporter of international copyright. A Senator from North Carolina, Robert Strange was also a budding novelist. He negotiated an unusual publishing contract with Peter Force of Washington, D.C., whereby the profits from the novel would be divided equally between them, and Strange would receive $600 before publication in what eventually became known as the now familiar publisher's advance. Even more interesting was the stipulation that they would share the profits from the English as well as the American sales. The novel, *Eoneguski: or the Cherokee Chief; A Tale of Past Wars*, made its appearance in two volumes in 1839. Clearly Strange was aware of the implications of an Anglo-American copyright, and like other American authors he probably felt that American literature would thrive best in an atmosphere free of literary piracy.[33]

Unfortunately we do not know how often the Patent Committee met nor how they arrived at their negative report. When it comes to analysing this document, however, one thing becomes very apparent. The arguments against international copyright bear a striking resemblance to P. H. Nicklin's *Remarks on Literary Property*. The preface of this work was dated 17 March 1838 and its publication was clearly designed to influence the Committee's deliberations.

Nicklin enjoyed a long-established relationship with one of the chief opponents of international copyright and a leading reprinter of English works, the firm of Carey & Lea of Philadelphia. In 1822 Henry C. Carey explained the connection:

We have consolidated all the law [books] of Riley, Nicklin and our own into one stock under the management of Nicklin as our agent. By this arrangement nearly all the law in the Union has come under our control and as Mr N. has devoted nearly the whole of his attention for many years to this business we think it may be carried on to great advantage. We have the exclusive control of nearly 200 volumes of law.

Since many of their publications as well as others handled by Nicklin were American reprints of British works they had a distinct vested interest in the *status quo*. In 1829 when Carey & Lea decided to discontinue handling lawbooks and to concentrate on general literature Nicklin more or less fell heir to the law side of the business. Thus, when he wrote his *Remarks on Literary Property* he was hardly an impartial observer.[34]

Both Nicklin's book and the Patent Committee report concentrated on the British authors' petition which Clay presented to the Senate. Each claimed this as interference from abroad and predicted that a copyright agreement would promote higher book prices and smaller editions. The point was driven home by comparing retail prices of new books in England and America, for it was universally acknowledged that English books were disproportionately more expensive. One of Nicklin's key arguments was that

an immense amount of capital is employed in publishing books [in America], in printing, in binding, in making paper and types, and stereotype plates, and printing presses, and binders' presses and their other tools; in making leather and cloth, and thread, and glue, for binders; in copper plates, in copyrights, and in buildings in which these various occupations are conducted.

He estimated that 'the whole of this investment' amounted to $30 to $50 million and that 200,000 Americans were employed in various branches of the book trade, of whom 50,000 were women and children.[35]

It is probable that one-fourth of the business done by the publishers is in re-printing foreign books and this large portion of their business would be reduced perhaps as much as nine-tenths, certainly as much as three-fourths, if copyright be granted to foreign books.

The Patent Committee report leaned heavily on Nicklin's statistics but ignored the fact that foreign reprints comprised only one-fourth of the total American printing and publishing output. Both Nicklin and the report also agreed upon the lack of reciprocity which would exist under an international copyright treaty since the term of domestic copyright could extend to forty-two years while England's lasted for only twenty-eight. They went further. Many more English authors stood to gain by such a treaty because American authors rarely if ever received favourable publishing terms in Britain. The report cited Nicklin: 'It is stated in a recent publication that two hundred and fifty copies of Marshall's Life of Washington' had to be returned to America for lack of interest in the English market. Finally the Patent Committee echoed Nicklin's warning that a copyright agreement would still not prevent cheap foreign reprints from flooding the American market due to the reduction in the 1833 tariff on imported books.

Only in one major respect did the Patent Committee depart from Nicklin's line of argument. He urged a limited right of exclusive control over publications followed by perpetual copyright during which anyone could reprint by paying a small royalty. It is hard to know how serious Nicklin was, for he must have known that the whole tendency of the time was away from perpetuity and in favour of statutory limitation on copyright. His plan was in fact a way of justifying reprinters sharing in domestic as well as foreign productions. Understandably, the Committee took little interest in this aspect of Nicklin's treatise.

On its own, the Patent Committee presented several negative arguments not prompted by Nicklin. Although not alluding specifically to the report of Clay's Select Committee of 16 February 1837, it sought to refute one of Clay's leading contentions and in its report made special mention of Saunders & Otley's attempt to establish a branch in New York.

as between nations, [copyright] has never been regarded as property standing on the footing of wares or merchandise, nor as a proper subject for national protection against foreign spoliation. It has been left to such regulations as every government has thought proper to make for itself, with no right of complaint or interference by any other government. . . . It is true the proposed [copyright] bill provides for the printing of the first edition in this country; but that does not remove the objection. The memorial of foreign authors states that there is already established in New York an English house of publication, to whom they have endeavoured to secure the exclusive benefit of publishing their literary productions, 'by declaring them to be the sole authorized possessors and issuers of the works of the said petitioners; and by publishing in certain American newspapers their authority to this effect'. [British authors] only want the aid of an act of Congress to enable them to monopolize the publication here as well as in England, of all English works for the supply of the American market!

Most emphatically, it took exception to those who would confuse copyrights with patents. Chairman Ruggles had distinguished himself in the reorganization of the Patent Office and was not about to ignore this dimension of the issue.

American ingenuity in the arts and practical sciences, would derive at least as much benefit from international patent laws, as that of foreigners. Not so with authorship and book-making. The difference is too obvious to admit of controversy.

The negative report of a Senate Committee was bound to colour people's attitudes for years to come and due to the economic hardships of the time it overshadowed the positive one of Clay's Select Committee.

During the next few years Henry Clay introduced his Copyright Bill three more times: on 17 December 1838; 6 January 1840; and 6 January 1842. On all three occasions it was referred to the Senate's Committee on the Judiciary. In December 1838 the composition of the Judiciary gave no clear indication as to its likely reaction. Although Robert Strange had now become a member of this Committee and was presumably favourably inclined, the other members probably were ill-disposed in view of the recent negative report of the Patent Committee. Garret D. Wall of New Jersey was Chairman, joined by Thomas Morris of Ohio, Thomas Clayton of Delaware, and Franklin Pierce of New Hampshire. With the exception of Strange, none of these Senators had previously been involved with the copyright issue. They apparently decided to do nothing until the end of the short session and then on 1 March 1839 requested the Senate's permission to cease consideration of the question.[36] At the end of 1839 Clay had to admit that things were not going well.

I am afraid the prospect is bad for the passage of an international copyright law. The two last Committees to which it was referred were adverse to it; and the activity of some of the large publishers has been such as to make strong impressions against it on the minds of many Senators.

Nevertheless he persisted and reintroduced his Bill ten days later. It was again referred to the Judiciary Committee, which was composed of essentially the same members. This time their tactics seem to have been more forthright. On 8 January they reported it out of Committee carrying neither a recommendation for or against. This left it up to the Senate as a whole to decide.

Supporters outside of Congress urged Clay on. Some, like George

Adlard, the New York bookseller, were prepared to make concessions in the interest of securing further support. Clay resisted but was ultimately willing to compromise.

I received your letter transmitting a sketch of alterations which the opponents of the Copyright bill are desirous of effecting. I do not think that which would limit the holding of copyright to American citizens is just or liberal. Without the restriction, that would however probably be the practical operation of the measure. And, rather than do nothing, I would accede to these alterations.

When the Bill came up for debate before the whole Senate on 15 April 1840, Clay asked that it be postponed for a week. Subsequently he never called for the debate, and the Bill was eventually tabled in July shortly before the end of the session.

Clay's tactics are intelligible if one assumes, as he no doubt did, that the Bill could not pass. This is why the Judiciary Committee was willing to report it out of Committee. Apparently, Clay did not dare risk a formal rejection by the whole Senate, preferring instead to smother the measure by procrastination. If this is so it again calls into question the seriousness of Clay's support of international copyright. Why did he continue to introduce a measure year after year if its chances were exceedingly slight? Repetition only strengthened the hand of the opposition by demonstrating its ability to secure defeat of the measure. One is once more led to conclude that Clay valued the gesture of championing the issue with its attendant publicity identifying him with the cause, but placed little faith in the practical outcome.[37]

Clay's last effort on behalf of copyright was almost farcical. When he next introduced the Bill on 7 January 1842, he had already made up his mind to resign from the Senate the following March. He set forth his reasons in a letter to the General Assembly of the State of Kentucky.

I have for several years desired to retire to private life, but have been hitherto prevented from executing my wish from considerations of public duty. I should have resigned my seat in the Senate at the commencement of the present session [December 1841], but for several reasons, one of which was, that the General Assembly did not meet until near a month after Congress, during which time the State [of Kentucky] would not have been fully represented. . . . The time has now arrived, when I think that, without any just reproach, I may quit the public service, and bestow some attention on my private affairs, which have suffered much by the occupation of the largest portion of my life in the public councils.

Clay's private affairs were indeed in jeopardy. He had loaned one of his sons $20,000 to finance an experiment in hemp manufacture which went bankrupt in 1843. He also wished to retire from the Senate in order to prepare for his possible Presidential candidacy in 1844. His influence in the Senate had also waned. When Harriet Martineau met him in 1835–6 and entrusted him with the British authors' petition a year later he was still the acknowledged leader of the Whig Party. But having failed to become his party's nominee for President in 1840, he was especially bitter when the Whig candidate, William Henry Harrison, won the election. In the early days of the Harrison Administration Clay tried to exert his customary power but to no avail. He complained,

And it has come to this! . . . I am civilly but virtually requested not to visit the White House – not to see the President personally, but hereafter only to communicate with him in writing. The prediction I made to him at Ashland last fall has been verified. Here is my table loaded with letters from my friends in every part of the Union, applying to me to obtain offices for them, when I have not one to give, nor influence enough to procure the appointment of a friend to the most humble position.

President Harrison died suddenly in the spring of 1841, and Clay anticipated better relations and more influence under President Tyler. However, they soon fell out over the issue of a national bank and Clay again found himself in a position of comparative weakness.[38]

The final irony came in the early months of 1842 when Dickens, on tour in America, decided to make an issue of copyright. He naturally looked to Clay to provide the motive power in the Senate, but Clay had already resolved to retire. Not that Clay was naïve about the difficulties of passing a copyright bill:

The difficulties which have been encountered, and will continue to be encountered, in the passage of a liberal Copyright law proceed from the trade, especially the large book printers in the large Cities. It is very active and brings forward highly exaggerated statements both of the extent of Capital employed and the ruin that would be inflicted by the proposed provision for Foreign authors. These statements exercise great influence on members of Congress, many of whom will not enquire into the truth of them. These are the difficulties to be overcome; and they can only be subdued by enlightening public opinion, or causing it to flow in a correct channel. To this end, petitions numerously signed, the agency of the press and all other practicable demonstrations would be highly useful. And if a Committee of authors, well informed, sensible and judicious men could be got to attend Congress to answer and remove objections, before Committees of that body, I think it would be attended with the best effect.

Clay's implied criticism was just. There had been little or no co-ordination of effort outside Congress. Occasionally someone, like George Adlard, would collect signatures for a petition, as was the case in early 1839. Or, some editor would pen another plea for international copyright. Yet time and time again the efforts of copyright advocates were allowed to work at cross purposes and cancel out one another. George Palmer Putnam, the young publisher, was supposed to be the Secretary of a committee of interested parties in 1837, but his activities were so obscure as to have left no trace, except in the vague recollection of his son. A leading author like Washington Irving might sign one petition but then, as in 1838–40, decline to sign another because he did not like its phraseology. It was not enough for him to protest his support of the cause in general. Clay was right. Authors must go to Washington, as Noah Webster had done in 1831, and attach themselves to members of Congress. It was no good writing in literary periodicals about one's advocacy. That was merely preaching to the converted.

Symptomatic of the problem was Francis Lieber's efforts in 1839–40 to stir up interest in a copyright bill. He met discouragement from Clay and Preston, two of the staunchest supporters in the Senate. Eventually the most Lieber could do was write a pamphlet on the subject as a vehicle to analyse the theoretical dimensions of the problem. From a practical point of view this was exceedingly feeble when compared with the influence which opposing members of the book trade brought to bear on Congress. Clay knew how things worked and pointed the way. Much more effort and co-operation were needed by the friends of copyright outside Congress. He might also have added that a far greater effort was called for on the part of Congressmen like himself if the measure was ever to override the natural hostility or indifference of most legislators.[39]

Chapter IV

FURTHER EFFORTS TO INFLUENCE THE AMERICAN CONGRESS, 1842–51

Charles Dickens's trip to America in the early months of 1842 coincided with the depths of a depression. As one scholar has noted, 'Dickens could hardly have chosen a more unfortunate time to plead for copyright'.[1] He rarely showed any awareness of the economic plight which beset most Americans, and was bitterly contemptuous of the cheap newspaper and periodical trade which characterized these years. He assumed that rampant price-cutting was typical of the depraved state of American literature. Nevertheless his visit has understandably captured the interest of many Dickens scholars. Since it would serve no purpose to trace in detail that which so many others have carefully delineated, especially the recently published Pilgrim Edition of Dickens's letters for the years 1842–3,[2] I shall confine myself to describing Dickens's efforts in behalf of international copyright in the fuller perspective of the 1830s and 1840s. What emerges most strongly is his naïveté about influencing American literary and political life.

After Dickens returned to Britain in June 1842 many Americans claimed that he had undertaken the visit in order to supplement his own literary earnings by promoting international copyright. He stoutly denied this, and there is little reason to question the sincerity of his motives. However, his tactics were indeed ineffective. This is not to say, as many have, that he intentionally undermined the cause he sought to plead, but rather that he grossly underestimated the sources of opposition.

It seems fairly clear that no one could have persuaded Congress to approve an Anglo-American copyright agreement in 1842. Legislators were not about to jeopardize home industry and threaten the jobs of thousands of men and women for the sake of a few authors and publishers. Perhaps when prosperity returned and certain American states were not embarrassed by the default of their bonds, and when cooler heads could analyse the economic structure of book production and distribution, then copyright might have greater appeal.

Dickens's unwillingness to acknowledge the depression was coupled with his exaggerated confidence in the power of public opinion. Like the signers of the British authors' petition of 1837, he believed that literary popularity conveyed political power. He was confident that public speeches reinforced by declarations from distinguished American authors would command recognition. He was thus delighted when Frederick Saunders provided him with just such a petition signed by twenty-five leading New York literary lights with Washington Irving at their head. For good measure he wrote to John Forster in London asking that he prepare a seemingly spontaneous memorial from some of the same British authors who had joined with Harriet Martineau in 1837. The Saunders petition was presented to Congress in March 1842 and a Select Committee was appointed in the House of Representatives. John Pendleton Kennedy, an author himself, was designated Chairman. Dickens appreciated the distinct advantage of having a friend of literature in this key position. Meanwhile in the Senate Clay's Copyright Bill was still under consideration by the Judiciary Committee.

Neither the House nor the Senate Committee ever reported its findings. What went wrong? Could Dickens have been expected to do more? For his part, he blamed American authors for not supporting him more vigorously. He felt that his fight was theirs, and that if they believed in the cause of international copyright they should work for it. That they did not is patently true. Dickens was completely justified in this criticism. Nothing better characterized the years 1837–42 than the lacklustre efforts of American authors. An inverse ratio seemed to function in the literary community: the more illustrious one was, such as Irving, Cooper, and Prescott, the less he was involved. On the other hand, Dickens, like many others, had an exaggerated confidence in the political finesse and prestige of Henry Clay. His own distaste for political manoeuvring led him to rely on others, as is revealed in a letter to John P. Kennedy, to whom he offered assistance in drawing up the Select Committee report. He confessed, 'on consideration and on sitting down to the task I found I could not write anything which was at all likely to prove of service to you in the matter of your report'. Each time he tried to argue the practical merits of a copyright agreement he found that his keen sense of justice cried out for redress regardless of the specific issues involved. His unwillingness to come to grips with the tedious details of legislative procedure and pressure rendered his efforts futile. He later acknowledged the ineffectiveness of his gestures but shifted the entire responsibility on to the American character with its insatiable desire to get the better of foreigners, and its inability to produce a native American literature.

Clay must certainly bear a good deal of the onus for Dickens's misinformation about the state of Congressional opinion. Shortly before Clay retired, he had a conversation with the Chairman of the Senate Judiciary Committee, John M. Berrien of Georgia, who was prepared to report negatively on Clay's Copyright Bill. Clay prevailed on Berrien to postpone this pronouncement, and then proceeded himself to present the Irving petition which Dickens had brought to Washington. On that occasion he casually mentioned that his resignation from the Senate the next day would unfortunately prevent him from witnessing the passage of an international copyright law. Berrien then waited two more months until, in response to a question, he acknowledged that the Judiciary Committee was not prepared to recommend Clay's Copyright Bill.

Everything now depended on Kennedy's Committee in the House of Representatives. Dickens's brief presence in Washington was sufficient to encourage its formation, but that was all. No additional petitions were forthcoming and no campaign of co-ordinated letter-writing sprang into being. No public meetings were held. If anything, the opposition was more vocal than the supporters. The only thing Kennedy's Committee succeeded in doing was to elicit from the President the previous correspondence with Britain on the subject which was wholly inconclusive. The second session of the Twenty-Seventh Congress was still sitting when Dickens departed for England. Kennedy did not issue a report, but he did request a renewal of the Select Committee in the following December, and there the issue rested.

During much of 1843 nothing significant happened on the copyright front. Articles kept pouring from the periodical press but had no visible impact. Then in August a group of New Yorkers sent out invitations announcing that on the twenty-third a meeting would take place at the Athenaeum Hotel. In the course of that evening the American Copyright Club was formed. In the following few weeks additional invitations were forwarded to *literati* not only in New York but throughout the nation urging them to join. Branches were established in a number of cities, contributions were solicited, and a permanent executive committee was chosen. Five executive officers co-ordinated the Committee and the Club. William Cullen Bryant, the poet, was President; Guilian Verplanck, the former New York Congressman and staunch copyright advocate, was Vice-President; Evert Duyckinck, the editor, was Recording Secretary; Cornelius Mathews, the author and magazine editor, was Corresponding Secretary; and A. W. Bradford, the author-lawyer, was Treasurer.[3]

Two months after its inception the Club published an imposing document entitled 'An Address to the People of the United States on Behalf of the American Copyright Club' in which it not only set forth its aims and aspirations, but also printed a comprehensive list of its many members scattered throughout the country. Each member then knew who his fellow Club members were in his locality. Typical of the cordial response received by the Club was that sent by the historian, Jared Sparks.[4]

I have received your circular letter, informing me that I have been elected an associate member of the 'American Copyright Club'. I am glad that an association for so important an object has been formed, and shall be happy to aid in carrying out its designs as far as my opportunities and means will admit.

I fear little can be done, however, till the publishers shall be convinced that their interests are identical with those of authors. If their cooperation could be secured, I believe Congress might be brought to reasonable measures, but not otherwise. The argument of cheap books will outweigh in the public mind every appeal to equity and right.

By December 1843 Club members were being urged to take more active and concrete steps. To William Gilmore Simms, editor of the *Southern Literary Messenger*, Mathews wrote:[5]

On the other page of this sheet you will find the form of a memorial adopted by the American Copyright Club. It is believed to be as free from points of objection or debate as any that could be devised, and to state properly the leading interest of the question. With the hope that it will meet your concurrence it is requested that you date it as of your city, procure as great a number of signers as practicable, placing their calling or profession against the name, and forward it to Washington at as early a date as possible to your member of Congress, accompanied with a letter or letters from proper persons enforcing the same upon his attention. A counterpart of this letter and memorial has been addressed to each of the appropriate members in your city, a list of whom you will find at the back of the pamphlet address heretofore directed to you. This is mentioned so that the friends of copyright in your city may cooperate on a mutual under-standing of the business.

The Club secured a particularly valuable ally in George Palmer Putnam, the publisher. During the autumn of 1843 he travelled throughout the eastern part of the country soliciting the signatures of ninety-seven booksellers, publishers, printers, and other members of the trade to a petition which he eventually presented to both Houses of Congress. In the Senate it was initially referred to the Judiciary Committee but after-wards was transferred to the Committee on Printing. This was a fortunate change since Berrien was still Chairman of the Judiciary Committee and was just as likely to oppose international copyright as he had done the year before. The House of Representatives appointed yet another Select Committee. Two of its members are worth noting. The Chairman was Robert C. Winthrop of Massachusetts, a powerful figure in the lower Chamber who had served on John P. Kennedy's Copyright Committee in 1842. Also appointed was former President, John Quincy Adams. No more prestigious member could be imagined. Here were two men who could scarcely be identified with the usual opposition to copyright from small town lawyers or frontier rustics.

The following January the Club got another strong boost from Nahum Capen, a partner in the Boston publishing firm of Marsh, Capen & Lyon. It may be recalled that Capen, along with N. P. Willis, had urged Saunders & Otley of London to establish a branch office in New York in 1836. Now Capen resumed his active promotion of the copyright cause, a testimony to the willingness of members within the book trade to take positive action. No longer was international copyright the darling of a few struggling authors; most of the leading publishers now came out in favour of some sort of Anglo-American copyright agreement.[6]

Finally, in the spring of 1844 the American Copyright Club took the unprecedented step of paying an agent in Washington, D.C., to press the measure. As determined advocates of copyright they were beginning to fight fire with fire. They chose Rufus W. Griswold, someone well versed in the workings of the book and periodical trade, as their agent. At one time or another he had been an editor of Greeley's *New Yorker*, Wilson's *Brother Jonathan*, Winchester's *New World*, Roberts's *Notion*, and the highly successful *Graham's Magazine*. He was also a freelance literary agent and the best known anthologist of American literature of his time. If anyone knew the book trade, Griswold did.[7]

The year 1844 was one of prosperity, and the Congressional session was a long one stretching well into the summer. The American Copyright Club organized its resources well and had secured valuable allies in Putnam and Capen. Minimal opposition was encountered, and even the redoubtable champions of literary piracy, the Harpers, joined the Club in the person of Wesley Harper. With so much going for the international copyright movement, why was nothing ever heard from Winthrop's Select Committee or the Senate's Committee on Printing? Why, having taken all the right steps, were the results no more successful? To answer these questions one must look beneath the surface of the events. In reality the whole effort of 1843-4 was deceptively strong.

The key to much of the disappointment lay in the origins of the Copyright Club itself. One of its founders, C. F. Briggs, described the first meeting of 23 August 1843 in a private letter to R. W. Griswold.

The history of this business is often funny. I had invitations sent to a few individuals requesting them to meet at the Athenaeum Hotel to form a club for the purpose of promoting an international Copyright, etc.; when we met there was only Hoffman, Mathews, Duyckinck, and myself present. I proposed Hoffman for Chairman, Duyckinck for recording secretary, and Mathews for corresponding secretary; a treasurer was wanting and I proposed Bradford for that office, and so the Club was formed.

William Cullen Bryant was unable to attend that first meeting but had already consented to be President of the new association. Bradford was presumably told later of his election as Treasurer, and there is little indication that he ever found his duties very time-consuming. From these humble origins the Club managed to construct an impressive façade. When seeking members a few days later, Corresponding Secretary Mathews was careful to note that 'you were unanimously elected an associate member of the club, with the hope that you would find it in your power to cooperate with its objects'. Little did the recipients suspect that four New York authors comprised this unanimity! There were also some major literary figures like James Fenimore Cooper who were insensible to the honour.

I beg you to communicate to the club that I would cheerfully join them did I join anything. But an issue has been raised that induces me to stand aloof. I ask nothing from the American public and I owe them nothing. I wish to keep the account square.

No pressure group like the Copyright Club could have significant political power if very many leading authors similarly declined membership.

From such modest beginnings, how did the Club manage to collect its imposing list of supporters? A close perusal of Mathews's invitation to prospective members provides the answer. They were automatically and 'unanimously' elected associate members unless they specifically declined in writing. This way of defining membership may help to account for certain anomalies in the ranks of the Club, chief among these being the name of J. Wesley Harper, one of the four Harper Brothers of New York whose firm was notoriously opposed to the aims of the Club. A former Harper author, William Gilmore Simms, found no contradiction in Wesley's inclusion, describing him as an 'amiable and sensible fellow', whose signature implied that the Harpers now approved of the Club's aims, 'but were unwilling to show themselves active because of their former hostility'. Simms's view is not inconsistent with a later explanation: that the depression years 1837–43 had forced the Harpers to reconsider their opposition to international copyright. The supplements of the *New World* and *Brother Jonathan* had in effect frightened the Harpers into affiliating themselves, if only temporarily, with the Copyright Club.

Despite Simms's testimony and the presence of Wesley Harper's name among the associate members, it is extremely difficult to accept the evidence at face value. It was totally inconsistent with Harper policy both before and after the Club's brief existence. Not till the late 1870s were the Harpers to side with the advocates of international copyright. Several other alternative explanations suggest themselves. First of all, the Regrets Only invitation may have presented Wesley Harper with a chance to befuddle others, since it involved no positive commitment. It was also good publicity as far as their American authors were concerned. Furthermore, by late 1843 the country was recovering from its economic depression, and the Harpers must have realized that they were getting the better of the *New World* and *Brother Jonathan*. If they had really been serious about supporting international copyright they would have joined the ninety-seven others in the book trade who signed G. P. Putnam's petition to Congress, but they were one of the conspicuous holdouts; and at just about the same time that Mathews was recruiting members for the Copyright Club. This is even more significant when one examines the wording of Putnam's memorial. Not only did it call for the printing and binding of foreign reprints in America; it also required that foreign

DAP

authors sell their copyrights to American publishers, which guarded against a British firm like Saunders & Otley establishing a branch in New York. It was precisely because Putnam so substantially represented the interests of the American book trade that many printers and publishers signed. The Harpers did not. One can only assume that their affiliation with the Copyright Club was a convenient and rather cynical public relations stunt. In either case it did not materially enhance the prestige of the Club.[8]

As to the Club's pressure on Congress, there is no indication that it made any effort to co-operate with memorialists like Putnam and Capen. If anything it tended to perpetuate the division between authors and the members of the book trade rather than seeking to heal the breach. Neither is there evidence that Griswold's services as a paid agent in Washington had any results. During most of the winter and spring of 1844 he was preoccupied with his own editorial and publishing interests and rarely appeared in the Capitol.

Finally there was a clash of personalities among the leaders of the Club which did more than anything else to discredit its image in the literary community. In later years, C. F. Briggs had nothing good to say of Cornelius Mathews.

the Centurion (Mathews) has continued to monopolize all the audit of that Copyright Club business, when in fact I did, myself, get up the Club, organized it and kept it going until I saw that the Centurion was bringing disgrace upon it, and then I abandoned it . . . and had it not been for the ridicule brought upon the affair by the monkey shines of little Manhattan (Mathews), I believe that before this an international copyright law would have been passed.

There seems little doubt that Mathews came to dominate the Club and to alienate many of its supporters. Yet he had as good a claim as any to be identified with the cause. His talents as a publicist were not inconsiderable. Although many of his New York contemporaries found him a bore when he spoke at length on the copyright question in February 1842, Dickens and other Englishmen were gratified by his overt support. As already mentioned, Dickens never forgave the way most American authors held back on that and similar occasions. Well before the Copyright Club came into being, Mathews personally contacted authors and publishers on the subject. It may have been true, as some alleged, that he wished to bask in Dickens's reflected glory by associating himself with Dickens's copyright campaign. Nevertheless, he did more than most to keep the issue alive prior to the Club's formation. Typical of the support he received was that of Samuel F. B. Morse in 1842.[9]

Until such an act is passed, our literature and consequently to a great degree the formation of our national character is in the hands of Great Britain. We are not independent. We have cast off our political chains but in almost everything else we are yet in colonial bondage.

Mathews incorporated Morse's sentiments in the October 1843 *Address* of the Copyright Club. Referring to America he said, 'In all other circumstances and questions save that of a literature you have taken a high ground of freedom and self-reliance.' Mathews even managed to salvage something from J. F. Cooper's refusal to join. At that time Cooper had written:

Unless we have a copyright law there will be no such thing as American literature in a year or two. At present very few writers are left. With a copyright law we shall have not only a literature of our own but literature of an improved quality.

These thoughts were converted by Mathews into:

Do you know, have you marked how authorship in any worthy sense is almost utterly silent throughout the land – how day by day and dollar by dollar the revenues of writers known far and wide . . . have shrunk to nothing.

Mathews continued his interest in the copyright question into the late 1840s but his tendency was to publicize the issue rather than work for it through political channels. Writing to R. S. Mackenzie in 1846, he said:[10]

I send you through the post office a letter, in one of our newspapers, in which I have expounded the present state of the International Copyright Question – which for the sake of its statements and for the satisfaction of English authors I would like to see transferred to your London papers.

By this time the American Copyright Club was dead, and although contemporaries like Briggs and Griswold blamed Mathews for its failure, it was not that simple. Pressure exerted outside of Congress could never succeed without internal Congressional support. Little had ever been anticipated from the Senate Committee on Printing in 1843 but much was hoped for from the Select Committee of the House of Representatives. R. C. Winthrop was a conscientious Chairman but apathetic. He wrote to the American Minister in London, Edward Everett, seeking information and suggestions about international copyright, but did not hesitate to

admit: 'It is a vexed question from which I would gladly have escaped.'
Four years later when John Jay spoke to him in Washington Winthrop
was still undecided as to the wisdom of securing an international copyright agreement! What is more, he told Jay that John Quincy Adams had
been strongly opposed to international copyright and his views had overshadowed those of other members on the Select Committee. The pattern
of petitioning Congress, forming committees, and recruiting allies had
repeated itself only to find that nominal friends in Congress were luke-
warm at best, and as often as not, hostile. Quite naturally, most politicians
were unwilling to proclaim their opinions publicly when it meant
alienating one or another group of constituents.[11]

The year 1844 was a Presidential election year, and this may have
distracted Winthrop's Committee from considering copyright. No report
was ever submitted and the subject was allowed to drop for several years.
It briefly surfaced at the beginning of 1846 when Senator Reverdy Johnson
of Maryland made a motion that a Select Committee be appointed to
consider the numerous copyright memorials on file with the Senate, but
nothing came of this and it was not until John Jay exerted himself several
years later that the issue was effectively revived.[12]

Meanwhile, American publishers revived the practice known as
'courtesy of the trade' after an absence of nearly a decade. Prior to the
depression of 1837–43 it had been customary to respect certain informal
rules governing the republication of foreign works because of the vastly
increased interest in the reprints of Scott, Byron, Edgeworth and Porter.
To claim this privilege a publisher had only to secure the first copy of the
foreign work to reach American shores. This induced leading publishers
like Carey & Lea to arrange the prompt dispatch of new books by an agent
in London. Once such books reached America, publishers hastily decided
which ones to reprint and announced their intentions in the press, expecting that by so doing their brethren of the trade would acknowledge
this priority, and would not reprint copies themselves. It was understood
that they would then place orders with those publishers who had been
first in the market.

This unofficial system worked tolerably well until the mid-1830s,
though there were always new circumstances which presented difficulties. One of these occurred in 1822 when Carey & Lea began receiving
advance sheets of Scott's novel, *The Pirate*, in instalments. On the basis of
these they advertised the book as 'in the press' well before receiving the
completed text. Wells & Lilly challenged this application of trade courtesy

and reprinted the work. The Philadelphia firm retaliated by dismissing Wells & Lilly and appointing Thomas Jordan as their agent in Boston.[13]

Meanwhile Wells & Lilly were also preparing for battle. No sooner had Jordan's connection with the Philadelphia firm become known than Wells & Lilly, on April 28, 1822, had him arrested for debt. Since the finances of the booktrade were so involved and complex that at almost any given time almost every bookseller could be said to be indebted to almost every other bookseller, Wells & Lilly could do this with little trouble, but the fact also simplified Jordan's next move. The following day he had Lilly arrested for debt. Five days later Wells & Lilly attached Jordan's horse and chaise for debt.

And so continued claim and counterclaim until the case went to court in October. Mysteriously Jordan's lawyer failed to appear at the trial, and Jordan lost the suit. Jordan felt that his lawyer had been bribed, but it may be that his lawyer simply felt that he had no case, because Jordan was apparently vulnerable on several counts. In fact, it was not long before Carey & Lea began to regret having selected Jordan to represent them. Within a year he was released from their services, after which time they found it nearly impossible to obtain an accounting of the transactions he had made for them.

Time did much to heal the breach between Wells & Lilly and the Philadelphians. As early as July, 1822, when Carey & Lea were 'holding their breath' till the final pages of Scott's Nigel should arrive, Wells & Lilly offered to allow Carey & Lea to reprint from a complete copy that they had just received. Carey & Lea were impressed, but, since their own copy had arrived the day before, they refused the offer. Both houses were large, and it was a matter of economic convenience that they should transact business with one another. They soon resumed normal business activities with one another, but for some time thereafter each watched the other with a jaundiced eye.

When a breach of trade courtesy occurred, a firm like Harper & Bros took swift and terrible vengeance. About 1830 the Boston publishers Munroe & Francis ignored Harpers' claim to Moore's *Letters and Journals of Lord Byron* and reprinted it. This so enraged the Harpers that they retaliated by reprinting Munroe & Francis' most valuable property: a twenty-volume set of Maria Edgeworth's writings which they compressed into ten volumes priced at $7.50 instead of $19.50. Courtesy of the trade obviously favoured the stronger and larger firms and the smaller ones were generally kept in line.[14]

Each major publishing house tended to consider certain authors their own, and on the whole, this propriety was observed. For example, it was tacitly understood that Bulwer and James belonged to the Harpers and that they would have the exclusive right to issue new works from these writers. Similarly, Carey & Lea claimed Capt. Marryat, and in so far as they could, Sir Walter Scott. We have seen how Munroe & Francis thought they had cornered the market on Edgeworth until they ran foul of the Harpers. This sense of trade courtesy even began to include an effort to keep up retail prices, but before 'resale price maintenance' could really take hold the depression of 1837 struck. By then Harpers and Carey & Lea had also clashed over the works of Bulwer and Marryat.

By the mid-1830s the system of trade courtesy was showing distinct signs of strain. The panic of 1837 put an end to what remained of trade courtesy throughout the country, and we have seen how cheap weeklies like the *New World* and *Brother Jonathan* rejoiced in literary piracy and the absence of internal trade restraint. However, by the mid-1840s the mania for cheapness had abated and trade courtesy began to be revived. Improved trade conditions brought greater stability. Publishers could plan ahead, make new arrangements to secure advance sheets from England, pay more for these sheets, with the expectation that their fellow Americans would not invade their territory. Of course, there were petty breaches of good faith, and occasionally some upstarts sought to make their fortunes at the expense of the more established. But newcomers were usually taught a lesson and quickly brought into line. As a result, from about 1845 until the depression of 1857 the American book trade experienced a remarkable prosperity and tranquillity which augured well for an Anglo-American copyright agreement.[15]

During 1847 and 1848 the New York lawyer John Jay took a keen interest in the cause. He had been initially drawn to copyright matters in connection with Coxe's scheme to promote an American edition of *Blackwood's Magazine*. As Blackwood's agent in New York, he clearly enjoyed treating with parties on both sides of the Atlantic, and having once subdued the reprinter Leonard Scott, he now threw himself wholeheartedly into the much larger undertaking of securing an Anglo-American copyright agreement.

His first step was to become informed concerning recent developments on the subject in Congress, and for this purpose he set out for Washington on 12 January 1848.[16] Among those he interviewed in the House of Representatives were T. B. King of Georgia, G. P. Marsh of Vermont, C. J. Ingersoll of Pennsylvania, I. E. Morse of Louisiana, and P. F. Schenck of Ohio. 'All expressed to me', Jay reported to Blackwood, 'their warm interest in the subject.' Jay also sounded out the Speaker of the House Robert C. Winthrop of Massachusetts who, though somewhat non-committal, expressed his willingness to appoint a Select Committee if the question reached the floor of the House. Jay proposed to send a memorial to Winthrop calling for amendment of the existing laws of copyright. Winthrop would then observe the traditional Congressional practice of giving the petition into the hands of its friends; that is, appointing a committee composed of those known to be favourable to the aims of the petitioners. Jay suggested that the House members with whom he had already discussed the matter would make admirable appointees. At this time Jay had no memorial ready, nor any signatures of impressive authors and publishers supporting such a document, but since this had been the procedure in the past he observed the ritual in order to get a Select Committee. A Select Committee, unlike a Standing Committee, could be expected to take a more lively interest in the subject and issue a report recommending legislation.

His main task in Washington, therefore, was to gain access to the previous petitions, reports, and statements on copyright in order to compile a new and convincing memorial. Through Senator Calhoun, he was provided with the archival documents he needed. He took as many notes as time permitted and supplemented them with references to printed volumes of the Congressional papers. While in the Capitol he also interviewed the respected Whig leader, Henry Clay, and the up-and-coming Democrat, Stephen A. Douglas.

By the time he left Washington, Jay had allayed many of his own misgivings, and reassured Blackwood that the whole question depended upon going about it the right way with the proper amount of organization and effort. Besides petitioning Congress, Jay knew that substantial newspaper support would be essential. Especially important was James Gordon Bennett's *New York Herald*, one of the first cheap mass circulation dailies. He knew, too, that he would have to pay for the kind of publicity he wanted. This would also be true for the twenty to thirty so-called 'letter writers' or correspondents who represented out-of-town newspapers in Washington. Weekly and monthly periodicals favourable to international copyright would also have to be cultivated assiduously.

In addition to managing the news as much as possible, Jay saw that a concerted effort would have to be made to manage the members of Congress. For this purpose he recommended that the distinguished literary figure Rufus W. Griswold be sent to Washington to influence opinion and to assist the Select Committee in drawing up its report. In mentioning Griswold Jay showed that he had done his homework well, for, as we have seen, Griswold had served in a similar capacity for the American Copyright Club during the early months of 1844.

Of course there would be opposition, especially from a few leading publishers such as the Harpers of New York and the Careys of Philadelphia. Most printers were equally hostile. Rampant reprinting had meant more type to set and more pages to print. Jay realized that the only way to gain their favour would be to guarantee that they would continue to print the works of foreigners even under an Anglo-American copyright agreement. Only with a 'manufacturing clause' could their natural objections be overcome.

These, then, were the proposals which Jay advanced to Blackwood at the end of January 1848. The one thing still needed to carry the plan into execution was money. In a cover letter accompanying his lengthy report Jay indicated his willingness to serve as co-ordinator of all these efforts, but he admitted that he could not do it all as a private citizen. He asked to be retained professionally for the purpose. One thousand pounds ($5,000) discreetly expended would, he was sure, accomplish wonders. Could Blackwood and the other British publishers raise such an amount? Jay hoped so, and on the assumption that they could he continued to prepare plans for a campaign.[17]

Jay had his work cut out for him. He began by asking his friend Coxe in Hartford, Connecticut, to sound out the local publishers as to their interest in a copyright agreement. The result was not encouraging. 'Dickens dished that matter here', Coxe reported, alluding to the visit of 1842, and when he mentioned the matter to one of the most prominent houses, 'they gave me so little encouragement, that I was unwilling to press the matter'. There was no looking to places like Hartford, Coxe added. 'The small cities will not stir in the business.'[18]

Undaunted, Jay set to work on his memorial. Illness in early February delayed him somewhat, and when his brother-in-law and law partner Maunsell B. Field decided on the spur of the moment to take a trip abroad, Jay's increased legal work took most of his time. In addition, he had to carry on without any encouragement from Blackwood since it was winter and steamships sailed less frequently, leaving Jay without a reply to his January proposal.

On 18 March Jay finally was able to send the memorial to Washington directed to the attention of one of the Congressmen whom he had previously interviewed, Thomas Butler King of Georgia.[19] The memorial was actually a composite of several documents. First came a lengthy set of arguments on behalf of international copyright; then an appendix reprinting Putnam's petition of December 1843, followed by a detailed second appendix listing about six hundred books which had been written by Americans and reprinted in Britain, finally, a section bearing the signatures of William Cullen Bryant, Charles Fenno Hoffman, Theodore Sedgwick, and a dozen other New Yorkers.[20] Clearly this was the most elaborate and carefully argued defence of international copyright to reach the halls of Congress before the Civil War. It not only emphasized America's moral obligation to protect foreign authors and promote the rights of American authors abroad, it also reiterated that America was no longer a colony but an independent nation with a literature of its own. As convincing evidence of this, Jay presented a catalogue of American books reprinted in Great Britain. George Palmer Putnam was responsible for compiling the list from issues of the *London Catalogue*, and it included the names of authors and titles as well as the British publishers and the prices of the reprints. Had time permitted, Putnam might have added many others, or indicated those instances when more than one London publisher reprinted a work. Even so, it was the most eloquent testimony to the fact that America had books worth reprinting, and by implication worth protecting through an Anglo-American copyright agreement.

The other noteworthy part of the memorial was Jay's point-by-point refutation of the standard arguments against international copyright. The case for the opposition had been rather devastatingly set forth by the Senate Committee on Patents in its report of 25 June 1838. As was so often the case throughout the century, the arguments centred on two major objections: that American printers and publishers would be deprived of work and that prices of books would rise in order to compensate foreign authors. To the first of these Jay repeated what he had said to Blackwood at the end of January: that reprints of foreign works would be manufactured in the United States. To the second point he used contemporary economics to argue that an expanded market such as the United States would provide publishers with larger sales and consequent reductions in the unit price.

Finally, Jay tried to show that pirating foreign works benefited only a minority of the book trade.[21]

The business of reprinting the new and popular books that issue from the

English press is to a great extent monopolized by a few large houses whose
wealth and power enabled them to crush competition, and this monopoly if
profitable to the few is injurious to the many.

It was the same point which Washington Irving and Henry Clay had
made a few years before when they referred to two large firms, one in
New York and one in Philadelphia, leading the fight against international
copyright. Jay did not have to mention the Harpers nor the Careys by
name, for everyone knew they still spearheaded the opposition. All Jay
hoped to suggest was that Congress stop serving the special interests of
certain large publishers plus a host of smaller printers and begin to
take note of the rights of authors and the needs of the nation at
large.

Thus, by the middle of March, Jay and Putnam had done all that they
could. They had put together more than thirty pages of argument and
evidence on behalf of copyright. It was now up to T. B. King and others
in the House and to Blackwood in Edinburgh to take the next steps.
When Blackwood finally sent a reply to Jay it was only to say that he
was too busy to do anything at the moment, but that he would begin
making inquiries, as soon as possible. He questioned whether the money
could be raised, but agreed to shoulder a large part of the financial
burden if others could be persuaded. In the meantime he generously
offered to compensate Jay for the expenses incurred in behalf of the
copyright cause.[22]

Jay now realized that it would be a while until he heard again from
Blackwood, but he daily hoped to hear that Speaker Winthrop had
appointed the Select Committee. March turned into April and still no
word, so Jay got in touch with J. G. Palfrey the former editor of the
North American Review to make some discreet inquiries in Washington.
Unfortunately Palfrey found nothing to report. Jay had stressed the
urgency of the matter to King, not only because he wanted to promote
the cause of copyright, but also because he and his wife were soon
to leave New York on a trip to Great Britain and he wanted to assist
the Select Committee with its report. With still no word from King on
10 April Jay went over King's head and wrote directly to Winthrop,
reminding the Speaker of their conversation in January.

About a week later Jay at last heard from King. The Select Committee
had just been appointed. King was Chairman and the members were G. P.
Marsh of Vermont, C. J. Ingersoll of Pennsylvania, I. E. Morse of

Louisiana, H. W. Hilliard of Alabama, H. Mann of Massachusetts, Alexander D. Sims of South Carolina, William B. Preston of Virginia, and H. C. Murphy of New York. Winthrop had done well by Jay. Five of the nine members including the Chairman were nominees that Jay had suggested. It was a well-balanced committee of Whigs and Democrats, affording some prospect for bi-partisan support, and several of the members were familiar with the issue, having served on the Winthrop-Adams Committee of 1844. Things were ready to go, King told Jay, and a meeting of the committee would soon be called.[23]

Since Jay's departure for Britain was postponed till around 11 May, he was able to continue doing even more for the cause. His next undertaking was the preparation of a group of duplicate letters which he sent to influential acquaintances such as Francis Lieber, William Gilmore Simms, and Alfred B. Sheets, urging each of them to petition King's Select Committee. Jay asked them to express their memorials in their own words, making them seem unsolicited and spontaneous. Each petitioner was instructed to secure as many other signatures as he or she could, following the principle that quality (that is prominence or distinction) not quantity was preferred. Francis Lieber who had taken so active an interest in copyright earlier in the decade promptly acquiesced. Slower to act though equally well identified with the cause was William Gilmore Simms. By the beginning of July, he too was prepared to gather signatures. It was thus clear that the Select Committee would not lack for testimonials which would strengthen the hand of the members favourable to international copyright.[24]

By the time Jay sailed for Liverpool, he had done much to promote the cause of copyright: prepared an elaborate memorial to Congress, secured a Select Committee, and arranged for petitions. What he had been unable to do was to apply the financial muscle which he deemed necessary to maintain an agent in Washington and to influence the press.

As Jay learned once he reached Great Britain, the Blackwoods had gone to a good deal of trouble in his behalf. As early as the beginning of April Blackwood had copies of Jay's long letter of 28 January printed and circulated to a few publishers and leading authors like Bulwer and Macaulay. Jay had emphasized the need for secrecy so as not to implicate him or give away his plans, and Blackwood in turn enjoined secrecy on those receiving the letter. As a result, no embarrassing publicity was carried in the British press as had happened with Putnam's petition in 1843.[25] Blackwood put Jay in touch with a variety of authors and publishers including Bulwer, James, and Bohn, the latter a leading reprinter of inexpensive books of high quality.[26]

It did not take long to learn that there was not much enthusiasm in Britain for raising £1,000 on behalf of international copyright. Englishmen were too preoccupied with the revolutions on the Continent and the consequent disturbances at home. Authors like Dickens felt that American legislators could never be brought to do anything other than serve their own self-interest. Nevertheless Jay still hoped that the work he had done before leaving America might be enough to secure a favourable report from the King Committee. If this were so and things looked more promising the following winter, a renewed campaign might find British publishers and authors more inclined to support the cause, since it was, after all, significantly in their interest to do so.

In the meantime Jay continued to supply T. B. King with suggestions and information. At the beginning of May he had passed on Henry T. Tuckerman's idea of including protection for unpublished manuscripts, plays, designs, works of art, and models of sculpture in some future copyright law. Then from London he sent copies of treaties which Britain had made with Continental states as authorized by the International Copyright Acts of 1838 and 1844. Somewhat optimistically he told King:[27]

A good deal of interest is expressed by men of letters in London, in regard to your forthcoming report on the subject of an international copyright – and I am satisfied that the present is a more favourable time for the establishment of such an agreement if it can be effected – than has ever occurred before. Our republic, its institutions and its citizens, are regarded in Great Britain with an increased and increasing cordiality and respect. The upturning of things on the Continent and the lamentable failure thus far of the French attempt to establish a republic or appear different from our own, has induced our being looked upon, no longer as a radical and dangerous democracy but a great conservative power, guided and governed by that eternal principle of law, liberty and order, the disregard of which is now too painfully exhibited on the Continent of Europe. Hitherto we have been called 'the Model Republic' – by way of a sneer – but now in good faith are Englishmen exhorting the newly pledged democrats of France to follow our example – and to copy our Constitution.

Two weeks later Jay sent King additional arguments. After talking with the eminent geologist, Charles Lyell, he realized how much Americans were penalized when they purchased reprints of English scientific or professional works. Lyell pointed out that his early publications had been stereotyped by American reprinters and sold in large numbers. However, when major revisions were made, the Americans ignored them, being unwilling to scrap expensive stereotype plates and manufacture new ones. Jay thus observed that under these circumstances American readers were scarcely getting a bargain when they purchased obsolete reprints at a low price. His other argument had to do with the import duty which the British imposed on books printed abroad. This was cut in half for those states having a copyright convention with Great Britain. American publishers might be induced to negotiate a similar convention if their publications could be sent to Britain more cheaply.[28]

And what was Thomas Butler King doing while Jay was labouring mightily in the cause of copyright? Towards the end of June Coxe wrote to say that nothing was going on in Congress with respect to copyright primarily because everyone was preoccupied with the forthcoming Presidential nominating conventions and campaigns. On 12 July M. B. Field, Jay's partner and brother-in-law, wrote to King to find out how the report was coming. Still no answer. Not until Jay returned to the United States in early November was the awful truth known. Nothing had been done.

On 10 November Jay asked Marsh of Vermont, one of the members of the Select Committee, to find out whether his memorial had ever been printed or the Committee's report issued. Three days later he received the reply that no action had been taken. The Committee had met shortly after it was appointed, with nearly everyone present. After a brief discussion it instructed the Chairman to procure an order for printing Jay's memorial, but either King failed to act in time or the order was not executed. Another Committee meeting was scheduled but never took place. All Marsh could say to Jay was that he hoped that King would revive the issue in the next session (beginning in about a month).

Jay knew that the new session of Congress was a short one, lasting only from December until March. At least the all-consuming Presidential election was over. Zachary Taylor had been elected, and now the 'lame duck' Congress could settle down and finish off old business. He once more approached King in a letter expressing these thoughts and again offered the Committee whatever help it might need in drawing up a report.[29]

He continued to exert himself on behalf of the cause for a few more weeks. When one of the Committee members, Morse, spent a few days

in New York, Jay wrote for an appointment and when King passed
through in December he invited him to the family house in Bedford to
discuss copyright, but none of these efforts bore results.

It was a melancholy Jay who, even before the Congressional session
was over, signalled defeat to Blackwood. In drawing up his account of
debits and credits as their American agent, he decided to subtract the
$30 which had been included for expenses relating to the copyright
campaign, even though Blackwood had offered to cover these charges.
Jay would not accept payment now that there seemed little likelihood
that anything could come of his efforts.[30] He finally had to admit failure.
Just as Frederick Saunders, Henry Clay, Francis Lieber, Cornelius
Mathews, G. P. Putnam and others had already discovered, he realized
that a mere handful of devoted advocates were no match for the
indifference of Congress and the implied opposition of powerful interest
groups.

Chapter V

THE IMPACT OF FOREIGN REPRINTS ON THE DOMESTIC BRITISH BOOK TRADE

The problem of foreign reprints coming into Britain was not a new one. During the eighteenth century Irish printers had subsisted largely on the pirating of English books which they sold at home or smuggled back into England. The Act of Union of 1800, however, had the effect of putting many Irish printers out of work since Ireland ceased to be a colony and, as an integral part of the United Kingdom, had to abide by British copyright law. In the 1820s several Paris printers and publishers, principally Bossange and Galignani, specialized in supplying British tourists with cheap reprints of the latest London publications. Galignani produced the whole of Sir Walter Scott's writings in seven handsome volumes at a fraction of the original selling price. This and other such bargains greatly increased the demand for Continental reprints which tourists regularly purchased abroad to bring back home to England.[1]

London publishers resented the French pirates as well as Belgian and American ones, but there was little they could do about it. The law gave publishers protection against the mass importation of foreign reprints, but there was nothing to prevent individual tourists from carrying single copies as part of their personal baggage. In the mid-1830s foreign editions began to show up in bookshops, circulating libraries, and reading societies. This prompted stricter legislation which eventually was enacted in 1854 after a decade of constant legal battles. In the meantime British publishers had to resort to the cumbersome machinery of the law courts if they hoped to discourage such traffic.

The prolific English novelist, G. P. R. James, described the effect of foreign piracy in a paper contributed to the London Statistical Society:

'the unlimited influx of the pirated copies . . . totally annihilated the trade in the genuine editions'. He estimated that the leading Paris reprinters, Baudry and Galignani, had issued almost 400 of the most popular British works. Another 100 titles came from other Paris houses. For certain books there were as many imported copies as original ones in the hands of British readers: 'the fact is notorious that all the circulating libraries upon the coast, and for nearly 40 miles inland, together with a great number of the small libraries around London, are supplied entirely with these pirated editions'.

There were a number of other ways by which foreign reprints entered Britain besides via travellers. Smuggling was by far the most common. G. P. R. James described 'sending over the works in [printed] sheets placed in layers between sheets of French works, and as it is impossible to expect that custom-house officers should examine every sheet in a large bale, which pays duty by weight, this method has been very successful'. It even paid English importers to send clerks across the Channel to Boulogne or Calais in order to buy a single copy of several hundred works, which would pass through British Customs legitimately only to be sold later for a tidy profit. These subterfuges paid off handsomely since French reprints were anything from a half to one-sixth the retail price in Britain.[2] The *Publishers' Circular*, the semi-official organ of the London book trade, reported:[3]

The clandestine importation exceeds the belief of those who may not hitherto have paid that attention to the subject which the interests of authors as well as book-sellers imperiously demands. It is a notorious fact that Foreign editions are printed purposely for the English market; *the Foreign demand alone being far too limited to repay the cost.*

Many British authors and publishers were convinced that foreign reprints were ruining the market for English books, yet it was very difficult to measure the damage. By its very nature an illicit traffic was handled with discretion, and shopkeepers rarely displayed the foreign editions. G. P. R. James stated that 1,500 copies entered one British port during the course of a year as legitimate single copies in the possession of travellers, and invited his readers to imagine the number which were never declared at ports of entry or which were smuggled into Britain by other means. Others cited equally threatening statistics. However, the fact that all of these assertions were made as part of a polemical campaign to stiffen the Customs regulations or perhaps even to exclude foreign reprints entirely suggests a distinct bias. It was in the interests of British authors and publishers to magnify the evil and it was almost impossible for anyone to contradict their claims.

Thanks to the surviving records of the London publisher, Richard Bentley, it is possible to obtain a much more precise view of things. One can never have a truly accurate and quantitative picture of the reprint trade, but many of the details can now be sketched in. Bentley was a most litigious publisher who delighted in tracking down malefactors, and many of his publications such as fashionable novels, books of travel, and memoirs, readily lent themselves to republication in Paris. If Bentley could locate a pirated Baudry or Galignani edition in some English bookshop he could seek an injunction from the Court of Chancery by which the offending bookseller would be compelled to cease the sale of the reprint and compensate Bentley for his legal costs. The trick was in trapping the unsuspecting dealer in foreign piracies.

Paris reprints rarely appeared in London shops until 1834–5. Then all of a sudden there seemed to be an epidemic extending as far as the city of Bath. The records of the Court of Chancery in the Public Record Office tell their own story. Early in 1834 John Carrol, a merchant doing business at 25 Poland Street, Westminster, invited Henry Richard Colburn, Bentley's former partner, to examine a book on Ireland recently imported from France, entitled *The Rise and Fall of the Irish Nation*. Colburn immediately recognized it as a poorly disguised version of Johan Barrington's *Historic Memoirs of Ireland* which he had published in 1826. Some sentences were altered and passages transposed. Unhappily Carrol did not realize this when he invited Colburn to consider the work. He apparently had obtained about 150 copies from a man called Halliday who used to share his premises in Poland Street and who was currently in Paris. It is not entirely clear, but Carrol may not have been a bookseller but rather someone who thought he could interest a London publisher in copies of an inexpensive work printed in Paris. Colburn obtained an injunction against him and put a stop to the further sale of the French reprint in Britain.[4]

Bentley's turn came later that same year. It began in late September when a respectable London bookseller, John Rodwell of 46 New Bond Street, received a request for two French reprints from a provincial Reading Society. Rodwell sent his clerk to the shop of a foreign book importer, Jean Baptiste Baillière of Regent Street, in quest of James Morier's *Ayesha* and Maria Edgeworth's *Helen*. The clerk later stated in an affidavit that Baillière's shop supplied him with Paris reprints at the price of

7s. rather than the usual London wholesale price of 21s. Knowing that the books in question were the copyright property of Richard Bentley, Rodwell passed on the information to Bentley's assistant, Edward Morgan, in Bentley's absence. Morgan was not taken completely unaware, as another instance of piracy had already been discovered in Bath involving *Italy, with Sketches of Spain and Portugal* by William Beckford.

In London Morgan sent a clerk to Baillière to purchase *Ayesha* or *Helen* but 'they pretended not to know of such an edition'.⁵ None the less, Bentley's solicitors, Adlington, Gregory & Faulkner, felt that there was enough evidence to start proceedings. Bentley signed an affidavit swearing that he was the copyright owner of *Ayesha* and *Helen*; that these works were extensively sold in Britain; and that Baillière had infringed the copyrights. Rodwell's clerk swore to the accuracy of the events leading up to the purchase of the French reprints. A bill of complaint was also drawn up which asserted what Bentley did not know for a fact but surmised: that Baillière possessed other copies of the imported works, that he had already profited from their sale, that he kept bills and receipts relating to them, and that he knew where more reprints could be secured. The affidavits and the bill were registered at the Office of the Six Clerks in Chancery Lane on 7 October, about a fortnight after Bentley first learned of the situation.

That same day the Court of Chancery issued an injunction 'whereby the said Defendant was required within four days after the service of such writ to cause an appearance to be entered for him in this Honourable Court to a Bill of Complaint . . . and to answer concerning such things as should be there and then required of him'. Two days later Adlington's clerk served a subpoena on Baillière.

Baillière had one of two alternatives when confronted by the Chancery injunction. He could appear in court and answer the bill of complaint, or he could settle out of court. To pursue the former course, he would have to produce evidence which called into question Bentley's copyrights or the affidavit of Rodwell's clerk. If unsuccessful in this, he would have to abide by the injunction and pay his own as well as Bentley's legal costs. Even if the injunction were removed Bentley could sue for damages in a Court of Common Law and also claim double the legal costs. Baillière chose the line of least resistance, a settlement out of court. Although we do not know the details, they presumably followed a fairly well-defined path. He probably paid Bentley's legal fees incurred in securing the injunction; he undoubtedly turned over all copies of the French reprints in question to Bentley; and he most likely compensated Bentley for those copies which had already been sold. Needless to say, it was assumed that he would refrain from selling such copies in the future.[6]

With Baillière out of the way, Bentley pursued the offending booksellers in Bath. Here things went less smoothly, since the case was based on hearsay. In June 1835 one of Bentley's readers went to Bath, and as a comparative stranger succeeded in securing several reprints from Eliza Williams, the keeper of a bookshop and circulating library on Milson Street. By this time more works were involved: Beckford's *Italy*; E. L. Bulwer's *Last Days of Pompeii* and *England and the English*; Henry Bulwer's *France: Social, Literary, and Political*; *Trevelyan* by a Lady of Rank (Lydia Scott); *The Princess* by Lady Morgan (Sydney Owenson), and Morier's *Ayesha*.

At the same time two quite separate violations were unearthed in London by another of Bentley's agents, a glass and china warehouseman on Regent Street named George Bird, who apparently possessed the requisite humility and innocuous demeanour to allay suspicion. At the circulating library of Elizabeth Girity, 40 Silver Street, Golden Square, he borrowed Baudry editions of *Ayesha* and *Helen* for 4*d*. each per day, plus a deposit of £1. One week later he borrowed a Baudry copy of *Helen* for 4*d*. per day and a deposit of 5*s*. at the circulating library of Robert Walker, Jones Street, Berkeley Square.

The traps were now set in London and Bath, and toward the end of June they were swiftly sprung. Three separate injunctions were applied for and granted; subpoenas served; and out-of-court settlements concluded. Bentley and his solicitors had the satisfaction of making object lessons out of the offending shopkeepers. But they had the lurking feeling that they were viewing only the surface of the iceberg since there was no way of telling how many illicit copies escaped their keen notice. The numbers confiscated were disconcertingly small compared to the 150 copies which Colburn thought he detected in Carrol's possession. Unfortunately there are no specific figures for Baillière, Girity, and Walker, but there are for Eliza Williams: nine copies of *Italy*; three of *Ayesha*; three of *Trevelyan*; ten of *England*; five each of *France* and *The Princess*; and twelve of *Pompeii*.[7]

Numbers of copies aside, Bentley's preoccupation was to uncover the suppliers of foreign reprints. The trail led back to London and to Alexander Alexandere of 37 Great Russell Street. Through information supplied by Eliza Williams, Bentley's solicitors were able to instruct Sutton Sharpe, the barrister who presented all of Bentley's applications to the Court of Chancery.[8]

she states that she purchased the said works from Mr Alexandere, whom we believe to be the original importer of them, and as this is a point which Mr Bentley has long been desirous of ascertaining, because by going to the fountainhead he is more likely than by any other means to put a stop to the practice which is so injurious to Mr Bentley's property; and you will therefore be pleased to prepare a bill (of complaint) as quickly as possible in order to stop all further importation and sale.

The case never came to court but the presumption is that Bentley forced Alexandere to capitulate by a settlement out of court.

During that same busy year Bentley also successfully defended two of his American publications against importations from New York, Henry Wadsworth Longfellow's *Outre Mer: or Pilgrimage Beyond the Sea* and Charles Fenno Hoffman's *A Winter in the West*. Both were published by Harper & Bros and imported by Richard James Kennett of York Street, Covent Garden, who made a speciality of Americans. Bentley had previously purchased their copyrights and published them in London claiming an exclusive market in the United Kingdom. The right of foreigners including Americans to copyright protection in Britain had always been and would continue to be an uncertain thing at best, but a decision of Lord Abinger in the Court of Exchequer in 1835 strengthened Bentley's hand. In *D'Almaine* v. *Boosey* the way was made easier for foreign authors and composers to convey their copyrights to British publishers. Kennett was trapped in the same manner as the others, and it is significant to note the atmosphere of suspicion surrounding the sale. On 3 August William Robert Turnham of 38 Clarges Street, Piccadilly, Gentleman, entered Kennett's shop:

and there saw a female who appeared to be in charge of the shop and this Deponent further sayeth that he thereupon asked what was the price of the book entitled A Winter in the West which he saw in the window of the said shop; that she the said female then replied that he would find it marked in the book and then taking up one of the volumes herself stated that the price was 12 shillings; that this Deponent replied that he would take the book, when she the said female asked him 'who it was for'; and he this Deponent replied, 'for myself'; but upon her repeating the question with the observation that 'she wished to know as he the Deponent was quite a stranger to her and we are rather particular as to whom we sell books to or words to that effect'.

On 8 August the injunction was granted and Kennett preferred to settle out of court rather than risk protracted legal conflict.[9]

For the next five years Bentley was comparatively free from the trespass of foreign reprints. At least he was unaware of specific instances which lent themselves to Chancery proceedings. Then in 1840 he discovered the most interesting case of all. A cotton manufacturer in Bolton, Lancashire, assisted him in exposing a particularly ingenious arrangement between the local bookseller and two men who were his suppliers. Towards the end of March a Galignani reprint of Ainsworth's *Jack Sheppard* was discovered in the Bolton bookshop and circulating library of James Perry Law. As in the case of Eliza Williams of Bath, James Law was prevailed upon to reveal the source of his supply which turned out to be a father and a son, both named Samuel Bushell. For convenience I shall designate them Senior and Junior. The father lived in Dover and was the Master of a small vessel which travelled frequently across the Channel to Boulogne and Calais. The son was a 'shopman' in the Paris publishing firm of A. & W. Galignani. In his affidavit James Law explained that the arrangement had evolved when he was on a bookbuying expedition in Paris in June 1839. At Galignani's he met Bushell Jr and they agreed to do business together using Bushell Sr as intermediary. Two invoices from this venture survive: an undated one for the autumn of 1839 and another for 6 April 1840. Bushell Jr made them out, listing each title with two prices, the retail price in Paris and Galignani's wholesale price. To clarify these lists I have added the names of authors, publishers, and the original dates of publication. Each order itself came to about 250 francs or £10 and further charges were made by Bushell Sr for carriage and handling. From the invoices it is apparent that Law requested a variety of books at different times. There can be little doubt as to the savings he effected, considering that most of the works wholesaled in London for 14s. to 21s. and he was paying only 4f or about 3s. 2d. for the equivalent of a three-decker novel. It is also clear that Bushell Jr was supplying Law with merchandise other than books and engravings.

We are also fortunate to have the amount Bushell Sr charged for each. The customs duty on the books was £1 16s. 8d. for the first shipment and £1 10s. 0d. for the second. The 'tableaux' on the second list carried a duty of £1 10s. 0d. whereas the coloured lithographs on the first only cost 2s. Carriage, freight, and packing amounted in the first instance to 17s. 8d., and in the latter, 25s. 3d. The duty on the gloves and perfume was 8s. and 16s. respectively. On each occasion the charges above and beyond the cost of the items in Paris were slightly over £4, an amount Law could well afford to pay in view of the handsome profit he would

Invoice, October–November 1839

AUTHOR	TITLE	PUBLISHER	FIRST EDITION	RETAIL FRANCS	WHOLESALE FRANCS
Brougham	Statesmen in the Reign of George III	Knight	1839	5	4
Bulwer	Paul Clifford	Bentley	1830	5	4
Byron	Poems	Murray	1825	11	7
——	Courtier of Charles II	——	——	5	4
——	Crichton's Memoirs	——	——	8	5.60
——	Edinburgh Review	(not available as a Paris reprint)			
Hallam	Literature of Europe	Murray	1837–9	20	16
James	De L'Orme	Colburn & Bentley	1830	5	4
James	The Gypsy	Longman	1835	5	4
James	Henry Masterton	Col-Bent.	1832	5	4
James	John Marston Hall	Longman	1834	5	4
James	Philip Augustus	Col-Bent.	1831	5	4
Lloyd	Desultory Thoughts	Baldwin	1821	3	2.10
Marryat	Diary in America I	Longman	1839	5	4
Marryat	Diary in America II	Longman	1840	5	4
Marryat	Jacob Faithful	Saunders & Otley	1834	5	4
Marryat	King's Own	Col-Bent.	1830	5	4
Marryat	Pacha of Many Tales	Colburn	1835	4	3
Marryat	Peter Simple	S. & O.	1833	5	4
Montagu	Letters and Works of a Lady	Bentley	1836	10	8
Moore	Life of Fitzgerald	Longman	1831	5	4
Moore	Life of Sheridan	Longman	1825	10	8
Scott	Ivanhoe	Constable	1820	5	4
Scott	Kenilworth	Longman	1815	5	4
Scott	Peveril of the Peak	Constable	1822	5	4

Miscellaneous items: 6 large coloured lithographs at 4f each; 6 small coloured lithographs at 2.50f each; 8 portraits of actors and actresses at 3f each; 12 classical engravings at 5f each.

Total of books and miscellaneous items: 251.70f or £10.

Invoice, 6 April 1840

AUTHOR	TITLE	PUBLISHER	FIRST EDITION	RETAIL FRANCS	WHOLESALE FRANCS
——	*Advice on Teeth*			1.50	1
Ainsworth	*Jack Sheppard*	Bentley	1840	5	4
——	*Cotton Revolution*	——	——	5	4
——	*Diary of George*	——	——	8	5.60
James	*Richelieu*	Colburn	1829	5	4
Marryat	*Diary in America II*	Longman	1840	5	4
Moore	*Letters and Journals of Lord Byron*	Murray	1830	16	11.20
Moore	*Life of Byron*	Murray	1832	10	7.50
Moore	*Poems*	Carpenter	1822	20	15
——	*One Fault*	Bentley	——	5	4
——	*Paris Guide*	——	——	6	4
——	*Psalm and Hymn Tunes*	——	——	6	4.50
Sherwood	*The Governess*	Houlston & Son	1820	5	4
Tibbins	*Dictionary* (2 copies)	——	——	5	3.50
Trollope	*Michael Armstrong*	Colburn	1840	5	4
Trollope	*Widow Barnaby*	Bentley	1838	5	4
Wordsworth	*Poems* (6 Vols)	——	——	12	9

Miscellaneous items: two boxes of watercolours at 4f each; 2 dozen pairs of gloves at 1.50f a pair; 2 dozen bottles of Chantilly scent at 3f each; 1 black cravat at 8f; 2 engravings of monks at 6f each; 2 engravings of Fanblas and and Daphne at 4f each; one Napoleon on horseback. 5f; 4 yards of bonnet ribbon at 1.25f each.

Total of books and miscellaneous items 250.8of or £10.

Tableaux de la Révolution Française
   (engraving)   250f

make on whatever he chose to sell or circulate through his library.

There was one item in the first shipment which caused difficulty and required some adjusting: 'expense on getting over the 12 classical engravings *prohibited*, £1-4-0'. These were copyrighted in Britain and were supposed to be excluded in quantity according to Customs regulations which admitted single copies but forbade foreign reprints in bulk. Bushell Sr was thus importing the books quite in accordance with official practice, and with the exception of some engravings, running no risk of confiscation. Had he retained the works in his own possession, Bentley would have had no legal recourse, but their sale to Law, and Law's subsequent resale, rendered both men liable to prosecution. Bushell Sr claimed that Law was his only customer and that he and his son supplied no one else in Britain. This is possible, since their arrangement was of recent origin. On the other hand he was anxious to avoid any further harassment from Bentley, and to have admitted connivance in other cases would have increased his liability. Law's untimely apprehension put an end to this very promising venture.

Just how costly was it to settle out of court? In the case of *Bentley* v. *Bushell* an unusually detailed list of Bentley's legal expenses survives for which Bushell was potentially liable. The account was divided into three categories: the bill of complaint, the affidavits, and the injunction. In connection with the bill of complaint, Bentley's solicitors charged 13s. 4d. for drawing up the instructions for counsel; £3 4s. 0d. for drafting the bill, including a 'fair copy', £1 12s. 0d. for engrossing it into parchment; 8s. for two sheets of parchment; 7s. 4d. for filing it with the appropriate office; £1 1s. 4d. to 'abbreviate' it; and 3s. 6d. for the certificate showing that it had been duly filed.

Next came the affidivats or sworn testimony of Richard Bentley and James Perry Law which involved charges of nearly £5. These included: instructions to counsel, £1 8s. 8d.; engrossing, 7s. 4d.; correspondence, 6s. 8d.; opening the office where the oath was administered, 1s.; the fee for its administration, 1s. 6d.; filing the affidavit and supplying Bentley with an office copy, 14s. 8d.; eleven 'brief sheets', £1 16s. 8d.

Once these had been prepared the injunction had to be secured. Since in this case the Court of Chancery was not in session, the barrister, Sutton Sharpe, had to make a special appointment with the Vice-Chancellor at his home outside of London. For this inconvenience he added £5 10s. 0d. as well as 21s. for hiring a chaise.

At this point Bushell was informed that Bentley had been granted an injunction and that a subpoena would be served, expenses for which were: preliminary notice being drawn up and delivered, 8s. 6d.; the formal order, £2 10s. 0d.; entry of the order in the Chancery record, 7s. 6d.; drawing up the subpoena by the appropriate clerk, 17s. 2d.; and serving it on Bushell Sr, 18s. 6d.

Bushell could have contested the injunction in the Court of Chancery, but if he lost he would have to pay for his own defence as well as Bentley's legal expenses. Not surprisingly he decided to settle out of court which obligated him to pay for a conference between his and Bentley's solicitors at which Bentley eventually agreed to settle for costs. These amounted to somewhat more than £33, a penalty far exceeding the profits which the Bushells could anticipate from the foreign reprint trade.[10]

Once again the weapon of an injunction proved temporarily effective, but the flow of reprints continued and many felt that only new and tougher legislation would remedy the situation. Prices of new books in Britain were inordinately high and authors like Harriet Martineau insisted that something be done. In a memorandum to the Foreign Office she noted that 'cheap copies come over by hundreds and we are undersold before our eyes . . . our liability to piracy compels them [publishers] to make their appeals to the aristocracy alone . . . the pirates must supply the middle classes'.[11] Similarly, G. P. R. James informed Lord Aberdeen, the Foreign Secretary, why Continental and American pirates had such an advantage.[12]

Cheapness of labour, materials, and advertising, and the total saving of payment for copyright, enabled the piratical publishers to sell the works thus reprinted at a very low rate; and the system is so well organized, and so terribly extended, that not a week elapses between the publication of a work in London and its republication in Paris; and thus the sale of English editions is totally at an end on the Continent, in the Channel Islands, in America, and all our own colonies. Vast numbers are also now thrown into England itself.

The Vice-President of the Board of Trade, William E. Gladstone, also became convinced that foreign piracies enhanced the price of British books, and in response to a communication from James promised to raise the matter with the Commissioners of Customs. There were other factors to be sure, but here was at least one place where the Government might appropriately act.[13]

Before drafting new legislation, however, Gladstone thought it best to make the most of existing law. As early as the reign of George II an effort was made to forbid piracies, a policy incorporated in the Copyright Acts of 1801 and 1814. All of Bentley's cases were prosecuted according to Section 4 of 54 Geo. 11, c. 156 (1814), yet this statute was silent on whether Customs officers should seize reprints or allow them to pass. A section in 3 & 4 Wm IV, c. 52 (1833) entitled 'A Table of Prohibitions and Restrictions', specifically forbade foreign reprints of British copyright works entering Britain, implying that illegal importations could be seized.[14] Customs and Excise were also guided by a Treasury minute dating from 29 June 1830 which authorized the confiscation of any large consignment of foreign reprints, allowing only single copies to enter the country by way of travellers' baggage.

Early in 1842 Gladstone persuaded the Board of Trade to recommend tightening these regulations, and by April he was able to report to R. B. Dean:

I wish to call your attention to a recent minute of the Board of Treasury relating to the introduction into this country of works pirated abroad. Authors are exceedingly desirous that the minute should be strictly interpreted; and that no works should be permitted to be introduced in the luggage of Passengers unless it has been rendered unfit to go into Circulating Libraries by having a name written on the title page or by such use as to render it evidently an old and not a new book; and that it merely being cut open should be not enough to secure its passage. As the minute in question was adopted on the suggestion of the Board of Trade I know I have no hesitation in saying that our intention was that it should convey this stringent sense.

This satisfied James, although he would have preferred a total prohibition of reprints since he was convinced that it was books purchased abroad which cut into the sales of British works at home. Gladstone was sympathetic but felt that the Government had gone as far as it could. 'Let the new order have a trial for a reasonable time, and if it be found that it does not cut off large supplies and stop the channels through which the circulating libraries have been fed, we must then move again and that forward, not backwards.'[15]

By the end of May James thought he could detect a distinct improvement. As he reported to Bulwer, a number of Baudry reprints had been seized at Dover, 'and a goodly pile they make'.[16] For the time being he had achieved virtually all that he wanted short of total prohibition. Yet it was natural to covet that ultimate restriction as well, and therefore he and others did not dismiss the possibility of new legislation. In fact, in order to protect themselves against the eventuality that Gladstone's approach failed, a few authors and publishers pursued a parallel course of action. Ever since 1837 they had encouraged T. N. Talfourd, the eminent legal authority and Member of Parliament as well as occasional playwright, to sponsor a bill to amend the copyright laws. Though mostly dealing with the extension and registration of domestic copyright, Talfourd's Bill included several clauses touching upon piracies and foreign reprints. For five years he promoted such legislation only to have it ignored or blocked. By 1842 he was no longer in Parliament and the literary community transferred its hopes to Philip Henry Stanhope, Viscount Mahon.[17]

Born in 1805, Mahon received his B.A. from Christ Church, Oxford, in 1827 and entered Parliament a few years later, combining a legislative career with writing historical works depicting the seventeenth and eighteenth centuries. Before he actually introduced his amended version of Talfourd's Bill, several leading publishers sought him out and urged the total exclusion of foreign reprints. Mahon obliged by modifying the conditions of exclusion while not entirely prohibiting reprints. When John Murray objected that this would accomplish little more than the Treasury could thanks to the prodding of Gladstone and others, Mahon was disconcertingly obstinate.[18]

It will be very difficult I think for the Legislature or the Government to proceed further in the exclusion of foreign reprints than Sir George Clark [of the Treasury] has now announced the intention of doing. For although the case of chance travellers to which you advert might fairly admit of prohibition, there would be great hardship in the case of foreign residents. Suppose for example a man of slender fortune goes abroad for the education of his children; he buys for their use a large assortment of books, Hallam's Lingard, Milman's Histories, Southey's or Wordsworth's Poems – all in foreign editions. What is he to do in returning? Is he bound to fling from him all these literary treasures – enriched perhaps with his pencil-marks or annotations – from the packet-deck?

Despite Murray's concern, the Talfourd–Mahon Bill had a good many teeth in it. Penalties were prescribed for anyone who imported reprints for sale or hire and any books seized by Customs were to be promptly destroyed. Importers were subject to a fine of £10, half to the Customs officer and half to the copyright owner. Double the value of each offending copy might also go to the lawful proprietor. Mahon's Bill became law on 1 July 1842 as 5 & 6 Vict., c. 45.

Eight days later an 'Act to Amend the Laws Relating to the Customs' secured the royal assent. Identified as 5 & 6 Vict., c. 47 it specifically stated that foreign reprints of British copyright works were to be 'absolutely prohibited' and established means by which Customs officials could identify books claiming protection. These provisions (Sections 24–5), attached to the Bill as 'riders', greatly reinforced and strengthened Mahon's Copyright Act. Their inclusion was no doubt due to Gladstone who, on rather short notice, was asked by the Prime Minister, Sir Robert Peel, to take charge of the Customs Bill. Gladstone saw it through the House of Commons in a matter of ten days, and another ten days sufficed to secure the Lords' approval. Having pondered the question of foreign reprints for many months, he was admirably placed to act. Realizing that the Talfourd–Mahon Bill provided no mechanism whereby Customs officers could know which books claimed copyright, he did what Mahon was unwilling to do: excluded *all* reprints, including those purchased abroad by British subjects for their own personal use.[19]

Authors and publishers were genuinely gratified by the passage of both bills. Even the redoubtable London reprinter, Thomas Tegg, had no wish to protect foreign piracies, whatever his views on domestic copyright might be. Similarly, Lord Brougham whose own writings had been reprinted abroad made it clear that he favoured the provisions against foreign reprints even though he disliked the rest of the Copyright Bill. On the other hand, Lord Cottenham who like Brougham had once been Chancellor, strongly objected to the legal implications of Sections 17 & 25 of Mahon's Bill which opened the way for books to be seized inland as well as at ports of entry. He conjured up the unpleasant picture of excisemen combing bookstores and circulating libraries in order to collect their half of the £10 fine levied for harbouring foreign reprints. Equally distasteful to him was the provision which permitted a Justice of the Peace to issue a warrant for the seizure of pirated copies possessed by anyone, anywhere.[20] G. P. R. James found the same prospects pleasing. He felt a kind of proprietary interest in Section 17 of the Copyright Act since he had suggested that the word 'hire' be inserted by Lord Mahon in the Bill. This was aimed at the circulating libraries as distinct from those offering reprints for 'sale'. He eagerly anticipated the time when it would be possible to:[21]

formally call upon the officers of Customs and Excise to do their duty in seizing all copies of French editions whether new or old to be found in the circulating libraries within their districts and to fine the offenders. This the officers will not be slow to do when once put on the track as they gain five pounds by every copy they seize and there are few animals who like five pounds better than an Exciseman.

Reluctant to insist on the enforcement of this part of the statute by himself lest the book trade interpret it as personal vindictiveness, James asked Bulwer to join him in issuing a formal warning to circulating libraries and booksellers.[22] It occurred to James that it might be wise to ask at least one other author such as Marryat to endorse the scheme. That gentleman did not hesitate.[23]

I return the document signed. If you wish I will take it to Dickens and to Ainsworth for their signatures as I know those gents better I believe than you or James do. I attempted to return your call but was misdirected to No. 34 – and No. 34 as is usual in this metropolis knew nothing about No. 37.

Good to his word, Marryat contacted Dickens who was unwilling to sign, though not for the reasons anticipated by James and Bulwer. As he told Marryat, 'I have always been on friendly terms with Bulwer but I am by no means pleased with his having taken no notice of my International Copyright letter'. Dickens was apparently alluding to a letter which he had circulated to a number of authors and publishers during the previous July urging them to avoid the cheap reprinters in America and deal only with respectable firms.[24]

I held my Gauntlet somewhat toughly to Jonathan's [America's] nose, and should have deserved better of the Baronet though I had been a stranger. Therefore, I will not sign his paper.

The author's warning to circulating libraries went largely unheeded. Librarians may well have decided to cover their tracks more discreetly, but in any event, no army of eager excisemen suddenly appeared to enforce the new legislation. As Gladstone later explained to James,[25]

The system which prevailed before July 1842 was one which had the allowance of the Government: and although it was not recognized by the written law, yet you are aware that a very large discretion for all purposes of relaxation is constantly . . . exercised by the Treasury and by the Customs as the organ of that Board. . . . I feel that precluded the Government from applying the new and rigid enactments retrospectively [against circulating libraries], in the manner which you (very naturally and justifiably I admit) have desired. So also I apprehend that the enactment for the destruction of the books is one with regard to which there is an unusual and established discretion with the Executive Government. It is difficult to defend such a discretion (which causes us infinite trouble) otherwise than by saying that without it the operation of the revenue laws could be intolerable, and that we trust to the checks of publicity and Parliamentary responsibility to defend it from abuse.

In the end the only feasible place to seize foreign reprints was at ports of entry, but inevitably this caused a certain amount of individual hardship. In October 1843 Col. W. H. Clavering returned to Britain from an extended residency abroad. Among his personal effects were French reprints of Byron's works and Scott's *Life of Napoleon*. He claimed exemption from the new legislation because he had purchased the reprints years ago, had paid duty on them previously when conveying them to Britain, and had re-exported them on his last trip abroad. The Customs thought otherwise and confiscated the books, retaining them for only the minimum length of time before destroying them as authorized by the new law. The drama which followed was worthy of Charles Dickens's 'Circumlocution Office', for try as he might, Clavering could not get round Customs and the Board of Trade. When he was informed that his books were subject to seizure regardless of when he had originally acquired them, he petitioned the Board to have them re-exported to his residence in France. Unaware that the books had already been destroyed, he referred to a similar case where an American sea captain had been permitted to export confiscated reprints. HM Customs assured the Board of Trade that no such exception had been made in favour of an American captain.[26]

since the Act of the 5th and 6th Victoria, Cap. 47, came into operation, the provisions thereof relating to the Pirated Editions of English works have been most strictly enforced, and in no instances has the forfeitures of the Books been waived, although the indulgence of returning them to the Port of Shipment has been repeatedly solicited.

Clavering next produced a letter from a third party who testified that the books had indeed been re-exported by the American captain. Unfortunately for Clavering, his evidence predated the 1842 Customs Act. Apparently the Board of Trade never told him that his books were irrecoverable, but this episode may have persuaded the authorities not to be quite so hasty about consigning reprints to the flames.

For their part, the Commissioners of Customs tried to enforce the new laws as efficiently as possible. By an order dated 30 May 1843 they declared all confiscated books not claimed by their British copyright owners be burned at the end of each month.[27] This directive proved distinctly controversial and was modified within a year and a half. As announced in the *Athenaeum*:

It is thereby directed that pirated works found in the baggage of passengers shall not be immediately destroyed, but shall be retained three months, – an account containing a list of the same being sent quarterly to the Board, in order to obtain the order for their destruction. Which is not to take place till the expiration of a month from the date of the order. It is not generally known that there is a provision in the act [S. 23 of 5 & 6 Vict., c. 45], to the effect that the owners of the copyrights are entitled to import pirated editions of their works. Therefore persons who may be possessed of pirated editions, and are anxious to retain them, should apply for the sanction of the owner of the copyright to their admission; which being obtained, they will experience no difficulty in obtaining their delivery.

Such an idea dismayed authors and publishers who had visions of being besieged by hordes of irate travellers seeking permission to keep their acquired bargains. In protest 'An Author' wrote to the *Athenaeum:*[28]

It was, in a great measure, to prevent these very parties from seeking their books in foreign markets rather than at home, that, after long complaint and remonstrance, the protection act in question was passed.

None the less, by one way or another word got out and publishers had to put up with special requests for consideration. Typical of these was a plea from George Waterman to Blackwood & Co. 'I am an American clergyman recently come to reside in this country.' He went on to tell about one of the books in his possession, an American reprint of Pollock's *Course of Time,* being appropriated by the Customs pending permission from the copyright owners to admit it into Great Britain. In writing to Blackwood he hoped to rescue the volume. Another clergyman wrote to John Murray who admitted that he was reluctant to grant exemptions because the Customs officers had enough trouble enforcing the law as it was. However, Murray was occasionally willing to replace a confiscated reprint with a British edition.[29]

As with any such regulations, there were always ways to evade them. A correspondent to the *Literary World* offered his pet remedy against the probings of British Customs: 'Tear out the title page and forward it by post. The book will then pay duty as damaged and once within Her Majesty's dominions the title page can be restored as before'.[30] In the case of one of James's novels, *De L'Orme,* a more ambitious scheme was tried. Someone substituted a fraudulent title page which read *The Mysterious Cavalier.* The Customs were suspicious and consulted Richard Bentley who failed to recognize it. Later one of Bentley's printers figured out that its author was James and that Bentley had published it![31] There was a natural reluctance on the part of some Customs officials to inconvenience travellers.[32]

There is scarcely a person who comes now either from Europe, America, India or Australia, without bringing with them a greater or lesser number of copies of our standard English works of some sort or another, either Literary, Political or Scientific, and the difficulty of finding them [piracies] and stopping their intro- duction among other books, is not among the least difficult or ungracious tasks that fall to the lot of the customs officers. You may easily conceive the grumbling of an individual who has a trunk of books all of which he perhaps carefully wrapped up in separate papers to prevent rustling, when he finds that every one must be opened and scrutinized as to genuineness or otherwise and the chagrin frequently experienced by persons who in ignorance of the law have taken the opportunity of laying in a choice selection of works for their own use, when they find that these are all forfeited and condemned to the flames.

Due to a misunderstanding by both copyright owners and Customs officials, complications sometimes occurred involving certain books not apparently covered by the 1842 Copyright and Customs Acts, and it was necessary for Gladstone to point out that copyright registration at Stationers' Hall did not automatically ensure the protection of Customs.

The view with which these clauses relating to copyright in the customs act were framed was that those interested in the exclusion of pirated works would take care to supply the Board of Customs from time to time with lists of all works under copyright which were at all likely to be reprinted abroad; and that this would render the law upon the whole much more operative and more fair than an enormous catalogue of all the works entitled to the privilege of which it would be found very difficult for the officers of the ports to manage the use.

A few of these lists still survive in the Library of HM Customs and Excise, organized according to title, author, copyright owner, and date of expiration.[33] As an example of the kind of confusion which arose, G. P. R. James was baffled to learn that three of his most recent novels, *Morley Ernstein, Forest Days,* and *Arrah Neil* were seeping past the Customs barriers in 1s. and 6d. pamphlet-like editions, presumably the products of *Brother Jonathan* or the *New World.* Upon investigation it turned out that James's publishers, Bentley and Saunders & Otley, had not registered these titles because James had retained the copyrights himself and there- fore it was his own responsibility to notify Customs.

Despite occasional complications, the prohibitions against foreign reprints were enforced remarkably well over the next fifteen years. Travellers' complaints testified to this as did a British author, William Howitt, who commended the thorough examination of his baggage and books on his return from the Continent in 1855. Pleased with the apparent results of the policy of prohibition John Murray expressed his great satisfaction to Gladstone:[34]

The prohibition to import single copies of pirated English copyright works has been one of the greatest boons to English Authors and owners of copyrights in recent times. It has had the effect of stopping almost entirely the reprints of English works on the Continent.

And lest Gladstone forget, Murray reiterated a favourite theme:

The Pirates are thieves – they contribute no payment to authors. Consequently English publishers cannot contend with them on any terms of fairness. To stop a pirated copy therefore is no more than to arrest a pick-pocket and any return to the old system would create dismay in the realms of Literature from one end of the country to the other.

Murray's sense of satisfaction was short-lived, however. By 1860 the philosophy of free trade had eroded the policy of excluding foreign reprints. Curiously, both policies had been spawned by Peel's ministry during the 1840s, but twenty years later the paradox was finally resolved, as far as books were concerned, in favour of free trade. The laws prohibiting the importation of foreign reprints were still on the statute books, but Customs and Excise apparently relaxed their application. As reported to Murray by Alfred Turner, the solicitor retained by several London publishers:

I wrote on the 22 of March last to the Solicitor of Customs to inquire on behalf of yourself and Messrs. Longman and Co. as representing the Publishers of London whether Copyrights now subsisting in works published . . . will still be protected as heretofore persuant to the acts of 16 & 17 Vict., c. 107 and 18 & 19 Vict., c. 96 . . . and whether Search would still be made in passengers Baggage and otherwise for any copy of foreign Editions of such copyright works.

After a long silence Customs eventually replied that some search of passengers' luggage would continue but the scrutiny would be 'by no means so stringent as when almost all goods of value were liable to Duty. . . . pirated works . . . will be detained, but it will not be deemed necessary to continue so rigid an examination as heretofore.'[35]

Gladstone, one of the chief architects of the policy of exclusion, had long since had second thoughts about the absolute prohibition of foreign reprints. This left James the undisputed champion of the cause, though he was spared its eventual undermining by his death in 1860. Years before, in the dedication to his novel, *The False Heir*, he praised all of his allies in the good fight.

TO THOSE MEMBERS OF THE GOVERNMENT WHO, taking into consideration the injustice of suffering Foreigners to benefit by acts of piracy which the Law prohibits to Englishmen, and with a view to enable British Authors and Publishers to obtain a due remuneration for their labour and the employment of their capital, of which they had been almost totally deprived by the Introduction into this country and the Colonies of the Continental Reprints of English Works, GAVE THE FIRST REAL PROTECTION TO OUR LITERATURE AND THE GREAT BRANCHES OF NATIONAL INDUSTRY CONNECTED THEREWITH, THIS WORK IS DEDICATED BY THEIR MOST OBEDIENT AND VERY HUMBLE SERVANT, G. P. R. JAMES.

At least one fellow author, W. Harrison Ainsworth, acknowledged James's leadership in a letter prefixed to his volume, *St. James's, or the Court of Queen Anne*:

Your brother writers owe you a large debt of gratitude, though I fear it has been but imperfectly paid. It is mainly, if not entirely, to your influence and exertions, that Continental Piracy has received a check, and unauthorized foreign reprints of English works have been kept out of the market.

As we shall see in Chapter VI, James's efforts reinforced those being made simultaneously by Members of Parliament. However, in the early months of 1842 James was indeed alone; Dickens was in America, other authors were silent, and the book trade gave him little support. As he told William Jerdan, editor of the *Literary Gazette*:[36]

My visit [to London] had for its object to carry through the business at which, as you know, I have been labouring for five years: i.e. first the exclusions of French piracies from England by means of Customs-House regulations and secondly the active prosecution of negotiations for international treaties for the security of copyright. In the first point I have entirely succeeded no thanks to the booksellers who for years left me to fight the battle alone and only came in at the last when the whole thing was done. . . . It has cost me labour, health, expense and anxiety to accomplish this; and I dare say I shall have some Gentlemen say, if it had not been for Mr. James they would have got more.

James's shortcoming was perhaps in exaggerating the impact that foreign reprints by themselves had on the British book trade. Excluding them was a partial remedy at best. Only a series of international copyright treaties would ultimately begin to deal with the problem.

Chapter VI

EFFORTS TO INFLUENCE PARLIAMENT, 1838–44

During the course of 1838 two Copyright Bills were presented to Parliament. One, sponsored by T. N. Talfourd, got nowhere. The other, introduced by the Government, was easily passed. The former dealt with the duration of domestic copyright: the latter paved the way for copyright treaties with foreign states. On the surface of things, one might have thought that Talfourd's Bill would be the easier to pass, as domestic affairs are often more palatable to a legislature than the prospect of foreign commitments. That this was not the case had much to do with the determined opposition of the book trade. Correspondingly, the easy passage of a Bill regarding international copyright was due in large part to the almost complete indifference of the book trade.

On 16 January the government approved the idea of an International Copyright Bill, and formal leave to present such a Bill was obtained from Parliament on 20 March. Its first reading came on 11 April, its second on 12 May, and after some debate and amendment it passed the House of Commons on 27 June. With slight modification the House of Lords passed it a month later, and the royal assent was secured on 31 July.[1] Styled as 1 & 2 Vict., c. 59 the Act prescribed steps by which copyright treaties could be negotiated between Britain and other countries based on the principle of reciprocity. British authors would receive the same privileges abroad as foreign authors would receive in Britain. Each treaty could be negotiated without specific Parliamentary sanction, using the less time-consuming method of Orders in Council.

To be sure there was opposition to a measure which could have the effect of making books more expensive. Some of the Radicals argued that reciprocal international protection would put an end to the availability of cheap reprints from France and the United States. Precisely so, retorted Harriet Martineau, who had laboured so strenuously on behalf of Anglo–American copyright. According to Henry Crabb Robinson, she lost all patience with her friends in Parliament and was 'full of flap with the Rads. for opposing the proposed international copyright law'.[2] However, since the Radicals numbered a mere handful, even with Tory support they could not defeat a Whig Government measure. The Bill therefore met with little opposition.[3] Furthermore, the international atmosphere was propitious. The French Government had been reassessing its own copyright policy and was hinting at negotiation with Britain; in 1834 the Zollverein or Customs Union came into effect in the Germanic Confederation and there seemed to be a willingness on the part of the thirty-eight German states to negotiate as an entity; Clay's Select Committee issued a favourable report concerning international copyright.[4]

Following the passage of 1 & 2 Vict., c. 59, there was some delay before the Board of Trade mobilized itself and sent a copy of the Act to the Foreign Office with the suggestion that overtures be made to France, Prussia, Austria, Saxony, and the United States, through their respective diplomatic representatives in London.

In its turn, the Foreign Office procrastinated but by early March 1839 diplomatic representatives were contacted and urged to consider treaty negotiations. A complicated series of exchanges then took place with the German states, especially Prussia, but in the end the British Government was reluctant to accept the Prussian terms. France never made an official reply to the British initiative and the matter was allowed to drop. The American Minister to the Court of St James, Andrew Stevenson, promptly acknowledged the Foreign Office note of 6 March, saying that he would refer the matter to his government in Washington, but nothing was heard from the Americans for a year. At this point the Foreign Office decided to work through its own Minister in Washington, Henry S. Fox, who broached the subject with the American Secretary of State. Another year passed. Fox was again asked to raise the subject. Eleven years later the Foreign Office noted: 'It does not appear that any answer ever was received.'[5]

The Whigs' long tenure of office came to an end in 1841 and the Tories led by Sir Robert Peel took office. After a lapse of two years the abortive negotiations for international copyright had faded from view, and it is scarcely surprising that Lord Aberdeen, the new Foreign Secretary, knew nothing about them. When G. P. R. James asked about these treaties early in 1842, it took the Foreign Office several months to ascertain their fate. They asked the Board of Trade: 'what progress if any was made with any of the foreign governments who were invited to negotiate upon this matter; why the negotiations which were commenced were discontinued; and what were the obstacles which appeared to have prevented them from being successfully prosecuted'.[6] Others began to ask the same questions, and the clamour grew once the Domestic Copyright Bill, 5 & 6 Vict., c. 45, was safely through Parliament.

The subject of international copyright was discussed by authors and publishers in a public meeting at Freemasons' Tavern on 30 June 1842.[7]

while this Meeting feel most grateful to Government for the additional protection which has been lately given to Literature, they cannot but view with deep regret the long delay which has taken place in carrying out the intentions of the Legislature, expressed in the Act, 1 and 2 Victoria, cap. 59, passed July 31, 1838, called 'the International Copyright Act.'

And returning to a familiar theme it was argued:

that the means employed for Smuggling copies of Spurious Editions into Great Britain and its dependencies are so artful, and the opportunities so great, that the most effectual remedy which can be applied to this evil appears to this Meeting to be the conclusion of treaties with Foreign Powers for the mutual recognition of Literary Property.

Two days later pressure from a different quarter was applied to the Government. Lord Mahon informed Peel that he wished to avail himself of the question period in Parliament. Having refrained from introducing the topic of international copyright while the domestic bill was pending, he now wanted to query whether the Government intended to resume efforts to secure international copyright treaties, especially with France and America.[8] By this time the Government was able to report progress. Negotiations were again under way with Prussia, and the British Minister in Berlin was trying to counter the objections of the Prussian Government to the proposed terms. Hitherto the problems had centred around the discrepancy between the extent of coverage each nation anticipated. In Prussia, domestic protection included artistic as well as literary productions, while Great Britain was prepared to guarantee reciprocity only for books. Similarly, the maximum time protection under British law was twenty-eight years, far shorter than the Prussian guarantee. Production costs and duties on imported books were much lower among the German states, another threat to the principle of reciprocity.

In a series of communiqués between the Board of Trade and the Foreign Office, the British Government sought to counter these objections. During the years 1842–4 they pointed out that British production costs were not very much higher than those on the Continent, and although the English reading public preferred its novels in expensive three-volume editions, books for export need not be similarly bound. Cheaper editions manufactured in England had in fact done very nicely in Europe lately. Second, a promise to reduce the duties on imported books was tendered to countries willing to sign reciprocal copyright treaties with Britain. Henceforth foreigners were to be given the opportunity to offer reprints of non-copyright British works to the home market, whereas hitherto they had been substantially excluded. As to the duration of copyright, Britain could now point with pride to its new Act (5 & 6 Vict., c. 45), extending the term to forty-two years.[9]

The Board of Trade felt something more explicit had to be done to foster negotiations. They prepared a Bill for Parliament which Gladstone introduced in the House of Commons for the first time on Tuesday, 12 March 1844. Its second reading came the following Monday, and by the end of the week it had passed through the committee stage, was amended, and reported out of committee. The Commons passed it on 25 March; the Lords on 2 April; and the royal assent was affixed on 10 May. So rapid and smooth was its passage that John Murray III was still recommending changes in the proposed Bill when it had already been reported out of committee.[10]

'An Act to Amend the Law Relating to International Copyright' (7 & 8 Vict., c. 12) accomplished two main things. It modified the International Copyright Act of 1838 so as to make it consistent with the domestic copyright legislation of 1842, and it broadened the coverage of the 1838 Act to include not only books but also prints, sculpture, drama, and music. Later in the session of 1844, Parliament reduced the duties on books imported from countries having reciprocal copyright treaties with Britain (7 & 8 Vict., c. 73). In the meantime negotiations with Prussia dragged on while fresh overtures were made to other Continental states. Eventually a number of treaties were signed. The first was with Prussia on 13 May 1846, followed by: Saxony, 24 August 1846; Brunswick, 30 March 1847; Thuringian Union, 1 July 1847; Hanover, 4 August 1847; Oldenburg, 28 December 1847; France, 3 November 1851; Anhalt, 8

February 1853; Hamburg, 16 August 1853; and Belgium, 12 August 1854. The principle of reciprocity took a long time to gain acceptance, but it seemed the best way to serve the interests of authors and publishers.[11]

The years 1837–44 were indeed remarkable as far as Parliamentary legislation on behalf of the literary community was concerned: two successful Bills for international copyright were passed, domestic copyright was set upon a new footing, and new Customs legislation sought to keep foreign reprints out of Britain and her colonies. For a time it even looked as though there might be a rapprochement among authors, publishers and politicians.

Nothing more graphically illustrates the traditional fragmentation within the book trade than the problems faced by Talfourd's Domestic Copyright Bill as it was taken up by Parliament in the years 1837–41. First of all, there is little indication that Talfourd ever consulted the book trade and their interests at all when drawing up his measure. Neither did he seek the support of authors in any systematic way. Unprecedented numbers of petitions poured in to oppose the Bill, over one hundred of which came from 'publishers, stationers, binders, printers, journeymen, devils, and hawkers'.[12] Only one petition favouring the Bill was recorded in 1838. The following year Talfourd's supporters mustered only nineteen petitions. A few prominent authors and public figures such as Thomas Arnold, Thomas Carlyle, and William Wordsworth, came to Talfourd's aid, but significantly, no publishers had yet done so. In 1840 over two hundred hostile petitions reached Parliament, balanced by a mere five in favour, while in 1841 the Bill was defeated so early in the session that interested parties had no time to memorialize their legislators. By this time it was all too evident that the opposition was exceedingly well organized.[13]

Two features of Talfourd's Bill as it was originally presented provoked ardent opposition from the book trade. The duration of copyright was extended to cover the life of the author plus sixty years, an obvious gesture to the descendants of famous writers. Second, the Bill provided that an author who had already sold his copyright to a publisher for the maximum twenty-eight years currently allowed could recover his copyright after the twenty-eight years and pass it on to his heirs or sell it again in accordance with the revised provision above. Publishers naturally disliked these proposals, 'feeling that if this Bill were passed, they would either, in the case of a valuable work, have to purchase the remainder of the term, or be prevented on the death of an author from enjoying this implied Copyright any longer'. Reprinters also resisted any lengthening of the term of copyright since their livelihood depended to a large extent on reproducing out-of-copyright works. As Talfourd observed, Thomas Tegg, 'the leader of the present opposition, had a stock worth £170,000 derived chiefly from the republication of works of merit, the copyright of which had expired'.[14]

For five different sessions Talfourd failed to enlist the support of key Members of Parliament. He had anticipated disagreement on the part of Radicals like Warburton, Wakley, Hume, and Grote, since they regarded any extension of copyright as a way of increasing the price of books. But he was taken completely by surprise in June 1838 when Lord John Russell raised objections. Three years later, as a result of what he regarded as the watering down of his Bill by Macaulay and others, Talfourd assumed a stance of all or nothing, urging Members to defeat the measure outright rather than cripple it by amendment. Nothing speaks so eloquently of the frustration surrounding this last effort than Forster's request to Bulwer to write an article on copyright for the next issue of the *Examiner*.[15]

For God's sake don't spare Macaulay. Fonblanque quite agrees with me in thinking his arguments below contempt – and he tells me that his conduct has been baser than his argument. Is it true that he promised to take no active part against the Bill. And he, a cabinet minister, with his Cabinet Colleagues voting in its favour, moves its rejection! What a paltry business.

And oh! paltrier Talfourd! Don't spare him either – if it is true, as Fonblanque tells me, that you offered to answer Macaulay and were prevented by his request. That could only be the meanest envy.

Such an exhibition altogether was surely never seen. Not to have a word to say for himself! To give the matter up like a plaything! To declare, as he did in effect, that he had taken the subject up for a few fine tawdry speeches, and that as to the positive thing in issue, he hadn't a word to fling to even such a dog as the nasty Mr. Macaulay.

In my life I never knew a man cut so contemptible a figure. For heaven's sake put in a word for the real interest at stake. At the head of the literary men of the day, say one word on their behalf. Expose the absurdity of Talfourd as well as Macaulay, and show how the whole thing has failed.

Fonblanque will be greatly obliged, and of course strictest confidence will be kept.

In view of the dissension which existed among authors, publishers and politicians, it is a wonder that Lord Mahon had the temerity to introduce

Talfourd's Bill for a sixth time. As we have seen Talfourd was no longer in Parliament following the elections of 1841, and in Mahon's words: 'I have at the request and sanction of himself [Talfourd] and other promoters of the measure' undertaken to see the Bill through Parliament.[16]

Mahon's leadership inaugurated an unusual period of effective co-operation among those in and out of Parliament who favoured some sort of copyright legislation. As an author himself, he was well known to publishers and worked closely with several of the leading ones, especially Thomas Longman and John Murray, preparatory to introducing the revised Bill in the House of Commons. On 3 March 1842, the day before its first reading, he appealed to Murray:

the object you have in view of guarding London publishers from the Paris reprints now brought in by private travellers – would be as effectually obtained and much more easily [by including it in clause 18 of the present bill] than by a separate measure.

And with an eye to its eventual appearance in the House of Lords, Mahon supplied an early printed copy of the Bill to the quixotic but influential Lord Brougham.[17]

It is a subject on which you formerly expressed considerable interest, and should you be pleased to favour me with any suggestions as to its details and with a view to any improvements in committee, I assure you that they will be received with much respect and considered with much attention.

Before the usual opposition had time to reorganize Mahon saw to it that Murray and Longman furnished him with a set of petitions in support of the Bill. They were signed by authors, publishers, stationers, printers, and binders, and were presented to the House of Commons on the occasion of the Bill's second reading, 16 March 1842. Immediately following their presentation Mahon engineered a postponement of debate, thus deferring detailed consideration until the Committee stage. This manœuvre forestalled any possible premature rejection of the Bill while at the same time giving the impression that there was growing support coming from all quarters.

On 23 March the Commons resolved itself into a Committee of the Whole. Anticipating trouble over section 19 which dealt with whether or not publishers could retain the copyrights of encyclopaedia articles, Mahon kept in close touch with key publishers and even agreed to reword the clause so as to 'completely meet the views of Mr. Longman as it does

Mr. Macaulay'. The fact that he was consulting with so powerful a figure
in the House as Macaulay was auspicious in itself. To Murray he gave
assurance: 'I will take care that copies [of the amended Bill] shall be
forwarded to Mr. Longman and to you.'[18]

When the Commons began discussing the Bill paragraph by paragraph
sudden notoriety surrounded the proceedings due to the interest taken
in the measure by two prominent parliamentarians, Thomas Babington
Macaulay and Sir Robert Peel. As reported in the *Athenaeum*:

*Mr. Macaulay, strange to say, after his last year's speech, concurred in the
objects of the proposed measure, but thought they would be better accomplished
by granting protection for the author's life or for forty-two years, whichever
should be the longer term. Sir Robert Peel declared in favour of Mr. Macaulay's
amendment, but proposed to add an additional seven years, in case the author
should [not] survive the forty-two years; and Mr. Macaulay's proposition,
with Sir Robert Peel's amendment, was carried.*

The length of time an author could enjoy ownership of his copyright had
long been a subject of negotiation and compromise, and Mahon had already
reduced the duration from sixty to twenty-five years following an
author's death. But with such sponsors as Macaulay and Peel the amendments carried by a comfortable margin, and it was becoming abundantly
clear that the Bill had an excellent chance.[19]

On 20 April the remaining clauses were taken up by the Committee of
the Whole. Among these was section 24 which became a major stumbling
block. When Talfourd had originally drawn up his Bill he used some of
his legal expertise to assist copyright owners in their efforts to suppress
piracies and importations of foreign reprints. Mahon preserved the proposed changes which permitted Common Law judges as well as Equity
judges to grant injunctions, keep account of damages, and award compensation. One Member of Parliament who was sympathetic explained the
problem this way:

*Now if a plaintiff went into the Chancery Court he would get his injunction,
but he would get no damages, and the object of the present clause was to enable
him to get both his injunction and his damages in the same court.*

This was a rather substantial alteration in legal procedure, and consequently considerable opposition arose. Sensing the danger to the Bill as a
whole, Mahon observed:

As the new power given to the Common Law courts was so strongly opposed by Hon. Members who had given their support throughout, he felt bound to consent to the omission of the Court of Common Pleas.

Thus section 24 was dropped and the other parts were approved without difficulty.[20]

A few days later Mahon again approached Lord Brougham with a copy of the Bill, 'altered in committee and as likely to reach your House where Lord Lyndhurst has promised me to undertake the charge of it'.[21] Mahon chose well in enlisting the co-operation of Lyndhurst, the Lord Chancellor. Even if he had wanted to ask Brougham to manage the Bill in the Lords, Mahon could not have since Brougham was a Whig and the Tories were in power. Among the Tories Wellington commanded the greatest respect but was too infirm at this time to be considered. Lyndhurst, having served as Chancellor in several Tory ministries, exerted a good deal of influence although he was far from a favourite of Peel's and generally ignored by the Prime Minister in Cabinet meetings. However, since Peel had already signified his support of the Copyright Bill, Lyndhurst's principal responsibility was to persuade the Lords of its merit and to defend its legal implications.[22]

With all of Lyndhurst's qualifications for the task, there was still trouble ahead. Increasingly Brougham seemed ill-disposed to the measure and there was fear that his opposition would influence other Members. Mahon explained, 'Exertion is very necessary, for this being no party question, we must depend on individuals rather than on masses and might find the latter against us'. We have seen how easily the Government measures of 1838 and 1844 on behalf of international copyright were passed by Parliament, but a Private Member's Bill such as Mahon's was something else. With party discipline relaxed, it became essential to seek support from all quarters. In an effort to do this in the Lords, Mahon again resorted to soliciting further petitions. On 6 May he wrote to Murray:

I learned from the Lord Chancellor that a great opposition will be made to the Second Reading of the Copyright Bill in the House of Lords – with Lord Brougham at its head. It would be of very good advantage to the success of this measure if you could obtain four petitions to the Lords similar to those which you sent me for the Commons – namely from authors, publishers, printers and stationers.

Such petitions must be if obtained not later than 4:00 o'clock on Tuesday after-noon [10 May] in the Lord Chancellor's hands. Let me beg of you therefore to see about it immediately – *this very evening if possible, or the object of our exertions may yet be lost to us.*

The Petitions need not be long, but should express satisfaction with the Bill and entreat the House to pass it as it stands.

It was Friday, but Murray did not hesitate to comply despite the difficulty of collecting signatures during the weekend. He asked Mahon whether Members of Parliament could sign. 'There is no objection,' Mahon replied, 'though some persons in that position may object to it', adding, 'Remember above all that the petitions should be in time – a small petition at 4:00 o'clock on Tuesday will be valuable – a large one at 6:00 would be useless.'[23]

On 9 May Lyndhurst asked the House of Lords to postpone the debate on the Second Reading which was scheduled for the next day, citing the precedent set by the House of Commons when debate had been deferred so that 'the discussion could take place on the motion for going into committee'.[24] This had the effect of lessening the pressure to amass petitions. In the meantime, however, it was hard to gauge the opposition in the House of Lords.[25] 'Lord Brougham's purposes are so variable and unsteady that they may change twenty times one way or the other', remarked Mahon.

The House of Lords took up the Bill in Committee on 26 May when Lyndhurst presented four petitions: 'from several persons of great eminence in the literary world, . . . from the most eminent publishers in the metropolis, . . . from the printers and stationers throughout England.' Alluding to Brougham, he noted that he 'anticipated no opposition in view of the Commons' action' but that 'he was distressed to find formidable opposition in the Lords from a particular quarter'. Brougham may have taken a dim view of the Bill because in 1838 he himself had unsuccessfully introduced one which would have empowered the Crown through an Order in Council to extend the duration of copyrights possessed by eminent authors like Scott and Wordsworth. In the present instance Brougham, perhaps from a sense of frustration, asked why no Select Committee had been appointed as had been done in 1814 and 1818. For whatever reason, he was now unalterably opposed to a uniform extension of copyright to forty-two years. None the less, his views were not generally adopted and although minor changes were made, the Bill reached its Third Reading virtually unscathed.[26]

At this juncture another potential obstacle arose, but to Mahon's credit he managed to avoid it. Without warning on the day when the Bill should have come up for its Third Reading Gladstone suddenly urged Nahon to delay proceedings. A Customs Bill under consideration in the House of Commons provided for specific enforcement of regulations stipulated in the Copyright Bill before the Lords. Should not Mahon and Lyndhurst delay the Third Reading of the Copyright Bill and allow the Customs Bill to pass; then, by amendment, incorporate the Customs provisions into the copyright legislation? Wisely, Mahon took no chances. He had seen the Copyright Bill go down to defeat time and time again; now that it was on the verge of passing, he signalled Lyndhurst to call for the Third Reading. It passed that evening with amendments, was returned to the Commons for their approval of the changes, and received the royal assent on 1 July 1842.[27]

There is no doubt that Mahon's political astuteness combined with his willingness to work closely with leading publishers was the key to the final success of the measure. Because he knew when to concede, when to apply pressure, and when to act promptly, his Bill's fate was far different from Talfourd's. Whereas previously the book trade had been hostile and divided, this time it co-operated for a common cause. The *Athenaeum* acknowledged this in its June edition: 'The voices of the literati form a powerful and welcome addition to the cry set up for the protection against foreign piracy.'

The spirit of co-operation engendered by their success in passing the Domestic Copyright Bill stimulated increased efforts on the part of the literary community to continue pressing for improved legislation for international copyright. Accordingly a meeting was arranged for 30 June at Freemasons' Tavern. Authors and publishers were urged to be present. G. P. R. James wrote to Bulwer, 'Messrs. Longman entrusted me with the enclosed. You will see by the contents that it is to enduce you to attend a meeting about international copyright and I undertook to ask if you would propose one of the resolutions.' Longman also appealed to Dickens to come, but received word:[28]

If I could possibly have attended the meeting yesterday I would most gladly have done so. But I have been up the whole night, and was too much exhausted even to write and say so before the proceedings came on.

I have fought the fight across the Atlantic with the utmost energy I could command; have never been turned aside by any consideration for an instant; am fresher for the fray than ever; will battle it to the death and die game to the last.

This meeting was not as successful as had been hoped. Having been called at short notice, comparatively few attended, and there were still those who failed to see the desirability of working together in pursuit of similar goals. In remonstrating tones, the *Athenaeum* warned:

So far well, as a manifestation of opinion; but, do those interested, really believe that firing a few paper pellets [memorials] at the Board of Trade will accomplish their purpose – will put an end to foreign piracy. . . . If the parties desire justice, they must resolve to have it. The question is one involving the interest of all authors and all publishers all over the world. Let them then elect a committee, and as no one has time to throw away on other people's affairs, they must subscribe their money, and nominate an efficient and well-paid secretary, whose exclusive business shall be to put himself in communication with like committees in France, Germany, and America – and, the whole of these conjointly must keep up a perpetual fire, until governments become sensible that authors and publishers are a substantive something, no matter what – and then, no matter wherefore, as people, if you please, sometimes give a beggar a half penny to get rid of his importunities, they may choose to do justice, if only to obtain peace and quiet. Right and wrong are very pretty subjects for declamation, but if authors and booksellers mean to have justice done them, they must put their shoulders to the wheel, and not waste time in praying either to Jupiter or the Board of Trade.

In November the *Athenaeum* repeated its call for a formal association of authors and publishers prompting one to wonder who was so interested in prodding the book trade into action.[29] Perhaps it was the editor, Charles W. Dilke, However it may well have been Tom Hood, an author and recent contributor on the subject of copyright. By the autumn of 1842 Hood was certainly sharing his thoughts widely. To Dickens he sent the following note, referring to a flagrant piracy of *American Notes* 'by Buz':[30]

It is hard for an individual author or publisher to have to proceed against men of straw. There ought to be a Literary Association for the Suppression of Piracy – a fund subscribed by Authors, Booksellers and friends to letters – and of which to proceed against the very first offender – similar to the provincial Associations for the prosecution of felons. Eh!

Hood later reported to Dickens:

I sounded one or two Booksellers yesterday about the Association, and oddly enough, on seeing Longman Junior, G. P. R. James had been there just before on the very same subject – and Longman showed me a paper in which the plan was sketched. So I said what you and I thought of it, and offered to cooperate.

There was nothing new about literary associations or book trade organizations. Since 1829 booksellers and publishers had banded together to regulate retail prices, but this group was restricted to members of the business side of the trade. Authors, if they knew about it at all, were suspicious of its aims, and every so often would begin a society of their own in which booksellers and publishers were not welcome.[31] One of these, the Society of British Authors was being organized at about the time that Hood's scheme was taking shape. The contrast between the two is significant. The proponents of the Society sent invitations to a number of authors asking them to join together for their mutual benefit. The idea was to finance their own publications by paying printing costs out of sales, thereby by-passing conventional publishers altogether. Dickens found himself an unwitting sponsor of this project, and hurriedly wrote to fellow authors privately disclaiming any connection with it. In fact, the truth of the matter was that he felt that an authors' society was impractical and served no useful end. What was needed was an organization uniting authors, publishers and booksellers, not one which polarized them. With laws needing enforcement and copyrights requiring protection, concerted action was paramount. Dickens indicated that he would lend his support to the proposal which was being put forth by Messrs Longman and Murray.[32]

By mid-May plans were complete for establishing an association representative of all branches of literature. Longman sent out circular letters and Dickens urged key figures like Bulwer to attend the organizational meeting. On the day it was to take place, 17 May, Dickens wrote to Longman:[33]

If you and Murray should be together, before I come; pray consider the 'two principles' which Dilke informs me he intends to move in the opening. and outset of the business.

1. That a main object of the association is to advance the cause of International Copyright all over the world.

2. That as it protests against being robbed, it protests no less against robbing; and therefore pledges itself by all its Members, not to lay violent hands upon the property of any Foreign author whomsoever, without his permission in writing.

I cannot oppose either of these things, so far as I am concerned. Indeed I consider them unquestionably honourable and just, and calculated to give the association a high standing.

The meeting was chaired by Dickens. Capt. Marryat moved the first resolution, seconded by Dilke of the *Athenaeum*, which called for the formation of an association of authors, publishers, printers, stationers, and others connected with literature, art, and science, having as its purpose: 'to carry into effect . . . the provisions of the recent Acts in relation to infringement of Copyright and the introduction into England and her Possessions abroad of pirated copies of English works'. Dickens and the printer, Spottiswoode, then moved that the Association for the Protection of Literature be established immediately. Dr Pereira, the author, and Henry Colburn, the publisher, followed with the suggestion that a working Committee be selected from among the different segments of the membership. John Forster and P. Stewart then brought forward a slate of nominations: Bulwer, James, Dickens, and Marryat as representative authors; Dilke as a periodical editor; Spottiswoode, Bradbury, and McDowall as printers; Dickinson as a paper-maker. Publishers nominated were Murray, Blackwood, Colburn, J. Richardson, and T. Longman, the last to serve as Treasurer. This Committee was to meet monthly, submitting a report to the whole membership at least once a year. Longman and Murray strongly recommended hiring a secretary who would administer such operating funds as were gathered from annual dues of one guinea levied on all members. In addition, an open appeal was to be made to the public. Finally, the Committee was authorized to draw up by-laws for the whole Association.

Fortunately the initial list of members has survived together with a notation of the amount subscribed by each. Apparently most contributed something extra to help launch the organization. The first column includes authors, editors, and men of letters. The second lists firms of booksellers, printers, publishers, and paper-makers.

Bulwer, E. L.	£2.2.0	Blackwood & Sons	£5.5.0
Cole, H.	£1.1.0	Boone, T. & W.	£1.1.0
Dickens, C.	£5.5.0	Bowles & Gardiner	£5.5.0
Dilke, C. W.	£5.5.0	Bradbury & Evans	£2.2.0
Forster, J.	£2.2.0	Chapman & Hall	£5.5.0
Hallam, H.	——	Colburn, H.	£10.0.0
James, G. P. R.	£5.5.0	Cox, J. L., & Sons	£1.1.0

Lockhart, J. G.	£5.5.0	Dickinson & Co.	£5.0.0
Macaulay, T. B.	——	Gilbert & Rivington	£5.0.0
Marryat, F.	£5.5.0	Longman & Co.	£10.10.0
Milman, H. H.	£2.2.0	McDowall, W.	£1.1.0
Moore, T.	——	Murray, J.	£6.6.0
Pereira, J. M. D.	——	Murray, J., Jr.	£4.0.0
Turner, A.	£3.3.0	Savill, T. C.	£2.2.0
		Spalding & Hodge	£5.0.0
		Spottiswoode, A.	£5.0.0
		Whiting, C.	£1.1.0
		Wilson & Ogilvy	£2.2.0

Reports of what took place at the meeting vary widely. As is quite often the case behind the façade of co-operation and unanimity, dissension and controversy swirled. As John Blackwood wrote to his brother, Alexander:

Dickinson was in today. He says the meeting yesterday went off very languidly; the subscription still more so. Dilke of the Athenaeum made a furious attack upon Bentley who it seems has been giving an English title page to a Yankee book and pirating in the very way we complain of.

Dilke's *Athenaeum*, after observing that not much was accomplished, went on:[34]

Indeed, the only discussion of importance related to a Resolution which went so far as to declare that the members would not knowingly either edit, print, or publish any work in which copyright existed, whether such copyright be vested in a foreigner or an Englishman, without the consent in writing of the author or publisher, or sell a copy of any pirated edition of such work; and the justice of this Resolution was fully admitted; but it was shown by Messrs. Longman, Murray, Spottiswoode, and others, that there were practical difficulties which made it inexpedient to adopt so stringent a principle as a fundamental law of the Association. It was therefore resolved, for the present at least, the aim of the Association should be to carry into effect the provisions of the recent Act in relation to the infringement of copyright, and the introduction into England and her possessions abroad of pirated copies of English works.

The tension between Dilke and Bentley was typical of the longstanding friction among authors and publishers. Despite the best intentions of men like Dickens and Longman, it was an uphill fight to preserve harmony. Well before the 17 May meeting Tom Hood voiced his misgivings to Dickens.

I ought to tell you of two remarks from two Publishers, but to one effect – viz.,
that, in reference to the proposed association for the defence of Copyright, the
Authors being most interested ought to pay Double!!! How fond they are of
profitable practical jokes!

And because he felt the cards were stacked against authors he resigned
from the Association soon after the first meeting in spite of being nominated for the Committee. Asking Dickens to deliver his letter of resignation,
he added:

I send you a letter I wish you to lay before the Association. I do not care to be a
Committeeman, but feel convinced there was a juggle. There are plenty of the
trade would object to me, for I have published what I have thought of them.
Colburn as likely as any, who on the publication of my last Copyright
*Letter [*Athenaeum, *June 1842] attempted to call me to account for writing in*
the Athm. I had all along told him I should write there and had done so, till
then without an objection. . . . As to the society they knew that you and I and
Dilke should pull together, in the Committee. However I can act as a Free
Lance – help the society as I see fit, and if not, like an Irish Partisan I'll cooperate
against it.

Hood was in a difficult position since he was editor of the *New Monthly*
Magazine which was published by Henry Colburn whom he thoroughly
disliked and who was already on the Committee. Furthermore Hood felt
that the publishers were taking all the credit for establishing the Association, whereas it was originally his idea. Again he complained to Dickens:[35]

If you remember the arrangement of bodies at the first meeting [17 May], at the
lower end of the table were the Publishers Longman, Murray and Colburn, but
off from the rest by Dilke, and I think Turner. The proposition originated with
that Trio. I do not believe Murray, whose Father is the only Gentleman, in
the line, I have met with. I have already told you about Colburn and my
Copyright letters in the Athenaeum, *and as to Longman, considering that*
when the idea of such a Society occurred to me, I called and proposed the thing to
him (a compliment not impaired by Mr. James having anticipated me) I feel
warranted in saying that he has shown himself deficient not only in the courtesy
of a gentleman, but the common civility of a Tradesman.

By way of experiment I sent to the Printer [of the New Monthly] *an*
announcement of the Association – coupled with the bare fact of my retirement
from it – and he [Colburn] has suppressed it. Confirmation strong as holy
writ of my impressions both as to him and a section of the Society, which has

only now to order a seal, with a motto from Rolla's Address to the Peruvians.
– 'Such Protection as Vultures give to Lambs – covering and devouring them.'

When the Association came to choose an Executive Secretary it singled out Alfred Turner for the job, and because his influence on the copyright issue was so significant he deserves special notice. Born in 1797, Alfred was one of seven children. His father, Sharon Turner (1768–1847), began practising law in London at the time Alfred was born. In 1806 the family moved to 32 Red Lion Square where they took up residence and where the law office was also established. As early as 1818 Alfred assisted his father in the practice, although he was not formally admitted as a solicitor until Michaelmas Term 1823. The next year Alfred joined his father in partnership. In 1838 a younger brother, William, entered the firm at about the time that Sharon retired to spend his time writing history. Sharon died in 1847 and William in 1852, leaving Alfred on his own at Red Lion Square until his death on 3 April 1864.[36]

From 1808 until the late 1820s Sharon served as John Murray II's solicitor and John Murray III relied on Alfred. This gave both Turners the opportunity to influence these clients above and beyond the usual routine of drawing up publishers' contracts and handling the preliminaries to an occasional lawsuit. For example, when Washington Irving asked Murray to pay the unprecedentedly high figure of £3,000 for the copyright of *Columbus*, Turner was consulted and offered his opinion to Murray.

Will you pardon a well-meant line? Have you finally concluded about the Columbus? If not will you excuse me if from the extract I see in the Literary Gazette I am induced to ask what has it of that superb degree as to make it fully safe for you to give the price you intend for it. I see no novelty of fact though much ability, yet not that overwhelming talent which will give you a very great circulation to so trite a subject. I merely take the liberty of suggesting a precaution, which I do with great diffidence, for I know you have such an admirable tact of judgment about works and their probable success that there is no one on whose prospective opinion I should rely more confidently than on yours. Yet the sum, compared with the subject and with the small part that I have seen of the execution, makes me send you these hints as a mere question for your consideration. Could you make part of the price depend upon the edition or the number sold?

As it happened, *Columbus* still had not made its expenses four years later.

However, with Irving's next work, the *Conquest of Granada*, Murray took Turner's advice and offered £1,400 for the first edition plus £100 for each additional thousand copies printed until a maximum of £2,000 was reached.[37]

Both Sharon and Alfred Turner made a speciality of literary copyright law. In 1813 Sharon wrote a pamphlet on the subject, and five years later the Turners assisted the publishers in connection with a parliamentary inquiry into copyright.[38] In 1842 Alfred Turner counselled Longman and Murray about the legal implications of Mahon's Bill and afterwards gathered together a group to celebrate its successful passage.[39]

My brother and myself have planned that we shall have the pleasure of seeing the acting Committee on the Copyright Law at dinner that we may all take a glass of wine to the success of the new measure.

The Association for the Protection of Literature, with Turner as Secretary, was not given much of an opportunity to function before it was faced with a challenge from an unexpected quarter. The Leipzig publisher, Tauchnitz, came to Britain in 1843 and offered to pay British authors a modest but welcome sum for the privilege of reprinting their books in Germany. His 'Collection of British Authors' had been growing since 1841, and it was clear that he had discovered a market for English-language books on the Continent. In making his offer Tauchnitz pointed out that he was not obliged by law to do this, but that he anticipated the day when international copyright would be a reality and in the meantime he sought their formal 'authorization'.

Authors such as Dickens, Bulwer, and James took a lively interest in the proposal. Dickens wrote to John Bayley of the Temple asking how the recent Copyright and Customs Acts affected such an arrangement and learned that there was no problem in a British author licensing reprints of his works in Germany, or for that fact in any other country. The essential point was to ensure that reprints should not enter the United Kingdom without the author's consent. The price charged abroad was immaterial since it would not interfere with the domestic selling price.[40]

It might have been anticipated that the Association would greet Tauchnitz's overtures with great enthusiasm. Here was a Continental reprinter offering to reimburse British authors instead of plundering them but members were distinctly divided on the question. John Blackwood spoke for many publishers when he said:[41]

There is to be a meeting on the ninth of August of publishers to consider the expediency of licensing parties in the Colonies, etc, to reprint English books at cheap rates, on their paying a certain sum to be agreed upon. I think it would be a most dangerous measure, as it is obvious we could not object to parties who had bought such legalized copies bringing them into this country for their own use. There would be an end of our total prohibition at once. Bulwer, James and some of these lads have already been making arrangements with a German bookseller [Tauchnitz] for the simultaneous publication of an authorized edition of their books. If men publish abroad of course it cannot be prevented; but for publishers as a body to give up all chance of selling their editions abroad or in the colonies would be perfect folly, and it runs directly in the teeth of what Government is so anxious for – viz, cheap editions; and all we would get for our licence would be a mere trifle except in the case of periodicals. The Longmans are very much disposed to forward this plan, but I must go to oppose it.

Because G. P. R. James could not be present at the next meeting of the Association, Alfred Turner, as Secretary, passed on the following account.

I was sorry that you were unable to attend the meeting of the Society on last Thursday; much discussion took place on the subject of Foreign and Colonial Editions and the resolution copied on the other side was finally passed. It is considered much more advisable to print off some cheap copies here when the Type is standing and to contract with parties in this country to export them – this will employ home capital and industry and may be done on inferior paper on very reasonable Terms. The Meeting therefore strongly advises that the arrangements with Mr. Tauchnitz should not be carried out.

The resolution stated:[42]

– That upon considering the communication made [concerning] proposed arrangements with Mr. Tauchnitz, it is the opinion of this meeting that it will not be expedient that such arrangements should be generally adopted in as much as it is calculated to lessen the sale of the genuine Edition – but they are of opinion that other arrangements at present under discussion might be entered into which would be more advantageous both to the author and publisher.

Although we do not know for certain, it is very likely that the Tauchnitz issue irrevocably split the fledgling Association. Authors such as Dickens, Bulwer, and James called it gross interference on the part of printers and publishers to dictate where their books could be licensed, and many apparently resigned. With a slightly altered name and with Turner as Secretary the 'Society for the Protection of Literature' functioned until 1848-9 petitioning the Government on behalf of copyright owners, but the hope of achieving a united front had collapsed. Authors, publishers, printers, booksellers, and stationers again went their separate ways.[43]

However, for years to come a thread of continuity was provided by Alfred Turner who was retained by the leading publishers when it came to dealing with Parliament and Government offices. As we shall see later, he represented Longman and Murray in discussions with the Board of Trade regarding the Anglo-American copyright treaty in 1853-4, and we have already seen his role in interrogating the Solicitor of Customs in 1860. Following his death in 1864 his nephew, Sharon Grote Turner, carried on in much the same manner, underlining the dependence of the nineteenth-century book trade on three generations of Turners.

Looking at the years 1837-44 it is remarkable that despite the difficulties of sustaining a copyright association, the British were more successful than the Americans in passing legislation favouring authors and publishers. One reason for the discrepancy lay in the contrasting legislative procedures. When the British Government undertook to sponsor measures such as the International Copyright Bills of 1838 and 1844, there was little difficulty securing their passage. If these bills had been highly controversial like the Reform Bill of 1832 or the repeal of the Corn Laws, the Ministries would have had to proceed with caution in order to preserve their majorities, but international copyright was scarcely an issue of this magnitude. By contrast, the American Executive could openly favour international copyright, as successive Presidential messages indicated, only to have Congress ignore its views completely. The Congress of the 1840s behaved very much like the French Chamber of Deputies under the Third Republic, voting according to convenience and self-interest rather than party loyalty. Southern Whigs often had more in common with southern Democrats than with northern Whigs, and some northern Democrats felt more sympathy with the South than they did with New England and the West.

Political astuteness was paramount in steering a Private Member's Bill through either Congress or the Houses of Parliament. In the latter, Sargeant Talfourd struggled mightily for five years to no avail while Mahon introduced an almost identical Bill and secured its passage in five months. Mahon succeeded largely because of his political skill in combining the interests of authors, publishers, and politicians. In America Henry Clay failed to apply his talents to organizing an effective campaign for copyright and he lacked the active support of authors like Irving, Cooper, and Prescott. Even the book trade was slow to exert pressure on Congress. Furthermore America lacked the extended literary and cultural community which characterized Britain in the nineteenth century. Congress was remarkably deficient in members who could claim to be distinguished men of letters. Occasionally there was a Daniel Webster, an Edward Everett, or a John Quincy Adams. However, at any given time, Parliament seemed to have a generous supply of men like Bulwer, Macaulay, Mahon, and Grote. Parliament placed a premium on clever men; Congress on crafty men. There was a lurking feeling among many Parliamentarians that they must pay homage to the world of letters whereas Congressmen found this inexpedient since Britain dominated the literary world.

It may be an obvious cliché, but it is impossible to ignore the effects of geography and distance. The time it took in each country for publishers to communicate with legislators differed vastly. In England when Mahon needed four petitions to present to Parliament he dropped a note to Murray on a Friday knowing that it would be received later that day and that he would have a reply the same day or the next. Given this kind of timing it was not unreasonable to expect Murray to secure a number of signatures on petitions by the following Tuesday. And if there were a question as to when the petitions would be needed, Murray could even carry them to Mahon personally. The fact that in London Parliament existed essentially side by side with the centre of the book trade speaks for itself. Washington, on the other hand, was situated far from the centres of the American book trade. New York was several hundred miles away, as was Boston; and Philadelphia was not much nearer. In America there could be no getting up of petitions on the spur of the moment and trotting them down to Capitol Hill. Distance more than anything else accounted for the use of resident lobbyists in Washington to apply pressure on legislators and government officials in behalf of those unable to present their own cases.

Finally, the American book trade was far more divided than the British on the subject of foreign reprints and international copyright. During these years there was never the harmony of interest in America that characterized the British literary community briefly in 1842–3. The American Copyright Club, which claimed to represent so many and in fact drew support from so few, contrasts markedly with the behind-the-scenes activities of G. P. R. James, Thomas Longman, John Murray, Alfred Turner and Lord Mahon. Perhaps America should have passed an international copyright agreement at this time, but it is clear why she could not.

Chapter VII

THE CANADIAN MARKET

The Copyright and Customs Acts of 1842 had very distinct implications for the British colonies, especially the North American possessions: Canada, New Brunswick, Nova Scotia, Newfoundland, and Prince Edward Island, whose proximity to the United States allowed them to benefit from cheap American reprints of British copyright works. This had little effect on the French-speaking inhabitants of North America, but those of British descent who had become used to getting English books relatively cheaply did not appreciate in the least the new copyright and Customs legislation from Westminster. None the less these laws took effect on 1 July 1843 and thereafter all foreign reprints were supposed to be excluded from the colonies.

Among the five British possessions in North America, the Province of Canada stood to lose the most because it contained the major centres of wealth and population: Montreal, Quebec, Hamilton, and Kingston. However, all the other provinces took offence to a greater or lesser extent and there was general agreement among them that they had been sacrificed to the interests of British authors and publishers. What began as disgruntled murmuring in 1842-3 swelled to a torrent of complaint by 1845-6.[1] Their first appeal to the Mother Country focused on her obligation to foster education among her colonial subjects. Cheap books and periodicals were all that most Canadians could afford, they said, and if the supply were cut off from the United States, self-improvement and enlightenment would suffer. Coincidentally they would be forced to rely even more heavily on works by American authors, and according to the Nova Scotia House of Assembly the moral and political repercussions of this were dangerous.[2]

Now the practical operation of the present law has a tendency to encourage in these Provinces the wide circulation of the literary periodicals, newspapers, and other light literature issuing from the American press, and thus places in the hands of our population works often spurious in their morality and propagating political opinions not favourable to British Institutions; against the circulation of these, the laws raise no check, while British works of the same class, whose morals are unobjectionable, and whose political references are intended to inculcate sound loyalty and reverence to the Crown and the Constitution, are excluded from general circulation as issued from the English press, by prices and other causes, and in the form of reprints they can only be had by a violation of the law.

They further argued that since Canadians would not purchase high-priced British copyright editions even English authors would be better off and in the meanwhile the colonists would suffer from the exclusion of American reprints. A comparison between the retail prices of English books and periodicals in London, Halifax, and New York dramatically demonstrated why British editions were too costly.[3]

At the same time the Canadians[4] had to admit that high prices applied chiefly to British copyright works. Non-copyright editions were available at low prices due to the efforts of London publishers like Tegg, Moxon, and William Smith. Together with books in foreign languages and works from America they also benefited from a reduction in the colonial import duty from 30 per cent to 7 per cent.[5] No duty was levied on British copyright works imported into the colonies.

With some justification the Canadians felt that British works intended for the home market were unsuitable for the colonial market.[6]

In the first place the style of publication, the printing types and binding, are suited to a more aristocratic taste and a richer people than exist here; that their prices, including of course a suitable compensation to the authors, come far beyond the means of our population, and hence if our sources of literature were confined to them, the mass of the people would in fact be entirely deprived of the productions of the English press.

Neither could the colonists avail themselves of book sales and cash discounts so prevalent in London. Whereas the average English reader could get round high prices by joining a Reading Club or by borrowing from a circulating library, Canadians were denied these conveniences of civilization, living at great distances from one another and in an atmosphere rarely conducive to book collecting. Only the well-to-do could afford to import British copyright works, which accounted for the failure of British publishers to establish a market in North America.

Even if Britain could have supplied Canada with special and cheaper colonial editions, there were considerable obstacles in the way. To send publications across the Atlantic was a slow and costly business. Although newspapers were allowed to go by post at the reduced rate of one penny per printed sheet, no such concessions applied to books and periodicals. They had to be sent at the full letter rate and were limited in weight to sixteen ounces. An English magazine which might sell for 5s. in Canada required 2s.–4s. postage, so the only practical method was to send magazines and books by freight, which inevitably involved delays of up to six months, insurance charges, Customs clearance, and additional handling. From November to May Canadian waterways were frozen, making it necessary to go overland, and though the postal service managed this trek twice a week, freight companies only made deliveries sporadically.[7]

Meanwhile American reprints continued filtering into Canada. The Nova Scotia House of Assembly attributed this to the inescapable facts of geography which worked against the enforcement of the copyright law.

That from the proximity of these Colonies to the United States, and from the extensive and frequent intercourse maintained between the seaports of the Republic and the harbours of our Atlantic coast, the Bay of Fundy, Basin of Minas, Pictou, and Sydney, Cape Breton, American reprints are introduced here in large quantities, and so rapidly after their appearance from the American press, that your Committee are satisfied a new English work is often read here nearly as soon as it has reached the most distant parts of the United Kingdom. That complete copies of them appear in American, as well as provincial newspapers, causes which operate to render the law of copyright nugatory and void.

American reprinters seemed to be prepared to try anything. When it became likely that the Canadian Customs would intercept shipments, they switched to using the post. Jonas Winchester's editions of *Blackwood's Magazine* was printed on cheap paper and so resembled a newspaper that for a time it had no difficulty securing entry. This ruse was also used by the *New World* and *Brother Jonathan* not only for the regular issues but also for their novel-length supplements. The Montreal booksellers and publishers, Armour & Ramsay, privately sought the aid of

William Blackwood, hoping that he could prevail on the Government to put a stop to this.

it so happens that the Head of the Post Office Department in the Colony has a direct interest in permitting things to remain as they are. He has, as his private perquisite, the postage of all Newspapers, Pamphlets, Books etc. within the Province, and it is therefore not to be expected that he will suggest anything which will reduce his income. The United States postage to our lines is one penny per sheet and our Postmaster General's fee for transporting it to any part of Canada is one penny additional.

Blackwood lost no time communicating the problem to the Board of Trade which in turn notified the Treasury who indicated that they understood the situation in so far as they supervised the overall workings of the General Post Office. The person alluded to by Armour & Ramsay was the Deputy Postmaster General of Canada, F. Stayner. Since assuming this position in 1827 Stayner had enjoyed a newspaper franking privilege that brought an additional £1,000 income per year. This was not intended solely for his personal use but rather as a supplement to his regular salary when needed to cover unbudgeted operating expenses. For a variety of reasons, including Blackwood's petition to the Board of Trade, the Treasury finally revoked the franking privilege. At the same time Stayner tightened up his administration of the Canadian post. The *New World* and *Brother Jonathan* found themselves officially excluded, and only after *Brother Jonathan* ceased reprinting British copyright stories was it allowed into Canada via the post.[8]

Prohibiting American reprints was futile, however, unless British publishers could fill the gap. In spite of obstacles, they needed to be made aware that they had to produce colonial editions low enough in price to please the Canadians. Otherwise the colonists would justifiably revert to buying American reprints, patriotism notwithstanding. Gladstone, in his capacity first of Vice-President and later President of the Board of Trade, was in an admirable position to goad British publishers, and he did not shrink from reminding them that in point of fact they owed the colonists cheaper books in return for the prohibitions granted them by the Copyright Act of 1842.

For their part, the publishers saw the problem as one primarily involving postal regulations. On this point they were caught in a crossfire between the Board of Trade and the Colonial Office on the one hand and the Post Office and Treasury on the other. The former felt a certain responsibility to make reading matter available relatively easily and at reasonable cost. The latter believed that economy and efficiency should be used as guidelines when it came to distributing literature. These two points of view clashed concerning the postal subsidy given to publishers for overseas mailing. As we have noted, British books and magazines were to all intents and purposes excluded from the overseas post because they had to pay the full letter rate. Five of the leading publishers[9] protested against this and petitioned the Treasury at least to allow magazines to be sent free on the same mail packets that carried newspapers without charge to North America. When the Post Office was consulted about this it agreed to lower magazine rates but not by very much. In view of severe winter weather conditions in North America they discouraged any change which would 'increase the weight and bulk of these mails by the addition of a vast number of the printed publications'. Because such periodicals could not be allowed to slow down the conveyance of the letter post, the weight limitation of sixteen ounces was retained. Ultimately the Treasury sustained the reservations expressed by the Post Office and concluded that the requested change in policy was unwarranted.

my Lords consider it expedient that you should be left to your private resources in the matter; availing yourselves of opportunities as they occur for the transmission of your publications otherwise than through the Post Office. Such works do not come within the monopoly of the Post Office in the same manner as Letters, but may be forwarded by private conveyance and my Lords consider it is obviously unfair to retard the Public correspondence, . . . solely for the advantage of printed Publications.

Here then was a minor but classic confrontation between the principles of *laissez-faire* and paternalism. The Treasury and the Post Office thought more of their budget and the efficiency of their operation and were unwilling to subsidize private businessmen in the interest of colonial consumers. Yet the Board of Trade under Gladstone as well as the Colonial Office felt that the Mother Country had some obligation to its colonial subjects and if private enterprise could not supply cheap enough editions, the Government should intervene.[10]

In spite of being rebuffed by the Treasury, magazine publishers continued to produce colonial editions of British periodicals. Armour & Ramsay became their chief distributor, and as long as prices were kept down and American reprints were disallowed they met with some degree of success.

Colonial editions of books presented another set of awkward problems not encountered by the periodicals. There was nothing in the law which prevented books published in Britain from being sent to the colonies and subsequently re-introduced back into the home market. British publishers lived in fear that this might happen and that these editions would undersell the domestic product. Periodicals were not a worry in this regard because their contents would likely be out of date by the time they were re-imported whereas books would retain their timeliness. Against this eventuality publishers could do nothing but seek promises from Canadian booksellers and publishers not to be a party to such a scheme. This threat continued to plague the British book trade for decades. A Royal Commission in 1876–8 found it as live an issue as it was in the 1840s.

An alternative solution for supplying the colonies with books was to grant licences to colonial printers authorizing them to reprint a certain number of British copyright works. This had the obvious merit of avoiding costly charges for freight and insurance, but it had the disadvantage of taking employment out of the hands of British printers and binders. Once again the issue which seriously undermined the fortunes of the Association for the Protection of Literature emerged, rekindling the controversy between authors and publishers. Most authors liked the idea. But the majority of the publishers were staunchly against it because only by printing large impressions could they increase their profit, and cutting down this number would make each copy cost more both at home as well as abroad. Thus they insisted on retaining control of both printing and publishing and forced the Canadians to import English editions at reduced prices.[11]

Among British publishers, John Murray made the greatest effort in behalf of the colonists. From his correspondence and conversation with Gladstone he became all too aware that certain concessions were expected of the London book trade in return for the Copyright and Customs Acts of 1842. Alone among his fellow publishers Murray responded to this expectation. His Colonial Library appeared in 1843 with the stated purpose[12]

of offering a substitute to the Canadas and other Colonies for the Yankee publications hitherto poured into them and which besides damaging the copyrights of British Authors by the piracy of their Works, are sapping the principles and loyalty of the Subjects of the Queen by the democratic tendency of the native American publications.

In opposition to these I hope to create a class of works inculcating good principles and loyalty, which shall possess interest for readers at home as well as in the British Foreign possessions.

Eventually known as the Home and Colonial Library, the thirty-seven volumes were weighted heavily on the side of patriotism and stressed noble virtues. The opening volume was an heroic life of Nelson by Southey, and there were also biographies of Clive, Cromwell and Drake. Murray tried to commission several prominent authors to write an account of the Battle of Waterloo before C. R. Gleig, a less well-known historian, agreed. When Murray asked J. G. Lockhart to write about Clive in India he assured him that it could be done with a minimum of exertion by relying heavily on the existing standard biography.

However, a glance at the following list of authors and titles will show that Murray's wish to indoctrinate was strongly tempered by commercial considerations. Since he rarely published fiction, his bread-and-butter publications consisted of travel narratives, voyages, and descriptions of exotic places. Into this category fell Darwin's *Voyage of the Beagle*, Melville's ostensibly autobiographical *Typee*, books on the Jesuits in China, travels up the Amazon, and tales of distant Persia.

MURRAY'S

HOME AND COLONIAL LIBRARY

SOUTHEY'S LIFE OF NELSON. 5/-

BORROW'S BIBLE IN SPAIN. 5/-

HEBER'S JOURNALS IN INDIA. 10/-

IRBY AND MANGLES' TRAVELS. 2/6

DRINKWATER'S SIEGE OF GIBRALTAR. 2/6

HAY'S MOROCCO AND THE MOORS. 2/6

LETTERS FROM THE BALTIC. 2/6

THE AMBER WITCH. 2/6

SOUTHEY'S CROMWELL AND BUNYAN. 2/6

MEREDITH'S NEW SOUTH WALES. 5/-

BORROW'S LIFE OF DRAKE. 2/6

FATHER RIPA, COURT OF PEKING. 2/6

LEWIS'S WEST INDIES. 2/6

MALCOLM'S SKETCHES OF PERSIA. 5/-

THE FRENCH IN ALGIERS. 2/6

BRACEBRIDGE HALL. 5/-

DARWIN'S NATURALIST'S
VOYAGE. 7/6
THE FALL OF THE JESUITS. 2/6
MAHON'S LIFE OF CONDE. 5/-
BORROW'S GYPSIES OF SPAIN.
5/-
MELVILLE'S MARQUESAS
ISLANDS. 5/-
LIVONIAN TALES. 2/6
MISSIONARY LIFE IN CANADA.
2/6
GENERAL SALE'S BRIGADE. 2/6
LETTERS FROM MADRAS. 2/6
ST. JOHN'S HIGHLAND
SPORTS. 5/-
HEAD'S PAMPAS JOURNEYS.
2/6
FORD'S GATHERINGS FROM
SPAIN. 5/-
THE TWO SIEGES OF
VIENNA. 2/6
SKETCHES OF GERMAN LIFE.
5/-
MELVILLE'S SOUTH SEAS. 5/-
GLEIG'S BATTLE OF
WATERLOO. 5/-
EDWARDS' VOYAGE UP THE
AMAZON. 2/6
MILMAN'S WAYSIDE CROSS.
2/6

ACLAND'S CUSTOMS OF
INDIA. 2/6
GLEIG'S CAMPAIGNS AT
WASHINGTON. 2/6
RUXTON'S ROCKY
MOUNTAINS. 5/-
CARNARVON'S PORTUGAL &
GALICIA. 5/-
GLEIG'S LIFE OF LORD CLIVE.
5/-
HAYGARTH'S BUSH LIFE. 2/6
STEFFENS' PERSONAL
ADVENTURES. 2/6
TALES OF A TRAVELLER. 5/-
CAMPBELL'S ESSAY ON
POETRY. 5/-
MAHON'S HISTORICAL
ESSAYS. 5/-
RAILROAD & ELECTRIC
TELEGRAPH. 2/6
ST. JOHN'S LIBYAN DESERT.
2/6
SIERRA LEONE. By a Lady. 5/-
GLEIG'S LIFE OF SIR THOMAS
MUNRO. 5/-
SIR FOWELL BUXTON'S
MEMOIRS. 7/6
IRVING'S LIFE OF
GOLDSMITH. 5/-

The wish to make these volumes saleable was so strong that Murray sometimes declined works that were offered to him. In a rejection letter to the distinguished historian Lord Mahon he confessed,[13]

I am obliged in the selection of books to study the taste of the middle and lower orders among whom my readers lie in a great degree, and I have some doubt whether they have sufficient knowledge of Spain and its history to enter into the spirit and interest of the Stanhope papers.

Murray was continually being caught between his intention to supply the colonies with works which they could afford and his wish to make the venture profitable. In the early 1840s he was quite sanguine ot success. Southey's *Nelson* sold 10,000 copies, and with this evidence Murray was able to persuade his regular authors to consent to cheap colonial editions of their works. In this way books whose sales were declining in their original expensive editions were finding new markets both at home and abroad. When Melville complained that his latest book was being published in a cheap edition Murray pointed out that other volumes in the series were selling as many as 6, 10, or even 15,000 copies. This was not the whole story, however. True, the occasional volume sold that well, but as Murray later confessed, most editions averaged 1,000.

In 1849 Murray abandoned the Colonial Library. Why? One disillusioned Canadian bookseller, William Greig of Montreal, grumbled at the outset of the series:

Murray, the great London Publisher, has put forth the prospectus of what he calls his cheap Colonial editions – and what are the great advantages which he offers? Why, instead of issuing cheap editions of his latest works, he reissues those that the 'run' is chiefly over for, and which have been reprinted and extensively circulated on this side of the Atlantic long ago; and then he offers for 2s Sterling equal to 3s in Canada, what is sold in the United States for 25 cents, equal to 1s 10½d currency in Canada.

Others in Canada faulted Murray on the selection of titles which they said were too serious for the average colonist who looked for light reading. A committee of the Canadian Assembly, endeavouring to show how inadequately the Colonies were being supplied from Great Britain, even took an opinion poll of booksellers and publishers as proof of the widespread dissatisfaction felt by many.[14]

Once the importation of American reprints was prohibited most Canadian firms gave grudging lip-service to the law, but in practice they procured them by fair means or foul, feeling an obligation to their Canadian customers rather than to British authors and publishers. Armour & Ramsay represented but a small minority of firms who came out forcefully in favour of importing authorized editions from Britain. However, the public bought only a few British exports such as Cadell's reissue of the Waverley Novels which were obviously good literature as well as being cheap.

Perhaps the blame for the demise of the Colonial Library, in addition to its essentially English character which put off the Canadians, should rest with the London book trade itself. After all, the 1842 legislation deferred to their interests and yet few of them made any effort to implement its provisions. In this respect the Board of Trade was justified in criticizing British publishers for not compensating the colonists for the loss of their cheap American reprints. Offering dead stock at reduced rates or reissuing out-of-print works in a new format was not what the Canadians wanted. Rather it was new publications at substantial price reductions, and here British publishers were reluctant to respond except in the case of periodicals.

Eventually the failure of Britain to deal with this problem led the Canadians to start thinking about a revision or revocation of the 1842 Imperial Copyright Law. Criticism of its provisions grew steadily. Gladstone sympathized with many of the objections and privately advised Canadian booksellers to make their own arrangements with British publishers. Acknowledging that the postal services were in need of reform, he also urged the Board of Trade and the Colonial Office to persuade the Treasury and Post Office to act quickly. Colonists were informed of the possibility of some amelioration: 'My Lords are directing their attention to the state of the Copyright law, in order to discover whether there are any particulars in which its details may be so amended as to afford any relief to the Colonists.'[15] In June 1846 Gladstone levelled the *coup de grâce.* Answering the complaints sent by the Lt Governor of New Brunswick, he acknowledged that 'the present stringent provisions of the law did not proceed originally from any proposal of Her Majesty's Government but were adopted by Parliament on the suggestion of an individual member of the House of Commons in deference to a strong public sentiment'. This was tantamount to repudiating Lord Mahon's Bill and the policy of excluding cheap foreign reprints from the colonial market.

Later in June, Gladstone left the Presidency of the Board of Trade and occupied briefly the post of Colonial Secretary where he lost no time bringing pressure to bear on his former colleagues at the Board. As Colonial Secretary he directed them to inform the book trade:[16]

that it is the opinion of Her Majesty's Government that unless vigorous and decided efforts be made by the publishers, to meet the views . . . of the Committee of Assembly at Halifax, the result will be an increase in dissatisfaction on this subject in the North American Provinces and a diminution of whatever limited benefit the English authors and publishers now derive from the exclusion of the American reprints of English works.

By October the Board of Trade reached a decision. Referring to itself as 'they' the Board indicated its readiness to consider a major change.

they are extremely desirous to adopt any measures consistent with justice, which may place the Literature of this Country within the reach of its dependencies on easier terms than at present. With this view my Lords have attentively considered the possibility of modifying the Imperial Law in such a manner as to meet the just demands of the Colonists without sacrificing the rights of the Author; ... For devising such an arrangement a knowledge of local feelings is required which they are conscious they do not possess in a sufficient degree, and they entertain great apprehensions that, were they to attempt to legislate with a view to it, they might create alarm or dissatisfaction here, without accomplishing their purpose of benefiting the Colonies.

In conclusion they proposed to introduce into Parliament a Bill which would suspend the Copyright Act of 1842 for any colony which would make provision to adequately compensate British authors; the Queen-in-Council would be the arbiter regarding adequate compensation; and only when an Order in Council was issued would such a colonial Act come into force. The Colonial Office gave its approval of this quite readily and sent instructions to the colonial Governors telling them of the Government's intention to recommend new copyright legislation, informing them that it was up to each colony to draft its own provisions, have them passed by the Imperial Parliament, and finally to secure their approval from the Privy Council in London.[17]

Unofficially entitled the Foreign Reprints Act (10 & 11 Vict., c. 95) it required less than a month to pass both Houses of Parliament. Introduced into the Commons on 2 July 1847, it received the royal assent on 22 July. Even with Government backing it is hard to imagine a Bill making its way through the legislature with greater ease and speed. Clearly, few of the Members gave much thought to it, and there was virtually no time for outside forces to mobilize any opposition. In fact, British authors and publishers were scarcely if at all aware of its existence until after it had become law.[18]

The Canadians were not slow to avail themselves of the Foreign Reprints Act. Even before it had made its way through Parliament the Province of Canada came forward with its own statute[19] which received the royal assent only six days after the signing of the enabling legislation. Entitled 'An Act to Extend the Provincial Copyright Act to Persons Resident in the United Kingdom', the Canadian act was a marvel of subterfuge. Nothing in it directly alluded to the Foreign Reprints Act but instead granted copyright protection to British authors who 'printed and published' their works in the Province. Since British authors were under the impression that they already enjoyed such a privilege under the Imperial Copyright Act of 1842 they took little notice. Neither did the Board of Trade which approved the Canadian Act. The only problem was that the Canadians were so subtle that no one at Whitehall realized that it was necessary to request from the Queen an Order in Council suspending the prohibitions of the 1842 Copyright Act. Nine months elapsed before the Provincial Government through its Governor-General Lord Elgin formally requested the Colonial Office for an Order in Council. At this point Gladstone was no longer in the Government and the Board of Trade was prepared to show a kinder disposition towards British authors and publishers. With this in mind John Murray was sounded out on the advisability of issuing an Order in Council. Murray in turn brought the matter before the Committee of the Society for the Protection of Literature, and the Society's Secretary, Alfred Turner, eventually notified the Board of its opinion. Turner's letter is missing, but the gist of it clearly emerges from the decision of the Board not to acquiesce in the Canadian request. Although they admitted that the Provincial Act was perfectly legal, they refused to endorse the issuing of an Order in Council which would suspend the Act of 1842. There was distinct concern that British authors would receive little or no compensation for the loss of an exclusive colonial market. Had a duty of 20 per cent on American reprints been stipulated, all would have been well. As it was, the Board declared that:

the Canadian Act now under discussion is framed upon a totally different principle. Its effect, were it followed up by an Order in Council, would simply be to take away from British authors, unless they republished in the Colony, protection which they now enjoy, without making them any compensation for the injury.

Using arguments put forth by the Society for the Protection of Literature, the Board of Trade accused the Canadians of subsidizing their own book trade at the expense of the British. Moreover, since the purpose of the Foreign Reprints Act was to make books available more cheaply they claimed that it did not make sense to condone higher production costs in the Colony. The Canadian book trade was thus sacrificed to the interests of the Canadian reading public on the one hand and to

British authors and publishers on the other, a plight it endured throughout the nineteenth century.[20]

There was nothing to do but begin all over again. Canadians took the better part of two years to secure the passage of a new Act which conformed to the provisions of the Foreign Reprints Act, and in the meantime conditions became increasingly chaotic. Foreign reprints were allowed to enter Nova Scotia, New Brunswick, Prince Edward Island, and Newfoundland, but not the Province of Canada, and this became a nightmare for Customs officials. Even in the Province of Canada confusion abounded. According to the prevailing Copyright and Customs Acts of 1842 British authors and publishers had to notify the Customs of their latest copyright works which were then incorporated into lists forwarded to the colonies every three months. Clever booksellers and publishers in Canada recognized the time-lag between the date of publication and the receipt of quarterly lists and simply imported all the American reprints they wished during the interval. Thereafter who was to know which reprints were imported before or after the Customs lists reached North America?

J. W. Dunscombe, the Province's chief Customs officer, saw the impossibility of enforcing these provisions and sought to prove just how unworkable the 1842 laws were. He chose to intervene in a case involving a Montreal Customs officer named Pratt who had confiscated a quantity of foreign reprints. Poor Pratt found himself caught between the regulations of HM Customs and Dunscombe's interpretation of them. Learning of the destruction of the books, Dunscombe ordered Pratt's salary to be appropriated to compensate the Canadian importer for his loss. The Canadian and British Customs, the Treasury, the Board of Trade, and the Colonial Office each analysed the points in dispute but could not agree. By the autumn of 1850, *six* months later, the case was still pending, although unsolved. In the meantime the Canadian legislature had passed another copyright bill which rendered the seizure of foreign reprints unnecessary. The new Act, 13 & 14 Vict., c. 6, mercifully extricated all the parties embroiled in the Dunscombe–Pratt affair.

The Canadians were not to slip through smoothly, however. The Board of Trade, having been caught napping once was determined not to make any mistakes this time. Accordingly, when the new Act reached Whitehall in October 1850 it was scrutinized suspiciously. True enough, it resembled those already in effect in the other Provinces of North America, yet the phrasing which concerned the duty to be levied was ambiguous.

A duty not to exceed 20 per cent was provided, but no mention was made of a minimum figure. Mistrusting the implications of this, the Board refused its sanction and recommended that an Order in Council suspending the Acts of 1842 be authorized only if the exact duty was stated. The Canadian Provincial Government ultimately capitulated and proposed 12½ per cent, a figure high enough to compensate British authors and low enough to discourage smuggling. In March 1851 the Board approved this and the Colonial Secretary put the finishing touches on the protracted negotiations.[21]

By 1855–6 the effects of the Orders in Council began to be felt. An absurdly small amount of money was being collected by Customs officials as payments due to British copyright owners. During a trip to Canada in 1851 Sampson Low Jr, son of the London publisher, already detected trouble. In conversations with booksellers there he learned the worst.[22]

In answer to my remark – 'at least the [British] author obtains a portion of the duty' (as intended by the law), – it was stated that no amount had yet been realized by any English author, the whole proceeds of the impost being engrossed by the expenses of stationery and salaries.

In 1856 the official returns from Customs became available. For the approximately five years during which the colonies had availed themselves of the Foreign Reprints Act they had collected £587. Nova Scotia reported scarcely more than £10 from American reprints which would have meant, at a rate of 20 per cent on the wholesale price, scarcely £50 worth of reprints! The figures for the Province of Canada were equally absurd. Between June 1851 and the end of 1855 a total of £514,746 worth of books had been imported. Of these, £97,770 were supposed to have come from the United Kingdom; £26,506 from countries outside North America; and £390,470 from the United States. If these figures are to be trusted, Canadians were importing four times as many books from the United States as from the Mother Country. Allowing for the fact that not all of these American imports were reprints of British copyright works – there were bound to be a significant number of American copyright books plus a large number of British works whose copyright had lapsed – nevertheless there must have been a substantial number of reprints of British copyright works on which a duty of 12½ per cent was due. Assuming that at least one-fourth of the estimated £390,470 worth of books was subject to this duty, there still should have been about £12,500 collected. In fact duty was levied on only £3,656 of these American books, amounting to the princely sum of £456 14s. 0d. Even this sum shrank to £252 11s. 3d. after the Canadian Customs deducted their collection costs.²³ The Colonial Office thus received only £206 12s. 10d. Sterling to be allocated to British publishers and authors. Richard Bentley received a mere £44 14s. 11d. as compensation for his scores of copyright books. Ten years later Edward Lytton Bulwer, with all of his copyrights still in force and with his popularity as strong as ever, received £1 19s. 10d. as his year's due from the entire British Empire!

It is no wonder that British authors and publishers repeatedly asked themselves why they had been so negligent as to allow the Foreign Reprints Act to pass through Parliament without a whisper of protest. Similarly, Canadian publishers felt no satisfaction from its passage because they still could not reprint British copyright works without obtaining the consent of British authors and publishers. Only the American reprinters and the Canadian consumers gained. As was true in the United States, the mania for cheapness won out over the interests of the literary community.²⁴

THE BRITISH LAW COURTS: A POSSIBLE REMEDY FOR THE ABSENCE OF INTERNATIONAL COPYRIGHT

During the first half of the nineteenth century, British authors had little prospect of protecting their publications abroad, especially in America. However, depending upon the state of the law as interpreted by the British courts, foreign authors including Americans could secure a valid copyright in Britain. During the years 1815–54 publishers and their solicitors were never quite sure how the Court of Chancery or the Common Law Courts would rule in a particular case, and this disconcerted everyone on both sides of the Atlantic. Broadly speaking, up to 1835 legal decisions went against foreigners securing a copyright. Then with *D'Almaine* v. *Boosey* and later with *Bentley* v. *Foster* (1839) the balance tipped in favour of foreign authors. The only prerequisite was that a work had to be published in Britain prior to or simultaneous with its appearance abroad.

The passage of the International Copyright Act of 1838 introduced additional complications. Some solicitors construed it as displacing all previous legislation and legal opinion, and maintained that reciprocity was henceforth the only basis upon which Britain would confer copyright on foreigners. But there were those who did not agree with this strict construction and so uncertainties continued.

For the British book trade this meant that American books were a risky speculation. Three types of publishers and booksellers took an interest in American literature. First, there were those like Bentley, Murray, and Blackwood who took special pleasure in promoting American authorship. Of these Bentley was the most heavily committed, often issuing a half dozen American titles a year. The second group was attracted to American authorship not so much for the prestige it might bring them but rather due to the ease of reprinting non-copyright works. These firms were the so-called 'pirates' whose methods were usually the same as their counterparts in North America. Their interests were contrary to the other two groups because they thrived on copyright uncertainty whereas the others championed the rights of foreign authors. The third group were principally importers of American books although they also published a few, copyrighting them if they could. Firms like John Miller, John Chapman, and Sampson Low made a speciality of Americana just as other firms specialized in law, medical, or other foreign books.

British literary piracy is usually lost sight of beside Dickens's well-publicized criticism of the American reprint trade.[1] But the same economic depression which created a market in America for cheap books and periodicals also gave rise to a similar though more modest effort in Britain. Publishers such as George Routledge, Henry George Bohn, H. G. Clarke, and William Smith capitalized on the increasing number of British readers whose main criterion for buying literature was its low price. Sometimes they would 'borrow' from their own countrymen like Dickens, but it was generally considered safer to go farther afield and publish pieces with dubious copyrights which were written by American authors. In addition to putting out periodicals and one-volume works, series of volumes labelled Railway Libraries, Cheap Series, or Popular Series began to pour from their presses. Mostly fiction, these series sold for a shilling or two per volume and were run off in as many as 5,000 to 6,000 copies at a time. When one considers that every other reprinter could also have issued the same work this is not an insignificant number. Occasionally the reprinters would strike it rich as they did in 1852 with *Uncle Tom's Cabin* by the American authoress Harriet Beecher Stowe. Within just a few years one million copies had been sold, dwarfing the sales of any contemporary work on either side of the Atlantic. In 1853 the *Illustrated London News* reported:

At present . . . the whole race of English booksellers, with few exceptions worth mentioning, are greater literary pirates than the Americans. No sooner does a tolerably good book appear in America, than the whole tribe of English publishers pounce upon it, and rival each other who shall first stock the market with it. There is nothing to pay the author. The book trade goes on swimmingly; and the English public have cheap 'Uncle Toms'. In the meantime

the English writer is at a greater discount than ever in his own country, and
sinks a step lower in the social scale.

Somewhat more typical was Nathaniel Hawthorne's *Scarlet Letter*.
Scarcely known in Britain, Hawthorne was unsuccessful at first in
securing a London publisher and British copyright. But once his book
proved popular in America it was not long until British publishers
took notice. Within several years two London importers, Delf and
Chapman, advertised the American edition; Routledge, J. Walker, and
Bohn republished the book under their own imprint; and reprints were
issued in Edinburgh as well as in Dublin. Fortunately Routledge's records
specifically mention their commitment in this case, indicating the sales
of at least one of the reprinters involved. His initial edition in the spring
of 1851 was 2,000. In August another 2,000 copies were struck off, and
the same number were again called for in September. November
saw an issue of 4,000 copies. The next July 2,000 more were ordered,
followed by the same number in both August and September. In 1853
the demand finally began to slacken, necessitating only two printings
of 2,000 in February and July. However, these numbers so impressed
Routledge that he even ventured to try 2,000 copies of Hawthorne's
campaign biography of Franklin Pierce![2]

Three other American authors, Emerson, Irving, and Melville were
unwitting contributors to one of the major legal battles within the
London book trade. It began in February 1850 when Henry G. Bohn
arranged to publish an English edition of Ralph Waldo Emerson's
Representative Men as the first number in his new Shilling Series only to
discover it shortly thereafter in Routledge's Popular Library. Bohn
regarded this as a breach of trade courtesy by a fellow reprinter and
decided to retaliate. Knowing that Routledge's new series was to include
a number of works by Washington Irving, Bohn simply helped himself
to one of them.

Soon the two rival firms were in a race to reprint other Irving titles,
especially the revised editions which were being issued by G. P. Putnam
of New York and John Murray of London. They flooded the market
with 1s. or 1s. 6d. volumes, overlooking what John Murray, whose father
had paid handsomely for their copyright in the 1820s, and Richard
Bentley, who became Irving's publisher in the 1830s, might do about it.

Murray and Bentley knew that the courts differed on the subject
but they determined to take their chances. During June and July 1850

they gathered evidence in the time-honoured fashion of sending innocuous-looking clerks to the shops of Bohn and Routledge with instructions to purchase copies of the disputed books. Bills of complaint and affidavits were sworn to, and at the end of July Bohn and Routledge were advised by the Court of Chancery that they would be forced by an injunction to cease publication of the offending works unless they could submit sufficient evidence to prove their innocence. Hearings were held on 7–8 August and the defendants managed to raise so many awkward points that Vice-Chancellor Knight Bruce felt that he could not grant an injunction against them.[3] The only consolation left to Murray and Bentley was the knowledge that they could still seek damages in one of the three Common Law Courts, and in the meantime Bohn and Routledge would be forced to keep accurate accounts of the profits made from the sale of the books in question.

The case is significant because it embodies so many of the legal issues faced by the courts during the first half of the nineteenth century. Fortunately a good deal of the background correspondence survives between plaintiffs and their solicitors and between plaintiffs and defendants, permitting a close analysis of the situation. Always implicit were the rights of foreign authors, the growth of cheap reprints, and the survival of trade courtesy within the London book trade. And as time went on each party became more obstinate, expended more money and energy, and even showed a determination to take the case all the way to the Court of last resort, the House of Lords.

By the time the Vice-Chancellor had denied an injunction to Murray and Bentley, the situation was grave indeed. Both Bohn's and Routledge's cheap series had grown to alarming proportions, and there was no telling which works they would appropriate next. As long as the courts were ambiguous the pirates were willing to risk appropriating American books which were readily available and required no translation. By the end of July 1850 the two series contained the following:[4]

Bohn's Shilling Series

AUTHOR	TITLE	1850
1. Emerson	*Representative Men*	February
2. Irving	*Life of Mahomet*	February
3. Sparks	*Franklin's Autobiography*	March

4.	Willis	*People I Have Met*	April
5.	Irving	*Successors of Mahomet*	April
6.	Irving	*Goldsmith*	April
*7.	Irving	*Sketchbook*	May
*8.	Irving	*Tales of a Traveller*	May
9.	Irving	*Tour of the Prairie*	May
*10–11.	Irving	*Granada*	May
*12–13.	Irving	*Columbus*	June
*14.	Irving	*Companions of Columbus*	June
*15–16.	Taylor	*Eldorado*	June
**17.	Irving	*Capt. Bonneville*	July
18.	Irving	*Knickerbocker's History*	July
**19.	Irving	*Alhambra*	July
20.	Irving	*Conquest of Florida*	July

Routledge's Popular Library

1.	Irving	*Goldsmith*	January
2.	Emerson	*Representative Men*	February
3.	Irving	*Mahomet*	March
*4.	Irving	*Bracebridge Hall*	March
5.	Melville	*Omoo*	March
6.	Melville	*Typee*	April
7.	Irving	*Successors of Mahomet*	April
*8.	Irving	*Tales of a Traveller*	April
*9.	Irving	*Sketchbook*	May
*10–11.	Irving	*Columbus*	May
*12.	Irving	*Granada*	May
13.	Irving	*Crayon Miscellany*	May
*14.	Irving	*Companions of Columbus*	May
15–16.	Taylor	*Eldorado*	June
17.	Irving	*Salmagundi*	June
18.	Irving	*Knickerbocker's History*	June
**19.	Irving	*Captain Bonneville*	July
**20.	Irving	*Alhambra*	July
**21.	Irving	*Astoria*	July
22.	——	*Life of Sir R. Peel*	July

One of the reasons Murray was denied an injunction by the Court of
Chancery was the uncertainty regarding the dates of publication of the
books in dispute. The courts had long since decided that one of the
essential prerequisites for a British copyright was prior publication in
the United Kingdom. Some of Irving's early works appeared in the
United States before their publication in London, while others such as
the *Sketchbook*, *Mahomet*, and *Goldsmith* came out in parts, sometimes
issued first in America and other times in Britain. Murray ultimately
rested his case on six of Irving's works, as designated by the asterisk
in the lists, as well as two of Melville's stories. Bentley sought to protect
three of Irving's other books, marked with a double asterisk.

The problem was to prove that these works had been published in
Britain prior to their appearance in the United States, an ostensibly
simple matter. But when Murray applied for assistance to Irving and
his New York publisher, G. P. Putnam, his answers were far from
reassuring. In June 1850 Putnam wrote:[5]

*So far I have not been able to procure documents that would be legal evidence
of time of publication in this country – for the record of the entry of copyright
does not prove the* day of publication *– inasmuch as three months latitude
is allowed by law – and no legal proof can be had from official persons on that
point.*

He sent Murray some advertisements of Irving's early works and trusted
that more could be learned from the publishers who had originally
issued the books. Putnam soon learned, however, that one of the publishers
was dead and another had lost his business records in a fire. Besides,
Putnam explained, the problem of contested copyright arose so infre-
quently in America that authors and publishers were not accustomed
to keep detailed account books and publication notices. Ultimately
it was up to Irving and Melville themselves to sign affidavits attesting
to the validity of the information they provided for Murray and Bentley,
and even this might not satisfy a judge and jury in a British Court of
Common Law.

Even if Murray and Bentley could prove, as was not always the case,
that their editions of Irving and Melville appeared first in Britain, they
still could not avoid the equally important issue of residency and nationality. The British courts were divided on the rights of foreign authors,
and who was to say that the recent decision of *Boosey* v. *Purday* (1849)
which was so unfavourable to foreign authors would not be upheld

again. Yet here was an area of ambiguity which Murray hoped to exploit at least in the case of Irving if not Melville. Melville had lived in Britain occasionally but not when *Typee* and *Omoo* were going through the press. However, Irving had spent a good deal of the 20s and early 30s resident in Britain and on the Continent, so much so that contemporaries sometimes wondered if he was not an American expatriate. Between 1829–31 Irving had even served with the American Legation in London. Residency was very important, as many British legal authorities felt that a foreign author considerably strengthened his copyrights if he was present when the works appeared. Murray wished to go one step farther and argue that Irving could even claim British citizenship on the basis of having parents who were British subjects. Murray's solicitor, Alfred Turner, and his barrister, Fitzroy Kelly, both doubted that a court would accept Irving's claim to British citizenship, but they thought it worth a try as long as it did not involve excessive expense in gathering the evidence.

In addition to the claims of prior publication and Irving's nationality, there was the basic question of Bentley's and Murray's title to their own publications. This was easiest to prove because they each kept good records and could produce contracts, original manuscripts in some instances, and letters exchanged between themselves and authors. Murray had further to demonstrate that he had duly inherited part of his father's business in 1843 and later bought out the other part of it from relatives.

As might be expected, Bohn and Routledge based their case on the obverse of the above. They denied the right of any foreigner to a copyright in Britain and challenged the dates of publication. They noted that Irving had been living in America more or less continuously since the 1830s except for a few years as American Consul to Spain. On the issue of nationality Bohn and Routledge were on particularly strong ground, for Irving had made it patently clear to the reading world that he was an American by birth as well as inclination and privately he told Murray that he would not become a direct party to litigation in Britain.

The task of Bohn and Routledge was a good deal more difficult when it came to publication dates. After all, they had no direct access to Irving or his current publisher, Putnam, and the burden of proof ultimately rested with the reprinters. If they could not show that the works in question first appeared in America, then Murray's and Bentley's account books would be taken as *prima facie* evidence. Bohn managed to extract some biographical information about Irving from the Secretary of the

American Legation in London until he was put on his guard and thereafter refused further co-operation. An even better lead proved to be two authorities on American bibliography, John Chapman and Thomas Delf, who as booksellers were importing Irving's works from America. If Bohn could prove that Murray had knowingly tolerated the sale of imported editions, Murray's case would be undermined seriously because the law held that a plaintiff was required to bring action against a reprinter within one year of the reprint's appearance. Since Chapman and Delf had been importing American editions of Irving for the past few years, Murray's only plea could be ignorance that these were on sale in London.

To buttress his position, Bohn tried to show that Murray had actually neglected Irving's works since the 1830s, reissuing only two books prior to the revised edition published in New York by Putnam in which Murray only shared. Again since Murray presumably imported these, it raised the problem of the status of an import.

Eventually all the arguments came back to whether a foreigner or his London publisher could secure a valid copyright in Britain. If this were admitted, then the evidence fell into place and both Bentley and Murray were confident that they could prove their allegations. Herein the plaintiffs had an advantage because they were prepared to co-operate in litigating the question. The defendants, on the other hand, mistrusted one another and were always in ruthless competition.

These were the arguments and the state of the case in August 1850 when the Court of Chancery granted Murray permission to seek satisfaction in another court. The Vice-Chancellor explained that he could do little else because his Court of Equity was not in a position to deal with serious conflicts of evidence. If Bohn and Routledge had failed to answer the bill of complaint or had responded feebly, an injunction would have been issued as a matter of course. But the defendants had introduced too many knotty problems which only a judge and jury could arbitrate.

Murray's solicitor, however, was dissatisfied. Turner felt that the Vice-Chancellor had rushed the case and given too much credence to Bohn's and Routledge's answers. Not only that, but in failing to grant an injunction the court was allowing the situation to get worse pending the case coming to trial. On the other hand, he confided to Murray: [6]

We gained however considerably by the Chancery proceedings, because it has shown the whole of our opponents case and disclosed to us many facts which we were ignorant of and which, if they had suddenly come out at a Trial of Law, might have at once thrown us out of Court – and we have obtained these without disclosing our case which we should have done if the matter had been more fully argued – a thing which was to be avoided. . . . It is now for us to make best use we can of the next two months.

Copyright cases could be brought before any of the three Common Law Courts: Queen's Bench, Common Pleas, or Exchequer. Since 1845 the Barons of the Exchequer had been consistently turning thumbs down on the rights of foreign authors, so there was no point in approaching them. Common Pleas had upheld a foreign author in 1848, which recommended it, but Queen's Bench, under its new Chief Justice Lord Campbell, seemed to offer an even better prospect. Not only was it caught up with its arrears of business and therefore promised a quick decision, but more important, Campbell was a distinguished scholar and biographer whose publisher happened to be John Murray.

The case was thus scheduled in Queen's Bench for November 1850. Sir Fitzroy Kelly, the eminent barrister and QC, was asked by Turner to plead Murray's case. Kelly was a Member of Parliament as well as a former Solicitor General and had gained a reputation for trying cases before the House of Lords. This was probably in the back of Turner's mind should Murray's litigation be carried all the way to the highest court.

November came and went without a trial. By February 1851 Kelly decided to take an extended holiday in the Mediterranean. Turner observed: 'it is equally impossible to say when the Actions may be read – as our opponents of course will not facilitate, and it is most likely that Melville's case from its being the most simple may be tried first'.

At the beginning of April a new wrinkle was introduced by Bohn's legal counsel. As Turner explained to Murray: 'The pleadings have by the course he [Bohn] has pursued assumed the form of a Demurrer and this is put down for argument of this month.' A Demurrer was, as one contemporary defined it, 'a kind of pause or stop, put to the proceedings of an action upon a point of difficulty, which must be determined by the court, before any further proceedings can be had therein'.[7] In effect Bohn was questioning Murray's right to a trial if no law had been broken. If aliens could not secure a copyright, as suggested by recent decisions of the Court of Exchequer, and if Irving and Melville were clearly aliens, then there was no basis for litigation. It was a delaying tactic, Turner said, for 'whatever decision the Court comes to on this being only a point of formal pleading will not prevent either party from going on before a Jury on the general facts of the Case'.

The Demurrer was not heard by Lord Campbell in Queen's Bench until 9 May 1851, and by that time Sir Fitzroy Kelly was back in England and able to argue Murray's case. Lord Campbell did not decide the matter but requested time to consider the arguments, thus leaving the proceedings in a state of suspension.

Several weeks later another copyright case, that of *Boosey* v. *Jefferys*, intruded itself upon Murray's and Bentley's affairs. Almost a year before, Boosey, another publisher, had tried to protect the copyright of a foreigner, but failed. Now, in May 1851, he was carrying an appeal to a Court of Error. Whatever decision was rendered in this case on this level would certainly influence, perhaps decisively, the disposition of Murray's case. Alfred Turner gave vent to his own frustration.

I am vexed at the position of the Case of Boosey *v.* Jefferys *– however, it cannot be helped – We have done all we can, which is to supply the Counsel for Boosey . . . with Sir Fitzroy Kelly's argument . . . I have great hopes that our case will not be decided immediately as the Judges in* Boosey *v.* Jefferys *will probably take time to consider their decision.*

Turner fervently hoped that the Court of Error would uphold the rights of foreigners, thereby virtually assuring Murray's victory over Bohn and Routledge. With surprising rapidity the court made known its decision. On 20 May 1851 it reversed the lower court's ruling and unanimously acknowledged the right of an alien author to a British copyright.

At this point the tenuous alliance between Bohn and Routledge began to crack. Even before the announcement of the decision in the Court of Error Routledge had intimated his willingness to settle out of court, but Bohn had apparently managed to keep him in line. In late May and early June Routledge again contemplated an out-of-court settlement in view of the mounting legal costs and the worsened propects for a favourable judgment. On 12 June Turner reported, 'After some negotiation we have so far arranged with Mr Routledge that we stopped further litigation with him.'[8] Routledge agreed to cease the reprinting of Murray's copyrighted works; to destroy the stereotype plates; surrender the printed copies on hand; pay the legal fees for both sides; and allow Murray to announce publicly that Routledge had come to terms. It was estimated that Routledge had made £1,500 profit on the sale of Irving's works and £500 on those of Melville. On this basis Turner 'arranged the penalty [bond] of £2,000 if he violates his agreement'. A few days later Bentley was able to impose a similar settlement on Routledge. Months passed while Routledge procrastinated, trying to salvage things as best he could. Instead of destroying his stereotype plates he sold them as scrap metal, and after withdrawing his reprints from the British market he exported some of them to America. Periodic threats from Bentley and Murray had their effect, and by the end of 1851 Routledge had essentially complied with the out-of-court settlement. This in turn accounts for the rarity of his Popular Library volumes, together with Bohn's Shilling Series, in the bibliographies of Irving or Melville.

For a time Bohn proved obdurate, refusing to settle out of court. Even if the Court of Error had determined that a foreign author could secure a British copyright, there was still a wide range of uncertainty as to whether Murray's and Bentley's editions of Irving were published in England prior to their appearance in America. As we shall see, another of Bohn's motives for procrastination had to do with the possibility of another copyright case, *Boosey* v. *Jefferys*, being appealed to the House of Lords. This left Murray no alternative but to force the issue by requesting that a commission of inquiry be sent to the United States to get written affidavits from the authors concerned. Murray's counsel admitted that this would be expensive, although in the long run it might justify the outlay. Turner explained:

it will be most important that it should not be done on written questions but viva voce, that any uncertain or doubtful answer may be followed by a proper question to clear up the point and leave the final reply as much in our favour as possible, which no doubt will be the result if ably done. But to do this properly . . . a Counsel must go out, as less than that would not be safe.

Bohn did all he could to block the dispatch of a commission even though he had the right to choose some of its members. However, the Court of Queen's Bench approved Murray's request at the end of July and Joseph Needham, one of the barristers on the case, agreed to undertake the task provided that he was paid £200 compensation for his work, his absence from his family, and his sacrificed holiday. One begins to appreciate the spiralling legal costs that were being incurred when it is realized that this fee was equivalent to a year's salary or more for an office clerk. Turner apologized to Murray for causing him such worry and expense, 'but I am quite satisfied it is a just cause as a private matter and a most important one in a Literary and National point of view'. In the meantime, the pressure on Bohn was increased, as Turner reported: 'I have arranged with Mr. Bentley's Solicitor that he shall apply to the Court of Chancery for an injunction against Bohn in respect of such works of Washington Irving as he claims Copyright in – as Bohn's defence to this may be useful both to Bentley and you – and if he succeeds and gets his injunction it may influence Bohn's mind towards some surrender'.[9]

Details for the month of August are lacking, but on the 27th we have the undeniable evidence of Bohn's submission. In a formal agreement signed by both parties Bohn offered to purchase the copyrights of Irving's works from Murray for £2,000 provided that Murray drop all litigation. Each party paid its own costs. Murray would transfer his surplus stock of Irving volumes to Bohn but would still reserve the right to reprint certain titles in the Colonial and Family Libraries.

It was a hollow victory for Murray. He wrote disconsolately to Irving:

Mr Bohn has offered me terms that are satisfactory to me and not humiliating to him. He has destroyed for me all value in your works, and I make over to him the copyright.

I regret to part with them, but it seemed to me the only way to get out of the squabble, which was becoming very serious, my law expenses alone having run up to £850.

One good, at least, has been elicited out of the contest – it has settled the right of foreigners to hold copyright in this country: for I am assured by my counsel, Sir Fitzroy Kelly, one of the soundest heads at our bar, that the recent decision of our judges . . . is not likely to be reversed by the House of Lords, or any other tribunal.

Alfred Turner was in little doubt as to why Bohn ultimately capitulated. Although the commission to America cost Murray almost £400 in travel expenses, fees, and the like it was 'the blow which made Bohn strike [his colours]'. Turner admitted:

though I felt great confidence both in the justice and in the real Law of the Case, I was not free from much anxiety when I saw the fearful expenses which might attend the struggle – and I feel not a little indebted to you for the courageous and manly way in which you supported me in what you properly regarded as a struggle for principle against a dark attempt to infringe the rights of property.

It was not surprising that Murray regarded publishers like Bohn and Routledge as unscrupulous adventurers who despoiled the literary property of others in the name of cheap literature and getting even with American piratical publishers. When it was Bentley's turn to settle he began by dramatically accusing Bohn of scurrilous acts of literary piracy. But Bentley's solicitor warned him, however, to temper his language. 'Bohn is a pirate . . . but he is not a felon! Your illustration, therefore, of a man robbing you of your watch, seems to me to lack a very rank ingredient in order to work it into an analogy.'[10] Devey advised instead hard but respectful out-of-court bargaining, and by the beginning of October a settlement was reached. Bentley received £400 for his copyrights of the three Irving works in question, and the other terms were similar to those imposed by Murray six weeks before.

In view of Bohn's determined opposition to Murray and Bentley prior to his acquisition of the Irving copyrights, it is ironic to find him in 1855 defending his ownership on the very grounds he once argued against:[11]

The Works of Washington Irving, having for the most part been composed and published during his long residence in the Country, are, by the recent decision of the House of Lords, pronounced English copyright. The whole being, now, . . . the property of Henry G. Bohn . . . he is the only legal publisher of them, and will take the necessary measures against infringements of his rights.

The copyright case which ultimately was heard by the House of Lords was *Jefferys* v. *Boosey*.[12] It might well have been Murray and Bentley versus Bohn and Routledge, but these veterans were spared the strain and expenses of an appeal to the highest court and the burden fell instead on two music publishers, Thomas Boosey of 28 Holles Street, Cavendish Square, and Charles Jefferys, 21A Soho Square. It was not entirely coincidental that most of the copyright cases involving foreigners during the first half of the nineteenth century had to do either with American authors or European musical composers. In a sense, both wrote in a language common to the British or sufficiently universal to be understood by them. There was no need to translate either, and as a result they were the natural targets of unauthorized republication.

The facts in the case of *Jefferys* v. *Boosey* were these: In 1831 the Italian composer Bellini sold the copyright of his opera *La Sonnambula* to a fellow citizen of Milan, Ricordi, who in turn gave the British right of publication to the London publishers, Boosey & Son. Boosey took care to register the opera at Stationers' Hall in accordance with the Copyright Act of 1842 and to publish the work in England prior to its appearance in Italy. In 1848 another London publisher, Jefferys, printed 20,000 copies of one of the melodies from the opera and began competing with Boosey's edition. The latter had printed about 50,000 copies but felt none the less that the Jefferys's publication seriously undermined the authorized one. In the autumn of 1849 Boosey took the case to the Court of Exchequer and sought to collect damages of £500 from Jefferys. A judge and jury rejected Boosey's right to an exclusive copyright in a foreign composition. Boosey appealed against this verdict in a Court of Error, and as we have previously noted, the lower court's decision was reversed. Jefferys thus had the next move: either he could settle on the basis of the last decision, or he could appeal to the House of Lords which promised much delay and expense. Eventually he decided to try the latter.

The special significance of the case lies not so much in the legal argument as in the interplay of personalities and procedures. To begin with, fifteen Common Law judges, one Lord Chancellor, four ex-Chancellors, and numerous barristers and solicitors became involved during the five years of litigation. Equally noteworthy was the fact that the House of Lords was indeed the court of last resort, and solicitors warned their clients to avoid becoming entangled in its lengthy and expensive appeal process. This was especially true in the early 1850s when there was growing alarm within the legal profession over the Lords' handling of appeals. In 1856 this discontent culminated in a full-fledged Parliamentary inquiry and a report recommending reform of the appellate procedure, but by then *Jefferys* v. *Boosey* had already been decided. Had it reached the House of Lords a year or two earlier or later the decision might have been different. An analysis of the case stage by stage may indicate why.

Bellini's *La Sonnambula* actually involved Boosey in three lawsuits. The first took place in January 1849 and Boosey successfully defended his copyright against Davidson in the Court of Queen's Bench. The second was against Purday in June of the same year. This time the hearing was in the Court of Exchequer and Boosey lost. Toward the end of 1849 Boosey brought Jefferys to trial, also in the Court of Exchequer. Chief Baron Pollock who handed down the adverse decision in *Boosey* v. *Purday* was absent this time and Baron Rolfe heard the case. Again, however, the judge and jury decided that a foreigner was not entitled to a British copyright.

It is worth noting that by 1849 the Court of Exchequer had persistently ruled against foreigners in three major copyright cases: *Chappell* v. *Purday* (1845), *Boosey* v. *Purday* (1849), and *Boosey* v. *Jefferys* (1849). However, two Common Law Courts: Common Pleas in *Cocks* v. *Purday* (1848) and Queen's Bench in *Boosey* v. *Davidson* (1849) favoured the rights of foreigners. In addition, the Court of Chancery also supported a foreign author in the case of *Ollendorff* v. *Black* (1850), thus apparently equalizing the weight of legal opinion.

This was the situation in the spring of 1851 when the Court of Error received *Boosey* v. *Jefferys* on appeal.[13] The Court of Error met in a room at Westminster known as the Exchequer Chamber. Contrary to its name, it was not part of the Court of Exchequer but served as the place where appeal cases from the three Common Law Courts were held. Judges for such cases were drawn from the two courts not directly involved in the appeal. Thus, in *Boosey* v. *Jefferys* the judges were from the Queen's Bench and the Court of Common Pleas. Since each of the three courts was staffed by one Chief Justice and four puisne justices, ten of these were eligible to serve for a particular appeal case. For *Boosey* v. *Jefferys*, Lord Chief Justice Campbell and Justices Patteson, Wightman, and Erle represented Queen's Bench; and Justices Cresswell, Maule, and Williams came from Common Pleas. These seven judges surprised many by repudiating the decision of the Court of Exchequer and unanimously affirming a foreigner's right to bring various actions, including a defence of his copyright, into a British court. Lord Campbell observed that under statute law the British Parliament could even legislate on behalf of foreigners provided that such laws applied to the sale and distribution of literature within the United Kingdom. Why, he asked, should a foreign author have to cross the English channel and reside in Britain in order to secure a valid English copyright? The distance between Calais and Dover should not make any difference when it came to protecting literary property within the British market.[14]

When this decision was announced most authors and publishers assumed that the issue was settled. So many judges had supported Boosey's claim that it seemed most unlikely that a subsequent appeal would be made to the House of Lords. Yet Jefferys, Bohn, and others who were interested in the unrestricted publication of foreign works immediately began to take the necessary steps to appeal. They called a small preliminary meeting in May and made further elaborate plans for a large public gathering to be held at the beginning of July. Edward Lytton Bulwer was recruited as Chairman of this meeting, and it was carefully designed to attract as many prominent guests as possible. Few publishers would attend, of course, since most of them favoured authorized editions with duly registered copyrights. But authors were divided in their loyalties. Bulwer himself was most anxious to promote an Anglo-American copyright agreement, but at the same time he saw no reason why Britain should protect American authors if America was unwilling to reciprocate. He wondered whether perhaps a certain amount of pressure in the form of republication of American works by anyone in Britain would induce American authors, publishers, and politicians to take seriously the issue of international copyright.

At the time of the public meeting in early July, Henry G. Bohn was in the midst of his own struggle against Murray and was thus Jefferys's natural ally. He and the others present firmly resolved to appeal the copyright issue to the House of Lords, but at the same time they realized that it was not fair to expect one publisher on his own to bear the full expenses of such an appeal. Therefore they formed an association to assist the financing of the undertaking. It was called the Society for Obtaining an Adjustment of the Law of Copyright, and in its prospectus it declared: 'the Society is wholly free from any personal motive and does not desire to infringe upon the property of anyone'. But it looked critically upon the judgment of Lord Campbell and the Court of Error for 'their most mischievous decision'. The Society's Secretary was Charles Stevens, a barrister in Grays Inn who specialized in copyright law. It was not generally known that he was also Jefferys's counsel who had not only handled the appeal before the Court of Error but would also carry the appeal to the House of Lords.[15]

A preliminary hearing took place more than a year later in March 1852 with Richard Comyn representing Boosey and Stevens as counsel for Jefferys. Final permission was then granted and the two parties began to prepare in earnest for the formal presentation. There was no hurry, however, as at least two years generally elapsed before such a case reached the Bar of the House of Lords.

By the nineteenth century the appellate jurisdiction of the Lords was something of a misnomer. The whole House could listen to an appeal, but only those who were 'learned in the law' were permitted to vote, which in practice meant only the Lord Chancellor of England and any ex-Chancellor of either England or Ireland. Depending upon the vicissitudes of politics and the frequency of forming new cabinets, there were from one to four ex-Chancellors in the House of Lords at any given time. Each new Chancellor was automatically given an hereditary title which justified his presence thereafter in the upper chamber. Because Chancellors were essentially politicians with legal training who worked their way up through the ranks climaxing their careers with the Chancellorship, they often returned to power after spending some years in opposition. Occasionally there was no Chancellor at all for a few months due to the indecision or inability of the Government in power to appoint one. When *Jefferys* v. *Boosey* finally reached the Lords in 1854 there were six men eligible to judge the case: four ex-Chancellors – Brougham, Lyndhurst, St Leonards, and Truro; one ex-Chancellor of Ireland – Chief Justice Campbell; and the current Lord Chancellor – Cranworth.

Indulging in a bit of historical conjecture as to what might have happened had *Jefferys* v. *Boosey* come before the Lords in either 1850, 1851, or 1852 one can imagine a very different outcome. Had it been tried in 1850 Brougham might have been the sole Law Lord hearing appeals, a situation troubling to many including Lord Campbell who wrote in his diary for 7 July 1850:

Most portentous of all, Lord Brougham sits alone deciding cases in the House of Lords! I prevented him from summoning the Judges – but he has been hearing several writs of error and appeals without any assistance. This is a mere mockery, and must bring the appellate jurisdiction of the House of Lords into sad discredit. . . . Brougham says truly that he is as good as when he was Chancellor – but then he made very indifferent work of it. Now he resembles a man who, having escaped from Bedlam, thinks himself a great judge.

A few months later Thomas Wilde became Chancellor and assumed the title of Lord Truro. When he was Chief Justice of the Court of Common Pleas he rendered a decision in *Cocks* v. *Purday* favouring the rights of foreign authors. Had *Jefferys* v. *Boosey* come up in the latter part of 1850 or the beginning of 1851 the likelihood would have been that Truro would have sided with Boosey.

From February to December 1852 St Leonards was the Lord Chancellor.

He was, according to Lord Campbell, 'a consummate master of his art but the most vain, conceited and arrogant of mankind'. There was nothing in his background which predisposed him one way or the other with respect to the law of copyright, and, in any case, he soon relinquished the Great Seal.

Lord Cranworth was in office when *Jefferys* v. *Boosey* came before the Lords. Among the recent Chancellors, Lord Campbell held him in highest respect as a jurist who was diligent though admittedly 'not a man of powerful intellect'. There was something else about Lord Cranworth: formerly, as Baron Rolfe of the Court of Exchequer he had rendered the initial decision in *Boosey* v. *Jefferys* in the spring of 1850, and at that time he felt that foreigners living abroad had no right to an English copyright.[16] This gave heart to Jefferys and clearly strengthened his determination to appeal.

During the years 1853–4 those Lords besides Cranworth who took the most active part in hearing appeals were St Leonards and Brougham. According to Lord Campbell:

Brougham coalesced with Cranworth, so as to bring about a decision by a majority; but when he was absent, the two others disagreeing, the vote was one to one, and they unwisely resolved, instead of having the case re-argued before all the law lords, to allow on such occasions the judgment always to be affirmed [i.e. reversing the Court of Error]. But when Brougham was present, he attended so little to what was going on, and so indiscreetly betrayed his ignorance by irrelevant questions put to the bar, that the joint opinion of himself and the Chancellor carried little weight with it, and the law was more and more unsettled by every fresh decision of the court of last resort.

This sort of dalliance brought the appellate jurisdiction of the Lords increasingly under fire. As Richard Bethell, the Solicitor-General, observed in 1855: 'judicial business was conducted before the Supreme Court of Appeal in a manner which would disgrace the lowest court of justice in the Kingdom'. He elaborated further in his testimony before the Parliamentary Select Committee, as described by Lord Granville.

The Solicitor-General was examined yesterday as to the defects of the Appellate Jurisdiction. He, with his most mincing manner and most perfect aplomb, supposed the case of two learned Lords, one of whom [Cranworth] gave judgments without hearing the arguments, ran about the House, conversed with lay Lords, and wrote notes and letters; the other [St Leonards], who made declamatory speeches, thumped the table, asked whether anyone would venture

*to say that was law which had just been laid down by the Lord Chancellor,
and who in short entirely forgot the dignity of a judge of the highest Court
of Appeal.*

The subjects of Bethell's innuendoes were present at the time and were
understandably furious, while Lord Derby and ex-Chancellor Lyndhurst
were reported to have sat back and laughed quietly to themselves.[17]

Despite these allegations the House of Lords' jurisdiction spelled
serious consequences for all litigants, and Jefferys and Boosey were
aware of this as they prepared their cases during 1853–4. At this point
they had no idea which of the Law Lords would attend. There could
be as few as one or as many as six. In the interim, the Chancellor, viewing
the subject of copyright sufficiently complex and significant requested
the Common Law judges to be present for the three-day formal pleading
of the 'cause' which was another hurdle to get over before the case
could proceed. Accordingly, ten of the fifteen judges obliged, although
their function was purely advisory since they had no vote in the final
determination. From the Court of Exchequer were Pollock, Parke,
and Alderson; from Queen's Bench, Coleridge, Crompton, Erle, and
Wightman; and from Common Pleas, Jervis, Maule, and Williams.[18]
These ten judges read their opinions before the Law Lords on 29 June
1854. As might have been expected, the three Exchequer Judges who
had already heard the cases of *Boosey* v. *Purday* and *Boosey* v. *Jefferys* a
few years before stood firm in their denial of British copyright to a
foreigner. They were joined by Jervis, the Chief Justice of the Court
of Common Pleas. Six justices favoured Boosey's position, four having
already listened to the arguments in the Court of Error: Justices Erle,
Maule, Wightman, and Williams. They reiterated their original support
of Boosey, and were joined by Coleridge and Crompton.[19]

In spite of the numerical preponderance of six to four the Lord Chancellor was later to say: 'I do not go into the particular facts of these [copy-
right] cases: they are fully commented upon in the very able opinions
of the judges. I consider it quite sufficient to say that these cases seem
to me only to show that the minds of the ablest men differ on the subject.'
Like his fellow Law Lords, Cranworth merely acknowledged the
opinions of the Common Law judges but did not admit being influenced
by them. Law Lords deliberated exclusively among themselves and
wrote their own briefs, finally rendering their independent and irre-
vocable decision.

Of the six eligible Law Lords, three took an active role in the copyright case: Lord Chancellor Cranworth, Lord St Leonards, and Lord Brougham. This was consistent with their general level of attendance to law business. During 1853 Cranworth had been present for 67 days relating to legal affairs, St Leonards for 36 days, and Brougham for 40. In 1854 their respective attendance was: 78, 43 and 71.

The other three ex-Chancellors were far less involved. In 1853 Lyndhurst devoted five days to law business in the Lords, Truro thirteen, and Campbell three. None of them had taken part in a single appeal case during 1854 while *Jefferys* v. *Boosey* was under consideration.[20] Whether their interest would have changed the outcome is difficult to say, because Cranworth, St Leonards, and Brougham rendered a unanimous decision. However the absence of Lord Campbell might have made a difference. His previous involvement with the case may have influenced him to stay away and possibly the other Law Lords inadvertently scheduled hearings and conferences which conflicted with his responsibilities as Lord Chief Justice of the Queen's Bench. Had he and Truro been involved it is reasonable to assume that they both would have sided with Boosey. We cannot know how Lyndhurst would have voted.

For the three Law Lords active in the case, the issue of residency ultimately assumed greatest importance. Alluding to the distance between Calais and Dover, Lord Cranworth admitted that it was not great but he argued that the law had to draw arbitrary lines and what better demarcation was there than the frontier of a nation? Any suggestion that there was a residual Common Law right to copyright was quashed, and the sole applicable criterion for copyright protection was declared to be statute law. They agreed that only if a foreigner travelled to Britain and remained there long enough to witness the publication of his work was he entitled to copyright protection. Otherwise he could neither claim a copyright himself nor sell the right to a British subject, including a publisher. Their verdict, rendered on the first day of August 1854, sustained Jefferys's position and denied British copyright to foreign authors.

The effect of *Jefferys* v. *Boosey* was to throw open the floodgates to the republication of American works. Reprinters no longer feared court injunctions, and publishers like Sampson Low could only appeal to a sense of honour within the trade not to reprint a new work assigned to him by Harriet Beecher Stowe.[21]

In ordering copies of this work [Sunny Memories of Foreign Lands], *the public are respectfully requested to specify the Author's Editions; as, in consequence of a recent decision in the House of Lords, finding that Foreign Authors had no* LEGAL *protection for their works in this country, the Author has no redress except such as is afforded by public discrimination in purchasing Authors' editions.*

On their part, Mrs STOWE's Publishers have taken care to print such Editions of the present work as can satisfactorily compete with any that can be brought against them.

Many other American works were also subjected to rapid reprinting, among them Ann Stephen's *Fashion and Famine* and Maria Cummin's *The Lamplighter* each of which saw seven imprints!

Publishers of American books like Richard Bentley were overwhelmed by the decision of the Lords. They had counted on a reiteration of the decision by the Court of Error in 1851, and now they were faced with having to renegotiate all their contracts with American authors. While so doing they tried to stay afloat by producing cheap editions of their own earlier works in order to compete with reprinters like Routledge. During the autumn of 1854 Bentley published five shilling editions of Prescott's three major works, *Ferdinand and Isabella*, *Mexico*, and *Peru*, printing 5,000 copies of each only to have Routledge follow suit and issue the very same works in similar quantities.

Prescott had become Bentley's most valuable literary property since the death of J. F. Cooper and so this was a particularly bitter blow. Prior to *Jefferys* v. *Boosey* Bentley had contracted with Prescott to publish the first two volumes of *Philip II*, agreeing to pay the substantial sum of £1,000 per volume. Now this contract was void. Prescott was anxious to salvage as much of the fee as possible and was therefore annoyed by Bentley's revised and what seemed to him trifling offers. Negotiations dragged on, and in an effort to placate Prescott and at the same time protect his own investments, Bentley turned to legal counsel. His solicitor, Devey, together with Alfred Turner and an eminent barrister, James Willes, agreed that a valid copyright could perhaps be secured if Prescott visited London at the time of publication. Bentley even offered Prescott the original £1,000 per volume plus £200 travelling expenses if he would agree to come. However, Prescott was growing old and was in poor health. His vision continued to fail. Having made a trip to Britain as recently as 1850 he felt it too soon to return, and besides he knew there were other publishers like Routledge who would make him handsome offers which he would find hard to resist. Thus, during the summer of 1855 Bentley released Prescott from any remnant of binding contract and obligation. Later Prescott discovered that he could only secure £100 a volume from Routledge, and so, because of their publishing relationship which had dated from 1837, Bentley reconsidered and offered Prescott £125 a volume. Nevertheless, Prescott became increasingly restive. He heard rumours about Bentley's impending bankruptcy and asked his literary agent in London, the banker Russell Sturgis, to investigate. When Bentley discovered this blatant mistrust he was incensed.

Had the mischief you supposed happened to me you certainly should have heard from me and here perhaps you will permit me to say that it would have been more in accordance with the long-continued friendly terms of our correspondence if, when any injurious reports about me reached you, you had addressed yourself to me direct.

On the following day after the receipt of your letter I called on Mr. Sturgis and explained to him that you were entirely in a mistake in supposing that 'I had found it necessary to place my property in the hands of trustees'. I beg to assure you that I have not done so. It is true that at a certain time of my spontaneous act and before any claim on me was unsatisfied, I consulted my principal creditor Mr. Spalding and he and a few others at once kindly accorded to me the time considered requisite to meet my engagements with them – no accommodation from others being required and all Authors paid.

In spite of these assurances, Prescott continued to be wary and increasingly gravitated towards Routledge's orbit, eventually accepting Routledge's offer to publish Volume III of *Philip II*. By this time Bentley could do little other than transfer to Routledge the stereotype plates together with his stock and moral claim in Prescott's earlier works. Routledge paid Bentley £2,600 on the assumption that henceforth Bentley would acknowledge Routledge's title in name if not in law. For Bentley it must have been the final irony to have the arch-pirate, Routledge, claiming the *de facto* right to publish his last successful property in American literature.[22]

Bentley's financial position in the years 1854–8 was not secure. He was forced to take on trustees not of his own choosing who met regularly to make decisions and to supervise the transaction of almost every contract. Thanks to a Minute Book that recorded these proceedings it is possible to trace the somewhat melancholy state of his affairs. His problems stemmed from several sources. Since the late 1840s the business had significantly worsened. Cheap reprints and price-cutting eroded profits. His 'Standard Novels' had once been an innovation, but in time almost every publisher copied the idea and undersold him. Finally, the loss of his copyright property in American authors hurt him irreparably.

In the years immediately following *Jefferys* v. *Boosey* Bentley did everything he could to obtain redress for his losses. To begin with, he wrote to Denis Le Marchant, chief clerk of the House of Commons, asking for suggestions. Was there no way for Parliament to remedy the situation? Le Marchant replied: 'I quite agree with Mr. Gladstone in considering your case one of singular hardship with respect to the American copyright, and yet unhappily no minister could bring it within the category of public wrongs. It is as irremediable a calamity as the illness of your poor son.' Bentley next approached Lord Brougham for assistance, which may seem curious, but it must be remembered that by 1855 Brougham had a reputation, whether deserved or not, of a political and social reformer as well as a prominent author. In two lengthy letters Bentley described his dilemma. Over the years he had paid considerable sums to American authors: James Fenimore Cooper had been the most highly remunerated, to the amount of £12,590; next came Prescott with £2,495, followed closely by Irving with £2,450; Melville received £660; Bancroft, £600; and Rush, £300. This £19,095 could be supplemented by a dozen smaller payments to lesser-known American authors. He continued:

I was the most largely engaged of any London publishers in the purchase of the copyright . . . of American authors, paying for them at the same rate as those of English authors. . . . These contracts were made in reliance on the decision of the various courts [prior to Jefferys v. Boosey]. Some of the works then purchased by me were only recently acquired, and therefore have not repaid the consideration given for them. By the late decision the provision which I had thought . . . I had made for my family in the latter years, has been at once taken from me. Editions upon editions of the works purchased by me are now issued by pirates, and an annual amount taken from me which I am not able to ascertain exactly, but I know to be very large. [Bentley later estimated that he stood to lose about £1,000 income per annum.]

I know that it is only necessary to point out a hardship like this to you, who are known to have interested yourself very kindly on many occasions to

*befriend those whom your Lordship considered to suffer unjustly, to pardon
me for troubling you with this long letter.*

*If you would kindly interest yourself for me, I feel convinced that your
Lordship would be able to point out the peculiar hardship of my case; and that
some compensation should be awarded to me for thus throwing open to the
public what was at the time of the several purchases believed to possess all
the value of English copyrights.*

Brougham was sympathetic but could do nothing.[23] Neither could
Gladstone *eleven* years later.

*As far as I can judge the question really raised is whether the right which you
thought – (and apparently thought with good reason) that you possessed can
be revived.*

*The circumstances seem to involve great hardship! But I am not aware
of any analogous case in which Parliament has given compensation in money
for damage accruing through the decision of a Court of Law.*

As the largest publisher of American works in Britain, Bentley lost
most by the decision of the House of Lords. In the absence of an Anglo-
American copyright agreement, he and other publishers once looked
to the law courts for the defence of their foreign copyrights. But now
that avenue was blocked. As with the United States and Canada, cheap
reprints won the day. Anglo-American copyright seemed farther away
than ever.

Chapter IX

AMERICAN LOBBYISTS IN THE EARLY 1850s

During the years 1849–51 the cause of international copyright became inseparable from the Bulwer family. As we have seen, Edward Lytton Bulwer the novelist was directly involved. His eldest brother Henry was a distinguished diplomat, and as British Minister to Washington in 1849, in a unique position to promote an Anglo-American copyright agreement. Bulwer's only son Robert sailed from Liverpool in October 1850 at the age of eighteen to join his uncle in Washington as an unpaid attaché in the British Legation.[1]

Not long after Robert arrived in Washington his father broached the question of copyright.[2]

I have been working hard lately and much want a holiday, but I fear that is impossible. Alps upon Alps lie before. And I shall have to write much for I fear that I shall not get a shilling from Knebworth [the family estate] this year. . . . Is there any chance, think you, of getting a Copyright for English Authors in America? Pray urge Henry to it. It might make me a rich man.

Robert's reply was discouraging. It reflected his uncle's pessimism as well as his own. They both feared that the American reading public had grown so accustomed to the convenience of buying low-priced reprints of English editions that there would be little or no support for any legislation fostering international copyright. Several months went by before Robert raised the subject again.[3]

The Government is no visible part of the legislative assemblies; they have no direct influence and can bring forward no measure of themselves. Even the

GAP

Secretary of State has no seat in Congress. Consequently the only plan to adopt is to . . . prevail upon some Senator or member of the House of Representatives to bring forward the 'bill of International Copyright'. This it would be almost impossible to do because in this country the reading population is very large and the writing population very small; and no man (for here public men are like candidates on a hustings and everything they do or say is done and said to their constituents), no man would peril his popularity by bringing forth so unpopular a measure.

The happy coincidence of uncle and nephew in Washington soon came to an end. In August 1851 Henry found it necessary to return home temporarily because of ill health. In his absence John F. Crampton who was Secretary of the Legation took charge. Early in the new year it became clear that Henry would not be able to resume his post, and so Crampton was formally appointed British Minister.[4] Crampton was well prepared for his new assignment. He had joined the staff of the legation in Washington in 1845 and following the removal of Sir Richard Pakenham had served for two years as *chargé d'affaires* until Bulwer arrived. Born in 1805 of a distinguished Anglo-Irish family, he matriculated at Eton and then went to Trinity College, Dublin. His father Sir Philip Crampton was a Baronet and surgeon in Dublin and therefore in a position to assist his son to embark upon a diplomatic career. As British Minister in Washington John Crampton was a congenial bachelor who was well liked by most Americans, and Robert Lytton found him a worthy substitute for his uncle. The only reservation he may have had was whether Crampton would favour his father's cause: securing an Anglo-American copyright agreement.

A curious series of events from an unexpected quarter revived the issue. The impetus came indirectly from Thomas William Charles Moore, a special courier attached to the British Legation in Washington who found himself in a unique position to help.[5] Moore was born in Nova Scotia in 1794 and did not take up residence in the United States until 1817 at the request of his uncle Thomas William Moore, the British Agent for Sailing Packets in New York and Boston. The uncle had lived in America since 1800, staying in British-occupied parts of the United States during the War of 1812. In his position as packet agent he performed a variety of commercial and semi-diplomatic services, and after the war found his business thriving due to the renewal of Anglo-American diplomatic and commercial relations. His need for extra help induced him to ask his nephew in Nova Scotia to come and join him. The younger Moore agreed. Initially he carried private mail and diplomatic correspondence for the British Legation from Washington to the port of Boston. Eventually he extended his route to parts of Upper and Lower Canada, riding on horseback during the long winter months when the rivers were frozen. As he became known, the diplomatic staff trusted him with more varied tasks. Thus in 1843 he was asked to accompany the newly appointed Governor General of Canada on the long trip from Boston to Kingston.

Because the uncle was unable to remunerate his nephew adequately, he was always on the lookout for other ways in which T. W. C. Moore might augment his resources. It was natural, therefore, to plead for a job as a government mail carrier when the Post Offices of Britain and America concluded a new agreement in 1845. Unfortunately, appointments of this kind were made from Whitehall without consulting the packet agent in America, and so Moore's candidacy was unsuccessful. A year later his uncle died. T. W. C. Moore then applied to succeed him as a packet agent of the Crown. Again, however, he was disappointed. The best that was eventually arranged was to attach him more closely to the British Legation in Washington as a semi-official courier rather than the more prestigious and remunerative 'Queen's Messenger', and this was his position in 1851 when Sir Henry Bulwer left Washington and Crampton took over as British Minister.[6]

To supplement his income T. W. C. Moore became involved in expediting certain claims that British subjects wanted to bring against the American Government or private American citizens. Two such cases involving Moore were brought to the attention of the Foreign Office. The first involved a young British subject named Thomas McVaye who was drowned while serving with the American Navy. The United States Treasury informed his mother in Liverpool that she could recover her son's back wages if they were applied for by an American resident who held a power of attorney from her. Moore agreed to take on this responsibility and collected the money. However, a year later the woman still had not received her money and could get no satisfactory answer from Moore. The second complaint came from James Harnett whose son had died while serving with the American army in the war against Mexico and who was due not only wages but also land options which were guaranteed to all veterans. Moore offered to settle these claims, but later admitted that after receiving the money he had 'remitted it to my agent in New York (with other monies) to purchase a bill of exchange', and apparently the agent 'absconded to California with nearly a thousand dollars in his hands'. As a result of these mishaps Moore was left 'quite unable to liquidate the debt', although he expressed his intention to repay the money, including interest, in a year's time. In the long run, this experience as a claims agent in addition to his job as a semi-official courier proved just the combination needed by those interested in promoting an international copyright treaty.[7]

Two things seemed to recommend T. W. C. Moore: he was a man of modest finances who was seriously in debt, and since coming to the United States he had had ample opportunity to observe the workings of politics. Taken together these go a long way towards explaining why he became involved in what we would now call influence-peddling. Although no definite proof exists there is evidence that because of his wide circle of acquaintances, a group of American claims agents (who would now be called lobbyists) persuaded Moore to act as an inter-mediary between them and the British Legation in hopes of persuading the latter to employ them as promoters of British interests in America. First and foremost this meant influencing Congress, and more particularly, expediting the passage of a proposed Reciprocity Treaty which would lower tariffs and facilitate commerce between the United States and Canada. Moore may not have been interested in a 'kickback' from these men but it is reasonably certain that he did put them into communi-cation with John F. Crampton who in turn wrote a long letter to Lord Elgin, Governor General of Canada, describing the current state of politi-cal morality and revealing for the first time the existence of a formidable group called the Organization.[8]

A proposition has been made to me with regard to the 'Reciprocity Bill' of so extraordinary a nature that used as I am to the ways and means by which things are carried on here, I did not believe it to be serious until I ascertained beyond the possibility of doubt the source from which it came, and the power of those who made it to fulfil their Engagement should we agree to their terms.

The proposition is simple enough, and is this: – that certain persons engage to carry or procure to be carried through both Houses of Congress, during the next session, the Reciprocity bill upon the payment by me to them or their agent of the sum of 20,000 Pounds, to be divided and used by them for the purpose: – twenty or thirty per cent of the same as a sort of retaining fee; – the rest to be paid after the bill shall have finally passed.

I communicate this to you much more with a view of giving you a specimen of the 'style' of Politics at Washington, than with a view to any practical use that could be made of the information. Even if our Government could dispose of such a sum for such a purpose, I am quite aware that I should scarcely succeed in persuading them that I had not been completely humbugged by whoever brought me the proposal. Indeed I was disposed to look upon it myself as mere nonsense until, to my infinite surprise, I found that it was a perfectly practical proposal, and well considered by those who made it. The worst feature of the case however is that it is accompanied by an intimation that a non-compliance with the terms will ensure the opposition of the 'Organization', as it is called, who make the offer, and they are unfortunately quite powerful enough to cause it to be rejected.

I was always aware that a great deal was done in Congress in this way, and thought that something might be done in regard to the Reciprocity Bill by such means, though I imagined at the same time that we should have peculiar difficulties in applying there were it ever thought expedient to have recourse to them. I was therefore little prepared to have the affair proposed to me 'en bloc' with everything foreseen and prepared, and nothing to be supplied but the moving power – but the truth is that what they call 'Organization' has within the last five or six years been brought to such a System that what may be called the outside Congress is more powerful than the Congress itself, and that there is scarcely a measure the passage or obstruction of which is not previously arranged by mutual compact long before it comes before that body and even before the session begins.

It would be very difficult for me in the compass of a letter to explain to you the nature of the 'Organization' which has made the present overture to me a very reason for knowing the proposal to be seriously intended: it would besides oblige me to mention names which I would not like to trust to the accidents or risk of post offices etc.: I will only say that knowing who they are, and what are the means at their disposal, I am fully convinced that they can pass this bill if they choose, and that they can secure its rejection if they choose. Indeed even their inaction would ensure that.

Crampton then went on to describe his conversation with a powerful member of Congress; one who was not a member of the Organization but knew all about it. Although the allusion is veiled, it clearly refers to Senator Stephen A. Douglas of Illinois, head of the so-called 'Young America' faction of the Democratic Party.

In short as things now stand, I fear that we have not the smallest chance of our getting this question settled by fair means. This has been intimated to me by the only person on whom I have to depend for managing and bringing forward this bill in Congress, in a way which I could not misunderstand, and this makes me anxious to put you in possession of the whole state of the case this early, in order that the Canadian Government may not, under the notion that the recommendation of the Measure in the President's Message at the next Session will ensure its success, be unprepared for what I cannot but think certain, viz. that it will meet this session exactly the same fate as it did on every previous occasion.

The gentleman to whom I allude is the same who had charge of the Reciprocity Bill in Congress last Session: he is the rising man of the rising Party, in the United States, and has by far the best chance of being placed at the head of affairs at the next Presidential Election. At all events as majorities now stand, he is by far the most powerful person in Congress. He is just come to Washington, and I of course took the earliest opportunity of calling upon him, and it was suggested that I should do so by the Parties of whom I have spoken above, in order to see how the land lay with regard to the Reciprocity Bill. We had a very long conversation on the matter, the substance of which it may be interesting to you to know. He began by expressing himself and thought, more strongly than he had ever done before, in favour of the measure, the real advantages of which he set forth in the clearest manner. The next question therefore which arose, was how the Measure was to be got through Congress. He then went into detail into the obstacles which were to be overcome and the means of overcoming them, and in doing so displayed an acuteness and a knowledge of the politics of this Country, which, although I had a high opinion of his talents, surprised me. This is a measure, he said, for or against which there cannot be got up any National or Party feeling. We cannot therefore hope to carry it by a hurrah! It is one which requires great study to understand its advantages or even its bearing on the different Interests of the Country: its supporters are friendly to it, not on any general Principle, but from various local and peculiar considerations; the opposition to it is of the same varied character; the only means of getting it is therefore one which involves great knowledge of men's characters, of their local and personal interests and prejudices – great knowledge of the question in its bearing on each of these interests – great tact in the manner of approaching the subject with different men – and above all great labor in keeping account of the 'ayes and noes' etc. And when we are assured of a majority, keeping it up to the mark at the moment required. I have, he said, carried measures in this way myself, and I know the hard work it requires. With regard to the present

Bill, much as I desire its success, I have too much on my hands to render it possible for me to undertake much of that sort of work. With respect to what you [Crampton] yourself could do, it would no doubt be useful that you should speak to some of our People with regard to certain political bearings of the measure, particularly as regards its bearing on annexation: but your attempting to do more than this would, from your position, do more harm than good. An agent from Canada, particularly if a man of any prominence in the Canadian Government, would also do more harm than good – although if some Gentleman well acquainted with the details of the Question should happen to be at Washington at the time, it would be useful.

This of course brought me straight up to the Question – whom then are we to employ? To whom are we to apply?

This is the difficult part of the business. It is difficult to fix upon one person: – one man may be good to influence a particular set of men, who, if he attempted to act upon another set, would, although he should use the proper arguments, do more harm than good. We then ran over some names – I seemed to find objection to them on some account or other: – but at length, after several minutes leaning his head on his hand in apparently profound reflection, he said there is a man, who, if we could get him to act – with the assistance of some others whom he could command – might do what we want better than any other in the U.S., and who, if he would take up these things in earnest, I think, would ensure our carrying the Bill. He then, to my surprise I confess, though I somewhat previously prepared for it, named the very person from whom the proposal stated at the beginning of my letter was brought to me. Now this man I also know to be the great 'faiseur' for the person I was talking to, in his capacity of Candidate for the Presidency and also to be chief mover of the sort of secret 'organization' I have mentioned by which almost any measure whatever, unless it happen to have a decided National Character, can be carried. I leave you to draw your own conclusion as to the way things hang together here, but I have even much more direct evidence of the means which are employed to bring about measures in this great Republic.

I fear I have troubled you with rather a long epistle on the subject without any more practical result than a little insight as to the blessing of Democratic Republics and their superior purity.

At the time Crampton sent this lengthy dispatch to Lord Elgin, Robert Lytton was serving as clerk in the British Legation and may well have transcribed the letter for him. Five days later he wrote to his father, mentioning the topic of copyright for the first time in six months and hinting that there were 'persons in New York who I think likely can give me the best information, as to what can be done or cannot be done'. This was apparently another reference to T. W. C. Moore.

It would be hopeless to get a bill through Congress about International Copyright, unless indeed the authors in England were willing to subscribe among themselves for a certain amount – perhaps ten or twelve thousand pounds – for a sum to buy the American Congress, and then seriously and without joking – but in sad and sober earnest, I think the thing might be done. This however is confidential, and I fear the possibility turned to no practical use. I cannot very well explain my reasons for making this suggestion, in a letter, but you would be amused I think by a peek behind the cowslips of politics here.

Robert's next communiqué to Bulwer echoed many other of Crampton's points and explained why the seemingly whimsical suggestion in his last letter was now a serious proposition. He said that he realized that the scheme would appear 'humbug and an impossibility', yet in view of the way Americans did things it was a 'perfectly simple and practical proposition'. If his father could raise the requisite funds in England, Robert was confident that a copyright bill 'could be brought forward, carried and passed this next session of Congress'. He then returned to the subject of the Organization.

So powerful and widely spread is this system of 'Organization' that the fate of almost every measure is generally known and settled long before it is brought into the House and before even the session commences. I was at first inclined to consider the whole thing a 'mare's nest' and a 'humbug', but overtures which have lately been made to our Legation by the 'Organization' with reference to other matters, have disclosed beyond the possibility of a doubt the power of those who make these propositions to effect what they undertake and to 'burke' any measure they choose.

As to those American authors and publishers who had previously supported international copyright, he said: 'these men can again be brought forward and will answer very well as a cover for the real working of the ring'. Above all, strict secrecy must be maintained or else there was the risk of some Anglo-American diplomatic crisis intruding itself upon the deliberations of Congress 'before the bill is smuggled through'.[9]

Those who knew about the Organization were always careful not to mention any names or reveal its methods, thus the discovery and reconstruction of what contemporaries intentionally kept secret has provided one of the most intriguing challenges of this research. Details are sometimes lacking, but enough have come to light so that we can fairly accurately surmise what happened. Contrary to Crampton's and Lytton's initial impression, the Organization was comparatively new. Had it existed for several years past, the likelihood was that Sir Henry Bulwer would have made use of it in his efforts to promote the Reciprocity Bill in July 1850. That he was clearly unaware of its existence can be seen from the following private dispatch to the Foreign Secretary, Lord Palmerston.[10]

With reference to my private letter of the 17th of June . . . relating to the employment of secret service money for the purpose of securing or expediting the passage of the Reciprocity Bill through Congress, I beg to say that I have since my former communication reflected much upon the subject, and made some inquiries. There can I believe be no doubt that members of Congress could be found subject to venal influences and a portion of the press might in the same way be controlled.

But my opinion is against any direct attempts of the kind: – what I should recommend is employing a skillful lawyer accustomed to manage bills in Congress.

To give him a good fee and promise him an additional one in case of success.

Such a person knows members intimately, has them to supper, their wives visit each other, and a measure having of itself a strong support, is thus considerably facilitated.

I think it might also be advisable to promise the American Consul in New Brunswick a handsome consideration as his testimony will go for something, if the bill passes . . .

I should leave every other matter in the hands of the lawyer employed.

The *prima facie* evidence suggests that the Organization was less than a year old when it approached T. W. C. Moore. If this is true its power must have come from its membership, not its longevity. From later sources we know that the head of the group was a Tennessee lawyer and claims agent in Washington named Joseph Knox Walker. Fortunately for our purposes one of his few surviving letters reveals the probable genesis of the Organization.

In December 1850 he wrote to William L. Marcy, former Governor of New York State and more recently Secretary of War under President Polk, suggesting that an association be formed to assist American inventors and patent-holders to sell rights to their discoveries in London at the Great Exhibition of 1851.

The effort of this association would be to present these specimens and patents favorably, have them noticed abroad and in some instances disposed of advantageously – charging them a cash retaining fee and a contingent fee dependent upon the disposal of their patents abroad, etc.

The association would be composed of two types of men: prominent ones like Marcy, R. J. Walker, Judge Mason, and Edmund Burke; and lesser known younger men like Beverley Tucker and Knox Walker himself. If the notion appealed, Marcy was asked whether he would be interested in being one of those sent to London. Robert J. Walker and J. Y. Mason countersigned this proposition, clearly indicating that two key personalities had already been enlisted.

Marcy's initial reaction was favourable, judging by an entry in his diary:

J. K. W. has made me a suggestion to go to the Great world convention at London. I am inclined to accept the invitation provided the arrangements can be made to my satisfaction. . . . I must be assured that all my expenses will be paid.

When Marcy arrived in Washington, D.C., in early January 1851 he set about prosecuting claims before the Government, interspersed with dinner meetings with both Walkers and Beverley Tucker. After one of these he noted, 'met the associates concerning patents. Was placed on the Committee to report outlines of the association. Mr. Ashmun made the sketch.'[11] The patent work abroad did not prove as successful as anticipated, but the men who were involved found that they had another interest in common: many of them acted as claims agents for people seeking land grants or other government dispensations. Knox Walker had been Recorder of land warrants since 1847 and no doubt realized the potential of group pressure on Congress in this area.

One of the reasons why claims agents were necessary was that there was no way a private citizen could directly sue the United States Government to collect damages or recover property. Each such claim had to go through both Houses of Congress either as a separate bill or in disguise as a rider on another measure. Individuals almost invariably had to employ the services of an agent unless they were lucky enough to obtain the sympathy of one of their elected representatives. The latter route was slow and uncertain at best, whereas it was in the interest of a claims agent to earn his fee. One of their number described his work:[12]

I am an agent for the prosecution of claims, arising under existing laws of Congress . . . I suppose there are some thirty or forty agents resident of this City, besides ex-Members of Congress and others, who visit the seat of Government to represent individuals who live at a distance, before the Departments and Congress.

An advertisement in a Washington directory by an attorney and counsellor at law further elaborated:[13]

Prosecutes Claims of all kinds against the United States, including Pension Bounty Land and Land Title Cases, either before Congress or any of the Executive Departments or Bureaus, and likewise Claims of our citizens against Foreign Governments, either before the State Department or Boards of Commissioners established for their adjudication:

Solicits the issuance of Letter Patent for Inventions, from the United States and from Foreign Governments. . . .

Their fees varied. Some charged a retaining fee regardless of their results, but more commonly they based their charges on a commission or percentage of the amount awarded to their client. Daniel Webster once explained to his son how he arrived at what to ask.[14]

In all former cases of recovery of claims against foreign governments, I have received the commission of five per cent. I have known no smaller charge in general either in the English, Spanish, Danish, or Mexican cases, but as Mr. Dorr paid a good deal of personal attention to this case I should be content to charge only one half the customary commission.

Other agents charged as much as ten per cent or more, depending upon the size of the claim and the extent to which incidental expenses were advanced by the client. Gradually it became clear to those with vested interests, business or otherwise, that they would have to pay lobbyists if they hoped to get things done. A correspondent from Boston addressed Senator Charles Sumner concerning tariff regulations:[15]

It is reported here that there will be some modification of the Tariff before Congress rises – doubtless to satisfy the important interests of Pennsylvania, meaning doubtless votes. Now the Foreign Importers of New York, have a large fund, out of which they support agents at Washington, to attend to their interests and most admirably they are attended to, witness the Tariff of 1846, which if it had been made [by] the Parliament of Great Britain could not have been more favourable to English interests.

The kinds of claims which agents customarily exploited involved compensation for lost property, applications for land, requests for patronage and office, and arranging contracts and subsidies. One of the most notorious subsidy cases was handled in an almost flamboyant manner by Edward Knight Collins, a prominent owner of sailing vessels on the East Coast. He made no secret of his attempts to gain government support for the construction and operation of trans-Atlantic steamships. From his point of view it was a matter of patriotic pride that America should have a steamship service to rival that of Samuel Cunard. With this conviction he enlisted the aid of a number of other people whose interests might be served by such a service, and in 1847 they were successful in securing an annual subsidy of $385,000 from the United States Post Office. To express his appreciation for their help Collins anchored one of his new steamships on the Potomac River and entertained large numbers of government officials, Congressmen, and leading Washingtonians. Later that year his subsidy was increased to $853,000 per annum in further recognition of his services to a grateful nation![16]

Among the claims involving compensation for lost property, one created a scandal which unnerved even the most inveterate congressional manipulators. It was known as the Galphin Claim and part of its impact was that it touched the Zachary Taylor Administration so closely. Like many claims against the United States Government, it went back to Revolutionary times. In 1773 the British Government incurred a debt to the Galphin family. After the War this obligation devolved on the new state of Georgia, and in time was passed on to the Federal Government. By 1830 no action had been taken, and so it was decided to engage a private attorney to prosecute the claim. The value of the original land plus the interest which was accruing must have been a distinct inducement to undertake the task since the agent stood to gain half of the amount recovered. A lawyer named George Crawford was awarded the job, and under his relentless pressure Congress finally authorized the Secretary of the Treasury, R.J. Walker, to pay $43,518 compensation to the Galphins, of which Crawford received $21,401. This amount covered only the value of the land, however. Crawford therefore continued to press the Government for the accumulated interest of $191,352.

Walker balked at this, but his successor, William M. Meredith, with the advice of the Attorney General, acquiesced. Crawford thus received a total of $115,577. When the settlement was made in 1850 Crawford was no longer a lowly claims agent but had risen to be the Secretary of War![17]

By far the greatest proportion of a claims agent's time was devoted to settling disputes involving land. The 1840s and 1850s saw an incredible expansion in the territory annexed to the nation. In rapid succession came the acquisition of the Oregon territory, the War with Mexico, the annexation of Texas, and the almost overnight conversion of California from a foreign possession to a State of the Union. These new territories transformed not only the nation's geography but its economy as well. East coast manufacturers had new markets to supply; immigrants needed outfitting on their way westward; steamships were envisioned as links between the Atlantic and the Pacific; an Isthmian Canal was projected. It became difficult for Americans to separate dreams from reality. And behind it all was heavy speculation and intrigue in land.

Military bounties caused many of the problems. Ever since the American Revolution soldiers had been induced to join the army by a promise of land. Depending upon how long they served and in what capacity, they were entitled to warrants which they could redeem either for cash or for acres of unsettled land. It was recognized by some that a profit could be made by selling these warrants for as much as the market would bear. Wall Street eventually stabilized their price, but speculators managed to get around this by purchasing them on the East coast and later disposing of them at much higher prices in the West where the land was located and consequently had meaning and value.

In the 1850s a number of land bills were passed which significantly increased the number of those who qualified for warrants. As one modern scholar quipped, 'not only officers and fighting men but musicians, militiamen, marine clerks or landsmen, wagonmasters and teamsters, chaplains and Indian-fighting volunteers' became eligible. Concurrently more than 61,000,000 acres were added to the national domain as bounty land.[18] Located mainly in the states and territories of Iowa, Illinois, Missouri, Wisconsin, Minnesota, Kansas, and Michigan, it was comparable in size to all of New England plus New Jersey, Delaware, and Maryland. Western Senators were hostile to this bounty legislation since many of their constituents were 'squatters' who had no legal claim to the property they had settled on and were therefore in danger of being dispossessed by the land warrants of Eastern veterans or speculators. Southerners were equally upset by the increased distribution of bounties and put considerable pressure on the Government to limit their sale. New Englanders, on the other hand, welcomed their increase because they stood to gain as a result of their families having served in all the wars since the beginning of the Republic.

The Bounty Law of 1850 tried to curb the obvious abuses. The Secretary of the Interior issued a memorandum directing local communities to insure that:[19]

a bounty [goes] to the soldier and not to agents and speculators. . . . The policy of this law in all its provisions is to discourage speculation in the claims of soldiers. . . . Speculators are therefore admonished that they can acquire no right by purchase which will be recognized by this Department.

However, even before the session of 1850 was finished the advocates of saleable warrants were hard at work trying to suspend the provisions of the new law. They alternately succeeded and failed at this throughout the decade. Only later with the Homestead Act of 1862, was the tradition of military bounties finally jettisoned.

The War with Mexico and the resulting Treaty of Guadelupe Hidalgo spawned countless claims for property compensation. In return for the large amount of land acquired from Mexico, the United States assumed some of the claims which American citizens had upon the Mexican Government.[20] Congress allocated $3,250,000 for this purpose and established a Commission to adjudicate the many claims and disperse the funds. Its most spectacular award went to George A. Gardiner who received $428,750 for the 'loss' of his mining interests. The truth was that they weren't worth anywhere near this amount, and so as soon as Gardiner received the money he skipped the country to evade arrest on charges of gross fraud. Sentenced to ten years *in absentia*, he ultimately committed suicide. This and similar incidents seriously undermined confidence in the Government's Claims Commission, and years later those claimants who felt they had been neglected or vastly undercompensated, were allowed to apply to Congress for further redress. However, to do so meant hiring a claims agent, reverting once again to the all too familiar pattern.

The claims against the new State of Texas were even larger and more numerous than those against Mexico.[21] Before becoming a part of the Union, Texas issued its own currency and bonds which were jeopardized by the Mexican War and annexation. As part of the 'Compromise of 1850' the United States Congress agreed to assume the Texas debt up to the amount of ten million dollars. An initial five million was paid by the Treasury, but the Texas legislature decided to use this amount for internal needs rather than settling claims. By January 1852, with $8,330,000 in claims outstanding and only five million still due the Texas legislators decided to scale down all awards, some to receive only 87½ per cent on the dollar, others, 20 per cent. During this period the value of these claims was so uncertain that many people were willing to gamble on their worth. Speculation was rampant, and hordes of agents were being paid to influence members of Congress. Letters from constituents to their Congressmen were common;[22] as, for example, this one to James Buchanan:

Permit me to ask what you think are the chances of the present or the next Congress redeeming the Texas debt? There has been a great deal of money made by the improvement of notes here, and I have a great inclination to enter into the speculation a few hundreds.

Senator Hannibal Hamlin, who was approached by one of his colleagues with an offer to supply bonds at half the going rate, recalled:[23]

When the representatives of Texas were trying to induce the government to assume the heavy debt of their State, there was more than one member of Congress who profitted financially through unscrupulous lobbyists who offered them Texas bonds at a low figure. One prominent Democrat, [later] identified with the scheme to bribe Kansas to adopt a pro-slavery constitution by offering her land, and who afterwards was an unsuccessful candidate for Vice-President, laid the basis of his private fortune by buying up Texas scrip at this time.

In August 1852 Senator Sam Houston of Texas thought it time to call for an official inquiry and resolved that a Committee be appointed:[24]

to inquire into abuses, bribery or fraud in the prosecution of claims before Congress, Commissions or Departments, or in passing through Congress bills embracing private, individual or corporate interests or in obtaining or granting contracts, and that said committee have power to send for persons and papers and examine witnesses on oath. . . .

The Committee took more than seven months to collect evidence, during which time Senator Borland replaced Houston as its Chairman.

The resulting report, published in March 1853, thus carried Borland's name.[25] It consumed more than two hundred pages and was a fascinating mixture of self-righteousness and hypocrisy. Although legislators had good reasons to mistrust claims agents, all too often they had come from their own ranks. Only one month before the Borland Report was released Congress had passed legislation to prohibit members of the Government from accepting payment for the prosecution of private claims and bills.[26] The dilemma was clear:[27]

Let once the belief be impressed upon the minds of the people that the justice or the generosity of this government is sold, either directly or through agents, to those who claim it; let it be known to them that, intermediate between them and the government, there is a mercenary political priesthood through whom alone, and by the private payment to whom of a tax in money, in addition to the public tax already paid for the support of the government, the benefits of its legislation or administration can be obtained; let them become convinced that personal interests, and not the general welfare, control its functions; let these signs of degeneration, depravity, and corruption, give form and pressure to popular opinion – what would the government be worth to the people? What good purpose, moral, social, or political, would it be capable of serving? In place of confidence, it would be regarded with distrust. Instead of respect, it would merit contempt. It would not be loved, but hated. And then the people, finding the government a thing apart from themselves, as despotisms are in other countries, and in its operations antagonistical to their true and legitimate interests, would no longer need its services nor tolerate its existence.

Claims agents, acting on their own or in association with each other, came in for particular criticism.[28]

It is shown in this case (which is but an epitome of the results of general observation) that a system of agencies exists; and there is reason to believe that it is extending farther and growing stronger with every succeeding session of Congress, whereby the national legislation is more or less influenced and controlled, (or is held to be so by those interested in its results,) not so much by principles of public justice, or regard for the general welfare, as by considerations of personal interest. And the effect of this, in one respect at least, is the encouragement by public expense, of a class of persons who are not only useless in their vocation to society, making no contribution to its welfare, but who hang like parasites upon its industry, and tend, by their daily practices, to poison the very sources of its prosperity.

Finally, on 24 February 1855, Congress took legislative action to stem the tide of influence-peddling and to unburden Congressional committees of the responsibility to process and evaluate every private claim against the Government. Under 'An Act to Establish a Court for the Investigation of Claims Against the United States', the President was empowered to appoint three judges and a solicitor to hear cases and to represent the interest of the Government respectively. Regular sessions began in October 1855 and thereafter all claims had to conform to stipulated procedures.[29] Rather than forcing witnesses to reside in Washington during hearings, written testimony was taken by Commissioners travelling throughout the country and attorneys representing claimants would argue the merits of each case before the court.

Here was the opportunity inadvertently given to former claims agents, and they were not slow to recognize it. Because someone had to represent plaintiffs and prosecute claims before the newly-created court, who could better do the job than those most familiar with the ins-and-outs of the business. Among the attorneys who plead before the court we find the familiar names of Joseph Knox Walker from Tennessee and Robert J. Walker from Washington; also F. P. Stanton who was later to be a partner of both Knox Walker and R. J. Walker. Admittedly there was much less scope for influencing Congress. However, the Court of Claims' jurisdiction was merely advisory and therefore there was always room for agents to intercede before Congress acted on the court's recommendations. Thus, in spite of their province being narrowed, claims agents still carried on. The Civil War years and the ensuing decades amply demonstrate that lobbying was far from over.

Chapter X

THE ORGANIZATION

Membership in the Organization was intentionally kept a secret, but it is likely that the following belonged: J. Knox Walker, R. J. Walker, W. L. Marcy, Beverley Tucker, Edmund Burke, John Y. Mason, George Ashmun, L. C. Levin, and G. M. Dallas. All but the last two were what might be called original members. There may also have been others, but their names have not come to light. The acknowledged leader was Joseph Knox Walker (1818-63). His contemporary epithet, 'Prince of the Lobbyists', belies his comparative anonymity. Standard works of reference and biography ignore him. If his name appears in a work of history it is usually as a nephew of President James K. Polk, since Walker's father, James, was married to one of Polk's sisters. Walker entered Yale University in 1835, graduating in three years. One of his Yale classmates later made a revealing comment about him in his diary:[1]

Had a visit in the afternoon made me by William Stuart Fleming and Joseph Knox Walker two of my Late College classmates. . . . (Knox has perhaps less genius, but occasionally more industry, – besides, he has a practical business kind of sense which will make him succeed anywhere in any business.)

Knox then began to study law with Gen. Gideon J. Pillow in his home town of Memphis, Tennessee, but soon became involved in Polk's efforts to be elected State Governor. During two unsuccessful election campaigns he served as Polk's private secretary, and when Polk eventually returned to Memphis in 1841 to resume practising law Knox joined him. For the next few years life remained quiet. However, in the Presidential election of 1844 Polk was the 'dark horse' nominee of the Demo-

cratic Party, and the following spring Knox found himself in Washington
as the Private Secretary of a President. At this time he was in his late
twenties and although trusted by Polk he never really settled down,
as Polk recorded in his diary in 1847.[2]

*I learned with surprise that, without giving me any notice, he had gone to
Annapolis on a party of pleasure. I was vexed at the occurrence, and think
it so thoughtless and inexcusable on his part that I must require an explanation
when he returns. In truth he is too fond of spending his time in fashionable
and light society, and does not give that close and systematic attention to business
which is necessary to give himself reputation and high standing in the estima-
tion of the more solid and better part of the community. This I have observed
for some months with great regret.*

Knox's sociability was one of his chief assets when he turned his
attention to lobbying after Polk's term of office was over. In the spring
of 1849 Polk departed from Washington, but Knox stayed on. Having
made numerous political contacts while assisting the President with
backstairs negotiations, he saw before him a promising career as an
attorney and claims agent. The extent to which he was already involved
in lobbying is brought out in a letter to Lewis Coryell dated May 1849,
in which he described the summer as a slack season with small political
profits. However, he urged Coryell to join him in Washington as there
were still things to be done.[3]

*Anthracite and Cumberland Coal are articles much in demand and advertised
for. What will it cost you to deliver the best of each kind here, and also what
in Philadelphia? And what is the bidding price at which you would be willing
for me to contract for you on joint account. The Mississippi Steamer is ordered
to the Mediterranean – soon sails and must have coal there. Can't you come
down and look after this?*

*I am anxious to have settled up our unfinished venture to California –
can't it be arranged? There ought to be about $2,000 coming from this source.
Did you ever look to it?*

During the next few years he built up an apparently successful claims
agency. There was no doubt that he was one of the upper crust among
influence-pedlars. A fellow agent indicated that he considered him too
casual and slipshod, but this judgment did not seem to hinder his dividing
the profits of a Mexican claim with him. That Walker was able to
persuade three of Polk's former cabinet members, R. J. Walker, J. Y.

Mason, and W. L. Marcy to join the Organization speaks for itself. Walker's prestige was further enhanced when he and Beverley Tucker served as unofficial managers for Stephen A. Douglas's campaign to become the Democratic nominee for President.

One of Walker's cases was cited in the Borland Report as an example of the kind of corruption prevailing among claims agents. He had collected over $4,000 from naval officers and seamen in return for securing legislation whereby they would receive extra pay for having served off the West Coast of North America during the Mexican War. For doing this he charged an average of $10 per sailor and $50 per officer. When the Senate Committee of 1852–3 learned of this they accused him of defrauding his naval clients and exerting improper influence on Congress. The fact of the matter was that no member of Congress had taken any interest in the sailors' claims until Walker came along. Grudgingly the Report admitted that Walker had performed the services for which he had been hired and had signed no contract with the sailors but left his fee up to their discretion. Confident that without his efforts the sailors would have received nothing, his defence rested on the assertion that his legal activities were no secret but were publicly advertised in the Washington press. Eventually the investigating committee acknowledged that Walker had exerted no more influence than others similarly employed and concluded that if anything was at fault it was the system of influence which pervaded American politics and society.

Towards the end of 1852 Walker left Washington to return to Memphis where he continued his agency for claims. A few years later a city directory listed Brown, Stanton, & Walker as Attorneys at Law with offices in both Memphis and Washington. Frederick P. Stanton, their Washington partner, was a former Tennessee Representative to Congress.[4]

Walker himself finally held public office in 1857 when he was elected a State Senator. Like many faithful Democrats in the South he was against secession, but when the Civil War broke out he sided with the Confederacy. As a Confederate colonel he had his own regiment. When severe illness overpowered him in 1863 he was treated as an officer and gentleman by the commander of the Northern troops that occupied Tennessee and given safe conduct to Memphis where he died at the home of his brother-in-law. His career was thus cut short, as had been so many others, before its promise materialized. Although a contemporary described him as one of the worst bank managers Memphis ever had, if he had lived Walker would probably have played a major role in either state or national politics.

Of the younger members of the Organization, Beverley Tucker like Knox Walker had built up a considerable reputation peddling influence. Born in 1820 and named after his uncle Nathaniel Beverley Tucker, the well-known judge and author, he always went by his middle name. Brought up in Virginia, he attended school in Richmond and entered the university there in 1835. Apparently he was an indifferent student and soon left to take a job with some construction engineers. After a short while the lure of the land brought him back to his family and he managed one of his father's plantations. Married in 1841, he continued as a gentleman farmer until in 1844 a fateful change occurred. His wife told the story years later.[5]

I don't know how the desire for a change came about. Crops had failed . . . some security debts . . . pressed for payment; and an offer to go into business in Richmond was made . . . and accepted. He saw afterwards that it was a mistake. Wholly unsuspicious, not trained to careful business habits, confiding implicitly in the honor and integrity of others, he entered into mercantile life with a firm that was afterwards found to be already tottering. He put in his capital and he gave enthusiastic work and energy to this new business. He was sent by the partners to New Orleans, and on his return found that failure was imminent and that the house would have to close up. The other partners had no moneys – creditors came forward to compromise; but [Tucker] . . . said he would pay one hundred cents on the dollar, and thus after six months' effort his whole life and career was changed, and he was, besides, under promise to pay this large indebtedness.

The Mexican War created new opportunities for Tucker. He contracted to supply the Government with munitions, afterwards finding someone who could make them, displaying a natural inclination to arrange matters first and then persuade people that he could perform whatever he undertook. This penchant worked strongly in his favour as a lobbyist. Through John Y. Mason, a friend of the family who happened to be Polk's Secretary of the Navy (and later a member of the Organization) Tucker secured another valuable war contract to supply the Navy with coal, again serving as middleman between the suppliers and the Government. His financial position remained desperate, however, and to help remedy this he made frequent trips to the Capitol in order to meet influential members of Congress and the Administration. Late in 1847 he moved to Washington to become a partner with another young attorney, practising law and acting as a claims agent. A year later he apologized to his uncle and namesake for not spending Christmas with him as planned.

It is not for one just rising from my prostrate condition of three long and weary years, inflicted by Debt and embarrassments, to follow the bent of his inclinations and his pleasures! . . . My Business since my return to Washington has quadrupled itself – and it is Business which allows not a moment for Holidays.

The seriousness of his efforts to extricate himself from debt could also be measured by his not having gone hunting all fall, and when another Christmas season came around (December was also the month when Congress convened) he again disappointed his uncle by not joining him for the holidays: 'Alas! however, a poor man is the slave of circumstances and the vassal of necessity'.[6]

Not long before his uncle's death Beverley wrote him the following letter, remarkable for its insight into the activities and attitudes of a lobbyist.[7]

> *Washington, D.C.*
> *April 1851*

I have postponed answering your letter until I felt determined definitely to go to California. This I have now done and there remains but one contingency, and that the arrangement of some matters, so as to leave with an easy mind. I prepare to sail from New York in the steamer of the 11th, and shall be gone five months, which will give me two months in that country! I have acquired considerable property there in the way of fees, and go there mainly to look after it. I expect too, to get a heavy business here for the next Session, and as I have resolved to take no cases unless attended with a retainer fee, I hope to gather in some cash by the Excursion. Even these two considerations might not form a sufficient inducement to make me leave my family and encounter the other risks of such a journey, were I not lured by the fact that I can go and return free of charge.

As to your sending any money out, I frankly say if you have to borrow it at any or much inconvenience, don't do it – if otherwise and if you can entrust me with $2,000, I will promise to make it 'another two' or 'five' if possible. My own private opinion is that I might do well with it. But of this be the judge yourself and estimate in your calculations only by my own integrity *and fruitful stewardship. I do much wish to see* you *easy and comfortable in your old days, . . . to see your latter and all your days peaceful and happy and your brilliant mind undimmed, and your generous heart unoppressed, by the belittling theme and struggle after the ways and means, that induce me to hold out to you the Bird of promise in that distant Eldorado. So do as you* think right, *only write to me.*

I have sometimes thought that if it were possible, *even for a man of my limited capacity, to devote all his time and energies 'soul, mind, body, passions, feelings, strong and weak,' to any one subject of literature, science, or philosophy,* as I have had to do *for ten years to this arduous and lowering struggle after the almighty Dollar – that Daniel Webster would have been an* idiot to me! *My Sir, it is my waking, my sleeping, my walking, my talking, my sitting, my eternal, all-absorbing, and haunting, yet* hateful *thought. I can't help it! Would to God I could.*

As it turned out, Beverley never made the trip to California. Instead he and Knox Walker threw themselves into organizing Senator Douglas's campaign to secure the Democratic nomination for the Presidency as well as trying to persuade R. M. T. Hunter of Virginia to be his running-mate. Somewhat defensively he wrote to the latter:

Young America *is to speak out and is to be* heard *and* heeded *too at the coming election, and we intend to prove to you that it is not necessary to be professional men* in Politics or Science *to be felt in the country. I know that is the estimate* you *among others have put upon a parcel of us, who were driven (in my case at least) to seek our daily bread by* Lobbying in Washington. *We therefore enter this contest with a* little feeling.

Tucker devoted much of 1851 and early 1852 to promoting Douglas's candidacy prior to the Democratic nominating convention but it was to no avail for the Party again fastened on a dark horse, Franklin Pierce, rather than the more prominent and notorious Cass and Douglas.

During this period Beverley was far from idle as a claims agent. His financial situation steadily improved but he longed to free himself completely from past burdens, especially as ill health overtook him at the end of 1851. He confided to his brother, Randolph, that he was not afraid to die but dreaded the thought of leaving his wife and family unprotected. Someone must know how his affairs stood, in particular those ventures which might materialize in future commissions if they were successful. Reflecting on his great expenditures of energy in both politics and handling claims he lamented: 'I never have had such a year of anxiety and trouble in all my life.' He went on to say that he was insured for $10,000 which would go to his wife and children if anything happened to him. As for his debts, they amounted to about $10,000 but this figure could be reduced to about $6,000 if his household possessions, horses, and carriage were sold. His wife Jane could always return to Virginia and live with her mother, and he was particularly proud that amidst all the debts he had taken upon himself he had never jeopardized 'all Jane's interest in her father's *Real Estate*'. If all went well during the coming year he hoped to realize $20,000 to $25,000: a bond worth $5,000 from a Philadelphia firm when the Texas debt was settled; another $5,000 from a client who would pay as soon as money and credit eased sufficiently; $2,000 to $10,000 from a business speculation; and as much as $8,000 once the contract for supplying marble for the Capitol was signed. Beverley explained to his brother that he would certainly be able to discharge the last of his debts and once again be a free man could he but live a year or two more. If, on the other hand, the worst should occur, 'Knox Walker is intimately acquainted with these things', and could help collect what was due him.[8]

When Douglas failed to secure the Democratic Party's nomination, Tucker threw his support to the official candidate, Franklin Pierce, hoping for some kind of patronage reward. Through an old family friend, Jefferson Davis, he applied for the post of Marshal for the District of Columbia, and although Davis was a member of Pierce's Cabinet Tucker was passed over, reflecting the fact that he was still sufficiently impecunious that party patronage was beyond his reach.

Probably resenting this, he allowed himself to become the centre of a nascent revolt within the Democratic Party when the full session of Congress met for the first time under the Pierce Administration in December 1853. One of the minor patronage decisions which each House traditionally made at the commencement of a new term was the appointment of a printer. Ordinarily the job went to the proprietor of the Washington newspaper that was acknowledged as the spokesman for the majority party. Often the same printer enjoyed contracts from both the House and the Senate. However, in December 1853 the House contract was renewed, while the Senate's contract went to Beverley Tucker, highlighting the presence of a split within the party. Tucker qualified for the contract because in September he had become the proprietor of a new Washington daily, the *Sentinel*. Whether the paper was established in anticipation of securing the printing contracts of both Houses is uncertain, but mystery surrounded its financial backing and its Congressional support.[9]

By this time Tucker was *persona non grata* with Pierce's followers who realized that he was beginning to cast about for a candidate to support for President in 1856. He finally chose James Buchanan who strongly urged him to keep the *Sentinel* going in spite of the heavy financial burden. Buchanan knew that Tucker represented strong Southern states' rights sentiment and he wanted this support in order to offset the attitudes of Northern Democrats. The paper continued as long as Tucker could manage, for though he disclaimed opportunism, he no doubt anticipated eventually running the Administration's official paper. However, a brief illness in June 1856 followed by Tucker's absence from Washington for four days in August sufficed to close down the impoverished *Sentinel*.

As President Buchanan was more mindful of his obligations than Pierce had been, Tucker finally received an appointment. He would have preferred something near Washington so that he could maintain his claims agency, but he accepted what was offered: the Consulship at Liverpool. In the autumn of 1857 he sailed there to replace Nathaniel Hawthorne, the novelist.

The remainder of Tucker's life resembled a second-rate melodrama more than the career of a first-rate lobbyist. When the Civil War broke out he resigned his post in Liverpool to return to Virginia via Canada. There he offered his services to the Confederate President Jefferson Davis and was sent back to Europe to purchase supplies and negotiate loans for the South. Once again he eluded the Northern blockade, transacted various commissions in Britain and France, and eventually returned home. Towards the end of the War he was sent to Canada to negotiate an exchange of Southern cotton for Northern meat. Shortly afterwards President Lincoln was assassinated, and because Tucker was in Canada he was implicated in the plot. Canada seemed the natural destination for one who had conspired with John Wilkes Booth, and although he vehemently denied any involvement he dared not return to the United States since there was a price on his head. The temper of the times was such that he was not safe even in Canada, and so eventually he and his family reunited in Great Britain. Finding little to do there he tried Mexico for a while but his sojourn there coincided with the withdrawal of French troops and the consequent execution of Emperor Maximilian at the hands of Juárez. Next he went back to Canada to manage a resort hotel, quite a comedown for a leading Washington lobbyist of ten or fifteen years before. Finally the charges of treason were dropped in the early 1870s and he was permitted to return to the United States where he soon resumed the only profession he really knew, that of a claims agent in Washington, and this occupied him until his death in 1890.

Of the three former Cabinet members who were attached at one time or another to the Organization Robert J. Walker was clearly the most successful speculator and financier. Born in Pennsylvania in 1801, he was no relation of Knox Walker of Tennessee. He was far better known than Knox, and lent considerable prestige to the Organization. After studying law at the University of Pennsylvania he went south to set up a joint practice with his brother in Mississippi. There he made some shrewd investments in plantations, slaves, and undeveloped land. He also became a staunch supporter of Andrew Jackson and looked to him for political favours. Walker's election to the Senate in 1836 and subsequent re-election in 1841 stemmed in part from this connection.

As early as 1837 he showed annexationist tendencies in urging the acquisition of Texas, and by so doing undermining Van Buren's bid for the Presidency. By the same token it secured him a prominent place among the coterie who succeeded in getting the Democratic nomination for James K. Polk in 1844. When Polk was elected he appointed Walker Secretary of the Treasury. This troubled some who felt that Walker's well-known banking connections and financial manipulations would pose a conflict of interest, but on the whole he managed to avoid this predicament.[10]

By the spring of 1849 Walker, together with other members of the Polk Administration, was out of office. However, he decided to remain in Washington, prosecuting claims and enhancing his personal finances. It may be recalled that the original purpose of the Organization was to secure patents for American inventors at the Great Exhibition. As it turned out, Walker was the only representative of the group willing to go to London, and his principal client was Samuel Colt who invented the 'repeating pistol' and wanted help convincing the British that his revolver was superior to any weapon then available.[11] When Walker arrived in London in August 1851 his interests and those of the Organization had broadened considerably. Having undertaken to raise $15 to $17 million for the construction of the Illinois Central Railroad, and realizing that investment capital was more plentiful in Europe than ever before, they aimed to raise one-third of this amount abroad. Accordingly, Walker asked W. W. Corcoran, the Philadelphia banking magnate, for an introduction to the British banking family of Baring and to George Peabody, the American merchant banker who had made such a success in London. He stayed in London from September 1851 to January 1852 meeting Baring and Peabody, becoming a guest member of the Athenaeum Club, and through its Secretary being introduced to Cabinet officials and other Members of Parliament. Besides collecting a $20,000 retaining fee from the railroad, Walker stood to gain $150,000 if the venture ultimately succeeded. As far as one can tell, however, little was achieved in London. Had it been otherwise, the Organization would then have played its part in securing Congressional support.

A year later when Crampton broached the topic of a Reciprocity Treaty, Secretary of State Marcy suggested that he get in touch with Walker. Not being a member of the Pierce Administration he was free to assist Crampton in a way which a Cabinet member like Marcy could not.[12]

Like Beverley Tucker, Robert J. Walker had a falling out with President Pierce. Initially he accepted an appointment as Special Envoy to China, but because he felt that Pierce deceived him, he declined it shortly thereafter. In the Presidential election of 1856 he joined other members of the Organization in supporting James Buchanan. Buchanan's gratitude was double-edged, however, for it was a dubious honour to offer Walker the Governorship of the explosive Kansas Territory. Though not an ardent abolitionist, he had freed his own slaves as early as 1838 and had openly advocated national unity which ran counter to states' rights. His tenure as Governor lasted less than a year and by the end of 1857 he had resigned. The South charged him with treachery for becoming reconciled to self-determination for Kansas as a free state.

During the Civil War Walker strongly supported the cause of the Union and devoted much of his time to raising $250 million in Great Britain. His old financial touch had not left him. Neither did it after the War when he assisted Secretary of State Seward in negotiating the purchase of Alaska from the Russians.

Of equal prominence with R. J. Walker in Democratic Party circles was William L. Marcy. Born in 1786, he was the oldest man in the Organization. After graduating from Brown University he settled in upstate New York, gradually making his way into state politics and eventually becoming Governor in 1833. President Martin Van Buren, a fellow New York Democrat, appointed him to the Mexican Claims Commission of 1840–2 before their estrangement over the issues of Texas and slavery. With the election of President Polk in 1844 Marcy was chosen Secretary of War, but he was acutely unprepared for the hostilities which broke out a year later with Mexico and made a number of political enemies during the war. At the conclusion of the Polk Administration he returned to New York as a private citizen.[13]

However, Marcy had Presidential ambitions. He witnessed the fragmentation of the Democratic Party in 1848 and the subsequent electoral victory of the Whigs, and harboured the hope that as a moderate he could restore party harmony. Like R. J. Walker he was a strong believer in preserving the Union against the extremes of rabid Southern slaveholding and radical Northern abolitionism. In order to finance his political ambitions he resumed his legal career, supplementing his income by advocating claims although his biographer says 'he was deeply prejudiced about claims agents and their business'. Nevertheless, by the opening months of 1851 Marcy was to be found in Washington pressing several claims, 'despite his hostility to such employment', and it was at this time that Knox Walker, R. J. Walker, and J. Y. Mason approached him about the Organization.

A scrutiny of both his correspondence and his working diaries for the years 1849–51 does not necessarily bear out the notion that he shrank from prosecuting claims, using influence, and speculating in business.[14] According to these, he spent the first part of November 1850 overseeing the affairs of the Canal Bank of New York State and then he attended the meetings of two Boards of Directors of which he was a member; the possibility of opening a railway line from Toledo, Ohio, to Chicago, Illinois, prompted him to invest about $25,000 in the two companies: the New York Railroad Co. and the Northern Indiana Railroad Co. In December he made some notes on Christmas Day concerning his moral and financial assets, listing among the former that perhaps he should have spoken out more for the cause of moderation in the great political turmoil associated with the Compromise of 1850. But then he admitted that being in the limelight was a mixed blessing. 'Though my life has been decidedly that of a public man, I have a disrelish for public affairs.' As for his financial balance sheet he commented: 'I have turned my labour during the year now closing to some account in a pecuniary point of view.' Besides his business and legal services which would net him about $3,000 he would receive $500 for pressing the Leggett claim and there was the prospect of a further $2,000 from a number of claims which he agreed to handle for James H. Causten of Washington. Causten was a successful claims agent who had operated in the Capitol for a number of years representing certain of the Latin American states diplomatically and specializing in claims against other Central and South American republics. Marcy had the experience of the 1840-2 Mexican Claims Commission. Together they were in an excellent position to co-operate in the pursuit of their clients' claims following the Treaty of 1848 ending the war with Mexico. A Commission established by Congress to arbitrate these claims met briefly in June 1850 but Causten told Marcy not to bother coming to Washington then since the main adjudication would occur from December 1850 to April 1851. Accordingly, Marcy was sent for in late December and arrived in Washington on 6 January. On 13 January he noted in his diary: 'prepared to go at the cases which I am to examine for Mr. C. Went to the Capitol, saw many of the Senators, but few of the members [of the House]'. That evening he dined with Robert J. Walker and the next day wrote: 'entered on the examination of Mr. C.'s cases. Dined with Beverley Tucker.'

A month later he was still working on Causten's cases by day and attending parties every evening. This pattern continued through March when he was finally able to get away from Washington, and in May drew upon Causten for $2,000. That June he went to Chicago on railway business, returning only briefly to Washington. Most of 1851 he spent in Albany, but he continued working on the Mexican claims. In November Causten informed him of clients who were dissatisfied with their awards from the Commission and wanted further compensation directly from Congress. Some of these claims came via J. Knox Walker who wanted to split the expected proceeds three ways.

Marcy may not have liked the business of a claims agent but he certainly worked hard at it and had good results. Since nothing could be less certain than securing the Democratic Party nomination for President, he had to do something in the meantime which would provide for himself and his family as well as keep his political lines of communication open. With the election of Franklin Pierce in 1852, Marcy was in a strong position for a Cabinet appointment since he had not done as several other members of the Organization like Knox Walker and Beverley Tucker had, and supported Stephen A. Douglas's candidacy. Pierce offered him the most prestigious Cabinet post, Secretary of State, which he readily accepted. When Pierce left office Marcy also stepped down, having no special claims on the new President, James Buchanan. He died later that same year.[15]

John Y. Mason became involved in the Organization by much the same route as the others: a combination of political activity and pecuniary need. Born in Virginia in 1799, he took his university degree at North Carolina and was admitted to the Virginia Bar in 1819. In 1831 he was elected to the House of Representatives, and served there until 1837. For the next seven years he was a federal judge, but in 1844 he returned to political life as President Tyler's Secretary of the Navy. Under President Polk he held the office of Attorney General for a year and then was reappointed head of the Navy Department for the remainder of Polk's Administration.

For the next few years he lived in Richmond, resumed his legal practice, and presided over the Virginia Constitutional Convention of 1850–1. He also became President of the James River and Kanawha Co. with the expectation that a canal would be built connecting Virginia and West Virginia with the Ohio River. At this time Mason was apparently in debt and seeking ways to improve his position. According to a letter dated September 1850 he was obliged to assure one of his debtors, H. B. Grigsby, that the interest on a loan would be paid promptly twice a year. He wrote an even more revealing letter to James Buchanan: 'Since May 1849 I have been incessantly occupied and even as much annoyed, and always anxiously employed, under pressure to meet engagements and provide for a numerous household'.[16]

Like other members of the Organization, Mason may have turned lobbyist primarily to improve his financial position. However, he clearly enjoyed playing an active role in politics. As Chairman of the Democratic Party's Committee for the State of Virginia, he exerted considerable influence on party affairs and doubtless had a hand in swinging his delegation to Pierce at the convention in Baltimore in 1852. Presumably as a reward Pierce appointed him American Minister to Paris where he died unexpectedly in 1859.

Still another member of the Organization once served under President Polk. This was Edmund Burke. Born in 1809, he was admitted to the Bar in 1829 and soon thereafter took up residence in Newport, New Hampshire, where for many years he controlled and edited the *Argus and Spectator*, one of the leading state newspapers. In 1838 he was elected to the House of Representatives and began to spend increasing amounts of time in Washington. At the end of his third and final term in the House, Polk appointed him Commissioner of Patents which lasted until the spring of 1849, when he accepted the co-editorship of the Democratic Party newspaper, the *Washington Union*. Burke was supposed to restore party unity regarding slavery and the admission of new states. However, the Party was already too badly split, and Burke was soon forced out.[17]

After this he devoted most of his time to New Hampshire affairs although he also maintained a law office in Boston. He was the first member of the Organization to work for the nomination of Franklin Pierce which was natural since both of them were from New Hampshire, and as much as anyone Burke was responsible for Pierce's success at Baltimore in June 1852. Burke's expectations of gratitude from his Party leader were dashed, however, because Pierce chose not to support him as Senatorial candidate the following autumn, thereby helping Burke's local political enemies who claimed most of the party patronage. Increasingly he became critical of the Administration and finally broke completely with Pierce by publishing some correspondence which showed that the President was far from the unsuspecting, last-minute candidate he had made himself out to be.[18]

George Ashmun of Massachusetts (1804–70) was the only Whig among the original members of the Organization. Like almost all of the others he was a college or university graduate (Yale) and then studied law. By 1828 he had established himself in Springfield, Massachusetts, where he resided till his death. During the 1830s he served in both Houses of the Massachusetts legislature, later going to Washington as a US Representative, whose term coincided with Polk's and many of his claims agent colleagues. However, his views strongly contrasted with those of R. J. Walker, Marcy, and Burke who were compromisers on the issue of slavery. Ashmun was strongly against the extension of slavery and consequently against the war with Mexico. As a Whig he tried to curb Polk's power of patronage although he didn't necessarily condemn all such political influence. In fact he may have lost his Congressional seat because he publicly defended Daniel Webster against charges of bribery and corruption. In 1860 he presided over the Republican Party convention at Chicago which nominated Lincoln, and was also the last person to discuss a matter of business with him on 14 April 1865 before the President went to Ford's theatre. The subject of this last meeting confirmed Ashmun's continuing activities as a claims agent since it dealt with whether Lincoln would be willing to set up a commission to judge the case of one of Ashmun's clients in Massachusetts.[19]

A somewhat later recruit to the Organization was George M. Dallas who figured prominently as Vice-President in the Polk Administration. After his term of office he returned to Philadelphia to prosecute claims and represent the interests of the Pennsylvania Railroad. In 1852 he was a strong contender for Secretary of State, but Pierce decided to choose Marcy instead. A year later he was asked by one of the members of the Organization to help with the Reciprocity Bill. Alternating as a friend and rival of Buchanan, he was appointed Minister to London in 1856.[20]

Although not an original member of the Organization, Lewis Charles Levin deserves particular attention since he became personally responsible for trying to get a Copyright Bill through Congress. Born in 1808 in Charleston, South Carolina, he availed himself of the opportunity of an education at South Carolina College. In his early twenties he taught school in Mississippi, and later studied law. Eventually he made his way to Philadelphia and was admitted to the Bar there in 1840. He practised law sporadically for the rest of his life, but it became apparent that his real vocation was as an entrepreneur, especially in politics. In the 1840s he published two newspapers. The first was called the *Temperance Advocate*, but this was soon replaced by a penny daily called the *Sun*. The *Sun* became the official spokesman of a new political coalition with which Levin had become involved, the Native American Party.

The Native American Party came into being as a reaction against the growing numbers of immigrants who began to arrive on America's shores. Since many of these were Roman Catholic, the Nativists combined their anti-foreign sentiments with anti-Catholic ones. They regarded the Democratic Party as an arch enemy because it made a special effort to recruit immigrants into its ranks, and they viewed the Whigs as nominal friends who were, however, unable to adequately represent working-class people threatened by the tide of immigration and resulting competition for jobs. In July 1844 riots broke out in Philadelphia directed against Catholics, and although Levin tried to restrain his followers he was implicated and later indicted for treason by a Grand Jury. This only served to enhance his popularity among those supporting him as a candidate for the House of Representatives. Efforts were made by his enemies to bring him to trial but he was duly elected from the First District of Philadelphia and took his seat in Congress the following year.[21]

As a lobbyist he came into his own as a result of a lengthy and involved case that arose during the course of 1849–50. He was still a Representative at the time and therefore the natural recipient of many requests for assistance from his Philadelphia constituents. One of those seeking his support was William D. Lewis, a banker and Whig party member who wanted to be Collector of Customs for the Port of Philadelphia. As a member of the House Committee on Naval Affairs Levin was a logical Congressman to approach, and it was known that he had been instrumental in promoting the construction of a dry dock for Philadelphia in 1848. The Collectorship represented more than a lucrative job. It carried with it the responsibility of dispensing a number of lower-level appointments, thus endowing the office with political power through local patronage. With the Whigs in power in Washington, men like Lewis looked forward to sharing the political spoils, but so did other influential Pennsylvania Whigs who were not about to let the Collectorship go unchallenged.

Although not a Whig himself, Levin found it convenient to co-operate with them at election-time. This had been especially true in 1848 when the Native Americans struck a bargain of mutual assistance with the Whigs whereby the Nativists would support Whig candidates throughout the State in return for support by them in the First District of Philadelphia where Levin's strength lay. The compact succeeded and Pennsylvania went both Whig and Nativist: moreover the State was one of two crucial determinants in the election of Zachary Taylor. Thus, when the new Administration assembled for the first time in March 1849 Levin anticipated wielding more power than he had during the previous Democratic régime. Office-seekers like Lewis were anxious to solicit Levin's support because he presumably had more influence than the newly elected Whig Senator from Pennsylvania, James Cooper.

A political appointment such as the Collectorship of Philadelphia had to go through two phases. One was securing nomination by the new Cabinet and the other was confirmation by the Senate. Accordingly Levin began making the rounds of the new Cabinet members, urging them to consider the merits of William D. Lewis. At the same time he began to establish himself as a man of influence who was willing to assist members of Congress with their pet projects if they would acquiesce in Levin's requests. It was axiomatic that during the first few months of a new Administration much time was taken up with political patronage. A measure of this preoccupation was finding President Taylor

HAP

interrupting a conference with the British Minister in order to chat with Levin about the Collectorship of Philadelphia! Because the name of Lewis had been slandered it was essential that the President as well as the Cabinet be told the truth. Levin advised Lewis: 'a committee of merchants, upon whom you can *certainly rely*, should come on (to Washington), and if they will see me in advance, I will arrange all matters for an interview with the President'.[22] Not satisfied with his dexterous manipulation of patronage, Levin had a compelling desire to believe in the righteousness of his cause and conversely the perfidy of his opponents. The perpetration of gross calumnies about Lewis provided this pretext, and Levin threw himself wholeheartedly into clearing Lewis's name.[23]

I need not tell you how my heart leaped at this declaration which showed that your good name, like polished steel, had flung off from its bright surface the opprobrious breath that sought to stain it. What a vindication! What a triumph! How true it is that slander, take what form or shape it may, not only furnishes its own antidote but, like empty sound among barren hills, receives its best answer from its own dying echo.... I scarcely know to what cause to attribute the deep interest I have felt in this matter, for if it had been my own father I could not have done more. A friend first stirred my blood and awakened and aroused my energies in behalf of a much injured man. My reward will be the consciousness of having discharged my duty.

As Levin reported to Lewis, 'I continued to pile influence upon influence, cautiously watching and tracing the effect of every move . . .', but though he succeeded in lining up the tacit support of about half of the Cabinet members, the Secretary of the Treasury, William Meredith, was not so easily won over, and it was under his jurisdiction that the Collectorship fell. Meredith's tactic was to delay whereas Levin sought to push through Lewis's nomination as quickly as possible. Delay would allow time for the anti-Lewis Whigs in Pennsylvania to settle on an alternative candidate, while at the same time dismissing the claims of those who were pro-Lewis. It was a typical intra-party struggle, but Levin hoped that as an outsider he could tip the scales in Lewis's favour.[24]

The fact is, that with the co-operation of a few active-minded and energetic men, I have succeeded in bringing about an entire change in the policy of the Administration, so far as appointments are to be made. They begin to see the importance of appointing men to office who can concentrate political power and combine dissident elements. They began to see and feel the difference between appointing a man merely qualified to discharge the duties of the office and one who, while he will discharge its duties, will also look to the considerations of political power.

There was another explanation for Levin's influence, and he was the first to acknowledge it. If a Whig other than Lewis were appointed, Levin would withdraw his own as well as the Nativist Party's support from the Administration, or alternatively, if the Administration appointed a member of the Native American party over Levin's head, so to speak, Levin would be forced to repudiate such a candidate, split his own party, and destroy the effectiveness of the Whig-Nativist alliance. In either case the Democrats would carry the First Congressional District in the next election and perhaps the whole state. Only by approving Lewis's nomination could the Taylor Administration sustain the support of the Native Americans as well as most Whigs. It was not exactly political blackmail but it served the same purpose, and on 9 May the Cabinet gave their approval.

Congress reconvened in December 1849 at which time the Senate's Committee on Commerce was formed. Lewis's nomination was now in their hands. Memorials for and against him poured in to the Committee. But trouble loomed from another quarter. During the previous spring the Whig Senator from Pennsylvania, Cooper, had tacitly supported Lewis's nomination. However, during the intervening months Lewis and Cooper had a falling out over local patronage. Cooper had made a list of party faithfuls who he felt deserved jobs from the prospective Collector and Lewis preferred to make his own choices in the interest of Whig party harmony and co-operation with the Nativists. Cooper resented this and determined to block Lewis's Senate confirmation.

By January 1850 it was all-out war between the supporters and the enemies of William D. Lewis; and by extension between Levin and Cooper. In his struggle to influence the Commerce Committee and ultimately the entire Senate, Levin's true personality came out. A combination of demagogue and crusader which had manifested itself on the public platform before large crowds now found an outlet in the corridors and ante-chambers of the nation's Capitol. In secret letters sent to Lewis by a trusted friend he gave full vent to his animosity and frustration. Of Cooper he wrote:

the poor, miserable, unscrupulous scoundrel is hard at work and will have his labor for his pains. . . . [He is] an infamous and unprincipled liar. . . . You

see how the infamous villain is cutting his own throat, or more aptly, pre-
paring a gallows on which he is destined to swing. How I should like to reach
his sensorium, by the application of a raw-hide to his recreant limbs.

A few days later he reported: 'Oh! How I love this fight! It braces
my nerves! It operates like a shower bath upon my entire system!'
And again,

I am breaking Cooper's political neck, and before I am done, he will not have
a political bone in his body, unmashed. It has become what I supposed it would –
a fight – bold, fearless, manly, and honest on one side – cowardly, sneaking
and stealthy on the other. He will soon be hemmed in on all sides, and when
he begins to beg – why, I may take pity on the wretch and teach him a lesson
of humility. . . . Never since the origin of this Government has there been
such a struggle.

Ordinarily the Senate respected a member's recommendation not to
confirm, but Levin managed to show that Cooper's opposition was
personally motivated.[25] Matters dragged on for month after month
because the Commerce Committee was reluctant to alienate either
faction. In the meantime Lewis recruited additional lobbying support.
By April Levin reported to Lewis that Cooper was becoming desperate.

Cooper evidently relies on a bargain which I am sure cannot be carried into
effect, simply because the Southern Senators are not willing to degrade them-
selves. His plan is as follows. He came into the Senate a strong anti-slavery
man, and now thinks that by a surrender of his fixed political principles on
that subject, he can so commend himself to the South as to secure certain votes
against you.

And a few weeks later: 'The low cunning of Cooper is overmatched by
superior skill, while his groveling malignant purposes are hourly thwarted
by the efforts of those whose motives are pure and whose objects are
lofty.'[26]

In July President Zachary Taylor suddenly died and Vice-President
Millard Fillmore assumed office. A thorough reshuffle of the Cabinet
took place. This in itself did not directly affect Lewis's nomination,
but it did prolong the session of Congress as did the 'Compromise of
1850' which dealt with the expansion of slavery and the balance of power
among the states. Thus Congress was still sitting in September, a good
month after it might otherwise have adjourned, and during that month
the Commerce Committee finally and unanimously recommended

Lewis. Cooper did all he could to prevent a vote, even absenting himself a week. Out of courtesy the Senate waited until he returned and then approved Lewis's appointment by a vote of 37 to 7. Cooper was the only Whig in opposition. After this victory Levin seriously considered leaving the House of Representatives to concentrate on lobbying as a full-time occupation. On 6 August 1850 he confided to Lewis:[27]

I have determined not to run. But I desire the nomination because Cooper has reported that my advocacy of yourself has destroyed me in the first district. . . . I do not wish it known that I intend to decline, for then they would give me he empty compliment in anticipation of it. I want it bona fide, and then decline.

The Native American Party re-nominated him and he agreed to run again for a fourth term. His prospects were good as long as the Whigs and Nativists co-operated, but if Cooper's wing of the Pennsylvania Whigs supported its own candidate, he was in trouble. This was precisely what happened, predictably splitting the Whig-Nativist vote and thereby throwing the election to the Democrat.

Out of Congress but far from out of influential Washington circles, Levin tried briefly to play the part of king-maker. It was an open secret that Daniel Webster, Fillmore's Secretary of State, coveted the Presidency. Learning that Webster would be passing through Philadelphia he offered to promote his candidacy.[28]

I am anxious for you to spend the evening at my house, and will undertake to have ten thousand friends in front of my house to greet you. A demonstration, on your arrival, is not the thing; our friends, are the working men, the bone and sinew, and they cannot be brought out during the day. It will all be done, in a quiet way, and the effect will be startling.

Webster failed to secure the Whig party nomination in 1852 but was supported for the Presidency by the Native American nominating convention.

It was sometime in 1851 that Levin allied himself with the Organization. Although he lacked the prestige and status of ex-Cabinet officers like Marcy and Robert J. Walker, he made up for this in determination and contacts. Whereas most of the other members were Democrats at a time when a Whig held the Presidency, Levin still carried influence among the Whigs. No matter what the topic he seemed to know the right people from whom to elicit help and advice. How he became the liaison between Henry Bulwer's nephew, Robert Lytton, and the Organization is difficult to say, but as was so often the case it probably stemmed from a personal acquaintance with Thomas William Charles Moore, the courier for the British Legation in Washington.

In 1856 Levin was seriously afflicted by mental illness which plagued him periodically until his death in 1860.

The careers and attitudes of those who made up the Organization give some clue as to its nature and how it functioned. Judging by the way members came and went from Washington it was never a fixed quantity for very long and its exact membership was a subject of conjecture at any given moment. Most of the original members were closely affiliated with the Polk Administration and the Democratic Party: R. J. Walker as Secretary of the Treasury, Marcy as Secretary of War, and Mason as Secretary of the Navy. Knox Walker was Polk's nephew and private secretary. Tucker, though not an ardent Democrat, got his start in politics through the help of Mason and others in the party. Burke became Commissioner of Patents. Only Levin and Ashmun had no close ties with Polk, although they were both in Congress throughout his Presidency. By 1852 even Levin had swung over to the Democrats and for a time linked his political and patronage fortunes with theirs. As he explained to Marcy shortly before Franklin Pierce was elected President and well before Marcy had been chosen Secretary of State, 'When I consented to become a Candidate for Congress I well knew that neither of the old parties [Democratic or Whig] would give me their support, and hence, defeat to a local party was inevitable.' The Pennsylvania Whigs thought they had a bargain with the Catholics of Philadelphia to support one another, and thus the Whigs had no intention of backing Levin and his Native Americans. However, the Democrats were confident they still could control the Catholic vote. 'Knowing my position in the Native American Party, I determined to run in the face of defeat, for the purpose of transferring our whole strength to the support of Pierce and King.' Levin was sure that 14,000 of the 15,000 Nativist votes in Pennsylvania would go for Franklin Pierce.[29]

Ironically the strength of the Organization was greater under the Whigs than under the Democrats. Perhaps this was due to the need felt by the Taylor-Fillmore Administration to arrive at a better working understanding with the Democrats in Congress, especially after the elections of 1850 when the Whigs lost their slim majority. Although the Democrats retained a majority under Pierce, factional disputes within the Party reduced what effectiveness the Organization might otherwise have had.

Something else bound many of the members together: their impecuniousness. As we have seen, Tucker and Mason were especially badly off, but all except Robert J. Walker and William L. Marcy were in need of funds. Paradoxically, most of the lobbyists helped their clients to obtain great wealth, though they themselves were struggling attorneys and ex-politicians trying to stay afloat or get themselves out of debt. For example, a contemporary lobbyist for the Reciprocity Bill, I. D. Andrews, spent well over $100,000 and had to devote the rest of his life collecting about half that amount.

In general the Organization was in favour of preserving the Union and not giving way to the extreme demands of states' rights' advocates. On the other hand none of them except Ashmun was sympathetic to the Free Soil platform which they felt would equally tear the Union apart. Mason, Tucker, Knox Walker, and perhaps Levin were prepared to see slavery endure for an indefinite time, while R. J. Walker wanted to phase it out gradually and the others a bit more rapidly. Like many of their contemporaries they thought that slavery would eventually die because of economic and geographical reasons, therefore why precipitate a confrontation between the North and South.

Their stand on slavery in addition to their strong support of the Democratic Party meant that many of them found James Buchanan a congenial candidate in the election of 1856. As President he retained Mason as Minister to France, appointed Dallas Minister to London, assigned Tucker to the Consulship of Liverpool, gave R. J. Walker the dubious privilege of trying to govern the Kansas Territory, and might have found a post for Levin if he were not indisposed.

One further principle was at work for those who became Organization members: friendship and family connection. Tucker was a close associate of Knox Walker and a family friend of Mason's. His brother married one of Dallas's daughters, and Dallas's niece married Robert J. Walker. All shared the common experience of Washington life and society.

This was the group, then, that seemed so formidable to the British Legation in 1851 when it offered its services through T. W. C. Moore to Crampton and Robert Lytton for the purpose of pressing for copyright legislation. With the political climate in Washington such as it was, there is little wonder that the Organization's assistance was accepted, for a price.

BRIBERY, OR THE NECESSARY EXPENSES OF CONGRESSIONAL ACTION: NOVEMBER 1851–FEBRUARY 1853

The year 1852 began auspiciously for those advocating an Anglo-American copyright agreement. There was a tone of suppressed excitement combined with feelings of relief in Robert Lytton's mid-January letter to his father.

As to the Copyright I am very glad to hear the money can *be forthcoming. That is the great thing – it will now be very simple – I shall be able to hear whether these people will undertake it or no; if they* undertake *it I think they can* do *it, and I don't think they will if they* can't. *I shall be able to let you know more fully about it I hope by next post.*

He went on to explain why there were no good alternatives to working through the Organization. Henry Clay, who had been the nominal champion of copyright in earlier times, was a dying man and in no condition to assist. Neither could Robert consult James Mandeville Carlisle, the American attorney for the British Legation in Washington, about so private and delicate a matter. In this as in previous letters Robert implied that if one wished to play the game of American politics one must be prepared to play by the informal rules. Thus application was made to the Organization and Lewis Levin responded:

We shall call the members of the Organization together at an early day and decide whether it is advisable to accomplish the subject by treaty or by a bill before the Houses of Congress . . . if we decide upon a bill through Congress, we will have secured the Committee, and have everything in readiness for the Report and Bill, by the time you hear from your friends. . . . You know

enough of American legislation to know that a Report and Bill thus intro-
duced and backed by our force cannot fail.

Levin went on to state the terms. A total of $60,000 (£12,000) would
be required: $20,000 in cash upon presentation of the Report and Bill;
the balance upon their successful passage.[1]

Robert Lytton was unable to confirm the arrangements with the
Committee until 23 February by which time he learned that the first
instalment of $20,000 had to be paid in advance. To Bulwer he reported:

I am not to obtain any further guarantee of their good faith in the business
from the peculiar nature of the transaction. I fear none can be given. The
money advanced will therefore have to be advanced at a risk and you will
yourself be the best judge as to the advisability of running that risk to the
extent of £4000.

He continued with an argument which he and others came to rely on
time and time again.

I am also convinced that if the thing cannot be done by this means it cannot
be done by any other, since these very men, if they do not support it will oppose
and upset it in the committees. . . . I understood from those who are best able
to judge that the present session of Congress is for several reasons a very
favourable time to bring forward the measure.

Having done his best to smooth the way for a successful copyright
campaign, Robert returned to England. When he docked at Liverpool
on 19 March, he made his way directly to Knebworth to join his father.
Crampton had been left in charge of the matter in Washington and was
apparently pursuing it zealously according to a letter from T. W. C.
Moore. The campaign was to involve a two-pronged attack. One approach
would be made through the executive branch of the Government,
urging sponsorship of a treaty which could be ratified by a two-thirds
vote of the Senate. The other was to simultaneously approach the House
of Representatives requesting them to present a favourable committee
report and to support a proposed bill. Moore emphasized the need for
prompt compliance with the Organization's terms. 'Action has been
taken upon my assurance that the agreement should be scrupulously
fulfilled.' A few days later Crampton filled in the details. The Patent
Committee of the House had already been alerted and was in the process
of drawing up a favourable report; petitions in support of copyright

would now start arriving on Congress's doorstep; 'and the press will also be employed'. If all went well the Secretary of State, Daniel Webster, would notice the ground swell of support being manifested for international copyright and would propose the desired treaty. The advantage of a treaty was that it could by-pass the House of Representatives because it required only Senate approval. Furthermore it was an infinitely easier task to influence sixty Senators than several hundred Representatives. Its disadvantage was that it required a two-thirds majority for ratification.[2]

In March 1852 Crampton informed the Foreign Office of his wish to negotiate a copyright treaty. The topic had not arisen since 1848, but he stated that America was becoming more favourably inclined towards an Anglo-American agreement, and he had learned confidentially that Webster would negotiate provided there was not too much hostility from Congress and the American public. Without alluding to the Organization therefore he asked the Foreign Office for permission to proceed. He addressed his remarks to Lord Granville, but they were received by the new Tory Foreign Secretary Lord Malmesbury who gave Crampton full authorization to negotiate, suggesting that any copyright treaty with America be patterned on the one signed recently between Britain and France. Malmesbury then consulted the Board of Trade and received their views. On 21 May he forwarded an annotated copy of the Anglo-French Copyright Treaty with appropriate modifications to Crampton.[3]

Negotiations progressed nicely until Crampton received disconcerting news that there had been a gross misunderstanding about the amount of money to be raised. Robert Lytton sent an abject apology:

It seems that when I stated to you that the money specified by the Persons, who have undertaken the Copyright business in Washington, to be advanced in England – I misread the sum stated in my father's letter to me on that subject, and mistook hundreds for thousands – . . . This is of course very vexatious and indeed I regret, as much as I am sure you will, – having misled you on the subject by so ridiculous and unfortunate a mistake. It is the more annoying from the fact that the Organization at Washington have taken up the business in so prompt and energetic a manner – with the belief that the sums stipulated for by them would be produced as promptly. I also know well that if the support of these men cannot be secured – their opposition will be certain and insurmountable – and the Copyright will be a dead quest.

The confusion had arisen because in Robert's first letter to his father he inadvertently put hundreds not thousands of pounds sterling. Bulwer's response saying he thought this amount could be raised was thus based on the lower figure, and though in later correspondence the mistake was rectified the misconception had sunk deep and was not detected until Robert arrived in England.

Bulwer tried to explain the reluctance of British authors and publishers to subscribe anything like what the Organization required: 'the suspicion that the money would be wholly lost, the distrust of the American securities; and the strangeness of the whole transaction according to our English notions.' Dickens and Bulwer estimated that £1,000 to £1,500 could initially be raised, and then if the treaty passed a larger amount might be forthcoming. Seconding this suggestion, Robert Lytton commented:[4]

I still hope that our friends at Washington may think that half a loaf is better than no bread – . . . I am sure you will do all that can be done but I am in a horrid fright that they will have gone some way in the matter before my letter reaches you and complain of me and [bad] faith upon our part.

Crampton had apparently harboured doubts that Bulwer could raise as much as Robert requested and had warned the Organization that its terms might not be met. When he received confirmation of this he lost no time contacting Levin to ask how far things had gone and was there any hope of salvaging the situation. Levin replied that the Patent Committee had its report in hand, 'and only awaited a fulfillment of the agreement on your part to ratify it'. In fact, the Organization 'had the privilege of drawing up the report ourselves which the committee would adopt'. In addition, Webster had given Levin permission to 'prepare the terms of the treaty'.

When it was learned that Crampton could scarcely offer one-tenth of what had previously been agreed, Levin sought to be as accommodating as possible.

Still we are Mr. Crampton's devoted friends, and fully appreciate the embarrassment of his present position. . . . We desire to carry the treaty through on his account even if we are obliged to work for nothing, but we have made engagements to the amount of £2,000 to various printers whose influences were important to carry the measure. We expected also in addition to receive £2,000 for our own services.

In order to carry on, however, the Organization needed £2,000 to cover outstanding obligations. Their own compensation might await the ratification of the treaty and a further solicitation of funds. Crampton relayed Levin's report to Bulwer reiterating that half of the £2,000 had to be paid as soon as possible and the other half once the treaty was signed.

By mid-May Crampton received tentative though reassuring word from Bulwer saying that he was glad to know that the Organization would carry on. He also mentioned that Dickens was planning to sound out leading publishers for donations. 'If you succeed in this great work – you will have conferred a greater boon on English authors and literature than they have ever yet obtained from Parliament or diplomatists.'[5] Even before he received this reassurance, Crampton was busy soliciting petitions in support of a treaty. These were regarded as evidence of strong popular sentiment. On 25 April he wrote to Robert C. Winthrop of Massachusetts, former Speaker of the House of Representatives, to enlist his help. Could he quietly secure signatures from some prominent Boston authors? Without mentioning the Organization, Crampton outlined the progress thus far:

We have taken these measures quietly not wishing to bring the matter forward till pretty well matured, in order to give as little time as possible for getting up a popular opposition to it – by this I mean publishers from whom alone we apprehend any objections.

Similar requests were sent to Longfellow and Emerson by W. W. F. Synge, a Foreign Office attaché temporarily assigned to the British Legation in Washington. Although Synge had been in America for scarcely six months he had managed to meet both Emerson and Longfellow and wished to assure them that the current copyright campaign was far different from the futile effort of times past.[6]

I have reason to know that Mr. Webster is well disposed to carrying out such a measure . . . we have got a very favourable report preparing on the subject in Congress by the Committee on Patents. . . . It is most essential that this measure should be proposed to us as one affecting American interests and not as a British measure.

Winthrop's response was affable but pessimistic. He reminded Crampton that previous memorials to Congress had not proved very effective, and therefore he hesitated to try again for fear of stirring up opposition. However, he had tried to oblige.

It happened that a few days after your letter came, I had Everett, Prescott, Longfellow, Dr. Warren, and one or two others of our literary and professional men, to breakfast with me. I took the opportunity to consult them upon the subject; – but nothing has come of it, and I fear nothing will.

On the other hand, Longfellow had more encouraging news to report.

I have been as expeditious and secret as possible and if no good comes of it I hope at least no harm will. I have seen Winthrop, Everett, Prescott and Emerson. The last is by far the most interested and ardent in the matter and I have requested him to write a few words for the rest of us to sign. Some of the gentlemen think we shall mar more than make. Of this you must judge.

On 10 May Emerson sent Longfellow a draft of a memorial and asked him to secure what signatures he could. Longfellow returned it with twelve signatures. Emerson delayed forwarding it to Washington until Hawthorne's name could be added, finally sending it to Synge on 6 June. Thirteen prominent New Englanders' names were attached: W. H. Prescott; H. W. Longfellow; Louis Agassiz; C. C. Felton; George Ticknor; O. W. Holmes; Edward Everett; E. P. Whipple; Charles Sprague; G. S. Hillard; Andrews Norton; Nathaniel Hawthorne; and R. W. Emerson.[7] Secrecy was well maintained, and the only thing now lacking was confirmation from England that the initial £1,000 had been raised. Bulwer was finding the task of collecting money most arduous. Crampton had urged haste because the current Congressional session would be over in August, but there was little Bulwer could do to speed things up. Being a man of limited means in spite of his reputation as one of the most popular authors of the day, he was chronically short of cash. Most of his own surplus income went to maintain the family estate at Knebworth. Because he personally stood to gain a good deal from an Anglo-American copyright agreement he was willing to promote one even though he himself could only contribute £100. Therefore, once it was clear that the Organization would continue handling the project, Bulwer approached Dickens for assistance. Unfortunately Dickens took a dim view of the project, as did his close friend, John Forster. Both expressed doubt that Longman or Murray would co-operate. It was a time of great antagonism among authors and publishers because of an upheaval in the book trade involving the right of the Booksellers' Association to regulate the retail prices of new books. This question was due for arbitration just when Bulwer began to solicit funds. Many authors and a few publishers, including Dickens and Bentley, had come out against the Booksellers' Association, but most of the publishers, such as Longman and Murray, strongly defended it. Dickens probably found it distasteful to contemplate fund-raising when he and other authors were castigating the book trade for their inordinate profits and monopolistic practices.[8] However, in several weeks' time he was persuaded to test book trade sentiment. To John Murray he wrote that Bulwer had 'some very curious papers on the subject of copyright which he wished to share with a few trusted and interested parties. Could Murray attend a small meeting at Dickens's home to hear what Bulwer had to propose?' The same day he wrote to his own publishers, Chapman & Hall, suggesting that they might also wish to be present.

The meeting at Dickens's house took place, as did many other private conferences, but by the end of May it was clear that Bulwer had failed in his object. He had to confess to Crampton that it was extremely difficult if not impossible to raise the first £1,000, let alone the second.

Mr. Longman and most of the principal publishers refused flatly altogether – alleging their total disbelief in the success of the negotiation – other booksellers declare it to be . . . an Authors' question not theirs – for that Authors would contract with American publishers without profit to themselves. Authors on the other hand are too poor to subscribe enough.

Even among the publishers there were considerable shades of difference. Murray was willing to contribute but Bentley was not. The Blackwoods greeted the idea enthusiastically and offered their energetic assistance whereas the Longmans denied any help at all. John Blackwood felt particularly bitter regarding Longmans because not only had they failed to support the Booksellers' Association with sufficient vigour, but now they were also refusing to go along with the copyright scheme. To his brothers in Edinburgh he confided:

there will be no getting together the money for the American copyright movement. . . . It is a great pity and Longmans have as usual behaved like despicable shits – petty tradesmen they are, incapable of taking the broad generous [view] of anything.

In a letter to Crampton, Robert Lytton expressed his disappointment and disgust.[9]

Some days ago I saw the principal Publishers, Printers, and Booksellers, to whom it was thought safe to confide the subject, at the home of Dickens. . . . [Bulwer explained the matter and Robert] backed him up very strongly – dwelling upon the power of the Organization and their ability to perform what they now undertook – the necessity of immediate action, and the fact that this opportunity once lost none other would ever occur again – Dickens, who from the first had hung fire, . . . now threw cold water upon the thing. He said that he did not believe either in the good faith of the American 'Organization,' or in their power to oppose successfully the cry of the small publishers and especially the newspaper press, which would be certain to do all they could to prevent the passage of such a measure. . . . When however it came to the point of raising a subscription everybody buttoned up their pockets, and looked very glum. Then Mr. Bentley (who I believe is one of the greatest seigneurs in the fraternity of Publishers) – declared that he felt moral scruples, that it was a dirty transaction and that he wouldn't be a party to bribery and corruption. This statement was immediately echoed by Dickens and all the others – My father ridiculed such an idea very much and showed very elaborately that such things as the 'Organization' were looked upon in American political life, in a very different way from that in which they would be regarded here. . . . You can't be more vexed at the stupidity of the people from whom we expected such eager cooperation than I am myself – For, either the measure . . . would be of immense benefit to them, or it would not; if not, all the clamour and fuss they have been making for years to obtain it is nonsense.

The question of bribery clearly plagued those in Britain who supported the copyright scheme. Bulwer did his best to calm their uneasiness by explaining how he had resolved his own doubts. Before he undertook to raise any funds, he articulated his thoughts to Crampton:

In fact the way I should propose it at such a meeting [for fund-raising] would be to treat the proposed act as analogous to a private Bill before our own Parliament, (in which considerable expense is always incurred) and to treat the party to deal with, as a Parliamentary agent.

Crampton agreed with Bulwer's approach:

You are quite right in supposing that the way in which pecuniary consideration is administered in such matters is analogous to a fee to counsel for carrying a private bill through Parliament. There is a class of persons at Washington called agents for claims whose business it is to get bills of that sort through

Congress for a fee. The only difference is that secrecy must be observed here as to the amount.

Crampton went on to justify the need for secrecy in the present instance. On the one hand it would be embarrassing to the British Government diplomatically if there were any kind of public exposure. On the other, it was vital that the Organization maintain its anonymity or else it would cease to wield such power and influence.

Try as he might, Bulwer could never quite erase the tainted stigma which clung to the undertaking. Yankees had not acquired a reputation for sharp practices without cause. Although Britain had her share of political corruption and bribery, especially on the local level at election time, most Englishmen were unwilling to acknowledge that influence was used in Westminster as it was on Capitol Hill. In America political morality had been gradually eroded. Increasingly it was taken for granted everywhere that American politics was a dirty business; fire must be fought with fire. The effect was cumulative. The more this was accepted, the more it was justified. Having seen the various applications of political pressure both fair and foul, it was hardly surprising that Crampton and Lytton became convinced of its necessity. No matter how they explained it away the fact remained that bribery was bribery.

On a different level, there were those in England who were troubled by the federal structure of the United States. John Dickinson, a leading paper-maker, questioned the power of the American Government to impose a copyright treaty on the individual states. Would this not require a constitutional amendment which would have to be ratified by a majority of the states? The same problem had been posed and answered before in 1838 when the President of the Board of Trade, Poulett Thomson, stated, with regard to international copyright, 'that the power was specially reserved to the [federal] Government and was not left in the hands of the states'. For his part, Crampton found it hard to believe that intelligent Englishmen were still so ill-informed about the American Constitution.[10]

The month of June dragged on with Crampton still uncertain about the funds from England. Bulwer and his son reinforced by Blackwood and Murray doggedly persisted though thoroughly disgusted. They managed to get a reluctant Dickens to pledge £100 if they each did likewise. Bulwer also offered to double the largest single contribution as an inducement to encourage subscriptions. Crampton, sensing the predicament they were in, made an ostentatious offer. 'I would willingly come down handsomely out of my own pocket rather than let the thing misfire', he wrote. Five days later he pledged £500, expecting that he might someday be reimbursed by the book trade. It was a wonderful gesture, and it persuaded Bulwer to make one last effort even though his son was dubious.

I confess that I have heard so much driveling nonsense talked about it – and it has met with so much determined and unreasonable (and I must say unaccountable and unlooked for) opposition from the very people on whose co-operation we had so securely counted, that I am too disgusted and disheartened to expect any great display of common sense from those gentlemen now.

However, in another fortnight Robert sang a new song.[11]

I am at last able to write you better news about the Copyright. Your offer of the £500 was so Princely and handsome a thing – that it has somewhat shamed these gentlemen over here out of their 'moral scruples' – and it was also a satisfactory guarantee for the security of the transaction. . . . I need scarcely say that it was solely through your most liberal offer, and your positive opinion as to the certainty of success, that the money has been raised and you will therefore at once see that if the measure should be manqué and fail after all – we are all lost men and I shall never dare to put my nose amongst the Moral Fraternity again – whose scruples will return with ten-fold intensity – . . . If therefore the £1500 should arrive too late to be used to advantage this Session, it would be well to keep it for another opportunity, but that of course I need not mention to you. . . . When the Copyright is satisfactorily obtained – I have no doubt whatever that I shall be able to make up the full £2000, and I assure you that I would rather work night and day than let you be in the end a loser by such generous and noble conduct. . . . I cannot say how disgusted I am at what I have seen of the 'literary mind' here; I believe Dickens to be solely actuated by 2 feelings 1st. a distaste to open his purse – though he is making £1000 a month! – and 2nd. a lurking sentiment of jealousy or some ill feeling at not having obtained the Copyright himself – But perhaps I may wrong him.

The first £1,000 was sent off to Crampton as soon as possible in mid-July. On the basis of several tentative lists it is possible to reconstruct the amounts which each contributor gave. Other names were listed as possible donors, but nothing seemed to come of them. Printers like Spottiswoode and paper-makers like Dickinson; music publishers and booksellers; publishers like Rivington, Charles Knight, Edward Moxon; and authors like Ainsworth, Thackeray, Macaulay, Tennyson, Forster and Lewes.[12]

Contributions Toward the First One Thousand Pounds

Alison, Archibald. *Historian*	£100
Aytoun, William. *Poet and Editor*	£ 25
Blackie, John. *Glasgow Publisher*	£ 50
Blackwood, Wm & Sons. *Edinburgh Publisher*	£100
Bradbury & Evans. *London Printers*	£100
Bulwer, E. L. *Author*	£100
Chapman & Hall. *London Publishers*	£ 50
Churchill, John. *London Publisher*	£ 25
Clowes, William. *Printer*	£100
Dickens, Charles. *Author*	£100
Layard, Austen H. *Author*	£ 50
Murray, John. *London Publisher*	£100
Smith, Elder & Co. *London Publisher*	£ 50
Spalding & Hodge. *Wholesale Stationers*	£ 50

14 Contributors Total: £1,000

Murray and Blackwood bore the brunt of soliciting the additional funds because Bulwer was suddenly called upon to contest an election to Parliament thanks to a decision of the Tories to go to the polls. Before he relinquished his share of the responsibility to Murray he received pledges from Dickens and Blackwood for an additional £100 each, and he himself added a further £100. With £50 from Murray plus Crampton's £500 they were well on their way to the second thousand. Murray then returned to the Longmans for the *third* time, imploring their cooperation. They agreed to supply £200 provided that Blackwood, Bulwer, and Dickens contributed the same. However, they also stipulated that they would not pay a shilling in advance, but only reimburse the others once the treaty had passed.

In an effort to avoid publicity, Crampton instructed Bulwer to deposit the first thousand in the Bank of Ransom & Co., London, in the name of T. W. C. Moore, but the bank would not accept such a large sum because Moore had no account with them. Since Crampton did, there was no alternative but to place the funds in his name.[13] The money now in hand, the ball was in the other court and it was Crampton, Moore, and the Organization's turn.[14]

The good news from London did not reach Washington until the end of July, and Crampton had already been forced to act. Since he had long been authorized by the Foreign Office to negotiate a treaty, he decided to concentrate on this alone and avoid having to deal with the Patent Committee and the House of Representatives. Accordingly, he and Webster escaped from the intolerable July heat of the Capitol and went to Webster's farm in Marshfield, Massachusetts to confer privately. The secret nature of the negotiations precluded using the Emerson–Longfellow memorial as originally intended, and as anticipated. Anyway, Synge admitted that 'though such signatures are invaluable, still the grounds on which the memorial is based seem to us to be so far not quite what we wish, inasmuch as we should like the measure to be asked for on the grounds of justice to Americans and not of fairness to British authors', and later added: 'the time is not yet come for a memorial from the great authors of America to be sent into Congress'.

Crampton must have been taken aback when Senator Charles Sumner of Massachusetts presented a copyright memorial to the Senate on 19 July. The signatures were entirely different from those collected by Longfellow and Emerson. A perusal of the names – J. F. Cooper; Wainwright; Melville; Bryant; Putnam; Irving; Hawks; Robinson; Griswold; Taylor; and Jay – revealed the New York connection of each. The fact that Cooper was dead suggested that the names had been assembled a year or two before. Who prompted Sumner to deliver the petition is not known, though it is more than likely that John Jay took the initiative. Since Crampton's negotiations were not general knowledge Sumner's memorial seemed to come out of the blue.[15]

Meanwhile at Marshfield Crampton and Webster agreed upon a draft treaty. Because there would not be enough time for the Senate to ratify it before the end of the autumn session Webster recommended holding it over until the session starting in December. Then suddenly another circumstance arose which also suggested procrastination. Fishing rights off the Canadian shores came into open dispute and there was just enough anti-British feeling in the Senate to prompt rejection of any Anglo-American treaty.

Under instructions from the Foreign Office Crampton had to issue a warning to American fishermen not to come within three miles of the Canadian coast, as stipulated in a treaty of 1818. If they persisted, British warships would support the Canadian squadron in excluding Americans from the bays of the St Lawrence. Webster replied with a strong note of protest, but privately counselled moderation. Many in Congress thought differently, however, and took the opportunity to twist the Lion's tail, especially as there was a Presidential election coming up the following November and this sort of campaign rhetoric was very popular. By mid-August Everett was able to report to the American Minister in London, 'The alarm of trouble with the fisheries is blowing over.'[16]

At this point the unpublished diary of John Pendleton Kennedy is illuminating. He was Secretary of the Navy under Fillmore's Administration, though better known as an author of historical novels. We have already witnessed his interest in Anglo-American copyright in 1842 when he was the Chairman of a Congressional committee on the subject. In an entry on 11 August he noted that Webster was back in Washington and present at a Cabinet meeting. When the President brought forth the copyright treaty he asked Kennedy, as an author, to examine it and report his recommendations to the Cabinet. On 20 August Kennedy and Crampton went over its provisions together, and five days later Kennedy 'urged the International Copyright treaty. . . . But I find the President rather adverse, at least for the present.' In the same entry he noted: 'I find Crampton very anxious about the Copyright treaty. Webster begs me to see the President again and urge it upon him. I promise to do so.' Apparently Webster had changed regarding a delay and now advocated hastening the exchange of signatures. The next day Kennedy recorded: 'To my office – and then to the President to talk about the treaty. He suggests the propriety of letting it lie over until after the Presidential election: thinking it may be made an element in the canvass if acted on now.' That evening Kennedy reported this conversation to Crampton who relayed the news to Bulwer that all was not bleak; in fact the delay might even enhance the chances of passage through Congress.

Ironically Crampton could not urge immediate action because he did not wish to disclose what arrangements had been made for Senate confirmation. It was to be one of the great dilemmas of Crampton's position that he was never able to explain the basis for his optimism to those who disparaged the treaty's chances.[17] In the meantime he retained most of the money designated for the Organization, advancing it as necessary. In a 'statement of account' drawn up by T. W. C. Moore

£345 was paid out which left a balance of about £775 with 'A.B.', presumably Anthony Barclay, the British Consul in New York. Here again Crampton tried to keep his own name and bank account separate from the copyright fund.[18]

Crampton awaited the next session of Congress with composure. Then in October occurred one of those accidents which so bedevils men's lives and confounds historical inquiry. Daniel Webster died unexpectedly. He had been thrown from a horse, complications had set in, and he succumbed on 24 October. It was one thing for Crampton to have a cosy understanding with Webster; quite another to sign a copyright treaty with a new Secretary of State. Webster had known about the secret arrangements, but none of them could be intimated to his successor.

Shortly before his death Webster had recommended Edward Everett to succeed him. Everett had enjoyed a distinguished career as an author, an educator, and a diplomat. In the latter capacity he served as American Minister to Britain from 1841 to 1845 and was known to have anglophil sympathies. His interest in literature presumably made him well disposed to an Anglo-American copyright agreement, but he was more austere and puritanical than Webster which meant that there would be none of that intimacy which existed previously between Webster and Crampton. Whereas Webster had really liked Crampton and was pleased with his appointment as British Minister to replace Sir Henry Bulwer, Everett disliked him, which Crampton no doubt sensed. Shortly before Everett assumed his official duties at the State Department he attended a dinner in Washington and was seated next to Crampton. Later recounting the evening to his wife he complained bitterly of Crampton's talking behind his hand to his charming female dinner partner thus preventing him from overhearing. Adding a bit more spice, Everett related the current gossip about Crampton paying court to Anna Coolidge of Boston. After he got to know him better Everett continued to be censorious of this man-of-the-world and was embarrassed to walk along the streets of Washington with him because he smoked a cigar in public.[19]

When Everett assumed his duties as Secretary of State there were several Anglo-American treaties pending. Webster's private secretary, G. J. Abbot, outlined them to Everett and said of Crampton:

He was very anxious that Mr. Webster should have the credit of [resolving] by another great treaty all the questions with England respecting the fisheries,

the navigation of the St. John's and St. Lawrence, reciprocity, Hudson's Bay
Company, and copyright.

We have already seen how the fisheries question intruded itself. The
claim of the Hudson's Bay Company against the United States stemmed from circumstances following America's acquisition of the Oregon
Territory. The Company was insisting on continued rights of navigation
on the Columbia River and in part of the territory north of the river
which had been purchased by the Americans. It was prepared to relinquish these provided that adequate compensation was forthcoming
from the American government. As to the Reciprocity Treaty, this
dealt with commercial relations between the United States and Canada
in which the British proposed that American tariff barriers be lowered
in return for concessions from Canada.[20]

As if Webster's death were not enough, Crampton received another
unpleasant surprise at the beginning of November: the Organization
was breaking up and the members going their several ways. Although
Levin's allusions are not entirely clear, the gist of his letter leaves little
doubt:

It has been a source of deep mortification to me, to learn that Mr. Walker
[J. Knox Walker] has left Washington, without providing for his acceptance.
It stamps him as a man, alike destitute of principle and honor. As the drawer
of the draft, I hold myself responsible for its payment, and shall provide for
it, at no distant day, although greatly pressed for means, at this time.

Apparently Walker had returned to Memphis, Tennessee, without
paying some obligation, leaving Levin to do so. It is possible that this
was why Levin asked Crampton to advance some of the copyright
money. In any case, he wanted to reassure Crampton that all was not
lost.[21]

I shall be in Washington, at the meeting of Congress [in December]. I shall
go on, in good faith, to carry the International Copyright through, as well as
the Hudson Bay Company affair. I have reason to know, that Mr. Everett
will favor both, and I am rejoiced at his appointment.

I shall also, if you approve it, lay the foundation for the certain passage
of the reciprocity Bill, if the Canadian Government acts judiciously – that
is if nothing be done to exasperate our people. That measure, must be kept
separate and distinct from the others. I feel confident of carrying all three
measures, independent of Mr. Walker or his influence.

A fortnight later Levin gave T. W. C. Moore similar assurances. He would concentrate on the three treaties alone and would 'undertake no other business'.[22]

Mr. Tucker of Philadelphia has promised me his active co-operation in carrying the reciprocity bill through Congress and it is an all-powerful influence. I have been organizing a strong force during the recess and I am willing to undertake to carry it on a contingent fee without asking any retainer. The fee however ought to be a considerable one.

Why Knox Walker suddenly left Washington is a mystery. It may have had something to do with the Senate investigation of bribery and claims. The Committee was appointed on 6 August 1852, and although it did not take Walker's testimony until the beginning of 1853, it may well have been scrutinizing his activities as early as the previous October. If he had wished to, there was no reason why he could not have continued to be active in the Organization from a distance. He need only have arranged for an agent in Washington to look after the day-to-day affairs until he could be on hand to deal personally with special cases. However, he and some of the other members chose to leave, and from this point on the Organization as an entity ceased to function. A few, such as Beverley Tucker, were still very much in evidence in the Capitol, but they seemed to be substantially on their own.

Characteristically, Levin was sure that he could manipulate the sources of political power himself. It is perhaps appropriate to wonder at this point whether he was not simply indulging in a certain amount of self-delusion. A man of considerable charm and energy, he nevertheless exaggerated his own importance and minimized the obstacles before him. Apparently he felt that he could not vanquish his opponents too casually or his triumphs over them would seem negligible. The British representative of the Hudson's Bay Co., Sir George Simpson, conveyed some of his misgivings to Crampton.[23]

Although no doubt a man of talent, I must say from what I saw and heard of him, he does not appear so circumspect as could be desired in a negotiation requiring privacy and address. Your good opinion of him however induces me to mistrust my own judgment and to repose confidence in his management.

One wonders whether Crampton also began to have doubts about Levin in the late autumn of 1852, but whether he did or not Levin had been the original liaison with the Organization and Crampton could not repudiate him and hope to enlist another agent. He either abandoned everything or carried on as best he could with Levin. This became even more imperative once Levin undertook to manage three treaties, not just the one for copyright. By the same token there was much to induce Levin to carry on. He had put all his eggs in one basket as the sole agent for the British Legation and whatever fees he hoped to earn would have to come from them.

The key to success was Everett. Without his signature on the treaty all was lost. Crampton could refund the money to the interested parties in Britain, but after they had worked so hard he was reluctant to give up so readily. Alternatively, he could bide his time and allow the Fillmore Administration to come to the end of its term of office in March 1853. If this were done Everett would no longer be Secretary of State since he had accepted the assignment only while Fillmore was President. Under a new administration there might be time to organize things more carefully. Yet Crampton and Levin knew that some of the Senators on whom they depended were 'lame duck' office-holders whose terms also ended in March 1853. Once they were gone Levin would have to begin lining up support all over again, and his influence among new Senators would mean less than it did among the retiring old guard.

In fact, Everett was not opposed to a copyright treaty. Generally he favoured it. But both he and Fillmore were reluctant to sign a treaty which they feared the Senate would repudiate. It was odd that they should be so apprehensive about a rebuff from the Senate since neither of them were staying on in the executive branch of the Government and therefore had no particular need to placate the upper branch of the Legislature. Perhaps it was vanity which prompted them to procrastinate; a desire to leave enduring legislative monuments rather than a series of wrecked treaties. Replying to Senator Sumner's query concerning the progress of the treaty Everett said:[24]

Is there a fair chance that the Senate would assent to a copyright convention? If I thought there was I would try to arrange the details with Crampton and Sartiges [French Minister] who both desire it, but there is no use in hammering upon a nail which will not go.

Fillmore proved an even greater problem. Crampton bitterly described him as 'the most hesitating and timid of mankind'. Neither John P. Kennedy's recommendation to the Cabinet nor Webster's evident willingness to sign a copyright treaty satisfied him. He insisted on asking

James A. Pearce, a Senator from Maryland and Chairman of the Senate Library Committee, to assess the mood of the upper chamber and estimate the probable chances of such a treaty. This drew open scorn from Levin who readily shared his frustration with Crampton.

The extraordinary position of the President, upon the subject referred to, may lead to delay, but it cannot produce defeat. The very contingency, upon which his action depends, will insure its success. . . . The course of the President is absurd, and ridiculous. What sources of information can Mr. Pearce have upon a subject, perhaps suggested to him for the first time? Has he canvassed the Senate? Or will he canvass the Senate after Congress shall have met? After all, his reply to Mr. Everett will be but his opinion. The true and only legitimate way to test the sense of the Senate, will be by sending in the Convention for their ratification or rejection. All else is boy's play'– disgraceful and degrading – and I should think Mr. Everett would so consider it.

Levin continued with an analysis of the current situation as he saw it. Since there was no practical way for Senator Pearce to canvass his colleagues immediately, the only possible danger was Pearce's rendering a negative opinion without sounding out his colleagues. If this seemed likely Crampton was advised to urge Everett to insist on a meeting of the Library Committee. Levin was sure he could arrange the support of two members of the Committee, Jeremiah Clemens of Alabama and Augustus Dodge of Iowa. Meanwhile additional efforts were needed to ensure that the Senate as a whole would be friendly. Levin counselled Crampton to let it be known that Webster had been prepared to sign a treaty and had 'sent for various Senators, Whig and Democratic – who pledged their support, both to the Copyright and the Hudson Bay negotiation'. Webster's son, Fletcher, should also be asked to publicize his father's support.[25]

Not only did Senator Pearce eventually report favourably on the treaty, but in the meantime sympathetic parties unconnected with the Crampton–Levin conspiracy began to apply pressure on Senators and other members of the Administration. That redoubtable champion of international copyright, John Jay of New York, again became active. Probably as a result of his regular correspondence with Senator Charles Sumner he learned of the pending copyright negotiations and gratuitously supplied him with a copy of the 1848 memorial which had been sent to the House of Representatives. One of the most interesting parts of this document was an appendix which listed British reprints of American books, and Jay promised to ask G. P. Putnam, its compiler, to bring the list up to date so that Sumner could make current use of it. Jay still smarted because the House had never ordered his lengthy memorial printed, and what was more, it had never seen the 1848 Committee report because the Chairman, T. B. King, had been derelict in his duty. Jay now sent copies of his memorial to Nathaniel Hawthorne, Senator William H. Seward of New York, and Frederick Hudson, Managing Editor of the *New York Herald*, asking Seward if he could arrange to have it printed. To the Edinburgh firm of Blackwood's he reported: 'I am endeavoring to enlist the aid of a few gentlemen here to use their personal influence with the Senators likely to oppose us.' He also counted on the fact that the extreme popularity of *Uncle Tom's Cabin* in Britain would alert Americans to the pirating of their books abroad and make them more disposed to a copyright agreement. Coincidentally he was echoing the same sentiments that John Blackwood had expressed to Bulwer six months earlier. Jay also hoped that many Southerners would favour such an agreement since it might have the effect of excluding British writings on sensitive subjects like slavery; a curious argument for a staunch abolitionist like Jay.[26]

The question inevitably arises as to Jay's awareness of the Crampton–Levin scheme. Jay certainly knew that negotiations were going on, and from Blackwood he learned that Bulwer was in close communication with Crampton. But Blackwood was most circumspect in what he told Jay, and there is no evidence to suggest that Jay was in on the secret. He met Crampton once during these months but it was only a brief encounter, and on the whole Jay's sphere of influence was quite different from that of the British Minister and the other lobbyists.

Up to this point the opposition forces were negligible. The Harpers had been asked by President Fillmore what they thought of a possible copyright treaty, and they somewhat ingenuously declined to express a private opinion, acknowledging only that the question was important; that British and American authors were generally in favour; and manufacturers and the reading public were not.[27] However, by the end of January 1853 certain publishers and printers were beginning to take alarm, and several of them presented an elaborate memorandum to the Secretary of State enumerating their 'Objections' to a treaty. Everett showed these to Crampton and invited him to comment confidentially. With the help of W. M. Thackeray, who was in America at the time, Crampton composed a résumé of 'Observations' in response to the

'Objections' and by so doing hoped to satisfy Everett and strengthen his resolve to sign the treaty. Fortunately copies of these documents have survived, and they portray vividly the fears as well as the hopes surrounding copyright.

The 'Objections' originated with an anxiety that British authors and publishers would exercise 'complete control over the publication of their works in the U.S.'. Popular writers like Bulwer, Dickens, and Macaulay 'could then exact their own prices for their books when sold here'. Thus, copyright would not only enhance the profits of major authors, but at the same time protect and encourage second-rate foreign talent. It would also interfere with the laws of supply and demand because it encouraged monopoly which was never in the public interest. Tariff duties might be appropriate for some industries, but they were never intended to confer a monopoly on a producer. As for books, they were unlike other commodities; whereas it took the same amount of labour to create each new hat or boot, the multiplication of copies of a book meant a saving on each additional facsimile. Further, authors and publishers enjoyed rights in their literary property only by virtue of statute law, not 'absolute and natural ownership. . . . The right of individual property has always been held subordinate to the public good' which was best served through free competition and cheap reprints.

It is universally conceded that the American people are far more intelligent than the English, and this is the special mark and proof of the superiority of their condition and character. . . . As popular reading must always be the chief means of popular education, a restriction of it would be seriously and injuriously felt upon our population, enlightenment and prosperity.

America's intellectual superiority was cited as the product of public-supported education which in turn developed a reading public far larger than Britain's.

In commenting upon these arguments, Crampton had to nimbly pick his way through the profusion of truths and half-truths because if he revealed an insulting or condescending attitude he might offend the American Secretary of State. Therefore, he began by suggesting that the 'Objections' were somewhat contradictory. If Americans were as intellectually advanced as they claimed, why were they so dependent upon British literature. With ten British works being reprinted in America for every one American work reprinted in Britain, surely other issues were involved.

While the United States were colonies it was natural that they should seek a supply of their literary wants in England, but the rough work of colonization is now over; a state of advancement in every other art and science equal to that of any other of the countries of Europe has been obtained; and yet the practice of relying upon England for a supply of literature is, to a great degree, maintained. This cannot be accounted for in any natural cause now existing. An explanation of the fact must therefore be sought in the existence of some artificial discouragement to the cultivation of literature in America, which has prevented its natural development.

By 'artificial discouragement' Crampton clearly implied the Congress whose members had failed to legislate an international copyright treaty.

Crampton was not alone in defending the cause of copyright. Many others felt that the time was right for the passage of a treaty and that there was much more support throughout the country than was generally recognized. The *New York Herald* declared with its usual exuberance:

The country is unanimous in favor of international copyright. Whigs and Democrats, protectionists and freetraders, book-makers and readers, writers and printers, and even a majority of the publishers, concur in confessing that honesty is not only the most becoming but the most advantageous policy to pursue. Neither the arguments nor the numerical strength of the dissidents entitle them to much consideration when ninety-nine hundredths of the people are clamorous for copyright. The Senate may safely stamp its sanction on the treaty in spite of the whine of one or two grasping publishers, and the groans of their newspaper organs. . . . On the Senators . . . now rest the whole responsibility of the future pillage of foreign authors. They have it in their power to rivet still closer the mill stone round the neck of our literature, or to cut it loose, once and forever. If they falter or swerve from their duty, let the ignominy of literary piracies attach to them – let them be branded as men who have done their utmost to crush our native authors and retain this country in a state of intellectual vassalage to England.

Yet other 'Objections' required answers. There was a general acknowledgment that the low prices of American books would inevitably rise after the passage of a copyright treaty. Crampton admitted that an agreement 'would no doubt increase the price to some extent, but to a much smaller extent than is supposed. . . . The cheapness of the English editions of books lately published in England for railway and colonial consumption, and for which copyright is paid, is a convincing proof of this'. G. P. Putnam took essentially the same tack in a letter to the *National Intelligencer.*

The objection urged by some that it would largely increase the price of books in this country, and would be a burdensome tax on the reading community, I believe to be wholly unfounded. It can be shown I think conclusively, . . . the interests of publishers will prompt them to make books cheap – suited in price to the character of the market – and that in this country at least it is more profitable to publish books at moderate prices, within the means of the largest number of readers, than it is to make them expensive.

For some the question of prices was as much moral as economic. According to the *New York Herald*:

Books, they tell you, are cheaper now than they would be under an international copyright law. The statement may possibly be true, though we are not at all clear that the few cents a volume which the copyright would secure to the author, would come out of the reader's pocket. But is it in a civilized land that we are gravely told to steal instead of buy because it is cheaper? Is it among men of wealth, standing, and education, that the economy of a systematic theft is descanted upon, and the pick-pocket is commended because he has saved half a dollar by stealing the handkerchief he desired, instead of buying it? The Messrs. Harper may, very probably, find it more economical to help themselves to an author's labor than to offer him a fair remuneration for it; and we, and other book readers, would also find it cheaper to help ourselves to a book from Messrs. Harper's shelves than to buy it over the counter. If the rule be good in one case, it is equally good in the other. Far as they may excel the rest of the community in the boldness and the extent of their 'border forays', the Harpers cannot be suffered to enjoy a monopoly of rapine.

Both sides became enmeshed in contradictions when describing the likely effect of a copyright agreement on the American book trade. They agreed that British authors had essentially two alternatives: sell the reprint rights to American publishers, or export their books from Britain to America. Opponents to a treaty condemned either alternative, pointing out that in the first instance British authors would doubtless ask as much as they dared and the American reading public would suffer accordingly. In the second, British-manufactured books would flood the American market, jeopardizing the employment and security of thousands of native artisans. Clearly the former was preferable to the latter, as everyone admitted that home-produced books were better than importations. Besides, Crampton gave assurances that British authors were in no position to dictate terms to American publishers.

The amount of this price depends upon elements which he has no power whatsoever to fix. It will depend upon the intrinsic usefulness of the article, upon its scarcity, and upon the degree of competition which may exist in the market at the time the article is offered for sale.

Elsewhere Crampton put forth the argument that retail prices of British books need not rise excessively if British publishers printed large impressions and were thereby able to export cheaper copies. But this was the last thing American publishers wanted. As it was, one-fifth of British works were imported, and any copyright agreement which threatened the American book trade was not to be tolerated. In one way or another the trade insisted on cheap books on its own terms, which meant reprinting British books in America either through piracy or paying for advance sheets when it proved convenient. The policy partook of a curious blend of protectionism and free trade: protection for American industry but not American authors; freedom to reprint British works but not to import them.²⁸

While this controversy raged the President and the Cabinet were incredibly *blasé*. As late as January Fillmore was merely instructing Everett to discuss the 'expediency' of a copyright convention at a Cabinet meeting. Everett in turn made a mild request of J. P. Kennedy to attend in order to lend a helping hand. Another month passed without anything happening. On 2 February Levin informed Crampton that he had the required number of votes, and would he therefore bring the issue to a head quickly.²⁹

Will you have the goodness to see Mr. Everett tomorrow and say to him, that you have the strongest possible assurances that the International Copyright treaty, will be ratified by the Senate.

General Cass is now, all right! *You may say, to Mr. E., that Mr. Cass will secure its passing . . . or you may, if you think it advisable, ask him to consult General Cass upon the subject, and let his (General Cass) action decide the question of signing the Treaty, one way or the other.*

. . . We have on the Democratic *side, Judge Douglas, Senator Dodge and Son, I. P. Walker, Clemens, Bayard, Atchison, Rusk, – Hale (and his friends in the Senate) – as he himself told me today – and as soon as Mr. Dandrige [?] arrives I shall have Hunter, Mason and Judge Butler.*

If necessary *I can bring an influence from Pennsylvania. That will secure Brodhead, and another influence, if required, that will control Borland.*

This was indeed a formidable array of the Senate's majority party. Senator Lewis Cass of Michigan had been a Democratic Presidential contender in 1848. Stephen A. Douglas of Illinois had sought the Democratic nomination for President in 1852 and as leader of the 'Young America' movement was a man who inspired loyal friendship or bitter hostility, seen later when he became Abraham Lincoln's chief adversary. Andrew P. Butler (South Carolina), Robert M. T. Hunter (Virginia), and James M. Mason (Virginia) were probably the three most powerful Southern Senators. They were not only colleagues but close personal friends, sharing the same residence in Washington. As Chairman of the Foreign Relations Committee, Mason was crucial to the success of any treaty.[30]

In February rumours were rife that the copyright treaty had already been signed and sent to the Senate. Crampton of course knew this was pure speculation, but he feared idle gossip. On the twelfth Levin reported: 'In a conversation which Mr. Everett had a few days ago with a certain U.S. Senator, Mr. Everett said that the only point of difficulty was concerning stereotype editions, and that all *he* asked was a *truly* reciprocal Treaty.'[31] As for stereotype plates these were the perennial bugbear because it was feared that they would be manufactured in Britain and become the source from which cheap reprints would be exported to America.

On 14 February President Fillmore finally authorized Everett to sign the treaty. Crampton and Everett conferred on the following two days, and signed a treaty 'for the Establishment of International Copyright' on the 17th. It was then conveyed to the Senate for its advice and consent. A small scrap of paper dated 21 February 1853 concluded the story: – 'Received from John F. Crampton Esq., Hon. Envoy Extraordinary etc., £1,000 sterling. – Lewis C. Levin.'[32]

With a mixture of pride and apprehension Crampton reported to the new Foreign Secretary, Lord Clarendon:[33]

I send home today a treaty for International Copyright . . . I had a hard fight to get it signed, and it is yet to go through the fiery ordeal of the Senate, where I have done my best to prepare the ground for it. The assurances I receive would, in any other country, make me sanguine of success; but here political blasts and counter-blasts are so rapid and changeable, and honorable

Gentlemen slippery, that it is hard to count upon anything. Whatever becomes of it however it is something to have got such a Treaty signed and presented, for I believe the inherent fairness of the measure and the real advantage of it to American Literature will ultimately secure its success, altho' on the present occasion it may be staved off by the application of dollars by the rich piratical Publishing houses of New York and Philadelphia.

Chapter XII

~~~~~~

THE NEED FOR SENATE RATIFICATION: FEBRUARY 1853–JUNE 1854

When Crampton signed the Copyright Treaty on 17 February he was all too aware that time was running out on the second session of the Thirty-second Congress. The Fillmore Administration had only a fortnight before it expired and Congress adjourned. On 4 March the President, Franklin Pierce, was sworn in. In a letter to Clarendon, Crampton informed him that

Congress, after a great deal of speechifying, has separated without doing anything. The Senate however remains in session for a month or so for what is called 'Executive business': that is to say confirmation of appointments, consideration of Treaties, etc. which is conducted in Secret Session and does not require the presence of the other House of Congress. The Copyright Treaty will come under their consideration. I hope they will pass it.

But fresh obstacles arose. Senators whose terms expired did not stay in Washington for the special session, and though their replacements arrived, they were preoccupied with the novelty of their situation and unfamiliar with the residue of unfinished business. Senators who were neither retiring nor arriving and who composed about two-thirds of the upper chamber were none the less anxious to conclude business and leave Washington as soon as possible. Men who were attentive and hardworking in January were likely to be unavailable or absent by April. For these reasons, Crampton and Levin had fervently wished that the Treaty would come to a vote prior to 4 March. However, they were helpless witnesses to legislative drift.

IAP

When Everett delivered the Copyright Treaty to the Senate on 18 February he relinquished control of it and it became the concern of the Committee on Foreign Relations whose Chairman was James M. Mason of Virginia, and whose members included Douglas of Illinois, Mangum of North Carolina, Norris of New Hampshire, and Underwood of Kentucky. As far as one can tell they did not consider the Copyright Treaty prior to the 4 March adjournment. Between adjournment and the second session of Congress beginning in December some important personnel changes occurred. Everett left the Executive Branch of the Government but claimed a seat in the Senate as one of the newly elected Senators from Massachusetts. William L. Marcy, former Governor of the State of New York and Secretary of War under President Polk, replaced Everett as Secretary of State. It may also be recalled that Marcy was one of the founding fathers of the Organization. The Foreign Relations Committee was reconstituted, with Mason still as Chairman, and Messrs Everett, Clayton, Douglas, Slidell, and Norris as colleagues.[1]

By mid-March the prospects of Senate ratification seemed good. Everett's presence on the Foreign Relations Committee augured well. Marcy was thought to favour the Treaty, and Levin claimed close, almost intimate ties with Marcy's family. Crampton reported to Lord Clarendon that the fisheries issue had quietened down and without a Presidential election in the offing Anglo-American relations were improving. Of special significance was the signing on 15 March of an Anglo-American Treaty for the settlement of outstanding claims which established arbitration procedures for private claims reaching as far back as the American Revolution and the War of 1812.[2] Crampton and Levin also seem to have been successful manipulators of the newspaper press. Of the *New York Herald*, Crampton commented: 'I have been fortunate enough to get one of the most ferocious anti-British organs, but at the same time by far the most widely read and influential papers in the U.S., to *go along* in our favour.' Quite independently John Jay noted that 'the tone of our newspaper press has been more decidedly in favour of a treaty than ever before, and our publishers are I think generally in favour of it'. Jay's personal efforts reinforced the press campaign. Through his acquaintance with Frederick Hudson, Managing Editor of the *Herald*, he secured some valuable statistics that showed that the majority of British works reprinted in America were handled by a comparatively few printers and publishers. He passed this information on to Everett, who he hoped would make use of it in his new role as a member of the Senate Foreign Relations Committee. [3]

Despite these favourable indicators, there were signs suggesting that all was not well. In early March Jay reported to Samuel Warren, author of *Ten Thousand a Year*, concerning the Treaty:

its fate is doubtful. I have just returned from Washington where I passed a few days with no other object than that of advancing the copyright interest, but as it had not yet come before the Senate and most of that body were ignorant of the matter, I could form no certain opinion of its chance of ratification. Mr. Crampton however was rather sanguine and, as Mr. Everett goes from the State Department into the Senate, his large personal influence will be exerted in its favor.

As we have already seen Everett's timidity tended to undermine the cause since he was looked upon as an authority on copyright. Thus his presence on the Foreign Relations Committee was a mixed blessing. Unfortunately Marcy did nothing to help. Since assuming his cabinet post he had virtually ignored the copyright issue, claiming that the State Department had been besieged by office-seekers and patronage-pedlars. Crampton related to Clarendon: [4]

The Senate are still in Session occupied with confirming appointments. . . . Mr. Marcy still professes that he has not had time to look into a single state paper since he came into office. A good many of the Senators have dispersed, and can now barely muster a 'quorum': under these circumstances, Mr. Everett and the other friends of the Copyright Treaty have judged it better to let it lie over till next Session. I have every reason to believe however that the feeling in its favour is on the increase, and I have good hopes of our carrying it in December next.

If there had been any hope of Marcy's applying pressure on the Foreign Relations Committee it was clearly misplaced.

The mustering of a quorum in the Senate was also becoming increasingly difficult. On 14 March Everett noted in his diary: 'a meeting of the Committee on Foreign Relations at which the Copyright Convention was read, and agreed to report it without any recommendation of its passage or rejection'. Later that same day on the floor of the Senate

an attempt [was] then made to take up treaties but given up in despair in consequence of want of quorum. There is no disposition on the part of the

Senate to do business. Many of the members are light and frivolous persons without feeling of responsibility; more are absorbed in President-making and general electioneering. The public good is the last thing thought of.

The Copyright Treaty was reported out of Committee the next day, but insufficient quorums continued to frustrate Senate business.[5]

By mid-March the Copyright Treaty was further and perhaps fatally undermined by a prolonged debate in the Senate on Central America. Crampton set forth the issues in a letter to the British Foreign Secretary in London:[6]

News arrived here on the 16th of the supposed proceedings of the 'Devastation' at Truxillo & Limas, distorted & magnified as usual, and produced one of those violent Democratic Anti British Squalls in the Senate, during which neither reason nor common sense could be heard. The arrival of this report was very unfortunately timed, for as bad luck would have it, the Senate were still engaged in a Debate on the Clayton–Bulwer Treaty. The Democratic Party who were endeavouring to fix upon us an Infraction of the Treaty in regard to our Protectorate of Mosquito and the Colony of the Bay Islands, I need scarcely say, eagerly seized upon the report that the Mosquito Flag had been hoisted over Truxillo, a town within the limits of Honduras, and that Her M's Steamer 'Devastation' was then bombarding some other Place in 'Central America' as a full confirmation of their assertations. This news has been since contradicted, but it served the purposes of these Gentlemen much too well not to gain their belief. It is somewhat unfortunate too that on the same day there should arrive news of a squabble between the Municipality of Greytown & the American Transit Route Company there, but as in this case, both Parties are Americans & we have no possible interest in the matter, they are inclined to take a less angry view of it.

These storms are, I think, of a transitory nature, & arise very much out of the struggle for offices. 'Young America,' under the Leadership of Mr. Douglas, wishes to shew Mr. Pierce that he cannot pass over its Claims with impugnity.

To understand this tangled web one must isolate the individual strands and analyse each one. In one way or another, they all originate with the Clayton–Bulwer Treaty (July 1850). The circumstances leading to its passage go some way toward explaining future complications. John M. Clayton, Secretary of State under President Taylor, was eagerly searching for a way to prevent further encroachment by the British in Central America; and similarly, Henry Lytton Bulwer, the British Minister to Washington, was anxious to check America's expansion there under the rubric of Manifest Destiny. The Anglo-American development of a canal across the isthmus between North and South America seemed the answer to both these problems. However, five days after such a treaty was ratified President Taylor died, and within a short length of time Daniel Webster replaced Clayton in the State Department. At the same time adverse public sentiment began to build up in America because many people disliked the idea of sharing the development of a canal with Great Britain and voiced their opinion that America should act on its own. As the months passed the proposed canal became increasingly important. The discovery of gold in California was one ingredient, but far more consequential was the incredible territorial expansion resulting from the war with Mexico. Almost overnight America had acquired Texas, Arizona, New Mexico, California, Oregon, Washington, and Eastward to the Great Plains. Within a few years she became a Pacific Ocean power in connection with the Sandwich Islands, China, and Japan. Suddenly a canal across Central America was essential to her diplomatic and strategic interests.

According to the Clayton–Bulwer Treaty, both parties agreed not to establish fortifications, protectorates, and colonies in any portion of Central America. This self-denying principle seemed clear enough but proved to be a great stumbling block. At the time of ratification Britain claimed an interest in three areas: British Honduras or Belize, directly South of Mexico and forming the South-east coast of the Yucatan Peninsula; the Bay Islands off the coast of the Republic of Honduras; and an ill-defined area along the Atlantic coast of Central America from Guatemala to Panama inhabited by the Mosquito Indians. In drawing up the Treaty, Clayton and Bulwer ignored the ultimate disposition of these areas, Bulwer assuming the tacit recognition of British rights and Clayton inferring their repudiation.

In Britain attitudes varied concerning whether these areas should be supported or abandoned. The American Minister to London reported 'that the British Government was becoming tired of continuing the protectorate and would gladly abandon it if any method could be devised of saving the national honour'. Crampton agreed:

I don't know exactly what terms may be considered as an honourable release for us from our position of protectors of the Mosquitoes, but I sincerely hope we may be able to make a clean job of it and get out of that position for good and all.

Lord Aberdeen's equivocal position was typical of British Government officials.[7]

I apprehend however that the great difficulty [of British withdrawal from the Mosquito protectorate] would not be on account of the Indians, but a certain number of English, or rather Scotch adventurers, who have obtained for a gallon of brandy, large grants of land from a drunken Savage whom we have thought fit to call a King. . . . I looked into this subject five and twenty years ago, and I never could discover on what pretext we made San Juan, or as we now call it, Greytown, a part of the Mosquito territory. As for the Bay Islands, our title is little better than manifest usurpation.

Until the beginning of 1853 those in America who were disgruntled by the Treaty were fairly moderate in their opposition. Then on 6 January, in a speech on the Senate floor, Senator Lewis Cass of Michigan accused the former Secretary of State of having deceived the upper chamber when he presented the Clayton–Bulwer Treaty for ratification. Though Cass was forced to retreat somewhat from this allegation he unleashed a protracted debate on Central America. Other Senators took up where he left off, all roundly condemning the Treaty. Stephen A. Douglas of Illinois was one of the most outspoken as was James M. Mason of Virginia, both members of the Foreign Relations Committee, so it was not surprising that the Committee issued a censorious report on 11 February 1853.[8]

While the Senate hotly debated American and British interests in the area fresh news arrived from Central America. On 15 March the official Democratic newspaper, the *Washington Union*, reported that a British armed steamer, the *Devastation*, had forced the surrender of the Honduran port of Truxillo (Tampillo) and had shelled the nearby port of Limas in the name of protecting British property. Two days later word was received that an American naval ship entered the port of Greytown to reinforce the claims of an American Transit Company.[9]

Remembering Crampton's private letter to Clarendon, it is perhaps clearer what he meant by 'these storms . . . arise very much out of the struggle for offices'. Regarding the incident involving the steamship *Devastation*, Crampton continues:

Although this statement has since been in substance contradicted, belief of it subsisted sufficiently long to increase the excitement already existing in regard to the affairs of Central America. Certain Senators, who impugned the Policy of the Treaty of 1850, found it convenient to refer to this vague report as an ascertained fact and as a fresh instance of a violation by Great Britain of Her Engagements. Violent and unfriendly language was again made use of by Mr. Douglas, followed by loud applause in the Galleries of the Senate.

In another dispatch written the same day he reported:[10]

The Committee on Foreign Relations had, I am also confidentially informed, prepared a report on the Copyright Treaty favourable to the adoption of a measure, which they were about to submit to the consideration of the Senate; but under the circumstances they have thought it more prudent to hold it over until the unreasonable excitement now prevailing shall have subsided.

Once the excitement over Central America subsided, Crampton had every reason to hope that the Senate would give its full attention to the Copyright Treaty. It ratified the Anglo-American Claims Convention on 15 March which seemed to imply that other Anglo-American projects might fare equally well. However, Crampton had been told by Senator Clayton that the vote on the Claims Convention was so close that it would have been defeated had it not been for the votes of one or two Senators. This news had the effect of seriously shaking Crampton's confidence, and he became convinced that the Senate was so hostile to Britain that it would reject any other Anglo-American legislation.

From the Executive Journal of the Senate it is evident that the vote was actually not close at all. The tally showed thirty in favour and five opposed; well beyond the two-thirds majority requisite for the confirmation of treaties. What Clayton must have meant was that the Treaty almost failed for lack of a quorum. With sixty-two Senators potentially in attendance during the special session of 1853, a quorum consisted of thirty-two. Since the total number of votes cast on 15 March was thirty-five, Clayton's story was partially true, yet hardly an accurate description of the proceedings. The list of those who voted for and against the Claims Convention is revealing. Many of the Democrats on whose support Levin was depending had supposedly departed from Washington, as their names were not recorded. None the less, there were still a substantial number of potential votes for copyright to be seen on Capitol Hill, and among the five who opposed the Claims Convention only Douglas was a worry in terms of his power and influence in the Senate. Had Crampton felt more confident and able to prod both Everett and the

Foreign Relations Committee, the Senate might well have ratified the
Copyright Treaty in late March 1853.[11] As it was, his resolve was faltering
and the opposition forces which had thus far remained quiet began to
surface. In a letter of 7 March Crampton describes his first awareness
of this.[12]

*am somewhat alarmed at discovering that Messrs. 'Harper & Brothers', the
great Piratical Publishers at New York have sent an Agent to Washington
with 50,000 Dollars to be spent in opposition to the measure. I will do what I
can to counteract the literary 'filibuster' by letting it be known that we are
aware of what is going on. I suspected something of the sort, but it was only
by mere accident that I discovered it.*

Three weeks after this discovery Crampton found himself temporarily
deserted by Levin who went South due to illness in his family. He wrote
to Crampton on 22 March from Key West, Florida:[13]

*I shall be in Washington by the first of June. I am waiting most anxiously
to hear of the action of the Senate in regard to the International Copyright.
Changes were made in the Senate by the efforts of the Piratical Publishers
before I left Washington. Every Engine was brought to bear and we had no
time to counteract their insidious efforts. Under these circumstances, I venture
to suggest, that if there were no certainty of the Treaty being ratified, that it
had better lay over till next Session. I am singularly fortunate in having Mr.
Marcy Secretary of State. The accompanying letter will show you the relation
in which I stand to him. He will go as far as any man living to serve me, and
I hope, if the questions in which you are so deeply interested have not been
acted upon, that you will not press them, until I have an opportunity to see
him.*

It was certainly awkward to be without Levin's services just when
they were most needed. Perhaps trouble should have been anticipated
when too much time had been allowed to elapse and too many delays
unaccounted for. The threat was always present that the opposition might
some day exploit the same tactics to influence the legislators as Levin
and Crampton had employed. Everett suggested this when writing to
Putnam: 'great pains have been taken by outsiders to prejudice the Senate
against the treaty; and not much to counteract these efforts. . . .' On
5 April Senator Mason reintroduced the Copyright Treaty for its Second
Reading and promptly moved to table the measure. Since this special
Senate session ended on 11 April, the Treaty would not come up again

until Congress reconvened in December, and Crampton's slim hope was that the opposition would dissipate by then.[14]

Meanwhile, the Foreign Office and the Board of Trade were carefully scrutinizing the signed Treaty. Although modelled upon the 1851 Anglo-French version, the Anglo-American convention had some significant modifications. Crampton's instructions were to discourage any such changes because the Treaty would then need the approval of Parliament whereas otherwise sanction by an Order in Council would suffice. However, when Everett threatened not to sign, Crampton agreed to some alterations, later explaining to Clarendon: 'I have been led to hope that Her Majesty's Government will not disapprove of my having consented to embody them therein, without waiting for further instructions from your Lordship.' Most of the Treaty's articles were straightforward. British and American authors would enjoy reciprocal copyright protection 'of books, of dramatic works, of musical compositions, of drawings, of paintings, of sculpture, of engraving, of lithography, and of any other works of literature and of the fine arts' (Article I). Since drama and music were favourite targets of plagiarism, Article II distinguished between fair imitation or adaptation and illicit pirating, the courts in each country deciding doubtful cases. Registration in one country must take place within three months of a work's first appearance in the other. Unlike the Anglo-French Treaty, tariff duties were not imposed on imported books. Lord Malmesbury gave Crampton the option of retaining or dropping this provision, and later it was made clear why it was omitted:

an article involving . . . a rate of duty would have necessitated a reference to the House of Representatives as well as the Senate . . . and would thus probably bring on a discussion of the merits of the whole question in the former body, in which opposition to or procrastination were most to be apprehended.

Each country could prohibit undesirable forms of literature, such as works of sedition, blasphemy, and obscenity. No fewer than four Articles dealt with the exclusion of foreign reprints (Articles I, III, IV, and X), and here the principle of reciprocity proved especially convenient. Instead of specifying penalties such as seizure and destruction, piracies were subject to the respective laws of Britain and America which avoided the problem of reconciling differing legal traditions. Lastly it was specified that the Treaty had to be ratified within twelve months of its being signed and would remain in effect for five years with the option of further renewal.

Only Article VI drew universal disfavour. It had not been a part of the Anglo-French Treaty but was strongly urged by Everett despite Crampton's vigorous opposition. 'Mr. Everett seemed to be of opinion', Crampton noted, 'that without the addition of an article such as we have adopted, the chances of success of the convention, when brought before the Senate, would be so seriously impaired as to render him unwilling to submit it to their consideration.' The offending article is worth quoting not because of its elegant style but rather its impact on later events.[15]

It is hereby agreed . . . that if a work is published in either country and the copyright thereof secured by registration under the provisions of the present Treaty in the other country; and if two or more editions of such work shall have been published in either country at different prices; then such Author, his Representatives or Assigns shall publish, or permit to be published, in the other country, an edition of such work not more expensive than the cheapest of the said two or more editions published in his own country; and it is agreed that the publication of such edition shall be made within 12 months after the first publication of the work in the country where it was first published.

Though the language was complicated, the problem it was addressing was the American fear of being forced to buy high-priced British books. It was widely thought that British publishers would foist expensive copyrighted editions on the American market and by so doing would preclude domestic publication of cheaper editions. Most readers were accustomed to the phenomenon of the gradual lowering of the original price of a newly published work and the issuing of cheaper colonial editions, but there was a widespread suspicion that the British would try to extort as much as possible from America. Crampton tried to dampen such fears by publicizing the testimony of 'an English gentleman now at Washington, himself an author of great merit and popularity' (Thackeray), who insisted that Article VI 'could never prove injurious or inconvenient to British authors or publishers, and that in fact what it intends to prevent could by no possibility occur, for it would be clearly to the interest of every author or publisher of a work to supply the American market at the cheapest possible rate'. However, mistrust persisted, and when the Foreign Office reviewed the Treaty it joined the grumbling because of the likelihood that being a new provision it would necessitate an Act of Parliament. For its part the Board of Trade doubted that this would be necessary, and after six weeks' consideration 'approved generally of the provisions of the above convention and . . . they see no objection to its ratification by Her Majesty in its present form'.

A Foreign Office minute circulated in May observed:

Our usual course with regard to treaties with countries where the Executive cannot ratify without the previous sanction of the Legislature, is not to prepare the Queen's ratification until we know that the other side is going to ratify, so as to avoid the indignity of the Queen's ratification being thrown away in the event of a refusal of a requisite sanction.

Almost simultaneously the Foreign Office received a copy of a letter which Alfred Turner, Longman's and Murray's legal adviser, had sent to the Board of Trade challenging the exact meaning of Article VI. What was meant by the phrase requiring an author to 'publish or permit to be published' an edition as cheap as any in the country of origin? Could this not be construed as 'an absolute printing and publishing in America' which would have the effect of disallowing American copyright to copies printed in Britain? Turner continued:[16]

But as it is a very important point to the English trader that the employment given to paper-makers and printers should not be so transferred to a foreign state, I beg to submit . . . the insertion of a few words in the article . . . to make a sale or publication sufficient.

Turner's letter raised two significant matters. First, British printers and publishers were just as anxious to protect their trade interests as were their counterparts in America; and second, one of the main attractions of an Anglo-American Copyright Treaty from the British point of view was the prospect of increasing the number of books they exported abroad. With these concerns in mind the Foreign Office instructed Crampton:[17]

There are however in the 6th article of the Convention some expressions which it is apprehended by the legal adviser of some eminent publishers in this country, might be construed in a sense which they were not designed to bear. . . . although Her Majesty's Government will accept the Convention in the terms in which it was signed, and would not wish any difficulty to be raised on the point referred to . . . if the United States Government would also be willing to ratify as it stands, it would be well to adopt the alterations suggested by the publishers in the event that its being found necessary hereafter to introduce any other alterations in the Convention.

When Crampton voiced British concern over Article VI to Marcy and Everett the latter admitted that he was also becoming increasingly uneasy about it and as a result was going to propose a substitute amendment to the Senate.[18]

The right of property or copyright provided for by this Convention shall be enjoyed in the United States only in the case of such works of British Authors which shall be stereotyped or printed and published in the United States; and it shall be enjoyed in Great Britain only in the case of such works of the United States Authors as shall be stereotyped or printed and published in Great Britain. Where a work is first published in the country of the author, no right of property or copyright in the same shall be enjoyed in the other country, unless the republication takes place within three months from the time of the first publication; and if two or more editions of a work shall be published in either country, and at different prices, no right of property or of copyright shall be enjoyed in favour of the said work, unless the republication in the other country shall be of an edition not more expensive than the cheapest of the aforesaid edition published at different prices.

Clearly Everett was succumbing to the traditional insistence of the American book trade for a 'manufacturing clause'. Ever since 1837 when Senator Clay introduced the first international copyright bill, foreign books could obtain a copyright only when they were republished in America. This assured the American printing industry of business while preventing the British from cornering the reprint market. Opponents of copyright traditionally latched on to this issue, but it was significant that ever staunch advocates like G. P. Putnam, D. Appleton, R. Carter & Bros, C. Scribner, and Stanford & Swords sent a memorial to Everett stipulating:[19]

that the type shall be set up and the book printed and bound in this country. The necessity of this provision is obvious, for if an English publisher or author may print and bind the book in England and at the same time secure a copyright without being required to print and bind his book here, then more than one-half of the mechanics and women employed in the type foundries, printing offices, paper mills, book binderies and the various collateral branches will be thrown out of employment, and great distress must follow.

The combination of a manufacturing clause and a mandatory republication of the cheapest editions was too much for the leaders of the London book trade. Although they should not have known about Everett's contemplated amendment because the provisions of the Treaty were still secret, they were, in fact, made aware of it through close ties with the Board of Trade. At this juncture Longman and Murray sat down with Alfred Turner and set forth their reservations in a lengthy memorandum which ultimately formed the basis of future Governmental policy.

One of their concerns was whether a Treaty superseded all previous American legislation. That is, whether for example Congressional action would be necessary to revise the extant copyright law of 1831 which conferred protection only on American citizens or residents, or would the proposed Treaty granting reciprocity to British subjects take automatic precedence.[20] This problem was referred in the first instance to James M. Carlisle, the Attorney for the British Legation in Washington. Citing the second clause of the sixth article of the US Constitution, he noted that duly signed and ratified treaties embodied the 'supreme law of the land', and that a treaty was 'equivalent to an act of the Legislature'. However, the Supreme Court did distinguish between treaty contracts which required legislative enforcement and international treaties where no further legislation was necessary. Armed with these reassurances Crampton formally raised the issue with Secretary of State Marcy who in turn referred it to the Attorney-General, Caleb Cushing. In an Opinion dated 16 February 1854 Cushing unhesitatingly confirmed Carlisle's findings and added 'therefore the Convention is and must be during its continuance competent and sufficient . . . to secure the British subjects a right to all the capacities, privileges and property which have the objects, intent of the Convention'.[21]

Taking a lead from the Longman–Murray–Turner memorandum, the President of the Board of Trade posed several other difficult problems were Article VI amended as Everett wished. First, as to maps and engravings:

It would be impossible to have a facsimile of an engraved plate made in America, because the artist would not be there to do it, and if it could be so engraved there, the time limited by the Convention [three months] for securing a copyright would not admit of any work of consequence being done in that country. . . . The English proprietor of a plate of any value would not send it out to be printed from. . . . The recent and beautiful invention of imitations of oil and watercolour pictures printed from prepared stones or blocks [would preclude republication in America]. Here, not only the proper original drawing on the stone or block is required but the practical experience and judgment of the workman, to take off the impression accurately.

In addition many books such as Thomson's *Seasons*, Walton's *Angler*, and Gray's *Elegy* claimed no copyright for the letterpress but solely for the engravings. Other works like the *Poems* of Rogers or Tupper's *Proverbial Philosophy* claimed copyright for both. Since amended Article VI applied a formula which varied not only with respect to production but also to price, Turner wondered seriously whether the disadvantages didn't outweigh the advantages:

The English author or proprietor must either open a shop in America and publish himself, or sell the right to publish there to some party resident there. If as is most probable he adopts the latter course, what control can he have as to what editions the party may think it prudent or advisable to publish.

Even an American publisher took a risk if he issued a reprint, since he might at any time be liable to produce a cheaper edition if a British publisher lowered his selling price at home.

The effect that the amendment could have on the cost of books troubled the Board of Trade.

If enforced, it is calculated to unduly enhance the cost of printed books to the public of both nations. In this country it will deprive the publisher of the power of which he now avails himself, to reduce the price of a particular book by working off from the same types and illustrations an extra number of copies for exportation to the U.S., and it will have a similar operation in the U.S., where the current literature is largely derived from British authors, by requiring the repetition there of every process of printing. . . . Thus the public both of Great Britain and America will be unnecessarily taxed in order to establish a new species of protection for the restriction in favour of printers and publishers.

The Board further doubted whether finer and more elaborate editions could be sold in America if only the cheapest editions could claim copyright. A possible compromise might involve the letterpress being done in America with the exception of prints, engravings, and maps which could be run off in Britain from the original plates and copies sent to

America. Failing such a compromise, the Board of Trade was 'still of opinion that the Convention, notwithstanding these blemishes, should be acceded to by this country. We anticipate that the disadvantages will be speedily so apparent to the Government of the U.S., as to lead to an early abandonment of the obnoxious provisions.'

The Foreign Office's instructions to Crampton were stiffer in tone than the recommendations of the Board of Trade.

Her Majesty's Government would indeed regret that, upon a ground of doubtful protection, this measure, which has been so long desired and delayed, should be clogged with obstacles which must to a great extent neutralize its operation; and you will use your best endeavours to prevent the amendment from being proposed or adopted by the Government of the United States.

He was authorized to extend the time limit, but not to sign any amended convention until he received further instructions. In a private letter of the same day (13 January 1854), Lord Clarendon somewhat softened his tone, but most significantly he did not repeat the Board of Trade's opinion that an amended treaty was better than none.[22]

I send you some arguments respecting Copyright that I hope will have due weight with Mr. Everett. Pray tell him with my best regards how much importance we attach here to having an equitable working measure for the international protection of literature. The value and influence of American literature are becoming daily more felt in England.

In the meantime, what of Lewis Charles Levin and the remnants of the Organization? True to his word, he was back in Washington by June 1853, and after making some arrangements with the Hudson's Bay Co. he told Crampton: 'if I can serve you, in any other [way], I shall always be most happy to do so. I have not lost sight of the International Copyright question, to which I shall devote myself.'[23] This is the last we hear from Levin about the Copyright Treaty. From other sources it is clear that he was in Philadelphia or Washington during the autumn of 1853, but after that, he disappears. It is possible that Crampton despaired of accomplishing anything through his auspices and severed the connection.

By December 1853 the opposition had far from dissipated, as Crampton had hoped. A lengthy pamphlet by Henry C. Carey entitled 'Letters on International Copyright', had fanned the flames. Carey was the chief theorist and spokesman for American protectionism. His elaborate polemic ranged from contrasting the decadence of the Old World with the vitality of the New to comparing the centralizing tendencies of British Government with the decentralizing freedoms of American society. In his view the essence of America was popular education buttressed by cheap literature. Authors should content themselves with fame not fortune. International copyright threatened all this by way of monopoly and high prices.

Although there was little new information in Carey's pamphlet, and he tended to be long on argument and short on facts, one assertion struck home. He capitalized on the idea that international copyright was being imposed by a secret treaty in the Senate.

It is an attempt to substitute the action of the Executive for that of the Legis-
lative. . . . Finding that no bill that could be prepared could stand the ordeal
of the public discussion, a treaty has been negotiated, the terms of which seem
to be known to none but the negotiators, and that treaty [is to] be discussed in
secret session, by a number of gentlemen, most of whom have given little
attention to the general principle involved.

Moreover, the Senate itself was unrepresentative.[24]

A thoroughly adverse popular will having thus been manifested [in years
past], it was now determined to try the Senate, and here the chances for
privilege were better. With a population little better than that of Pennsylvania,
the New England states had six times the Senatorial representation. With
readers not a fifth as numerous as were those of Ohio, – Carolina, Florida,
and Georgia had thrice the number of Senators.

Carey's arguments carried weight because they were expounded systematically by a professional economist and public figure. Their appearance was particularly well-timed, as revealed by Everett's letter to Crampton on 9 December 1853 explaining that the contemplated change in Article VI owed something to Carey's pamphlet which had been circulated to members of the Senate.[25]

It is especially interesting to note who promoted the pamphlet. In its preface Carey refers to a request by Senator James Cooper of Pennsylvania to be enlightened on the subject of international copyright. It may be recalled from a previous chapter that Cooper was the arch political enemy of Lewis C. Levin. Very likely the opposition forces learned of Levin's sponsorship of the Treaty and persuaded Senator Cooper to co-operate with them and at the same time pay off an old political grudge.

In January 1854 members of the Philadelphia book trade began to collect petitions for Congress.[26]

You will observe that the petition is not adapted for booksellers exclusively, taking ground, as it does, against the intended extension of executive action over constitutional legislation, and therefore is suitable for all citizens who desire to prevent this dangerous innovation.

Not long afterwards the New York trade followed suit. Cyrus W. Field & Co., commission merchants and wholesale paper-dealers, collected signatures from the principal paper-makers in New York and forwarded them to Messrs Harper & Bros:[27]

The enclosed Petition against the International Copyright Treaty with the signatures of the principal Paper Houses attached.

We find the Booksellers are actively engaged in obtaining signatures to a similar petition, and we have therefore not interfered with them.

We have written a letter and enclosed one of our forms, to Mr. Edward Walker [a partner of Leonard Scott, the reprinter] and endeavored to persuade him to make a stir among the Bookbinders, and the same to Mr. J. F. Trow, to induce him to stir up the Printers.

Soon petitions against the Treaty began to pour in to Washington. On 9 February Senator Brodhead of Pennsylvania presented one bearing the signatures of 363 fellow citizens. The following day he introduced another, and Senator Fish of New York tabled one from Leonard Scott and 43 others. Three days later another two arrived, the larger one listing 71 citizens from Massachusetts. Senator Everett had the embarrassing task of having to present negative petitions from 127 people in his home state of Massachusetts. No petitions were forthcoming in support of the Copyright Treaty during the early months of 1854.

In addition to memorializing Congress, the opposition prevailed upon Senator Stephen R. Mallory of Florida to challenge the secrecy surrounding the Copyright Treaty. Rumours abounded as to what was contained in the Treaty, but no full text of its provisions had been made available. This was soon remedied, however, and in a somewhat unorthodox manner.[28]

[Resolved] that the President of the Senate be directed to address a note on behalf of the Senate to each Senator putting the following interrogatories. First, whether he has any information which will enable the Senate to ascertain in what way or by whose instrumentality the treaty with Mexico, and that

with Great Britain relating to copyright and the amendment to the latter offered by the Senator from Massachusetts, or either of them which are now pending before the Senate, had been disclosed in violation of the 39th rule and been published in the public journals?

Once the Treaty had been leaked to the press it was easier for the enemies of copyright to criticize specific provisions instead of having to address themselves to the Treaty as a whole.

By the end of February the prospects for ratification were bleak but not hopeless. It was ready for a Second Reading in the Senate whenever Everett saw fit to proceed, and provision had been made for extending the time limit.[29] There were, for the moment, no Anglo-American crises. The session of Congress extended until July or August rather than terminating in March, thus allowing plenty of time to gather the momentum necessary to carry the Treaty through.

The great obstacle, other than the mounting pressure of the opposition, was Everett's unwillingness to formally amend Article VI in view of Crampton's objections, and Crampton's inability to act without specific instructions from London. The deadlock broke on 12 May 1854 when Clarendon gave Crampton permission to go ahead.[30]

Much as H.M. Government would regret the substitution of the altered article, which as stated in your dispatch no. 195 of the 12th of December last Mr. Everett proposed should be substituted for article 6 of the Convention as signed, they would, in case your strongest representation should fail to induce the American Government to give way on this point, accept it as an alternative preferable to the entire abandonment of the negotiation.

By the time Crampton received these instructions events had again stolen a march on him. Everett had left Washington intending to resign from the Senate on the advice of his personal physician.[31] Writing from Boston he told Chairman Mason of the Foreign Relations Committee that: 'the International Copyright Treaty was left to my management', and before leaving Washington he had come to the conclusion that it could not secure ratification and therefore should be dropped. Too many Senators opposed it, and furthermore he had become personally convinced that a manufacturing clause was necessary. 'I gave notice to the Senate that I should move such an amendment, but this amendment is much objected to in England by the friends of International Copyright.' Under these circumstances Everett recommended that the

Committee not bring the Treaty to a vote, although the decision was now theirs.[32] On 3 June he wrote to Crampton repeating these considerations and adding:

My proposed amendment was not satisfactory in England and, on submitting to practical persons in this country the objections taken in London, I despaired of an adjustment that would be approved on both sides of the water. On conferring with Mr. Prescott, when I was at home in March, I found it to be his opinion that if the Convention was likely to be defeated, in the Senate, it would be much better in the present state of the copyright law in England not to take it up. No action at all he thought would be much preferable to rejection. In this state of things I have determined, unless you should have earnestly desired it, not to call up the Convention nor ask a vote of the Senate. I have informed Mr. Mason, Chairman of the Committee on Foreign Relations, that I had come to this conclusion, and I have reason to think that no movement will be made by the Committee towards taking it up.

On 7 June Crampton replied that he agreed it would be useless to 'press the treaty to a rejection'. Ten days later he informed Lord Clarendon that unfortunately Americans were not yet ready for a Copyright Treaty and apparently preferred to exploit cheap foreign reprints rather than foster their own authors and literature.[33]

Certain writers in America would have felt more of a sense of loss had they not assumed that Lord Campbell's decision in the Court of Exchequer in 1851 at least provided copyright protection for their works published in England. Prescott held this view so firmly that he was never a staunch advocate of the Treaty. Why, said he, risk its rejection when American authors already enjoyed copyright protection in Britain? When in 1854 the House of Lords passed judgment in *Jefferys* v. *Boosey* depriving American authors of this vestige of comfort, Prescott suffered greatly because he was one of the most highly paid American authors in Britain. It is tempting to speculate what effect the Lords' decision might have had if it had been handed down a few months earlier.

Dramatic irony such as this, however, pervaded the protracted negotiations to secure an Anglo-American treaty. From the outset they had been plagued by misunderstandings and poor timing. Initially there was the discrepancy as to the amount of money to be raised for the Organization. Who would have thought that English authors and publishers would balk at furnishing £2,000? Then followed the untimely death of Webster, and later the unexpected resignation of Everett from the Senate.

One couldn't have foreseen that Knox Walker's abrupt departure from Washington would fragment the Organization. It was even more unpredictable that Everett's temporizing would reinforce Fillmore's hesitations and cause endless awkward delays. The fisheries and Central American questions arose at particularly inopportune times. When Levin was most needed he was called away from the Capitol. Neither Crampton nor Everett was prepared for the kind of opposition generated by Longman, Murray, Turner, and the Board of Trade. Was it Lord Clarendon's intention to curb Crampton's power to negotiate, or did he merely procrastinate until it was too late to make it clear that a ratified treaty was better than no treaty?

There were other loose ends which may never be satisfactorily resolved. Did Lord Clarendon know about the secret arrangement with the Organization; and what became of the money subscribed? It seems unlikely that he was ever fully apprised of the Crampton–Levin plan. Nothing about it was ever mentioned in either the official dispatches or private correspondence. Only one person was so situated that he could have revealed the existence of the fund. Austen Henry Layard was not only one of John Murray's most successful authors but he also was in the employ of the Foreign Office and had been asked to contribute to the fund. His response to the solicitation was that it was absurd for private authors and publishers to raise such large sums of money when payments such as this could be taken from Secret Service funds administered by the Foreign Office. There is no indication that Layard's comments ever reached Lord Clarendon, however, and Crampton made no requests for Secret Service funds for this purpose.[34] As to what became of the money subscribed, the first £1,000 was paid to Levin soon after the signing of the Treaty in February 1853. At that time the understanding was that the second instalment would be payable once the Treaty had been ratified. Since this never happened, the balance was not needed and Bulwer, Blackwood, Dickens, and Murray were saved from having to contribute twice. Crampton was also relieved from having to pay his promised £500.

The causes of failure were manifold, but a letter from Herman Melville to Richard Bentley highlights the powerful underlying attitude which predisposed defeat.[35]

And here let me say to you, – since you are peculiarly interested in the matter – that in all reasonable probability no International Copyright will ever be obtained – in our time, at least – if you Englishmen wait at all for the first step to be taken in this country. Who have any motive in this country to bestir themselves in this thing? Only the authors. – Who are the authors? – A handful. And what influence have they to bring to bear upon any question whose settlement must necessarily assume a political form? – They can bring scarcely any influence whatever. This country & nearly all its affairs are governed by sturdy backwoodsmen – noble fellows enough, but not at all literary, & who care not a fig for any authors except those who write those most saleable of all books nowadays – i.e. – the newspapers, & magazines. And tho' the number of cultivated, catholic men, who may be supposed to feel an interest in a national literature, is large & every day growing larger; yet they are nothing in comparison with the overwhelming majority who care nothing about it. This country is at present engaged in furnishing material for future authors; not in encouraging its living ones.

In 1868 H. C. Carey offered his own explanation. Inscribing a copy of the second edition of his *Letters on International Copyright*, he boasted: 'With this I send you some letters on the copyright question that might interest you. They killed Everett's treaty 14 years since.' There is no question of the damage done by Carey's *Letters*, but they hardly merit this claim. The most that can be said is that, as a collection of grievances, they helped to focus the attack of various opposition forces.[36]

Looking back on the negotiations, Everett concluded:[37]

The measure suffered greatly from the apathy of its friends, particularly of the friendly press, while its opponents in the hostile press were indefatigable. Large sums of money . . . were expended by the publishing houses in printing and circulating pamphlets against the Convention . . . [and] . . . this was not the worst that was done if rumor can be trusted.

Echoes of the Organization and L. C. Levin reverberated throughout the visit of a young London publisher, John Cassell, who travelled to America in November 1859 in order to arrange for the expansion of his new publishing house. His biographer tells us:[38]

At Washington he endeavored to put in an argumentative word or two for internationl copyright. He found that what international copyright wanted in Washington was not argument but cash. When he pointed out to the politicians the justice and expediency of international copyright, they cut him off short. 'If you English publishers will only subscribe a sum of such-and-such to work the lobby', he was told, 'the measure could be carried. You know that there are certain houses here which are deeply interested in the reproduction of English books; what are a few thousand dollars to them, expended to defeat any attempt to interfere with the system by which they have become million-aires?'

Perhaps the final irony of all was that British authors, publishers, and politicians had to accept in 1891 what they resisted in 1854.

NOTES

Chapter I   The Depression of 1837–43 and its Implications for the American Book Trade

1 Harper to Bulwer 25 May 1837 and 31 July 1837, as quoted in J. J. Barnes, 'Edward Lytton Bulwer and the publishing firm of Harper & Brothers', *American Literature*, XXXVIII (March 1966), pp. 35–48.

2 A good general account of the depression of 1837–43 is D. C. North, *The Economic Growth of the United States, 1790–1860* (Englewood Cliffs, N. J., 1961), pp. 189–203. A very useful contemporary account of the state debts and political repercussions is to be found in the short-lived periodical which was published in London by an American: *Great Western Magazine*, II (September 1842), pp. 101–6.

3 H. Greeley, *Recollections of a Busy Life* (New York, 1869), p. 95.

4 M. M. Hoover, *Park Benjamin: Poet and Editor* (New York, 1948), pp. 89–90.

5 E. Exman, *The Brothers Harper, 1817–1853* (New York, 1965), pp. 23, 92–3, 151, 230 and 234.

6 W. S. Tryon and W. Charvat, *The Cost Books of Ticknor and Fields and Their Predecessors, 1832–1858* (New York, 1949). The yearly totals are a rough compilation, incorporating entries in the main body of the volume as well as the appendices.

7 D. Kaser, *The Cost Book of Carey and Lea, 1825–1838* (Philadelphia, 1963). The figures are a rough compilation of the main volume and its appendices. The annual totals which Kaser gives on pp. 72–3 do not include the books which Carey and Lea published in conjunction with other firms.

8 Quoted in J. Bayless, *Rufus Wilmot Griswold: Poe's Literary Executor* (Nashville, 1943), pp. 28–30. See also Hoover, *op. cit.*, pp. 96–100.

9 The best account of the *New World* is to be found in Hoover, *op. cit.*, p. 100 and following.

10 *New World*, 2 November 1839, p. 1; *Jonathan*, 16 May 1840, p. 3.

11 The last folio issue of the *New World* was 19 March 1842.

12 For such details see especially *New World*, 6 June 1840, p. 2; 4 March 1841, p. 4; quarto ed. II (23 January 1841), p. 64; quarto ed. VI (20 May 1843), p. 609.

13 *New World*, 28 November 1840, p. 1.

14 *Ibid.*, 13 March 1841, p. 2.

15 *Ibid.*, quarto ed. III (3 July 1841), p. 15.

16 *Ibid.*, 12 June 1841, p. 1; quarto ed. IV (19 February 1842), p. 130.

17 *Ibid.*, 26 October 1839, p. 1; 30 November, p. 1; 18 April 1840, p. 2; 29 May 1841, p. 3; 1 January 1842, p. 4. See also the MS journals of Jared Sparks, Houghton Library, MS 141K (15 November 1841), p. 22.

18 *New World*, 28 March 1840, p. 1; 1 January 1841, p. 1; 4 March 1841, p. 4.

19 *New World*, quarto ed. IV (23 April 1842), p. 271; IV (21 May 1842), p. 326; IV (11 June 1842), p. 382; V (6 August 1842), p. 93; V (17 December 1842), p. 399. *Brother Jonathan* supplement, 25 July 1842. Thanks to Hoover, *op. cit.*, pp. 201–6, it is possible to follow the course of all the *New World* extras for 1842–3. This is all the more valuable since the extras are comparatively rare in most libraries.

20 *New World*, quarto ed. IV (11 June 1842), p. 382.

21 *Brother Jonathan* supplement, 9 July 1842.

22 *Brother Jonathan*, quarto ed. III (26 November 1842), p. 375. See Hoover, *op. cit.*, pp. 123–4, for the *New World*'s claim to have fostered American authorship.

23 *New World*, quarto ed. VI (7 January 1843), p. 23. See also *New World*, quarto ed. V (10 December 1842), p. 386.

24 *Athenaeum*, no. 813 (27 May 1843), pp. 510–11.

25 *Ibid.*

26 *New World*, 17 October 1840, p. 1; 24 October 1840, p. 2.

27 *Ibid.*, quarto ed. V (13 August 1842), p. 111.

28 *Ibid.*, V (6 August 1842), p. 94.

29 *Ibid.*, quarto ed. IV (4 June 1842), p. 366.

30 *Ibid.*, V (27 August 1842), p. 143.

31 The most authoritative and reliable work on the Harpers is Exman, *op. cit.*, pp. 158–9. As to the responsibility for the fire, Exman expresses no firm opinion. It seems unlikely, however, that the *New World* had to resort to such measures. It was still riding the crest of popularity prior to any serious competition from others. It had its own agent in London who was quite as adept as Harpers' agent in forwarding the latest English publications to New York. Besides, its market at this time was different enough from Harpers', what with yearly subscriptions and cheap supplements, that it need not have sanctioned such a desperate act as theft and fire. One possible alternative was noted by *Brother Jonathan* a few months later when it pointed out that the Harpers' cash box had been broken into and that money may have been the prime motive: II (13 August 1842), p. 438.

32 *New World*, quarto ed. V (13 August 1842), p. 111.

33 *Ibid.*, quarto ed. V (12 November 1842), p. 319. For details of the Harper publications, see Exman, *op. cit.*, pp. 159–62.

34 *Ibid.*, p. 163. Harper had quite an investment to protect in the Alison book, issuing it first in sixteen parts and then all together in four volumes totalling 1,358 pages.

35 W. H. Prescott to Charles Dickens, 1 December 1842, as quoted in R. Wolcott (ed.), *The Correspondence of William Hickling Prescott, 1833–1847* (Boston, 1925), p. 323. In the phrases quoted above, Prescott was referring to a somewhat different situation but his point was applicable.

36 For details of the various Sue editions, see *New World*, quarto ed. IX (10 August 1844), p. 177; IX (7 September 1844), p. 311.

37 Exman, *op. cit.*, p. 143.

38 F. L. Mott, *American Journalism, 1690–1940* (New York, 1941), p. 267.

39 F. L. Mott, *A History of American Magazines*, I (Cambridge, Mass., 1930), pp. 320–9.

40 *An Act to Reduce into One the Several Acts Establishing and Regulating the Post Office Department*, 3 March 1825.

41 *Brother Jonathan*, quarto ed. II (7 May 1842), p. 43; *New World*, quarto ed. IV (7 May 1842), p. 305.

42 National Archives, letter books of the Postmaster General, vol. M/1, p. 351.

43 *Laws and Regulations of the Government of the Post Office Department* (Washington, 1843), pp. 19–22. Legaré's opinion was included among the *Regulations* for the benefit of local postmasters who had to assess rates of postage on various publications.

44 *New World*, quarto ed. IV (7 May and 14 May 1842), pp. 305, 319. *Brother Jonathan*, quarto ed. II (7 May 1842), p. 43. Supplement, 20 June 1842.

45 *New World*, quarto ed. VI (27 May 1843), p. 628.

46 *Ibid.*, quarto ed. III (17 July 1841), p. 46; III (4 September 1841), p. 157; V (6 August 1842), p. 93.

47 *An Act Amendatory of the Act Regulating the Post Office*, 2 March 1827. Section 3 prohibited foot and horse conveyance of the mail by private firms. Section 30 of the Act of 1825 permitted newspapers and magazines to be carried by those contracting to carry the mail.

48 'Report of the Postmaster General: Post Office Department; December 2, 1843', 28th Cong. 1st Sess., *Senate Documents*, I (Washington, 1844), pp. 593–632. The report was document no. 1.

49 *Ibid.*, p. 627. Wickliffe's letter to the Attorney-General is undated: National Archives, letter books of the Postmaster General, 10 December 1842–5 September 1843, p. 181.

50 *New World*, quarto ed. VI (27 May 1843), p. 628.

51 Although the *New World* and *Brother Jonathan* had discontinued their weekly folio editions, they still issued occasional mammoth folios at Christmas and

other holidays. Furthermore, they wanted the privilege of resuming the regular folio editions and sending them at newspaper rates of postage.

52 *New World*, quarto ed. IX (7 December 1844), p. 726. Other examples of the *New World*'s campaign against the Post Office are: VI (3 June 1843), p. 661; VII (7 October 1843), p. 424; VII (21 October 1843), p. 483; VII (28 October 1843), p. 510; VII (4 November 1843), p. 541; VII (9 December 1843), p. 687; VIII (6 January 1844), p. 22; VIII (30 March 1844), p. 406; IX (10 August 1844), p. 180.

53 *Ibid.*, quarto ed. IX (20 July 1844), p. 84; IX (10 August 1844), p. 180. *Littell's Living Age*, I (22 June 1844), p. 322.

54 *An Act to Reduce the Rates of Postage*, 3 March 1845.

55 *New World*, IX (10 August 1844), p. 180. 'Report of the Postmaster General', 29th Cong. 2nd Sess., *Congressional Globe*, XVI (Washington, 1847), pp. 22–5. Johnson's report was dated 7 December 1846.

56 F. L. Mott, *Golden Multitudes: the story of best sellers in the United States* (New York, 1947), p. 78.

57 Not until 1851 were bound books weighing 32 ounces or less permitted through the post.

58 11 December 1841, Houghton Library, Longfellow Papers.

59 Benjamin to B. Mayer, 23 June 1844, Maryland Historical Society, Mayer and Roszel Papers, MS 581.3.

60 Ward had previously acquired the *New World*'s interest in *Brother Jonathan* in June 1844.

61 In addition to various New York City directories for the period, see: Hoover, *op. cit.*, pp. 144, 156–60; Greeley, *op. cit.*, pp. 91–3; L. Scott to J. Jay, April [?] 1848, Jay Homestead.

62 *Dictionary of American Biography* and *Appleton's Cyclopaedia*; plus various New York City directories.

63 In addition to various City directories, see *Brother Jonathan*, 4 July 1848.

64 E. P. Norton, *Before the Commissioner of Patents: In a matter of interference between James G. Wilson and William H. McNary for patents* . . . (New York, 1862).

65 See *Dictionary of American Biography* and the following for Day's success with the *Sun*: F. Hudson, *Journalism in the United States from 1690 to 1872* (New York, 1873), pp. 117–18, and Mott, *American Journalism, 1690–1940*, pp. 222–4. For Benjamin's disclosures, see the *New World*, III (10 and 24 July 1841), pp. 29, 62.

66 For Weld, see *Appleton's Cyclopaedia*. See also H. A. Beers, *Nathaniel Parker Willis* (Boston, 1885). John Neal was apparently affiliated with *Brother Jonathan* in 1843, but his own autobiography is sufficiently muddled on this point to be of little use: *Wandering Recollections of a Somewhat Busy Life* (Boston, 1869), p. 351. Neal suggests he was a contributor and not an editor. It is not clear when Weld ceased editing *Brother Jonathan*. From May to August 1843 the

editors were John Neal, G. M. Snow and Edward Stephens.The last of these seems to have continued from September 1843 until the sale of the magazine at the end of the year.

67 For an example of Dickens's circular letter of 7 July 1842, see *Athenaeum*, no. 768 (16 July 1842), p. 636. See also: *Brother Jonathan*, quarto ed. II (6 August 1842), pp. 410–11; *New World*, quarto ed. V (6 August 1842), pp. 93–4 and VII (5 August 1843), p. 146.

Chapter II   British Periodicals in America

1 These and many of the other details which follow, about the American re-printing of British periodicals, come from a remarkable letter at the Jay Homestead, Katonah, New York. In early April 1848 the leading reprinter of British periodicals in New York, Leonard Scott, undertook to describe the various past efforts to supply the American market with reprints of foreign periodicals. Scott's letter was addressed to John Jay and forms the basis of much that follows in this chapter. Many of the gaps left in Scott's undated letter have been supplied by reference to contemporary magazines and city direc-tories. Other sources are cited when appropriate.

2 By the 1840s Clayton had given up his printing business and become a success-ful stationer and paper-maker.

3 Blackwood to Wilder & Campbell, 9 December 1824, National Library of Scotland, MS 4013, f. 293v–4v; and Wilder & Campbell to Blackwood, 10 December 1824, MS 4013, f. 293v.

4 M. C. Grobel, 'The Society for the Diffusion of Useful Knowledge, 1826–46' (unpublished doctoral dissertation of University College, London, 1932), III, p. 790.

5 An announcement of Jackson's undertaking is to be found in the *Albion*, I n. s. (8 June 1833), p. 183.

6 W. S. Tryon and W. Charvat, *The Cost Books of Ticknor and Fields and Their Predecessors, 1832–1858* (New York, 1949), pp. 445–6.

7 Shortly after selling their reprint business to Theodore Foster, Peck & Newton dissolved their partnership.

8 The later career of Theodore Foster typified the fragmented affairs of many printers and publishers in the 1830s and 1840s. As Leonard Scott noted in 1848: 'Foster has started several literary Enterprises since his failure, but generally without success – He published the "Plaindealer" edited by Wm Leggett until it was suspended for want of patronage – Subsequently he wrote and published some works in Phrenology – and at one time he was engaged in moulding "the human face divine" in plaster of paris and selling Busts. He was, for a year or more, afflicted with blindness – so much so as to render it impos-sible to do any business – He recovered from this, however, and then commenced

the publication of a paper called "The Family Visitor and Silk Culturist" devoted to the silk interest, which at the time was all the rage in this Country, as many Speculators in Morus Multicaulis may remember to their sorrow – This failed however, then he got up a society called the "National Society of Literature" whose business it should be to form Reading Associations in every Town and Village in the Country and furnish them with periodicals such as they might select to any amount [to which] such associations should subscribe – The plan of this National Society involved the employment of numerous travelling agents and lecturers – and for the first year it went on auspiciously, but it never lived to see the End of the second year, and many were the wailings of subscribers thereat who had paid for their works in advance and found them *not* forthcoming – The dishonesty of some of these itinerant agents, and the want of experience in the management of this new business, were doubtless the principal causes of its failure. Foster then published a Magazine called the "Indicator", an excellent thing it was too, but not popular, so he gave *that* up. He has more recently published a host of little shilling Pamphlets, out of which he has made some money, and he is still engaged in that business.'

9 For these and other details see the note to Leonard Scott above.

10 Murray to Wiley & Putnam, 3 October 1840, John Murray Ltd, letter book, p. 53. A good example of Wiley & Putnam's advertising of imported periodicals may be seen in the *New World*, quarto ed. V (15 October 1842), p. 258.

11 For announcements of these reprints see Winchester's *New World*, quarto ed. VI (4 February 1843), p. 150; VI (4 March 1843), p. 267.

12 Murray to Mason, 16 December 1843, John Murray Ltd, letter book, p. 139. Curiously enough Murray made no better terms to Mason than he had with Wiley & Putnam three years before. This may help to explain why the importation of British periodicals was never as successful as anticipated. The price was never quite low enough.

13 The advertising agency did not last long, and by 1846 Mason managed a reading room. His wife, Jemima, had died the previous year.

14 *Dictionary of American Biography*.

15 Biographical background for A. C. Coxe may be found in E. and G. Duyckinck, *The Cyclopaedia of American Literature* (New York, 1855), II, p. 656; R. W. Griswold, *The Poets and Poetry of America* (Philadelphia, 1842), p. 425; *The Builders of the Nation: Compiled from the National Cyclopaedia of American Biography* (New York, 1893), II, pp. 474-5.

16 Coxe to Blackwood, 29 April 1846, National Library of Scotland, MS 4078, f. 126.

17 *Blackwood's Magazine*, LXI (March 1847), pp. 337-49. The *Wellesley Index to Victorian Periodicals* substantiates that Coxe was the author of the article entitled: 'The cave of the regicides', as well as the other articles which Coxe subsequently published with Blackwood. See also Coxe to Jay, 23 March 1847, Columbia Univ., MS Jay Papers.

18 Coxe to Jay, 2 June, 28 June and 20 July 1847, Columbia University, MS Jay Papers; 9 June 1847, MS Jay Homestead.

19 Jay had two of Coxe's articles registered with the District Court under the general title of *Letters to Godfrey*. The first 'letter' appeared as ' "Maga" in America', LXII (October 1847), pp. 422–31; the second 'letter' as 'American copyright', LXII (November 1847), pp. 534–46. Copies of the copyright registration are in the Jay Homestead for the dates 12 October, 21 October and 6 November 1847. The Jay–Van Norden agreements are both dated 23 October.

20 Scott to Jay, 27 October; Jay to Scott, 29 October; and Jay–Scott agreement, 30 October 1847; MSS Jay Homestead.

21 *Ibid.* See also Jay to Blackwood, 30 October 1847. Behind many of Jay's arguments lay the advice of Coxe. See for example Coxe to Jay, 27 October, 20 November and 22 November 1847; MSS Jay Homestead.

22 Coxe's estimate of 10,000 came in LXII (November 1847), p. 537. For Scott's account of his expenses and profits, see his letter to Jay, 27 October and a copy of his letter to Blackwood, 30 October 1847; MSS Jay Homestead.

23 Scott estimated that the printing and binding cost for 2,000 copies was $3,156; the overhead costs were $650; giving a combined outlay of $3,806. Figuring subscriptions at $4 he could make 11½¢ on all copies sold beyond 2,000, and he was willing to allocate to Blackwood 3¢ on every such copy.

24 Scott's calculations were based on the tariff of 1846.

25 Thus the total composing bill for 3,000 copies was about $117 and not what Blackwood had supposed.

26 Scott to Jay, 15 November, 20 November, 30 December 1847; Blackwood to Jay, 1 December, 2 December 1847; copy of Jay to Blackwood, 30–1 December 1847.

27 *Blackwood's Magazine*, LXIII (January 1848), pp. 127–8. Scott's statement, dated 24 January 1848, was reprinted inside the back of the cover of the *Literary World* for 15 April 1848.

28 Scott to Jay, 16 March 1848; Jay to Blackwood, 1 May 1848; MSS Jay Homestead.

29 For the renewal of the Scott–Blackwood agreement, see extracts from letters of Scott to Blackwood, 4 December 1849 and Blackwood to Scott, 5 January 1850; MSS Jay Homestead. Between 1848–54 Scott's payments were handled by Jay and forwarded to the Blackwoods. See for example Jay to Blackwood, 11 February 1851, National Library of Scotland, MS 4094, f. 11; Jay to Blackwood, 14 March 1852, National Library of Scotland, MS 4098, f. 192; Jay to Blackwood, 8 April 1852, National Library of Scotland, MS 4094, f. 20; Jay to Blackwood, 28 January 1853, National Library of Scotland, MS 4102, ff. 179–82; Jay to Blackwood, 31 March 1854, National Library of Scotland, MS 4105, f. 158; and Blackwood to Jay, 24 April 1854, Columbia University, Jay Papers.

30 Jay estimated $100–150 per annum.

31 Jay to Chapman, 12 September 1851, copy in letter book, pp. 187–9; MS Jay Homestead. The history of eclectic magazines in America is worthy of a separate study; it is unfortunately beyond the scope of this present work. Suffice it to say that a great deal of British Periodical writing was made available to the American reading public under the scissors-and-paste auspices of the eclectics.

32 Chapman to Jay, 24 February 1852, Columbia University, Jay Papers; Jay to Chapman, 16 March and 23 April 1852, Jay Homestead, copies in letter book, pp. 35–6 and 48–9. The article in question was presumably 'American literature', *Eclectic Magazine*, XXV (March 1852), pp. 289–307.

33 The standard work on Henry Stevens is W. W. Parker, *Henry Stevens of Vermont: American rare book dealer in London, 1845–86* (Amsterdam, 1963). The only confusion in an otherwise valuable work is that Parker credits Stevens with originating negotiations with Scott. However, correspondence in the Clements Library of the University of Michigan makes it clear that Stevens worked out new arrangements only in 1853. See especially Stevens to Scott, 11 November 1853 and Stevens to C. B. Norton, 10 January 1854.

34 Two of Coxe's articles were in the form of 'Letters to Godfrey'.

35 Coxe's later contributions to *Blackwood's Magazine* were: LXIII (March 1848), pp. 328–39 ('My route into Canada'); LXIII (April 1848), pp. 425–35 ('My route into Canada', continued); LXIV (July 1848), pp. 31–9 ('American thoughts on European revolutions'); LXV (February 1849), pp. 190–201 ('American thoughts on European revolutions', continued); LXV (May 1849), pp. 529–41 ('The reaction, or foreign conservatism'). Bristed's article, 'Periodical literature of America', appeared in LXIII (January 1848), pp. 106–12. For the attitudes of Coxe, Jay and Blackwood respecting various contributors to the magazine, see Coxe to Jay, 15 November, 1 December 1847; 20 January, 29 January, 7 March, 27 March, 11 April 1848, Jay Homestead; Coxe to Jay, 15 August 1848, Columbia University; Blackwood to Coxe, 29 December 1847, Jay Homestead; Scott to Blackwood, 23 March 1848, Jay Homestead; Jay to Blackwood, 24 March 1848, 19 June 1849, Jay Homestead, letter books, pp. 38–9 and p. 15; Jay to Blackwood, 1 February 1853, 12 July 1854, National Library of Scotland; MS 4098, f. 190 and MS 4105, f. 160; Blackwood to Jay, 4 May 1852, Columbia University.

Chapter III   Copyright In and Out of Congress, 1815–42

1 Cooper to Miller, 7–12 February 1826, J. F. Beard (ed.), *The Letters and Journals of James Fenimore Cooper* (Cambridge, 1960), I, pp. 127–8.

2 Most standard works on the American book trade and on copyright give brief accounts of these years. See, for example, H. Lehmann-Haupt *et al.*,

The Book in America (New York, 1939), p. 107. For a more specialized treatment, F. Goff, *The First Decade of the Federal Act for Copyright, 1790–1800* (Washington, 1951), *passim*.

3 G. C. Verplanck, *Discourses and Addresses on Subjects of American History, Arts, and Literature* (New York, 1833), pp. 217–19. For a general study of Verplanck, see R. W. July, *The Essential New Yorker: Guilian Crommelin Verplanck* (Durham, 1951).

4 Webster, *A Collection of Papers on Political, Literary and Moral Subjects* (New York, 1843), pp. 174–8; Webster to W. C. Fowler, 29 January 1831, in H. R. Warfel (ed.), *Letters of Noah Webster* (New York, 1953), pp. 424–5; E. E. F. Ford, *Notes on the Life of Noah Webster* (New York, 1912), I, p. 318.

5 Cooper to Carey & Lea, 9 November 1826, Beard, *op. cit.*, I, pp. 170–4.

6 The best account of these transactions is D. Kaser, *Messrs. Carey & Lea of Philadelphia* (Philadelphia, 1957), pp. 42–4, 67, 95–7, 102–3, 107–10.

7 *Knickerbocker*, VI (October 1835), p. 287.

8 The Harpers concluded a similar agreement with G. P. R. James on 13 July 1836, though the rate of compensation, £30 per novel, was considerably less than that accorded Bulwer. The Harper–James agreement is in the Greater London Record Office, Middlesex Records, Acc. 976D, no. 160a–b. Some of what follows about Bulwer and the Harpers is taken from my article, 'Edward Lytton Bulwer and the publishing firm of Harper and Brothers', *American Literature*, XXXVIII (March 1966), pp. 35–48. Unless otherwise indicated the quotations come from the Hertfordshire County Record Office, Bulwer Papers, MS Box 63. Edward Lytton Bulwer was created a Baronet in 1838, and thereafter referred to himself as Sir Edward Bulwer Lytton. In 1866 he became Baron Lytton of Knebworth, and was addressed as Lord Lytton. For the sake of clarity and convenience, he is referred to as Bulwer throughout this account.

9 16 February 1836. At this time there were two related firms in Philadelphia: Carey & Lea and Carey & Hart.

10 15 January 1835.

11 7 April 1835.

12 *The Duchess de la Valliere.*

13 Harper to Bulwer, 16 (?) February 1836; Appleton to Bulwer, 5 March 1836; and Harper to Bulwer, 12 September 1836.

14 Capen to Bulwer, 29 August and 17 October 1836.

15 See chap. I, where Willis was a contributing editor to *Brother Jonathan.*

16 *Melanie and Other Poems* (London 1835,), and *Inklings of Adventure* (London, 1836).

17 The best account of Frederick Saunders and his attempt to establish an office in New York is A. L. Bader, 'Frederick Saunders and the early history of the international copyright movement in America', *Library Quarterly*, VIII (January 1938), pp. 25–39. See also J. A. Rawley, 'An early history of the inter-

national copyright movement', *Library Quarterly*, XI (April 1941), pp. 200–6; *Publishers' Weekly*, XXXIII (30 June 1888), p. 988, for a brief statement by Frederick Saunders. In 1890 Saunders dictated his 'Recollections' to his grandson, a copy of which is in the Manuscript Department of the New York Public Library. I am grateful for permission to quote from this latter account.

18 Frederick Saunders, 'Early history of the international copyright movement in America', p. 24v, part of an undated 1836 newspaper clipping, New York Public Library, MS Department.

19 12 September 1836.

20 Martineau to Brougham, 5 November 1836 and two undated (November 1836) letters, University College, London, Brougham Papers, MSS, 8357–9. As far as one can tell Brougham never signed the memorial, since his name did not appear on the version printed by order of the United States Senate. On the other hand Charles Dickens claimed to have signed and yet his name is missing as well. Dickens wrote to J. P. Kennedy 30 April 1842, as quoted in M. House, G. Storey, and K. Tillotson (eds), *The Letters of Charles Dickens: Pilgrim Edition* (Oxford, 1974), III, pp. 221–2. 'When Miss Martineau came to me to sign the petition which was presented to the American Legislature a few years ago, I said, then, that I had an invincible repugnance to ask humbly for what I had as clear a right to, as the coat upon my back; and that I could not bring myself to sue to a Body which had so long sanctioned such a Monstrous and Wholesale Injustice, as if in seeking its correction, I asked a favour at their hands. I was persuaded to sign that petition, and did so. I have always regretted it since.' For a time I thought the explanation of this seeming contradiction lay in a hitherto unnoticed entry in the *Journal of the Senate*, 24th Cong. 2nd Sess., 1836–7, p. 203. Clay had presented the memorial of the British authors on 2 February 1837, but two days later he offered additional signatures on a parchment which had just reached him. It looked as though these supplemental names had been inadvertently omitted by the printer when the memorial was printed. Dickens may have been among those whose names were missing. The *Congressional Globe* makes no mention of the extra names, but mention is made in the competing *Register of Debates in Congress*, XIII (4 February 1837), pp. 696–7. However, the survival of the original supplementary list in the National Archives at Washington, without Dickens's name upon it, disposes of such conjecture. Still, it seems very unlikely that Dickens would have said what he did in 1842 if he had not in fact signed the memorial circulated by Harriet Martineau.

21 Martineau to Everett, 8 November 1836, Massachusetts Historical Society, Everett Papers, MS Box 5; Bader, 'Frederick Saunders', p. 33; P. Godwin, *A Biography of William Cullen Bryant* (New York, 1883), I, p. 315; Sparks to Martineau, 22 June 1837, copy, Houghton Library, Sparks Papers, MS 147–G, pp. 20–1.

22 Everett to Martineau, copy, Massachusetts Historical Society, Everett Papers, LXVII, p. 137.

23 *Public Documents Printed by Order of the Senate*, 24th Cong. 2nd Sess., II (1837), no. 134; *Register of Debates in Congress*, XIII (2 February 1837), pp. 670–1; *Journal of the Senate*, 1836–7, p. 192; *Journal of the House*, 1836–7, p. 400; the British authors' memorial was also reprinted by Saunders & Otley in their monthly periodical, the *Metropolitan Magazine* XVIII (April 1837), pp. 413–14.

24 *Journal of the Senate*, 1836–7, p. 203; *Register of Debates in Congress*, XIII (4 February 1837), pp. 696–7.

25 *Congressional Globe*, 24th Cong. 2nd Sess., IV–V (16 February 1837), p. 201; *Journal of the Senate*, 1836–7, p. 258; the report of the Select Committee, no. 179, was reprinted by the *Metropolitan Magazine*, XIX (May 1837), pp. 25–8; see also *Senate Documents*, II (1837).

26 A. J. Eaton, 'The American movement for international copyright, 1837–60', *Library Quarterly*, XV (April 1945), p. 103. Eaton's article is still the best brief survey of these early years.

27 The *Congressional Globe* did not report this debate in any detail, but fortunately the *Register of Debates in Congress* gave it considerable coverage: 24th Cong. 2nd Sess., XIII (2 February 1837), pp. 670–1.

28 Jay to Blackwood, 28 January 1848, copy, Jay Homestead.

29 Some publications appeared with Saunders & Otley's imprint in 1837–8.

30 As we shall see, the British Government took steps to remove the ambiguity the following year, in the form of the International Copyright Act of 1838. Martineau to Clay, 15 May 1837, in C. C. Colton, *The Private Correspondence of Henry Clay* (New York, 1855), pp. 413–14; Everett to Martineau, 10 May 1837, copy, Massachusetts Historical Society, Everett Papers, LXVII, p. 187; Sparks to Martineau, 22 June 1837, copy, Houghton Library, Sparks Papers, MS 147–G, pp. 20–1; *Congressional Globe*, 25th Cong. 2nd Sess., VI, p. 20.

31 The most convenient list of petitions ordered to be printed by the Congress, along with citations to the respective Congressional papers, is in T. Solberg, *Copyright in Congress, 1789–1904* (Washington, 1905), pp. 96–102. For references to some of these as well as petitions not printed, see the *Journal* of the House and the Senate for 1837–8 (25th Cong. 2nd Sess.). See also Clay to Sargent, 13 January 1838, Massachusetts Institute of Technology. Clay's remarks of 24 April 1838 are in *Congressional Globe*, VI, p. 326; Nicklin, *Remarks on Literary Property* (Philadelphia, 1838), p. vii.

32 *New World*, 16 November 1839, p. 2. The report of the Committee on Patents and the Patent Office was in *Senate Executive Documents*, 25th Cong. 2nd Sess., I (1838), p. 314.

33 Basic information about these Senators may be found in *The Biographical Directory of the American Congress* and *The Dictionary of American Biography*. For the Strange–Force publishing agreement of 10 July 1838, see State Dept. of Archives and History, Raleigh, North Carolina, Strange Papers. See also R. Walser, 'Senator Strange's indian novel', *North Carolina Historical Review*, XXVI (January 1949), pp. 1–27.

34 *Remarks on Literary Property* was published by Nicklin & Johnson. See S. A. Allibone, *A Critical Dictionary of English Literature and British and American Authors* (Philadelphia, 1859–71), III, p. 1427; Kaser, *op. cit.*, pp. 117–18.

35 More realistic statistics were set forth a few years later in a memorial to the Senate, *Senate Documents*, 27th Cong. 2nd Sess., IV (13 June 1842), no. 323. It estimated that the total number of people employed in the book and printing trades were about 41,000. The figure of 200,000 was arrived at by estimating that each employee would have four dependants: a very different impression from that left by Nicklin and the Patent Committee. The investment in plant and equipment was about $15 million, while the annual volume of business was $27 million. The facet of the trade most directly involved with foreign reprints was that having to do with 'publishing and bookselling'; with 4,000 employees, $4 million investment, and $7 million in sales.

36 *Congressional Globe*, 25th Cong. 2nd Sess., VII (17 December 1838), p. 34; *Journal of the Senate*, pp. 51, 55 and 305.

37 Clay to Lieber, 28 December 1839, Huntington Library, and Clay to Adlard, 17 March 1840, Houghton Library; *Congressional Globe*, 26th Cong. 1st Sess., VIII (6 January 1840), p. 193; *Journal of the Senate*, pp. 78, 87, 312 and 522.

38 *Congressional Globe*, 27th Cong. 2nd Sess., XI (6 January 1842), p. 96; *Journal of the Senate*, p. 73; Clay to the General Assembly, 16 February 1842, in C. Colton, *The Life and Times of Henry Clay* (New York, 1846), p. 404; C. Eaton, *Henry Clay and the Art of American Politics* (Boston, 1957), pp. 141–51, 161.

39 Clay to Lieber, 19 June 1839, in F. Freidel, 'Lieber's contribution to the international copyright movement', *Huntington Library Quarterly*, VIII (February 1945), p. 202; *New York Mirror*, XVI (19 February 1839), p. 263, for Adlard's petition; *New World*, 25 January 1840, p. 2, concerning Irving's reluctance to sign. G. H. Putnam, *Memoir of George Palmer Putnam* (privately printed, New York, 1903), p. 40; S. T. Williams, *The Life of Washington Irving* (New York, 1935), II, p. 215.

Chapter IV   Further Efforts to Influence the American Congress, 1842–51

1 L. H. Houtchens, 'Charles Dickens and international copyright', *American Literature*, XIII (March 1941), pp. 18–28. Houtchens is still the best treatment of Dickens's visit to America as far as the copyright issue is concerned. Perhaps Houtchens's chief shortcoming, and that of many Dickens scholars, is to assume that Dickens had a thorough understanding of the American literary and publishing scene.

2 M. House, G. Storey, and K. Tillotson (eds), *The Letters of Charles Dickens: Pilgrim Edition* (Oxford, 1974), III.

3 An example of the initial invitation is Duyckinck's letter to John Jay, 23 August 1843, Columbia University Library, Jay Papers. Typical of the letters which the Corresponding Secretary sent out was that of 26 August 1843 to R. W. Griswold, Boston Public Library, Griswold Papers; or that to Dr John W. Francis, 28 August 1843, Library of Congress, Rare Book Division. The Club's 'Address' was printed, bore the date 18 October 1843, and was sent to all the members.

4 Sparks to Mathews, 11 September 1843, copy, Houghton Library, Sparks Papers, MS 147-H, p. 26.

5 Mathews to Simms, 22 December 1843, Columbia University Library. As with the original canvassing of members in August 1843, so with the instructions about petitions, Mathews's correspondence was essentially a form letter.

6 *Journal of the Senate*, 28th Cong. 1st Sess. (15 December 1843), p. 33; *Journal of the House*, 16 December 1843, p. 58; an advance copy of the Putnam petition was printed in the *Athenaeum*, no. 835 (28 October 1843), p. 963. For Capen's memorial see *Journal of the House*, 15 and 19 January 1844, pp. 238, 260; it was also printed as a separate pamphlet by Capen. See also *House Documents*, I (16 December 1843), no. 10; I (15 January 1843), no. 61.

7 Mathews authorized Griswold to keep the Copyright Club's 'interests before the Committee of the House' in a letter of 21 February 1844, Historical Society of Pennsylvania, Amer. Lit. Dupl., MS Box 327. On 4 April 1844 Mathews told Griswold he would send him some money to cover necessary expenses in connection with copyright Boston Public Library, Griswold Papers.

8 Briggs to R. W. Griswold, 6 August 1848, Boston Public Library; Cooper to Mathews, 25 September 1843, in J. F. Beard (ed.), *The Letters and Journals of James Fenimore Cooper* (Cambridge, Mass., 1960–8), IV, pp. 413–15. For those who take Wesley Harper's membership at face value, see W. G. Simms's fourth letter on international copyright in the *Southern Literary Messenger*, X (August 1844), p. 469; E. Exman, *The Brothers Harper* (New York, 1965), p. 157; A. J. Clark, *The Movement for International Copyright*, p. 71. Clark may have a point when he argues that Wesley Harper joined the Copyright Club in order to infiltrate the enemies' camp. However he badly confuses H. J. Raymond's connection with Harper's in 1850 when he edited the new *Monthly Magazine* with his membership in the Club seven years earlier.

9 Morse to Mathews, 5 March 1842, New York Historical Society. For mention of those who blamed Mathews see Clark, *op. cit.*, p. 72.

10 29 July 1846, Pennsylvania Historical Society, Amer. Lit. Dupl., MS Box 327. Mathews was referring to a letter he wrote to the editor of the *Courier and Inquirer*, dated 22 July 1846. Mackenzie was an American residing in Britain, who served as a correspondent to American newspapers from time to time.

11 Winthrop to Everett, 27 December 1843, Massachusetts Historical Society, Everett Papers, MS Box 8; Jay to Blackwood & Sons, 28 January 1848, copy, Jay Homestead.

12 *Journal of the Senate*, 29th Cong. 1st Sess. (22 January 1846), p. 115.
13 D. Kaser, *Messrs. Carey and Lea of Philadelphia* (Philadelphia, 1957), pp. 146–8.
14 Exman, *op. cit.*, p. 24.
15 Carey to J. Miller, 19 June 1835, in Kaser, *op. cit.*, p. 150. Between Kaser and Exman one gains a good picture of trade courtesy as it functioned in the 1820s and 1830s. In some future work I shall hope to deal with the phenomenon for the 1840s and 1850s in considerable detail. Harper & Bros reprinted Marryat's *Stones of the Sea* and in retaliation H. C. Carey persuaded his younger brother in the firm of Carey & Hart to reprint Bulwer's *Rienzi*.
16 An account of Jay's visit to Washington and the conclusion he drew from it are set forth in a lengthy letter written to Blackwood on 28 January 1848 which was subsequently reprinted by Blackwood and cautiously distributed to interested parties. The original draft is in the Jay Homestead. One of the printed copies, entitled 'Copyright in America', is among the Lytton papers at the Herts County Record Office, MS vol. XVI, ff. 21–2. Another copy is among the Jay Papers at Columbia University.
17 Jay to Blackwood, 29 January 1848, MS Jay Homestead.
18 Coxe to Jay, 24 January 1848, MS Jay Homestead.
19 Jay to King, 18 March 1848, MS copy, Jay Homestead letter book, pp. 34–5; King to Jay, 20 March 1848, Columbia University, Jay Papers. King presented the memorial to the House of Representatives on 22 March.
20 For the Jay and Bryant memorials see *House Misc. Documents*, 30th Cong. 1st Sess. (22 March 1848), no. 76. Although ordered to be printed at the time, through a confusion it was not generally available for some years thereafter. This was of considerable annoyance to Jay, who had wished to convert the memorials into a vehicle of effective publicity.
21 *Memorial*, p. 6.
22 Blackwood to Jay, 24 February 1848, MS Jay Homestead.
23 Jay to King, 27 March 1848, Jay Homestead, MS copy in letter book, p. 41; Palfrey to Jay, 3 April and 6 April, Columbia University, Jay Papers; Jay to Winthrop, 10 April, Jay Homestead, MS copy; King to Jay, 15 April, Columbia University, Jay Papers.
24 Jay to Sheets, 8 May and Jay to Lieber, 11 May 1848, New York Historical Society, Jay Papers; A. D. Sims to Lieber, 25 May, Huntington Library, Lieber Papers; W. G. Simms to Jay, 1 July, Columbia University, Jay Papers.
25 The copy of Jay's 28 January letter which was sent to Bulwer was dated 5 April and had no. 5 on it.
26 James to Jay, 4 June 1848 and R. Blackwood to Jay, n.d. [June 1848], Columbia University, Jay Papers.
27 Jay to King, 1 May and 8 June 1848, University of North Carolina, Southern Historical Collection, King Papers.
28 Jay to King, 26 June 1848, University of North Carolina, King Papers. The Customs regulations in question were 8 & 9 Vict., c. 90, and 9 & 10 Vict.,

c. 58. The former had set a duty of £5 per hundredweight on foreign editions of works which had previously been published in Britain. Naturally reprints of books which still enjoyed copyright in Britain could not be imported from abroad. In the case of those states which had concluded a copyright treaty with Britain, the duty on foreign reprints of non-copyright English books was £2. 10s. 0d. The latter statute reduced these duties respectively to £2. 10s. 0d. and 15s. The 15s. was felt to be equivalent to what British publishers and paper-makers had to pay in excise to the British Government.

29 Coxe to Jay, 20 June 1848, Columbia University; Field to King, 12 July 1848, University of North Carolina; Jay to Marsh, 10 November, Jay Homestead, MS copy in letter book, pp. 112–13; Marsh to Jay, 13 November, Columbia University; Jay to King, 17 November, Jay Homestead, MS copy in letter book, pp. 123–4.

30 Jay to Morse, 28 November 1848, Jay Homestead, MS copy in letter book, p. 128; Jay to King, 11 December, University of North Carolina; Jay to Blackwood, 6 February 1849, Jay Homestead, MS copy in letter book, pp. 162–3.

Chapter V   The Impact of Foreign Reprints on the Domestic British Book Trade

1 The best account of the Paris reprint trade is G. Barber, 'Galignani and the publication of English books in France, 1800–52', *Library*, XVI (December 1961), pp. 267–84.

2 James, 'Of some observations on the book trade, as connected with literature in England', *Journal of the Statistical Society of London*, VI (1843), pp. 50–60. Although the article is not dated, internal evidence would suggest the late spring of 1842.

3 *Publishers' Circular*, V (1 April 1842), p. 97.

4 *Colbrun* v. *Carrol and Halliday*, P.R.O., Chancery, C. 13–2702; C. 31–508 (part II).

5 Morgan to Bentley, 22 September 1834, University of Illinois Library, Bentley Papers, authors' file, Morgan folder; *Bentley* v. *Baillière*, P.R.O., C. 31–514 (part I); C. 13–2702; Bentley Papers, B.M. Add. MSS 46633, ff. 18–27. The case and others of the time are briefly discussed in J. J. Barnes, 'Galignani and the publication of English books in France: A postscript', *Library*, XXV 5th ser. (December 1970), pp. 294–313. The article deals mainly with the efforts of London publishers to issue their books through agents in Paris.

6 These procedures are set forth in 54 Geo. III, c. 156. Section 4 of this Act provides for double costs when damages are claimed. The main reason to avoid a common law court, as distinct from Equity in Chancery, was that the legal expenses would far exceed an out-of-court settlement.

7 *Bentley* v. *Girity*, P.R.O., C. 31–528 and C. 33–865/651v; Bentley Papers, B.M. Add. MSS 46633, ff. 86–103. *Bentley* v. *Walker*, P.R.O., C. 31–528 and C. 33–865/658; B.M. Add. MSS 46633, ff. 105–22. *Bentley* v. *Williams*, P.R.O., C. 13–2039/13 and C. 33–865/658; B.M. Add. MSS 46633, ff. 37–84; University of Illinois Library, Bentley Papers, authors' file, coypright folder. Eliza Williams also comes into *Bentley* v. *Alexandere*, B.M. Add. MSS 46633, ff. 188–9.

8 *Bentley* v. *Alexandere*, Bentley Papers, B.M. Add. MSS 46633, ff. 181–9 and 214–18.

9 *Bentley* v. *Kennett*, Bentley Papers, B.M. Add. MSS 46633, f. 165 and following.

10 For the itemized legal expenses, see B.M. Add. MSS 46634, ff. 287–90.

11 P.R.O., F.O. 5–339/246v. The memorandum was enclosed in a letter from J. A. Murray to Lord Palmerston, 25 March 1839.

12 10 January 1842; P.R.O., B.T. 1–385. James's letter was enclosed in the F.O. dispatch 488 to the Board of Trade, 17 March 1842.

13 See a long memorandum in the Gladstone Papers, May 1842, B.M. Add. MSS 44730, ff. 106–13.

14 For the earlier legislation, see 12 Geo. II, c. 35; 41 Geo. III, c. 107.

15 Gladstone to Dean, 14 April 1842, Gladstone Papers, copy, B.M. Add. MSS 44527, f. 70v; Gladstone to James, 18–20 April 1842, copy, B.M. Add. MSS 44527, f. 72. The Treasury Minute in question was dated 25 February 1842. See also Customs to Board of Trade, 11 February 1842, Report, P.R.O., B.T. 1–382 for a good summary of the earlier policy.

16 James to Bulwer, 26 May 1842, Herts Record Office, Bulwer Papers, III, 32.

17 For a fuller discussion of Mahon–Talfourd Bill and its eventual passage, see chapter VI.

18 Mahon to Murray, 3 and 5 March 1842, in the possession of John Murray Ltd.

19 For Gladstone's role in steering the Customs Bill through Parliament, see *The Journals of the House of Commons*, XCVII (1842), pp. 394, 398, 418, and 430. See also Gladstone to F. B. Long, 17 June 1842, B.M. Add. MSS 44527, f. 82v; Gladstone to Mahon, 24 June 1842, Add. MSS 44527, ff. 83–4; copies.

20 *Parliamentary Debates*, LXIII (26 May 1842), pp. 794, 810–11.

21 6 November 1842, Herts Record Office, Bulwer Papers, III, p. 28.

22 James to Bulwer, 22 September 1842; Herts Record Office, Bulwer Papers, III, p. 31.

23 James to Bulwer, 23 November 1842; Marryat to Bulwer, n.d. (Wednesday, November–December 1842); Herts Record Office; Bulwer Papers, III, p. 30; IV, p. 10.

24 James to Bulwer, 6 and 23 November 1842; Marryat to Bulwer, n.d. (Wednesday, November–December 1842), Herts Record Office; Bulwer Papers, III, pp. 28, 30; IV, p. 10. Dickens to Marryat, 21 January 1843, as quoted in M. House, G. Storey, and K. Tillotson (eds), *The Letters of Charles Dickens: Pilgrim Edition* (Oxford, 1974), III, pp. 491–2.

25 Gladstone to James, 21 January 1845, B.M. Add. MSS 44528, f. 5v.
26 Clavering to Board of Trade, 9 December 1843, P.R.O., B.T. 1–420, no. 2078; Customs to Board of Trade, 21 December 1843, B.T. 1–420, no. 2152; Clavering to Board of Trade, 17 January 1844; Customs to Board of Trade, 7 February 1844, B.T. 1–423, no. 211; Clavering to Board of Trade, 25 June 1844, B.T. 1–432, no. 1078.
27 6 Customs 28/158 in the possession of the Library of Customs and Excise, King's Beam House, London.
28 *Athenaeum*, no. 885 (12 October 1844), p. 927; no. 890 (16 November 1844), p. 1052.
29 Waterman to Blackwood, 5 November 1852, National Library of Scotland, MS 4100, f. 237; Murray to Pigou, 16 July 1858, and Murray to Leslie, 3 April 1849, John Murray Ltd, letter book.
30 *Literary World*, XII (1 January 1853), p. 16.
31 R. A. Ogilvie to Fowler, 27 December 1844, Massachusetts Historical Society, French Papers, MS vol. for years 1843–7.
32 *Ibid.*
33 Gladstone to Murray, 6 February 1843, quoted in S. Smiles, *A Publisher and His Friends* (London, 1891), II, pp. 500–1. The Customs lists are filed, Customs 54/244, no. 41, 21 March 1843. I am indebted to Giles Barber for first calling my attention to these.
34 Howitt to Editor, *Athenaeum*, no. 1423 (3 February 1855), p. 148; Murray to Gladstone, 28 February 1860, John Murray Ltd, letter book.
35 Turner to Murray, 11 and 27 April 1860; Solicitor of Customs to Turner, 25 April 1860 (copy), John Murray Ltd.
36 James to Jerdan, 19 April 1842, Bodleian Library, MS Eng. Lett. D. 113, f. 263.

Chapter VI Efforts to Influence Parliament, 1838–44

1 P.R.O., Board of Trade, Ind. 14107/7 (16 January 1838), no. 6169; *Athenaeum*, no. 537 (10 February 1838), pp. 105–6. The measure may best be traced in the *Journals* of the Commons and the Lords for 1838. Comparatively little shows up in Hansard's *Parliamentary Debates*, but see Paulett Thomson's request to present the Bill, XLI (20 March 1838), pp. 1096–8.
2 E. Morley, *Henry Crabb Robinson* (London, 1938), II, p. 548.
3 J. J. Lowndes, *An Historical Sketch of the Law of Copyright* (London, 1840), p. 93.
4 For French interest in copyright negotiations see Foreign Office to Board of Trade, 12 May 1837, F.O. 5–1534/1–2.
5 Board of Trade to Foreign Office, 29 January 1839, P.R.O., F.O. 5–339/60–2. The Foreign Office summary of earlier transactions is in F.O. 5–1534/1–1v. In 1842 a summary of earlier negotiations was set forth in a memorandum

for Sir Robert Peel, 6 May 1842, Peel Papers, B.M. Add. MSS 40508, ff. 137–8v.

6 Foreign Office to Board of Trade, 17 March 1842, P.R.O., B.T. 1–385, Disp. 488, in which a copy of James's letter to Aberdeen, 10 January 1842, was also enclosed.

7 *Publishers' Circular*, V (1 July 1842), p. 186.

8 Mahon to Drummond, 2 July 1842, Peel Papers, B.M. Add. MSS 40511, f. 236.

9 Board of Trade to Foreign Office, 12 March, 3 May and 15 October 1842; 19 June 1843; 2 April and 20 May 1844; P.R.O., B.T. 3–30/461, p. 581; B.T. 3–31/258–70; B.T. 3–31/193–7; B.T. 3–32/98, p. 118.

10 *Journals of the House of Commons*, XCIX (1844), pp. 119, 147, 162, 168, 193, and 285. The *Parliamentary Debates* are particularly brief in their reporting of this measure and throw little light on its passage. See also Murray to Gladstone, 23 March 1844, John Murray Ltd, letter book.

11 A convenient list of the treaties is to be found in the *Parliamentary Papers*, 'Copyright commission', *Reports from Commissioners*, XXIV (1878), Appendix VI, p. 608. For more recent treatment, see S. P. Ladas, *The International Protection of Literary and Artistic Property* (New York, 1938), p. 21; S. Nowell-Smith, *International Copyright Law and the Publisher in the Reign of Queen Victoria* (Oxford, 1968), pp. 41–2.

12 *Athenaeum*, no. 763 (11 June 1842), p. 524; letter from Tom Hood.

13 The lists of petitions, though not the contents nor signatures of each, may be traced in the indices of the respective volumes of *The Journals of the House of Commons*.

14 *Parliamentary Debates*, XLII (9 May 1838), p. 1072.

15 *Parliamentary Debates*, XLIII (6 June 1838), p. 553; LVI (5 February 1841), pp. 344–57. Forster to Bulwer, n.d. (February 1841), Herts Record Office, Bulwer Papers, vol. XV.

16 Mahon to Brougham, 15 March 1842, University College, London, Brougham Papers, MS 6361.

17 Mahon to Murray, 3 March 1842, John Murray Ltd; Mahon to Brougham, 15 March 1842, University College, London, Brougham Papers, MS 6361.

18 Mahon to Murray, 23 March 1842, John Murray Ltd. The progress of the Copyright Bill can best be traced in the *Journals* of the Commons and the Lords for 1842.

19 *Athenaeum*, no. 754 (9 April 1842), p. 320.

20 *Parliamentary Debates*, LXII (20 April 1842), pp. 892–3. Godson supported the legal implications of section 24. See also Mahon to Murray, 21 April 1842, John Murray Ltd.

21 24 April 1842, University College, London, MS 6362. The Bill passed the House of Commons on 26 April.

22 Lyndhurst is given extended treatment in J. Campbell, *Lives of the Lord Chancellors* (London, 1869), VIII. The section on Lyndhurst covers approximately half the volume.

23 Mahon to Murray, 6 and 7 May 1842, John Murray Ltd; Mahon to Drummond, 7 May 1842, Peel Papers, B.M. Add. MSS 40508, f. 136.

24 *Parliamentary Debates*, LXIII (9 May 1842), p. 252.

25 Mahon to Murray, 13 May 1842, John Murray Ltd.

26 *Parliamentary Debates*, LXIII (9 May 1842), p. 252; LXIII (26 May 1842), pp. 777–813; *Journals of the House of Lords*, LXXIV (26 May 1842), p. 256.

27 Gladstone to Mahon, 24 June 1842, Gladstone Papers, B.M. Add. MSS 44527, ff. 83v–4. According to Gladstone section 17 of the Copyright Bill 'provided no means of ascertaining what works are under copyright and thus as it now stands seems to fail in part of the executory provisions necessary for giving it effect'.

28 *Athenaeum*, no. 763 (11 June 1842), p. 524; James to Bulwer, n.d. (28 June 1842), Herts Record Office, Bulwer Papers, III, p. 27; Dickens to T. Longman, n.d. (1 July 1842), in W. Dexter (ed.), *The Letters of Charles Dickens* (London, 1938), I, p. 461.

29 *Athenaeum*, no. 767 (9 July 1842), p. 610; no. 787 (26 November 1842), p. 1016.

30 A. Whitley, 'Hood and Dickens: some new letters', *Huntington Library Quarterly*, XIV (August 1951), pp. 399–400.

31 For a description of the Booksellers' Association see J. J. Barnes, *Free Trade in Books: A study of the London book trade since 1800* (Oxford, 1964), *passim*. For an account of different authors' societies see *ibid.*, pp. 85–91; J. G. Hepburn, *The Author's Empty Purse* (London, 1968), pp. 32–44.

32 Dickens to T. Beard, 7 April 1843; Dickens to Babbage, 27 April 1843; and Dickens to Bulwer, 27 April 1843; in Dexter, *op. cit.*, I, pp. 515–16. Gladstone to J. Robertson, 1 May 1843, B.M. Add. MSS 44527, f. 127v.

33 Dickens to Bulwer, 14 May 1843, in Dexter, *op. cit.*, I, p. 521; Dickens to Longman, 17 May 1843, as quoted in M. House, G. Storey, and K. Tillotson (eds), *The Letters of Charles Dickens: Pilgrim Edition* (Oxford, 1974), III, pp. 491–2. Whitley, *op. cit.*, p. 399 n. 59; *Athenaeum*, no. 812 (20 May 1843), p. 489; *Literary Gazette*, no. 1374 (20 May 1843), p. 337; *Meeting of Authors, Publishers and Other Gentlemen Connected with Literature Held at Messrs. Longman and Co.'s, 39 Paternoster Row, on Wednesday, the 17th Day of May, 1843*. Copies are to be found in the library of HM Customs and Excise and in the Parrish Collection of Princeton University. The latter collection also contains a list of members with their contributions.

34 J. Blackwood to A. Blackwood, 18 May 1843, M. Oliphant, *Annals of a Publishing House* (Edinburgh, 1891), II, p. 345; *Athenaeum*, no. 812 (20 May 1843), p. 489.

35 Hood to Dickens, n.d. (November 1842 and May 1843), in Whitley, *op. cit.*, pp. 402–4.

36 For background on the Turners the following have been consulted: the Last Will and Testament of Sharon Turner (27 November 1843) and of Alfred Turner (20 February 1864). A considerable file of letters from both

Turners to John Murray is in the possession of John Murray Ltd. Further information came from the Library of the Law Society.

37 S. Turner to J. Murray, December 1827, quoted in S. Smiles, *A Publisher and His Friends* (London, 1891), II, pp. 257–8; J. Murray to T. Aspinwall, 15 November 1828, John Murray Ltd, letter book, p. 44.

38 Although their exact role in the inquiry of 1818 is not entirely clear, it is apparent that the Turners aided Murray and the poet, Robert Southey, in seeking to amend the 1814 Copyright Act. In a letter to Murray of 25 March 1818 Alfred Turner wrote: 'I enclose you copies of the two general petitions against the existing copyright act for Mr. Southey if you think they will be of use to him.' Letter in the possession of John Murray Ltd.

39 Turner to Murray, 20 July 1842, John Murray Ltd.

40 By far the best account of Tauchnitz is S. Nowell-Smith, *op. cit.*, pp. 41–63. A copy of Bayley's opinion dated 15 July 1843 is in Herts Record Office, Bulwer Papers, MS Box 40. Dickens's inquiry does not seem to have survived. The licensing of foreign reprints of English copyright works was provided for by Section 17 of 5 & 6 Vict., c. 45.

41 Oliphant, *op. cit.*, II, p. 353.

42 Turner to James, 7 August 1843, Boston Public Library.

43 An example of the Society's effort to influence the Government may be found in a letter from A. Turner to the B. of T., 31 December 1844, P.R.O., Ind. 20446, p. 2. Five years later Turner was writing to the Board of Trade on behalf of interested publishers, but without mentioning the Society: 31 August 1849, Ind. 20451, p. 71. Unfortunately no membership list for these years seems to have survived.

Chapter VII   The Canadian Market

1 The following arguments are based on both private and official sources. Of particular value is the printed Parliamentary report of 1872, which reprints some of the inter-departmental correspondence for 1845–6: *Accounts and Papers*, vol. XLIII, document no. 339, pp. 1–14. See also Colonial Office to Board of Trade, 10 June 1845, 27 June 1845, 27 June 1846, P.R.O., Ind. 20446, p. 144 and Ind. 20447, p. 148; Board of Trade to Colonial Office, 5 November 1845, 19 October 1846, P.R.O., B.T. 3–34/64–6 and B.T. 3–34/99–102; Board of Trade to Colonial Office, 14 July 1843, B.T. 3–31/68; 28 August 1843, B.T. 3–31/73; C.O. 42–509/118–19. See also J. Murray to Editor of *The Times*, 28 August 1843, copy, John Murray Ltd, letter book; *Athenaeum*, no. 855 (16 March 1844), p. 249.

2 *Accounts and Papers* (1872).

3 *Ibid.*

4 Hereafter the term Canadian will be used in its more general sense to include all five Provinces of British North America.

5 5 & 6 Vict., c. 49.

6 *Ibid.*

7 During the winter British books were shipped to the port of Halifax, and then overland across Nova Scotia and New Brunswick to Montreal.

8 Armour & Ramsay to Blackwood, 7 March 1843, National Library of Scotland, Blackwood Papers, MS 4063, ff. 65–6; Blackwood to Board of Trade, 18 April and 1 May 1843, P.R.O., B.T. 1–408 no. 690 and B.T. 1–409 no. 782; Treasury, T. 1–4956 no. 14,751, which bundles together all the previous correspondence relating to Stayner; a copy of the Treasury Warrant of 11 October 1843 is in C.O. 42–511/311. See also *Brother Jonathan,* quarto ed. VI (11 November 1843), p. 298.

9 John Murray of the *Quarterly Review,* Thomas Longman of the *Edinburgh Review,* Henry Colburn of the *New Monthly Magazine,* Richard Bentley of the *Miscellany,* and William Blackwood of *Blackwood's Magazine* joined Armour & Ramsay of Montreal in requesting the Treasury to allow bulk mailings.

10 Murray *et al.* to the Treasury, 8 May 1844, P.R.O., T. 1–4947 no. 12,516; Colonial Office to Treasury, 25 May 1844, C.O. 42–529/148; G.P.O. to Treasury, 15 June 1844, T. 1–4947 no. 12,516; Treasury to Longman *et al.,* 29 June 1844, C.O. 42–529/147; Treasury to Colonial Office, 17 February 1845, C.O. 42–529/145. See also Murray to T. Freemantle of the Treasury, 11 May 1844, and Murray to G. Clark of the Treasury, 19 June 1844, copies, John Murray Ltd, letter book.

11 For the Association for the Protection of Literature, see chapter VI above. For the Royal Commission, see *Reports from Commissioners,* XXIV (1878). Canadian publishers were not given permission to reprint British copyright works until 1875, and then only under certain circumstances.

12 John Murray III to F. B. Head, 20 November 1843, John Murray Ltd, letter book.

13 Murray to Mahon, 8 December 1843, letter book. A printed copy of Murray's prospectus for the Colonial Library may be found in the Gladstone Papers, B.M. Add. MSS 44259, ff. 29–30. The best description of the Colonial Library and its intentions is in S. Nowell-Smith, *International Copyright Law and the Publisher in the Reign of Queen Victoria* (Oxford, 1968), pp. 27–30. The list of authors and titles is taken from Murray's statement for the *Publishers' Circular,* XII (1 December 1849), p. 414.

14 The opinion poll of booksellers and the comment by Greig are taken from Appendix PP of *The Journals of the Legislative Assembly of the Province of Canada,* III (1843), First Provincial Parliament, 3rd Sess. In the Public Record Office this is C.O. 45–216. For Murray's statements about the sale of Colonial Library volumes, see: Murray to G. Borrow, 18 January 1844; Murray to Melville, 3 December 1847; and Murray to Head, 7 April 1849.

15 Board of Trade to Colonial Office, 5 November 1845, P.R.O., B.T. 3–34/64. Also reprinted in the report of 1872.

16 Earl Grey succeeded Gladstone as Colonial Secretary. It is unlikely that the Board of Trade put further pressure on the book trade as Gladstone recommended.

17 Most of the correspondence between the Board of Trade and the Colonial Office relating to copyright is reprinted in the report of 1872. See also: Colonial Office to Board of Trade, 27 June 1846, P.R.O., Ind. 20447, p. 148 no. 1195; Board of Trade to Colonial Office, 19 October 1846, B.T. 3–34/99.

18 The *Parliamentary Debates* throw no light on the passage of the Foreign Reprints Act. However, its course may be followed in the *Journals of the House of Commons*, CII (1847), pp. 778, 807, 862, 868, 874, 931 and 951.

19 10 & 11 Vict., c. 28 (1847) applied *only* in the Province of Canada, not in the other four Canadian provinces.

20 For general background to Canadian copyright legislation, see: T. Solberg, *Copyright in Canada and Newfoundland* (Washington, 1903); H. G. Fox, *The Canadian Law of Copyright and Industrial Designs* (Toronto, 1967). Solberg reprints the texts of the various provincial copyright acts. For the exchange of official correspondence, see: Elgin to Colonial Office, 7 April 1848, P.R.O., C.O. 42–550/4; Colonial Office to Board of Trade, 12 May 1848, Ind. 20449, p. 139, no. 1361; Board of Trade to Colonial Office, 30 June 1848, C.O. 42–553/54 and B.T. 3–35/641; Colonial Office to Elgin, 7 July 1848, C.O. 42–550/302. The following Acts and Orders in Council imposed a duty of 20 per cent on foreign reprints entering their respective provinces: Nova Scotia Act of 21 March 1848 (11 Vict., c. 9) confirmed by Order in Council, 11 August 1848; New Brunswick Act of 30 March 1848 (11 Vict., c. 66) and Order of 31 October 1848; Newfoundland Act of 23 April 1849 (12 Vict., c. 5), Order of 30 July 1849.

21 See the following for the problems of enforcing the 1842 Copyright and Customs Acts, as well as the dispute between Dunscombe and Pratt: Treasury to Colonial Office, 31 July 1849, P.R.O., T. 7–1/129; Treasury to Colonial Office, 23 August 1849, T. 7–1/150; Elgin to Colonial Office, 8 February 1850, C.O. 42–565/53; Treasury to Colonial Office, 7 March 1850, with enclosures, C.O. 42–569/70–84; Colonial Office to Board of Trade, 25 March 1850, Ind. 20452, p. 94; Elgin to Colonial Office, 16 August 1850, C.O. 42–566/86; Board of Trade to Colonial Office, 20 November 1850, C.O. 42–567/56; Colonial Office to Board of Trade, 29 November 1850, C.O. 42–567/59; Board of Trade to Colonial Office, 9 December 1850, C.O. 42–567/62; Order in Council, 12 December 1850, C.O. 42–566/95–9; Privy Council to Colonial Office, 21 December 1850, C.O. 42–567/40; Elgin to Colonial Office, 4 February 1851, C.O. 42–572/182; Board of Trade to Colonial Office, 8 March 1851 and Board of Trade to Colonial Office, 18 March 1851, C.O. 42–575/150–3.

22 *Athenaeum*, no. 1254 (8 November 1851), p. 1174.

23 The Inspector-General of Canada noted that 'the annual expense attending upon the collection of the Copyright duty at 89 Ports, at which so much of the time of the officers is necessarily engaged in the scrutiny of Book Importations, the keeping of Separate Accounts and Entries, and the preparation of special Returns', far exceeded the duty collected. He estimated that the Province spent about £250 a year imposing and collecting the duty on books, while only £30 to £35 was deducted from the receipts to cover the printing of lists and forms. Only about 1 per cent of the possible duty on American books entering Canada was collected from 1851–5.

24 The best source for the Canadian figures is: P.R.O., Governor-General E. Head to the Colonial Office, 16 February and 12 July 1856, with enclosures, C.O. 42–603/283 and C.O. 42–604/319. See also: Bentley to C. Trevelyan of the Treasury, 8 July 1856, copy, Bentley Papers, B.M. Add. MSS 46642, f. 110v. For a discussion of the Foreign Reprints Act of 1847 and its effectiveness or lack thereof, see: *Athenaeum*, no. 1418 (30 December 1854), p. 1592; no. 1429 (17 March 1855), p. 324; and no. 1517 (22 November 1856), p. 1436. For some of the legal implications see the *Jurist*, VI n.s. (11 February 1860), pp. 44–6. Bulwer's income from the colonial duty comes from Herts Record Office, Bulwer Papers, Treasury to Lord Lytton, 31 October 1866, MS Box 40.

Chapter VIII   The British Law Courts: A Possible Remedy for the Absence of International Copyright

1 *Illustrated London News*, XX (12 February 1853), p. 122.

2 The Routledge figures come from one of the 'paper and print' volumes in possession of Routledge & Kegan Paul Ltd. Although the figures in these volumes were estimates of future commitments, they are a gauge of actual practice. For a history of the firm see F. A. Mumby, *The House of Routledge, 1834–1934* (London, 1934). A description of Hawthorne's writings and the publishers who reprinted them may be found in J. Blanck (ed.), *Bibliography of American Literature* (6 vols to date; New Haven, 1955–73). See also C. Gohdes, *American Literature in Nineteenth Century England* (Carbondale, 1944).

3 In July–August 1850 Murray formally applied for the injunction while Bentley gathered evidence and awaited the outcome of Murray's litigation. Thus, strictly speaking, Murray was the only plaintiff. However, it was made clear at the time that if Bohn and Routledge did not cease the republication of Irving and Melville, Bentley would also seek damages.

4 The most convenient listing of Bohn's Shilling Series and Routledge's Popular Library is in the *Publishers' Circular*, XIII (1850), in the Catalogue of Printed Books at the beginning of the volume. Bohn's list was numbered in the order

of appearance while Routledge's was not, but I have assigned numbers to the latter.

5 The following correspondence deals with Murray's requests to Putnam and Irving for information and their replies: Putnam to Murray, 5 June, 3 July, 16 July 1850, in the possession of John Murray Ltd: R. Cooke in behalf of Murray to Putnam, 9 August 1850, in G. H. Putnam, *A Memoir of George Palmer Putnam* (New York, priv. printed, 1903), pp. 341–2; and Irving to Murray, 18 August, 19 August and 22 September 1850, in B. H. McClary, *Washington Irving and the House of Murray, 1817–1856* (Knoxville, 1969), pp. 193–9, where these three letters are reprinted in their entirety. The letter from Irving to Murray of 22 September was particularly important since it provided Murray with literary and biographical information which Murray needed for his lawsuit.

6 Turner to Murray, 10 August 1850.

7 Turner to Murray, 11 February, 1 April and 20 April 1851, John Murray Ltd. The definition of a Demurrer came from a former solicitor of Richard Bentley's, J. H. Adlington, in his *Cyclopaedia of Law* (London, 1820), p. 217.

8 Turner to Murray, 12 June and 3 December 1851, John Murray Ltd; Bentley to Routledge, 3 June, 13 June, 8 July, 10 July, 14 July 1851, Bentley Papers, B.M. Add. MSS 46641, ff. 140v., 142, 147v., 151v–2v; Bentley to Devey, 31 January 1852, B.M. Add. MSS 46641, f. 207; Bentley–Routledge agreement, 17 June 1851, in the possession of Routledge & Kegan Paul Ltd (agreements and copyright receipts A–H). Bentley's dissatisfaction with the way Routledge abided by the agreement of 17 June 1851 is indicated by his solicitor's warning that legal proceedings might be resumed for breach of contract; Devey to Routledge, 6 December 1851, University of Illinois, Bentley Papers, business file, Devey folder. See also Devey to Bentley, 30 January and 6 February 1852, Devey folder. Eventually Routledge seems to have pacified Bentley by a penalty payment of £100, though Bentley wanted £300. By 1851 Routledge had reprinted three of J. F. Cooper's works in a Railway Series, thus forcing Bentley to protect his copyrights in Cooper as well as Irving.

9 Turner to Murray, 20 June, 22 July, 28 July, and undated (late July) 1851; and Murray to Irving, undated (late July) 1851; copy; John Murray Ltd; for Bentley's efforts to force Bohn's surrender see: Bentley to Devey, 23 May 1851, Bentley Papers, B.M. Add. MSS 46641, f. 134v; Devey to Bentley, 3 June 1851, University of Illinois, Bentley Papers, business file, Devey folder; Bentley to W. H. Prescott, 19 June 1851, B.M. Add. MSS 46641, f. 143v.

10 Murray to Irving, 19 September 1851, in P. Irving, *The Life and Letters of Washington Irving* (New York, 1862–4), IV, pp. 89–90; Turner to Murray, 8 April and 14 April 1852, John Murray Ltd. The Murray–Bohn agreement of 27 August is in the possession of the Murray firm. The total of Murray's legal costs came to £817 14s. 10d. For the Bentley–Bohn settlement see: Devey to Bentley, 11 September, 3 October 1851, University of Illinois,

Bentley Papers, business file, Devey folder; Bentley to Bohn, 27 December 1851, B.M. Add. MSS 46641, f. 189v.

11 McClary, *op. cit.*, pp. 204–5.

12 On appeal to the House of Lords this case was known as *Jefferys* v. *Boosey* rather than *Boosey* v. *Jefferys* as it had been referred to in the Court of Exchequer and the Court of Error.

13 References to the various cases cited in this chapter may be found in any of the contemporary works on copyright. Perhaps the most comprehensive and useful is R. A. Fisher, *A Digest of the Reported Cases Determined in the House of Lords and Privy Council, and in the Courts of Common Law . . . 1756– 1870* (5 vols; London, 1870); see especially vol. I, cols 1873–4 for copyright of foreigners. Not all cases were reported, especially if they were tried in the same court and were of a similar nature. Thus, *Boosey* v. *Purday* was reported and *Boosey* v. *Jefferys* was not. Information about the latter is taken from materials at the Public Record Office: Exchequer, E. 8–11 and E. 8–12 Exch. of Pleas Roll no. 63. These Exchequer materials provide dates and details for the years 1849–52 but not thereafter.

The appeal before the Court of Error was duly reported in several of the contemporary journals, as was the final decision of the House of Lords: *4 House of Lords Cases*, 815, which includes the opinions of the Common Law Judges as well as those of the Law Lords.

The Parliamentary Inquiry into the appellate jurisdiction of the Lords is in the Parliamentary Papers, *Reports, Committees*, VIII (1856), pp. 403–605. See also *Accounts and Papers*, L (1856), nos 272 and 298, concerning the number of cases brought to the House of Lords and those who heard them. The best, and most lively account, though by no means impartial, was Lord Campbell's *Lives of the Lord Chancellors*, especially the posthumously printed volume VIII (London, 1869).

14 The biography of Lord Campbell by his daughter, the Hon Mrs Hardcastle (2 vols; London, 1881), is another important source. She was heavily dependent upon the personal diaries of Lord Campbell, and I am especially indebted to the Rt Hon. Baron Stratheden and Campbell, for permission to peruse and quote from manuscripts of these which are in his possession. W. Holdsworth's *A History of the English Law* (new ed., 16 vols; London, 1966) is also valuable, as are: C. M. Denison and C. H. Scott, *The Practice and Procedure of the House of Lords . . . under the Appellate Jurisdiction Act 1876* (London, 1879); T. Beven, 'Appellate jurisdiction of the House of Lords', *Law Quarterly Review*, XVII (October 1901), pp. 357–71.

15 Bohn went to great lengths to publicize the open meeting of 1 July 1851 chaired by Bulwer. He hired a shorthand writer to take down the proceedings verbatim but when this arrangement failed he personally supervised the collecting and editing of the speeches and motions which became the basis for a long pamphlet entitled *The Question of Unreciprocated Foreign Copyright*. This

appeared in August 1851. The Society for Obtaining an Adjustment of the Law of Copyright also issued a printed circular encouraging membership. The only copy of this that has come to my attention is at the British Library, London School of Economics, Coll. G, 884 (2). The July meeting was also well publicized in the daily and periodical press.

16 Lord Campbell's comments about his contemporaries are in his MS journals for the years 1850–4.

17 Granville's description is quoted by Holdsworth, *op. cit.*, XVI, p. 59. Bethell's evidence before the Select Committee begins on p. 431 of the 1856 report, as cited above.

18 We do not know why the other five judges were absent, although it was a rule of procedure that a judge could deliver an opinion only if he were present at the outset of a hearing and was later present to read his opinion in person. Lord Campbell may have been precluded because he had written the decision for the Court of Error, though his absence may have stemmed from some other cause.

19 Justice Patteson, who had also supported Boosey's appeal in 1851, was in retirement by 1854, and Cresswell, another supporter in 1851, was absent. One other judge of Common Pleas might have taken part in both judgments but for some reason did not: T. N. Talfourd, whose name had for so many years been linked with the defence of copyright. The opinions of the ten judges are set forth in the report of *Jefferys* v. *Boosey* as cited above. They are also reprinted in the *Journals of the House of Lords*, LXXXVI (1854), pp. 299–322.

20 The statistics concerning the frequency of Law Lords attending to appeals were conveyed in a special statement by the House of Lords to the House of Commons, *Accounts and Papers*, L (1856), no. 272.

21 Sampson Low placed his announcement in his own publication, *Publishers' Circular*, XVII (16 August 1854), p. 376. See also *Athenaeum*, no. 1402 (9 September 1854), p. 1090.

22 The various figures for Routledge's editions are taken from the firm's paper and print book covering the years 1851–5. A copy of Bentley's sale of Prescott's works to Routledge is also in the possession of Routledge & Kegan Paul Ltd. There is a voluminous exchange of correspondence between Bentley and Prescott divided among the British Museum, the University of Illinois, Houghton Library, the Massachusetts Historical Society. The published works of C. H. Gardiner also contain portions of this correspondence. Bentley's statement about his financial position comes from a copy of a letter to Prescott, 22 June 1855, B.M. Add. MS 46642, f. 74. Statistics of Bentley's cheap reprints are in B.M. Add. MSS 46637, f. 76. The legal opinions of Turner, Devey, and Willes, dated 28 May, 9 June and 14 June 1855 respectively, are in the University of Illinois, Bentley Papers, authors' file, Prescott folder. By 1854 the only other potentially profitable American author attached to Bentley was George Bancroft. However, they had fallen out over the length of

Bancroft's multi-volume work even before the decision of *Jefferys* v. *Boosey*.
23 Le Marchant to Bentley, n.d. (August–September 1854), extract, University of Illinois, Bentley Papers, authors' file, copyright folder; Bentley to Brougham, 3 January and 23 February 1855, University College, London, Brougham Papers, MSS 19, 201–2; Gladstone to Bentley, 12 January 1866, copy, University of Illinois, authors' file, Gladstone folder.

Chapter IX   American Lobbyists in the Early 1850s

1 Much of what follows comes from materials in the Hertfordshire County Record Office, Bulwer Papers, red files marked 1831–64 and 1854. These contain the letters which Robert wrote to his father. Another volume, labelled 'Letters of the First Lord Lytton to his Son', are less useful for this study. The standard biography of Robert Lytton Bulwer who referred to himself as Robert Lytton and later assumed the *nom de plume* of Owen Meredith was written by his daughter, E. E. Balfour, *Personal and Literary Letters of Robert first Earl of Lytton* (London, 1906).
2 21 January 1851.
3 24 February and 29 April 1851, red file 1854.
4 For basic biographical information about Crampton, see *Dictionary of National Biography*; E. Walford (comp.), *The County Families of the United Kingdom* (4th ed., London, 1868).
5 A brief and somewhat unreliable obituary notice of T. W. C. Moore is in the *New York Times*, 25 November 1873, p. 8. Other details are in *The Foreign Office List* (London, 1871), pp. 145, 217; R. W. Bosburgh et al., *The Church of St. Andrew: Richmond, Staten Island* (New York, 1925), p. 185.
6 Metcalfe to Lord Stanley, 3 April 1843, P.R.O., C.O. 42–505/15; R. Pakenham to H. U. Addington, 29 March 1845, enclosing letter of T. W. Moore to Pakenham, 19 March 1845, F.O. 5–425/107–10; J. Harvey to Lord Palmerston, 14 December 1846, F.O. 5–455/96–7.
7 Palmerston to H. Bulwer, 21 November 1850, P.R.O., F.O. 5–510/167; A. McVaye to Palmerston, 21 November 1850; J. Harnett to Palmerston, 11 November 1850; Bulwer to Palmerston, 13 January 1851, enclosing Moore to Bulwer, 10 January 1851; F.O. 5–524/134 and 149; F.O. 5–527/13–14.
8 Crampton to Elgin, 3 November 1851, copy, enclosed in Crampton to Malmesbury, 12 September 1852; in possession of the Earl of Malmesbury; volume labelled 'Private Correspondence: Turkey . . . N.S. America, 1852'. In this letter Douglas is clearly alluded to in terms of his support of reciprocity and his aspiration for the Presidency. He had introduced a Reciprocity Bill on 11 February 1850: *Journal of the Senate*, 31st Cong. 1st Sess., p. 138.
9 R. Lytton to E. L. Bulwer, 8 November and 13 November 1851, Herts Record Office, Bulwer Papers, red file 1854.

10 Bulwer to Palmerston, 1 July 1850, Palmerston Papers, currently in the possession of the Historical Manuscripts Commission, Chancery Lane, London.

11 J. K. Walker to Marcy, 19 December 1850, Library of Congress, Marcy Papers, MS vol. XVIII; 'Literary diary', 25 December 1850, LXXXV, pp. 38–9; diary marked 1831–57, MS vol. LXXVII, pp. 3–4, for entries 13–15 January 1851, and p. 6, 25 January 1851.

12 Testimony of James G. Berret, *Senate Documents*, 33rd Cong. Special Sess. (22 March 1853), report no. 1, p. 208.

13 A. Hunter (comp.), *A Washington and Georgetown Directory* (Washington, 1853), pp. 100–4 for the listing of general agents.

14 Daniel Webster to Fletcher Webster, 20 December 1847, in C. H. Van Tyne, *The Letters of Daniel Webster* (New York, 1902), p. 730.

15 Austin to Sumner, 6 June 1852, Houghton Library, Sumner Papers.

16 R. G. Albion, *The Rise of New York Port, 1815–1860* (New York, 1939), pp. 326–7.

17 H. Hamilton, *Zachary Taylor* (Indianapolis, 1951), II, pp. 164, 345–7. Hamilton provides good references for further inquiry into the affair. See also *Stryker's American Register*, IV (July 1850), pp. 78–80, for a good contemporary account.

18 Most useful for the history of public lands and land warrants were: P. W. Gates, *The Farmer's Age: Agriculture, 1815–1860* (New York, 1960), vol. III; T. Donaldson, *The Public Domain* (Washington, 1884); G. M. Stephenson, *Political History of the Public Lands from 1840–1862* (Boston, 1917); V. R. Carstensen (ed.), *The Public Lands* (Madison, 1963); R. P. Swierenga, *Pioneers and Profits* (Ames, Iowa, 1968). The last two are particularly valuable.

19 *Stryker's American Register*, V (January 1851), pp. 572–4.

20 A good account of the Mexican claims is in A. Nevins, *Ordeal of the Union, 1852–57* (New York, 1947), I, p. 156.

21 For lobbying and the Texas debt, see: H. Hamilton, 'Texas Bonds and Northern Profits', *Miss. Vall. Hist. Rev.*, XLIII (March 1957), pp. 579–94. The best book on lobbying in general is: H. Cohen, *Business and Politics in America from the Age of Jackson to the Civil War* (Westport, Conn., 1971).

22 Nevins, *op. cit.*, I, p. 155.

23 C. E. Hamlin, *The Life and Times of Hannibal Hamlin* (Cambridge, Mass., 1899), p. 274.

24 *Congressional Globe*, 32nd Cong. 1st Sess., XXVIII (6 August 1852), pp. 2100–1.

25 'Bribery and claims', *Senate Documents*, Special Session of the 33rd Cong. (22 March 1853), report no. 1.

26 'An Act to Prevent Frauds upon the Treasury of the United States', 26 February 1853.

27 Borland Report, p. 31.

28 *Ibid.*, pp. 28–9.

29 *Congressional Globe*, 33rd Cong. 2nd Sess., XXX (1855), pp. 15, 24, 68, 94, 105, 127, 388, 636, 902, and 909. Above and beyond the Congressional debates

and papers, one of the best sources for the background and workings of the Court of Claims is J. C. Devereux, *Court of Claims: Report and Digest of Opinions Delivered since the Organization of the Court* (New York, 1856).

Chapter X   The Organization

1 MS Diary of William F. Cooper, 11 February 1839, pp. 5–6, Tennessee State Library; *Obituary Record of Graduates of Yale College, Deceased from July, 1859, to July, 1870* (New Haven, 1870); E. L. Watson, 'James Walker of Columbia: Polk's critic and compatriot', *Tennessee Historical Quarterly*, XXIII (March 1964), pp. 24–37; C. Sellers, *James K. Polk* (2 vols; Princeton, 1957–66). I am particularly grateful to the Tennessee State Library, the Memphis Public Library, and the Yale University Alumni Office for assisting me with these sources. Because Walker usually styled himself J. Knox or merely Knox Walker, some writers have mistakenly assumed that his Christian name was James. However the family Bible as well as other sources clearly indicates Joseph, not James.

2 M. M. Quaife (ed.), *The Diary of James K. Polk during his Presidency, 1845 to 1849* (Chicago 1910), II (21 January 1847), pp. 345–6.

3 15 May 1849, Library of Congress, Coryell Papers, IV, p. 80.

4 Borland Report, 1853, pp. 24–7, 190–205; *Rainey's Memphis City Directory* for 1855–6.

5 The chief source for Beverley Tucker is Jane Ellis Tucker, *Beverley Tucker: A Memoir, by His Wife* (Richmond, 1893). See also the *Dictionary of American Biography*.

6 Beverley to N. B. Tucker, 14 December 1848 and 10 December 1849, College of William and Mary, Tucker–Coleman Papers.

7 B. Tucker to N. B. Tucker, 25 April 1851, College of William and Mary, Tucker–Coleman Papers.

8 Tucker to Hunter, 5 April 1851, University of Virginia Library, Hunter Papers; B. Tucker to J. Randolph Tucker, 15 December 1851, University of North Carolina Library, Southern Historical Collection, Tucker family Papers.

9 Davis to Tucker, 1 [?] April 1853, University of Virginia Library; Tucker to Davis, n.d. (April 1853), Princeton University Library. The first issue of the *Sentinel* appeared on 24 September 1853. The best account of Tucker's appointment as printer is R. F. Nichols, *Franklin Pierce* (2nd ed., Philadelphia, 1958), pp. 315–16. For efforts to secure Douglas's nomination see R. F. Nichols, *The Democratic Machine, 1850–1854* (New York, 1923), pp. 107–15. Although Tucker is scarcely mentioned, Douglas's strategy is fully treated.

10 There is a particularly good account of Walker in the *Dictionary of American Biography* and there are several monographs dealing with Walker's later career. The most recent and generally useful is J. P. Shenton, *Robert John Walker: a politician from Jackson to Lincoln* (New York, 1961). See also: M. Eichert, 'Some

implications arising from Robert J. Walker's participation in land ventures', *Journal of Mississippi History*, XIII (January 1951), pp. 41–6; and F. H. Tick, 'The political and economic policies of Robert J. Walker' (unpublished doctoral dissertation, University of California at Los Angeles, 1947).

11 In 1849–50 Colt's personal attorney was Joseph Knox Walker, and thus it was natural to use the Organization's representative at the Great Exhibition in 1851. See H. Stevens, *An Account of the Proceedings at a Dinner Given by Mr. George Peabody to the Americans Connected with the Great Exhibition at the London Coffee House Ludgate Hill on the 27th October 1851* (London, 1851), at which both R. J. Walker and Colt were present. On 25 November Colt read a paper entitled *On the Application of Machinery to the Manufacture of Rotating Chambered-Breech Fire-arms, and Their Peculiarities* to the Institution of Civil Engineers in London. R. J. Walker was one of the Honoured Guests in attendance. The paper was published in 1853 with notes by the Institute's Secretary, Charles Manby.

12 Walker to Corcoran, 30 July and 16 August 1851, and Corcoran to Walker, 2 August 1851, Library of Congress, Corcoran Papers, vol. V and letter book, III, pp. 435–6; Crampton to Clarendon, 19 June 1853, Bodleian Library, Clarendon Papers, C. 11., f. 177–85. Walker also had a hand in the development of telegraphic communication, which nicely dove-tailed with his various railway and land investments.

13 The most recent biography is I. D. Spencer, *The Victor and the Spoils: the life of William L. Marcy* (Providence, 1959). For a brief account, see the *Dictionary of American Biography*.

14 Spencer, *op. cit.*, pp. 184–5, 193; MS diary, 1831–57, Library of Congress, Marcy Papers, vol. LXXVII, see for example p. 14 (7 March 1851), where Marcy works on the Leggett claim; A Leggett to Marcy, 16 July 1851, Library of Congress, Marcy Papers, vol. XIX. The difficulty with Spencer's approach may be that he is so preoccupied with political considerations in the narrowest sense that he ignores the role of personal influence through business connections and claims.

15 Various letters from Causten to Marcy are found in Library of Congress, Marcy Papers, vol. XVIII; Marcy's end-of-the-year account for 1850 is in his MS diary, 'literary and political', vol. LXXXV, section C.; his day-to-day work in Washington from January to April 1851 is in MS diary, vol. LXXVII, especially pp. 1–25. Causten is regularly listed in the city directories for Washington, D.C., for the late 1840s and early 1850s.

16 A brief account of Mason's life is in the *Dictionary of American Biography*. See also: Mason to Grigsby, 14 September 1850, Pennsylvania Historical Society, Gratz Collection; Mason to Buchanan, 8 December 1851, Pennsylvania Historical Society, Buchanan Papers, MS Box 74.

17 Brief accounts of Burke are in Appleton's *Cyclopaedia of American Biography* and *Biographical Directory of the American Congress*. For his connection with

the *Washington Union*, see C. H. Ambler, *Thomas Ritchie: a study in Virginia politics* (Richmond, 1913), p. 276.

18 Nichols, *Pierce*, pp. 174, 178, 218, 290–1; Sister M. M. C. Hodgson, *Calab Cushing: Attorney General of the United States, 1853–1857* (Washington, 1955), pp. 89–92.

19 *Dictionary of American Biography; Biographical Directory of the American Congress*; J. Bishop, *The Day Lincoln was Shot* (New York, 1955), pp. 188–90.

20 *Dictionary of American Biography*; plus references in Sellers's *Polk*; Nichols's *Pierce* and *Democratic Machine*.

21 The most comprehensive study of Levin is to be found in an article by J. A. Forman, 'Lewis Charles Levin: portrait of an American demagogue', *American Jewish Archives*, XII (October 1960), pp. 150–94. This traces the earlier years of Levin's career and elucidates Levin's political and social views. It does not deal with his career as a lobbyist, however. See also: *Dictionary of American Biography; Biographical Directory of the American Congress; National Cyclopaedia of American Biography; Dollar Newspaper*, 21 March 1860, p. 2. I am very grateful for the assistance which Professor Thomas Curran of St John's University (N Y) gave me in my search for information about Levin. Unfortunately the Levin family papers were lost in the Charleston earthquake of 1886.

22 Levin to Lewis, 15 April 1849, Huntington Library. Unless otherwise indicated, the following references and quotations are from the same collection.

23 16 April 1849.

24 30 April, 2 May and 3 May 1849.

25 10 and 19 December 1849; 26 January, 31 January and 1 February 1850. W. D. Lewis's charges against Cooper were set forth in an extended pamphlet: *A Brief Account of the Efforts of Senator Cooper of Pennsylvania . . . to Prevent the Confirmation of William D. Lewis, Collector of the Customs of the District of Philadelphia* (Philadelphia, 1851).

26 22 April and 8 May 1850.

27 Levin to Lewis, 6 August 1850.

28 Levin to Webster, 25 April 1851, Library of Congress, Webster Papers, vol. X.

29 15 October 1852, Library of Congress, Marcy Papers, vol. XXVI.

Chapter XI   Bribery, or the Necessary Expenses of Congressional Action: November 1851–February 1853

1 R. Lytton to Bulwer, 17 January 1852, Herts Record Office, Bulwer Papers, red file, 1854; Levin to Moore, January–February 1852, Bodleian Library, Crampton Papers; there is also an unsigned copy in Herts Record Office, Bulwer Papers, XII, p. 18. Both the original and the copy are unsigned, but the former is in Levin's writing.

2 R. Lytton to Bulwer, 23 February 1852, Herts Record Office, Bulwer Papers,

red file, 1854; Moore to R. Lytton, 10 March 1852, Bulwer Papers, XII, p. 11; Crampton to Bulwer, 15 March 1852, Bulwer Papers, XII, p. 12.

3 Crampton to Granville, 14 March 1852, P.R.O., F.O. 5–544/213–17; Malmesbury to Crampton, 19 April 1852, F.O. 5–544/218–19; Foreign Office to Board of Trade, 7 May 1852, F.O. 5–556/208–8v; Board of Trade to Foreign Office, 19 May 1852, F.O. 5–556/262–63v; Malmesbury to Crampton, 21 May 1852, F.O. 5–542/174–8v. Copies of the Anglo-French Copyright Treaty, signed 3 November 1851, altered for purposes of negotiation with America, are in: F.O. 5–542/180–4v; F.O. 5–556/264–8v.

4 R. Lytton to Bulwer, 13 November 1851, Herts Record Office, Bulwer Papers, red file 1854; Bulwer to Crampton, 25 March 1852, Bodleian Library, Crampton Papers; R. Lytton to Crampton, 28 and 29 March 1852, Crampton Papers.

5 Levin to Moore [?], 15 April 1852, original in Bodleian Library, Crampton Papers; copy in Herts Record Office, Bulwer Papers, XII, p. 12; this latter copy in the handwriting of T. W. C. Moore. The name of Levin was obliterated, presumably by Bulwer at some later date to maintain the American's anonymity. See also Crampton to Bulwer, 19 April 1852, Herts Record Office, Bulwer Papers, XII, p. 14; Bulwer to Crampton, 3 May 1852, Bodleian Library, Crampton Papers.

6 Crampton to Winthrop, 25 April 1852, copy, Bodleian Library, Crampton Papers; Synge to Longfellow, 26 April 1852, Houghton Library, Longfellow Papers; Synge to Emerson, 26 April 1852, Houghton Library, Emerson Papers.

7 Longfellow to Synge, 5 May 1852, New York Public Library, Berg Collection; Emerson to Longfellow, 10 May 1852, Houghton Library, Longfellow Papers; Winthrop to Crampton, 12 May 1852, Bodleian Library, Crampton Papers; Longfellow to Emerson, 26 May 1852, Houghton Library, Longfellow Papers; Emerson to Synge, 6 June 1852, Houghton Library, Emerson Papers. See also R. L. Rusk, *The Letters of Ralph Waldo Emerson* (New York, 1939), IV, pp. 292–3.

8 Dickens to Bulwer, 5 May 1852, in W. Dexter (ed.), *The Letters of Charles Dickens* (London, 1938), II, p. 293. The various aspects of the bookselling question of 1852 are set forth in J. J. Barnes, *Free Trade in Books: A study of the London book trade since 1800* (Oxford, 1964).

9 Dickens to Murray, 18 May 1852, copy in the possession of the Editors of *The Letters of Charles Dickens: Pilgrim Edition*. Dickens to Edward Chapman, 18 May 1852, in Dexter, *op. cit.*, II, p. 462; J. Blackwood to W. Blackwood, 24 May and 28 May 1852, National Library of Scotland, MS 4097, ff. 163–4 and 170–1; Bulwer to Crampton, 29 May 1852, Bodleian Library, Crampton Papers; R. Lytton to Crampton, 30 May 1852, Crampton Papers.

10 *Parliamentary Debates*, XLI (20 March 1838), pp. 1107–8; R. Lytton to Crampton, 30 May 1852, Bodleian Library, Crampton Papers; Crampton to Bulwer,

19 June 1852, enclosed in 9 July 1852 letter of Bulwer to Murray, at John Murray Ltd; J. Blackwood to J. Dickinson, 16 July 1852, Wm Blackwood & Sons, letter book, pp. 6–7.

11 R. Lytton to Crampton, 29 June and 14 July 1852, Bodleian Library, Crampton Papers.

12 Apparently one contributor paid in £5 less than indicated above, so that the actual total forwarded to Crampton was £995. The lists of contributors were scrawled on the backs of several of the following letters, while other letters referred to specific subscriptions. Crampton to Bulwer, 14 June 1852, enclosed with some letters from Bulwer to Murray, John Murray Ltd; Bulwer to Murray, 9 July 1852, John Murray Ltd; Blackwood to J. Dickinson, 16 July 1852, letter book, pp. 6–7, Wm Blackwood & Sons; Murray to Blackwood, 3 August 1852, National Library of Scotland, Blackwood Papers, MS 4013, f. 41.

13 Bulwer to Crampton, 27 July 1852, Bodleian Library, Crampton Papers; R. Lytton to Crampton, late July 1852, Crampton Papers.

14 For material concerning the fund-raising efforts see: Murray to Blackwood, 10 July 1852, National Library of Scotland, Blackwood Papers, MS 4099, ff. 165–6; Blackwood to Murray, 12 July 1852, Wm Blackwood & Sons, letter book, p. 4; J. Blackwood to J. Blackie, 12 July 1852, letter book, pp. 2–3; Murray to Blackwood, 14 July 1852, National Library of Scotland, Blackwood papers, MS 4103, f. 40; Blackwood to Murray, 16 July 1852, Wm Blackwood & Sons, letter book, p. 5. Some of these financial arrangements first came to light in K. J. Fielding, 'Dickens and international copyright', *Bulletin of the British Association for American Studies*, no. 4 n.s. (August 1962), pp. 32–3. Since Fielding had access to only a few of the letters pertinent to the subject, namely those at John Murray Ltd, he laboured under a considerable disadvantage.

15 Crampton to Bulwer, 28 June 1852, Herts Record Office, Bulwer Papers, XII, p. 16; Synge to Longfellow, 8 June 1852, Houghton Library, Longfellow Papers; Synge to Emerson, 28 June 1852, Emerson Papers; *Congressional Globe*, 32nd Cong. 1st Sess., XXIV (19 July 1852), p. 1832.

16 Webster to Fillmore, 4 August 1852, in C. H. Van Tyne, *The Letters of Daniel Webster* (New York, 1902), pp. 535–6; Everett to Lawrence, 15 August 1852, Massachusetts Historical Society, Everett Papers, CI, pp. 129–32. For useful background to the fisheries dispute, see S. F. Bemis (ed.), *American Secretaries of State and Their Diplomacy* (New York, 1928), VI, pp. 109–10; C. M. Fuess, *Daniel Webster* (Boston, 1930), II, pp. 262–3.

17 The Kennedy diaries are in the Peabody Institute, Kennedy Papers. See also Crampton to Bulwer, 28 August 1852, Herts Record Office, Bulwer Papers, XII, p. 17.

18 Statement of account, in the name of T. W. C. Moore, 19 February 1853, Bodleian Library, Crampton Papers.

19 Everett to Charlotte Everett, 6 November 1852, Massachusetts Historical Society, Everett Papers, MS Box 13; Everett MS Diary, 8 February 1853, CLXXII, p. 30.

20 The literature on the Reciprocity Treaty and other Anglo-American negotiations at this time is voluminous. Standard works on diplomatic history deal with these issues in detail. The forthcoming edition of Crampton's letters by Mrs Theodore Silverstein of Chicago, Illinois, will undoubtedly yield a good deal of new and valuable insight on these issues. See also G. J. Abbot to Everett, 28 October 1852, Massachusetts Historical Society, Everett Papers, MS Box 12.

21 Levin to Crampton, 2 November 1852, Bodleian Library, Crampton Papers.

22 Levin to Moore, 15 November 1852, Bodleian Library, Crampton Papers.

23 Simpson to Crampton, 28 December 1852, Bodleian Library, Crampton Papers.

24 Sumner to Everett, 19 November 1852, Massachusetts Historical Society, Everett Papers, MS Box 13; Everett to Sumner, 21 November 1852, Houghton Library, Sumner Papers; Crampton to Bulwer, 24 December 1852, Herts Record Office, Bulwer Papers, XII, p. 18.

25 Levin to Crampton, 20 and 23 November 1852, Bodleian Library, Crampton Papers.

26 Blackwood to Bulwer, 30 September 1852, Wm Blackwood & Sons, letter book, p. 24; G. P. Putnam to Jay, 28 December 1852, Columbia University, Jay Papers; Jay to Putnam, 29 December 1852, Jay Homestead, letter book, pp. 29–30; Jay to Sumner, 14 January 1853, Houghton Library, Sumner Papers; Jay to Hawthorne, 24 January 1853, Jay Homestead, letter book, pp. 58–60; Jay to Seward, 24 January 1853, University of Rochester Library, Seward Papers; Jay to Blackwood, 28 January 1853, National Library of Scotland, Blackwood Papers, MS 4102, f. 182; Jay to Hudson, 19 February 1853, Jay Homestead, letter book, pp. 107–9.

27 Fillmore to Harper, 9 August 1852, and Harper to Fillmore, 23 August 1852, in J. H. Harper, *The House of Harper* (New York, 1912), pp. 107–8.

28 The 'Objections' and Crampton's 'Observations' are in P.R.O., F.O. 5–563/312–21. Thackeray's memorandum is also undated and in the Bodleian Library, Crampton Papers. See also *New York Herald*, February 1853; *National Intelligencer*, 16 March 1853.

29 Everett to Kennedy, 10 January 1853, Peabody Institute, Kennedy Papers; Levin to Crampton, 2 February 1853, Bodleian Library, Crampton Papers.

30 Basic information on these and other Senators may be found in the *Biographical Directory of the American Congress*. Since the volume is cumulative, a twentieth-century edition includes nineteenth-century members. For further details about her father see V. Mason, *The Public Life and Diplomatic Correspondence of James M. Mason* (Roanoke, 1903).

31 Levin to Crampton, 12 February 1853, Bodleian Library, Crampton Papers.

32 Everett MS Diary, Massachusetts Historical Society, CLXXII (14–18 February 1853), pp. 36–7; Fillmore to Everett, 14 February 1853, Massachusetts Historical Society, MS Box 13; Everett to Seward, 18 February 1853, University of Rochester Library, Seward Papers; Everett to the US Senate, 18 February 1853, National Archives; Levin receipt, Herts Record Office, Bulwer Papers, XII, p. 18.

33 Crampton to Clarendon, 21 February 1853, Bodleian Library, Clarendon Papers, C. 11, ff. 29–9v. The French Minister to Washington, the Comte de Sartiges, also wanted to sign a similar copyright treaty. However he lacked instructions to do so and in fact his whole position as envoy was somewhat tenuous. Louis Napoleon had recently declared himself Emperor, accompanied by a further shake-up in government and diplomatic circles. The American Government was apologetic but declined signing a treaty until Sartiges's full credentials arrived. Everett MS Diary, Massachusetts Historical Society, (14–18 February and 3 March 1853), pp. 36–9 and 50; Everett to Sartiges, 18 February 1853, Everett Papers, LIII. Although it is not entirely clear it seems that Everett agreed to sign the treaty with France just before leaving office on 4 March 1853. The signed treaty was then presumably placed on file with the State Department archives awaiting Sartiges's full diplomatic powers. Nothing ever came of the treaty.

Chapter XII The Need for Senate Ratification: February 1853–June 1854

1 John Slidell of Louisiana joined the Committee in December 1853. Though John M. Clayton of Delaware was newly elected to the Senate, he was well known as Zachary Taylor's Secretary of State in 1849–50. As we shall see shortly, the so-called Clayton–Bulwer Treaty of 1850 was to impinge upon the fate of the Copyright Convention.

2 Crampton to Clarendon, 27 February, 7 March and 13 March 1853, Bodleian Library, Clarendon Papers, C. 11, ff. 38–9v, 44–5, and 48–9; The Claims Convention was signed on 8 February in London and then conveyed to Washington; *Journal of the Executive Proceedings of the Senate of the United States of America, Dec. 6, 1852–Mar. 3, 1855* (Washington, 1887), IX, p. 68, concerning the ratification of the Claims Convention of 15 March 1853. For the first reading of the Copyright Treaty and its referral to the Foreign Relations Committee, *ibid.*, p. 36. See also; MS Diary, Massachusetts Historical Society, Everett Papers, CLXXII (15 March 1853), p. 61; Levin to Crampton, 22 March 1853 and Marcy to Levin, 23 October 1852, Bodleian Library, Crampton Papers.

3 Seward to Everett, 28 February 1853, Massachusetts Historical Society, Everett Papers, MS Box 13; F. Hudson to Jay, 10 March 1853 and Jay to

Hudson, 10 March 1853, and Jay to Everett, 11 March 1853, Jay Homestead, letter book, pp. 125-7.

4 Jay to Warren, 5 March 1853, Jay Homestead, letter book, pp. 118-21; Crampton to Clarendon, 4 April 1853, Bodleian Library, Clarendon Papers, C. 11, ff. 80-1; G. T. Curtis, *Life of James Buchanan* (New York, 1883), II, p. 81.

5 MS diary, Massachusetts Historical Society, Everett Papers, CLXXII (14 March and 25 March 1853), pp. 60, 67; *Journal of the Executive Proceedings of the Senate*, IX (15 March 1853), p. 69.

6 Crampton to Clarendon, 21 March 1853, Bodleian Library, Clarendon Papers, C. 11, ff. 56v-7v.

7 There is a considerable body of literature on the Clayton–Bulwer Treaty and Central America. For the issues raised in this chapter see especially: H. Hamilton, *Zachary Taylor* (Indianapolis, 1941 and 1951), II, pp. 192-3; Lawrence to Webster, 2 January 1852, in C. M. Fuess, *Daniel Webster* (Boston, 1930), II, p. 260; Crampton to Clarendon, 23 January 1854, Bodleian Library, Clarendon Papers, C. 24, ff. 50-5; Aberdeen to Clarendon, 5 November 1854, in R. W. Van Alstyne, 'Anglo-American relations, 1853-7', *American Historical Review*, XLII (April 1937), p. 498.

8 Crampton to Malmesbury, 2 January and 10 January 1853, P.R.O., F.O. 5-563/5-13 and 37-43v; Clayton to Pearce, 7 January and 11 January 1853, Maryland Historical Society, Pearce Papers; Crampton enclosed a copy of the 11 February 1853 Senate report in F.O. 5-563/407-15. For Cass's speech see: *Congressional Globe*, 32nd Cong. 2nd Sess., XXVI (6 January 1853), pp. 237-8; J. P. Comegys, *Memoir of John M. Clayton: Papers of the Historical Society of Delaware*, IV (Wilmington, 1882), p. 212 and following; MS diary, Massachusetts Historical Society, Everett Papers, CLXXII (8 March 1853), p. 56.

9 *Washington Union*, 15 March 1853; *National Intelligencer*, 17 March 1853. The Accessory Transit Company belonged to the American entrepreneur, Cornelius Vanderbilt.

10 Crampton to Clarendon, 21 March 1853, P.R.O., F.O. 5-564/88-9v and 96-6v.

11 Crampton to Clarendon, 21 March 1853, Bodleian Library, Clarendon Papers, C. 11, ff. 55-9; MS diary, Massachusetts Historical Society, Everett Papers, CLXXII (15 March 1853), p. 61; *Journal of the Senate*, IX (15 March 1853), p. 68. The *Journal* lists the names of those Senators voting for and against the Claims Convention.

12 Crampton to Clarendon, 7 March 1853, Bodleian Library, Clarendon Papers, C. 11, ff. 41-2v.

13 Levin to Crampton, 22 March 1853, Bodleian Library, Crampton Papers.

14 Everett to G. P. Putnam, 25 March 1853, quoted in G. H. Putnam, *A Memoir of George Palmer Putnam* (New York, privately printed, 1903), pp. 374-5. *Journal of the Senate*, IX (5 April 1853), p. 146; Crampton to Bulwer, 25

April 1853, and Crampton to R. Lytton, 25 April 1853, Herts Record Office, Bulwer Papers, XVIII, pp. 97 and 98.

15 'Convention between Her Britannic Majesty and the United States of America for the Establishment of International Copyright, 17 February 1853.' The copies of the Treaty which Crampton sent the Foreign Office are in F.O. 93–8/32. Almost more interesting is Crampton's draft copy with the last minute changes including the new Article VI, F.O. 115–31/195–205. A copy is also in the National Archives: Notes from the British Legation . . . in the United States Department of State, microcopy no. 50, Roll T–30, vol. XXX, under date of 24 February 1853. Crampton's lengthy comments on the Treaty are in his dispatch to the Foreign Office of 21 February 1853, P.R.O., F.O. 5–563/294–306v.

16 Russell to Crampton, 25 January 1853, P.R.O., F.O. 5–561/97–97v; Foreign Office Memo., 10 March 1853, F.O. 5–563/308–11; Foreign Office to Board of Trade, 16 March 1853, F.O. 5–576/160; Board of Trade to Foreign Office, 30 April 1853, F.O. 5–576/247–47v; Foreign Office Minute, 9 May 1853, F.O. 5–576/249. Thackeray's undated memo is in the Bodleian Library, Crampton Papers, Box A–2, in a folder marked October 1853. Turner to Board of Trade, 9 May 1853, and Board of Trade to Foreign Office, 12 May 1853, P.R.O., F.O. 5–577/57–60.

17 Clarendon to Crampton, 13 and 20 May 1853, P.R.O., F.O. 5–561/222v, 224–5.

18 Clarendon to Crampton, 14 November 1853, P.R.O., F.O. 5–562/136; Crampton to Clarendon 12 December 1853, F.O. 5–567/192–9.

19 Appleton et al. to Everett, 15 February 1853, copy, University of Rochester Library, Seward Papers.

20 Cardwell to Clarendon, 4 January 1854, Bodleian Library, Clarendon Papers, C. 14, f. 544; A. Turner to Board of Trade, 5 and 6 January 1854, P.R.O., F.O. 5–607/54–7v; Board of Trade to Foreign Office, 11 January 1854, F.O. 5–607/44–50v.

21 Carlisle to Crampton, 4 February 1854, P.R.O., F.O. 5–594/21–9; Cushing to Marcy, 16 February 1854, and Marcy to Crampton, 28 February 1854, F.O. 5–594/7–19v. Cushing's own copy of the 'Opinion on international copyright' is in the Library of Congress, Cushing Papers, Box 234, February 1854 folder.

22 Clarendon to Crampton, 13 January 1854, P.R.O., F.O. 5–590/15–20; Clarendon to Crampton, 13 January 1854, Bodleian Library, Clarendon Papers, C. 127, f. 241. Crampton to Clarendon, 12 February 1854, P.R.O., F.O. 5–593/188–90v; the amendment is in the National Archives; see also the *Journal of the Senate*, IX (14 February 1854), p. 241.

23 Levin to Crampton, 22 June 1853, Bodleian Library, Crampton Papers.

24 H. C. Carey, *Letters on International Copyright* (Philadelphia, 1853), p. 6; *ibid.* (2nd ed., New York, 1868), p. 4.

25 Everett to Crampton, 9 December 1853, copy, P.R.O., F.O. 5–567/205.
26 A. Hart *et al.* to H. C. Baird, 31 January 1854, Pennsylvania Historical Society, Gardiner Collection, Baird section, Box 5. See also *Athenaeum*, no. 1375 (4 March 1854), p. 279, where the circular letter from Hart and others is cited.
27 Field to Harper, 8 February 1854, in J. H. Harper, *The House of Harper* (New York, 1912), pp. 108–9.
28 *Journal of the Senate*, IX, pp. 237–8, 240, 249 and 259. The original petitions are preserved in the National Archives. For a slightly earlier effort to prevent treaties from finding their way into unauthorized hands, see IX (16 February 1854), p. 247.
29 *Journal of the Executive Proceedings of the Senate*, IX (24 January 1854), p. 216.
30 Clarendon to B. of T., 30 March 1854, P.R.O., F.O. 5–607/258; Board of Trade to Clarendon, 2 May 1854, F.O. 5–609/208; Clarendon to Crampton, 12 May 1854, F.O. 5–591/29–31.
31 MS diary, Massachusetts Historical Society, Everett Papers, CLXXIII, pp. 78, 89, and 94; Everett to Warren, 17 April 1854, Everett Papers, CIII, pp. 141–2; Everett to A. Lawrence, 12 May 1854, Everett Papers, CIII, pp. 171–2.
32 Everett to Mason, 24 May 1854, Massachusetts Historical Society, Everett Papers, copy, CIII, pp. 200–1.
33 Everett to Crampton, 3 June 1854, Massachusetts Historical Society, Everett Papers, copy, CIII, pp. 210–12; extract of same enclosed in Crampton to Clarendon, 7 and 18 June 1854, Bodleian Library, Clarendon Papers, C. 24, ff. 376–8; Crampton to Everett, 7 June 1854, Massachusetts Historical Society, Everett Papers, MS Box 13.
34 Murray to Blackwood, 3 August 1852, National Library of Scotland, Blackwood Papers, MS 4103, f. 41; concerning Layard's suggestion to Murray. Crampton's Secret Service account is in P.R.O., Treasury, Ind. 12666.
35 Melville to R. Bentley, 20 July 1851, in M. R. Davis and W. H. Gilman (eds), *Letters of Herman Melville* (New Haven, 1960), p. 134.
36 E. P. Smith to Carey, 22 February 1854, Pennsylvania Historical Society, Gardiner collection, Box 77, Carey section; Carey's inscription to an unknown recipient is in the second edition of his *Letters on International Copyright* (New York, 1868), in the Library of Congress.
37 Everett to Hayes, 27 November 1855, Massachusetts Historical Society, Everett Papers, copy, CV, pp. 123–4.
38 *The Story of the House of Cassell* (London, 1922), p. 52.

INDEX

Authors, Publishers and Politicians

The quest for an Anglo-American copyright agreement was repeatedly thwarted throughout most of the nineteenth century, due to the effect of lobbyists and influence-peddlars on the American Congress. This meant that in the United States the question of international copyright was not decided on its own merits but rather by pressure groups who wielded great financial and private power upon the legislators.

The opposite was true in Great Britain, where Parliament was far more interested in the rights of authors and publishers and had already passed a number of statutes promoting international copyright. Copyright agreements, however, needed to be mutually agreed upon by both countries, and the United States would not reciprocate. In desperation, a group of British authors and publishers decided to play the game of politics American-style, and with great caution they raised enough money to defray the expenses of a secret lobby in Washington. A copyright treaty was duly signed by the Secretary of State and all that was required was Senate approval.

Authors, Publishers and Politicians describes these efforts to secure an Anglo-American copyright agreement. It explores the underlying causes of the failure of this quest, a failure which enabled literary pirates on both sides of the Atlantic to continue operations for a further forty years. It traces the effects this had on the writers and producers of books as well as their reading public. Few aspects of Anglo-American relations were untouched by the drama presented in this study. Its broader implications range from straightforward business transactions, official diplomatic manœuvres, endless legal complexities, and clandestine political intrigue, to the peculiarities involved in book smuggling, newspaper rivalries and industrial espionage.

$13.00